Tomorrow is Today

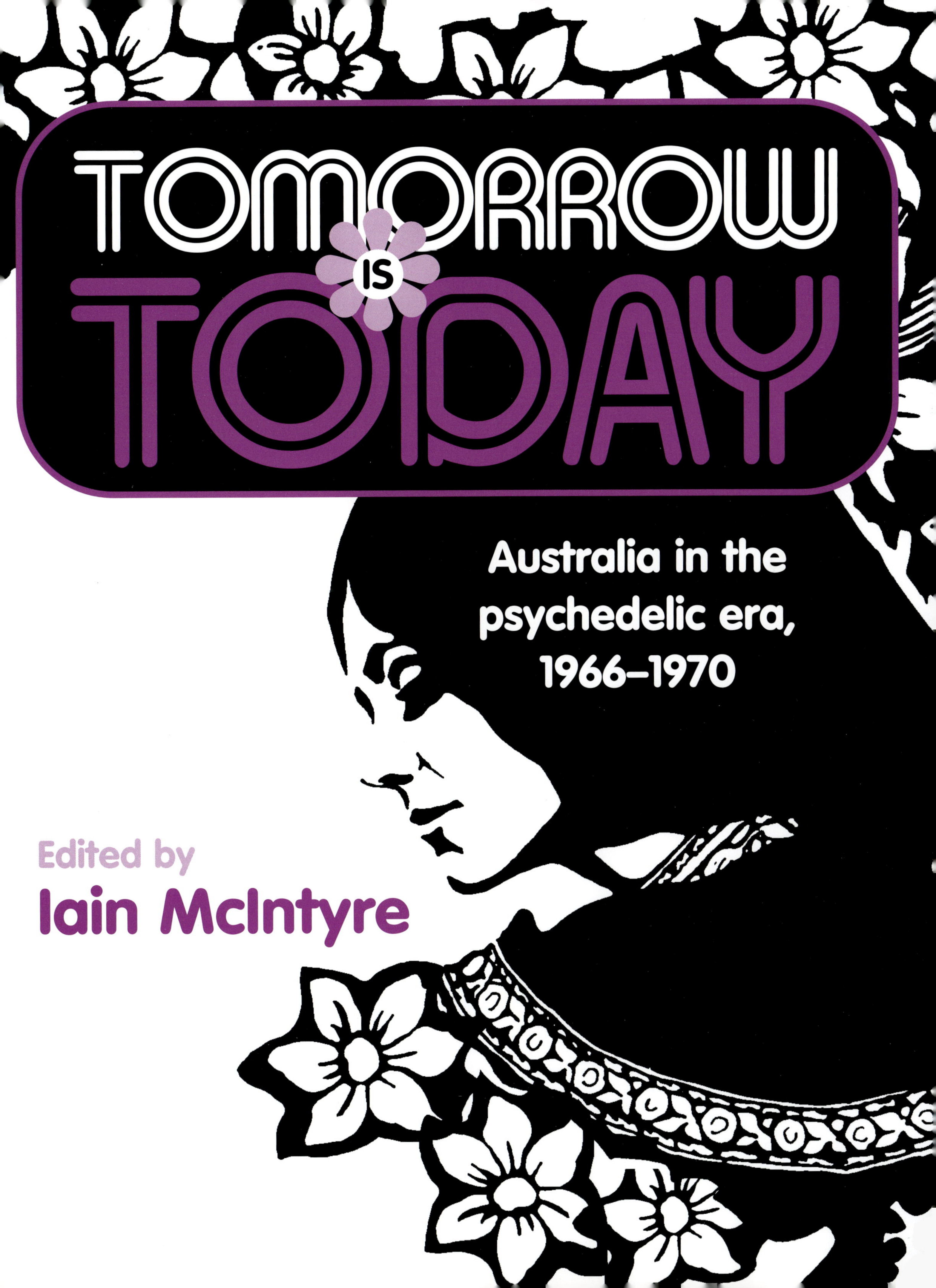

TOMORROW IS TODAY

Australia in the psychedelic era, 1966–1970

Edited by
Iain McIntyre

Wakefield Press
1 The Parade West
Kent Town
South Australia 5067
www.wakefieldpress.com.au

First published 2006

Designed by Liz Nicholson, designBITE
Printed in China at Everbest Printing Co. Ltd

Tomorrow is today: Australia in the psychedelic era, 1966–1970.

Bibliography.
Includes index.

ISBN-13: 978 1 86254 697 4.
ISBN-10: 1 86254 697 5.

1. Popular music – Australia – 1961–1970. 2. Popular culture – Australia – 20th century. 3. Australia – Social conditions – 1965–1972.
I. McIntyre, Iain, 1970– .

306.0994

3CR acknowledges the generous support of the City of Yarra in making this publication possible.

Contents

Introduction

Sociologically and fashion-wise, trends don't strictly follow the calendar. The 1960s really didn't start until around three years after the turn of the decade when the influence of the British 'beat' boom and all its associated trends took hold at an alarmingly fast rate. Then, almost in the blink of an eye, that innocent period was seemingly gone and the next era, perhaps best sign-posted by San Francisco's 'summer of love', began. What a very strange trip it was in the following few brief years for the willing participants.

Many resisted or were insulated from the changes that were gonna come. How else to explain a John Howard or a George 'Dubya' Bush! At the time, though, it really did seem as if a revolution was taking place, and in many ways it was. It was a straight jacketed intolerance for anything/anyone different that gave the 1950s a rationale for the emergence of rock 'n' roll, beatniks and teen culture, but now society had moved to another level where seemingly everyone wanted in.

Check hairstyles, Nehru jackets, pendants, beads and Richard Nixon appearing on the television show *Laugh In*. Celebrities declaring they had smoked pot and were willing to try LSD became predictable weekly newspaper headlines. The media got a little turned on if you were still tuning in. Changes were happening everywhere, even if still driven by a desire to make a buck. Watch the later Elvis movies for a subtle switch to the vibe of the Happening generation as The King tried to keep an eye on the kids under the terms of his White House secret service pact.

My gender and age group's prime mid '60s obsessions of (1) having sex and (2) staying out of the draft were joined by a third – participating in the psychedelic experience. This was harder than it may seem in terms of actually getting hold of mind-altering drugs, but as for obtaining the accoutrements – that was easy. Granny glasses and copies of *Are You Experienced?* and *The Politics of Ecstasy* would at least send the smoke signal that you were hip and willing to be groovy.

If other bands of the era were anything like mine then actually taking drugs was not required to create a so-called psychedelic musical masterpiece. It was the spirit of the times more than any hard core real life experience that mattered. Not having a clue what you were doing was also a definite plus.

Which is why looking at the time-lines in this book is so fascinating. In Fortean fashion, without additional comment, they delineate an era that is now so long ago that any attempt to explain it is going to fall short. Just gimme the facts ma'am. I hope you look forward to reading the essays here as much as I did, and if some of the information has morphed into faction so be it. They say history repeats itself, but it could be some time before we get the next psychedelic era. I haven't seen too many flowers in people's hair of late, and right now the world sure could use more than a little love.

Keith Glass, 2006

Part One
1966

ld bassist John Helman (Colbert)

1966 MUSIC

WORLD EVENTS

- The US bombs the North Vietnamese capital Hanoi.
- Ken Kesey and The Merry Pranksters set the nascent Bay Area hippy movement alight with their multimedia Trips Festival in San Francisco.
- The first meeting of the heads of the Catholic and Protestant churches in 400 years takes place in Rome.
- Swiss pharmaceutical company Sandoz stops supplying scientists and psychiatrists with LSD.
- The South African Prime Minister Verwoerd, a key architect of apartheid, is assassinated.
- The Cultural Revolution begins in China, with youthful Red Guards wreaking havoc across the country as they pursue 'revisionist elements' opposed to the rule of Mao Tse Tung.
- African-American civil rights activist James Meredith is shot and wounded in Mississippi.
- The Beatles play their last official live concert in San Francisco.
- Bobby Seale and Huey Newton launch the radical Black Panther Party in Oakland, California.
- *Time* magazine awards its Man of the Year honour to 'The Younger Generation'.

Throb guitarist Marty Van Wyk (Beard) • • •

The year in Australian rock music

1966 was the year that beat music began to get a little bit fuzzy and purple around the edges. It was also the year that Australian pop music truly came of age. The Easybeats – after having totally outgrown the local scene – flew out to London and wrote and recorded the finest Australian pop song of all time, 'Friday on My Mind'. Back in Oz there were hundreds of fabulous groups to catch live on any day of the week, from lunchtime till dawn. Melbourne band The Loved Ones released two of the most astoundingly original singles ever in 'The Loved One' and 'Everlovin' Man', and Adelaide's Masters Apprentices burst onto the scene with one of the greatest double-sided single debuts of all time in 'Undecided'/'Wars or Hands of Time'. Meanwhile, dozens of feral new bands such as The Moods, The Creatures, Wild Colonials, Last Straws, Pilgrims 5, Mystrys, The Five, The Morloch, The Union, The Gemini Five, The Pogs, Derek's Accent and The Chosen Few got themselves out of the garage and onto vinyl with varying degrees of success, but always 100% pure teen spirit.

Blues and R&B were still the hippest sounds in nightclubs, but a brassier soul influence was starting to come through in the form of Jeff St John and The Id, Max Merritt and The Meteors, Python Lee Jackson and The Ram Jam Big Band. Some groups stuck to the basic guitar/bass/drums format, but began to crank up and play with more intensity (and volume) than ever before. Pioneers of this style, The Purple Hearts, wouldn't see the year out, but Running Jumping Standing Still – featuring the fluid sustained guitar-work of Doug Ford – emerged from the ashes of the notorious Missing Links and took up where the 'Hearts left off.

The male solo pop star phenomenon was still alive and well. Normie Rowe continued his golden period, but other boy stars like Ray Brown, Tony Worsley and Billy Thorpe were on the wane (though in Billy's case this was only a temporary situation). Fresh new faces such as Mike Furber, Ronnie Burns, Johnny Young and Thorpie's former guitarist Tony Barber were paused and ready to snatch Normie's crown. But, for the moment at least, Normie was still King.

International Album Releases

The Rolling Stones – *Aftermath*
The Beach Boys – *Pet Sounds*
Bob Dylan – *Blonde On Blonde*
The Small Faces – *The Small Faces*
John Mayall with Eric Clapton – *Blues Breakers*
The Byrds – *Fifth Dimension*
The Beatles – *Revolver*
Jefferson Airplane – *Jefferson Airplane Takes Off*
The Kinks – *Face To Face*
Simon and Garfunkel – *Parsley, Sage, Rosemary And Thyme*
Cream – *Fresh Cream*
The Who – *A Quick One*

Normie Rowe (Beard)

AUSTRALIAN EVENTS

- Japan overtakes the UK as the nation's primary trade partner, accounting for almost a fifth of all Australian exports.
- The ban on married women gaining permanent jobs in the public service is lifted.
- The Australian census is conducted, with the result recording the population at 11 550 462.
- The Australian Sculpture Centre, the first gallery in Australia devoted entirely to sculpture, opens in Canberra.
- Australian television enters its tenth year with local stations launching new productions including *Playschool, Here's Humphrey, The Private World of Miss Prim, Wandjina, My Name's McGooley – What's Yours* and *Nice 'n Juicy.*
- Charles Perkins and Margaret Valadian become the first Indigenous Australians to graduate from university.
- Nat Young takes out the 1966 World Surf Titles in San Diego. Dubbed 'The Animal', Young displays a set of aggressive moves using the shorter, faster boards that have recently been developed in Australia. Over the coming months a whole range of products featuring the champion's moniker are released, including wetsuits, ice cream, sun tan lotion and shorts.

- Making a break with the common use of concrete and glass in city buildings architects Ancher, Mortlock, Murray and Woolley use traditional brown-toned bricks for the University of Newcastle's new Student Union Building.
- South Australia leads the country in being the first to legislate against racial discrimination in the service industry. It also becomes, with the passage of the South Australian *Aboriginal Lands Trust Act*, the first state to allow the return of some areas to Aboriginal ownership.
- *Dr Zhivago* opens in Australian cinemas.
- The New South Wales government repeals the *Sunday Observance Act*, allowing people to buy alcohol at clubs, visit cinemas and pay to see sports on the Sabbath.
- Australia's first parking meters are installed at the Gold Coast in Queensland.
- Various surfboard manufacturers donate boards to the Australian Army for use in Vietnam. Military propaganda

Bobby and Laurie (Beard)

The Charts

Melbourne

The Seekers started off the year at #1 on the Melbourne charts with 'The Carnival is Over', which finally ended its five-week run at the top spot in mid-January when it was replaced by The Beatles' 'Day Tripper'/'We Can Work it Out'. Perth band Johnny Young and Kompany had the biggest Melbourne hit of the year with their 'Step Back'/'Caralyn' double-sider (highest position #2; 36 weeks in the top 40). Most of 1966's international chart-toppers were in a traditional pop vein, although The Rolling Stones' 'Paint It, Black' (#1 in June) pointed out the way of the future.

Other Aussie singles to hit big in Melbourne in 1966 were 'Hitchhiker' by Bobby and Laurie (#1 for five weeks), 'Needle in a Haystack' by The Twilights (#1 for four weeks), 'Fortune Teller' by The Throb (reached #2), 'Let the Little Girl Dance' by Grantley Dee (#2), 'Tell Him I'm Not Home', 'The Breaking Point' and 'Ooh La La' by Normie Rowe (#2, #2 and #1) and 'Everlovin' Man' by The Loved Ones (#2).

Sydney

Local heroes The Easybeats dominated the Sydney charts in 1966. Their double-sided single 'Women (Make You Feel Alright)'/'In My Book' was the biggest Australian hit in the harbour city for that year. It made #1 (for one week) in March and stayed in the charts for 18 weeks. Then in June they hit top spot again (for two weeks) with 'Come and See Her'/'I Can See', and completed their hat trick of aces with the *Easyfever* EP (featuring 'I'll Make You Happy'), which stayed at #1 for three weeks. The Easys could have made it four in a row, but their October double A-sider 'Sorry'/'Funny Feelin'' stalled at #2. However, they capped off the year in fine style with 'Friday on My Mind'/'Made My Bed (Gonna Lie In It)', which hit #1 in mid-December and stayed up there for six weeks.

Adelaide and Brisbane

While Adelaide's charts tended to follow a similar line to their nearest neighbours Melbourne, it became clear that the city of churches was keen to embrace some of the more radical and obscure sounds on offer from overseas. Future *Nuggets* bands such as The Seeds, Count Five, The Standells and The Knickerbockers all scored major Adelaide hits in 1966. In fact, the city's sixth biggest hit of the year was the frantic raver 'I'm a Man' by The Yardbirds.

In Brisbane between January and November, The Easybeats managed to achieve what they couldn't in Sydney – score an incredible FIVE consecutive #1s ('Women', 'Come and See Her', *Easyfever* EP ['I'll Make You Happy'], 'Sorry', 'Friday on My Mind'). No other act in Brisbane chart history has ever managed to top the singles charts five times within a single calendar year.

The 1966 *Go Set* Pop Poll Winners (as voted by the readers of *Go Set*)

Male Vocal
Normie Rowe: Gold
Ronnie Burns: Silver
Merv Benton: Bronze

Female Vocal
Lynne Randell: Gold
Dinah Lee: Silver
Denise Drysdale: Bronze

Group
The Easybeats: Gold
The Twilights: Silver
The Purple Hearts: Bronze

1966 Hoadley's Battle of the Sounds Winners
The Twilights: Gold
Eighteenth Century Quartet: Silver
Chaos and Co: Bronze

Denise Drysdale (Colbert)

The Sonic Landscape

While Australian pop records of 1965 had tended to use a lot of reverb and tremelo, 1966 saw an increasing use of fuzz guitars and the first inklings of exotic Eastern-style musical scales – no doubt inspired by British groups such as The Beatles, Rolling Stones, Kinks and Yardbirds. Records were still being made on two track machines (vocals on one track, backing on the other), and so overdubs were only possible by 'bouncing' from one recording machine to another while recording an overdub live. Things were to change, though, as by the end of the year EMI, at least, had acquired a magical four-track machine. Still, creative producers such as Roger Savage, Ted Albert, Tony Geary, Pat Aulton, Sven Libaek, Nat Kipner, Robert Iredale and David Mackay were doing absolute wonders with the limited equipment they had on hand.

The Top 7 Proto-Psychedelic Australian Tracks from 1966

Title – Artist	Status (release date)	Label: Cat. No
1. 'Black' – The Throb	**Single (July)**	**Parlophone: A-8212**

Coming off the back of their massive nationwide hit 'Fortune Teller' Sydney band The Throb decided to throw all pop sensibility to the wind and unleash a dark and visceral sonic purge onto the innocent teen ears of Australia. 'Black' is actually a version of the traditional folk song 'Black is the Colour of my True Love's Hair' – but to compare The Throb's version of the song to say, Joan Baez's, is like comparing a flower to a volcano. 'Black' remains an intense listening experience almost 40 years after it was first recorded. Dense sludgy guitars, mournful harmonicas and moaning vocals are doused in oceans of reverb above a loping, sinister 3/4 rhythm. Despite its violently uncommercial sound, the single actually made #8 in Perth and the top 40 in most other states.
Killer Moment: 02.32, *when the band decide to drop everything and just PURGE.*

2. 'Early in the Morning' – The Purple Hearts	**Single (August)**	**Sunshine: QK-1448**

When Purple Hearts guitarist Lobby Loyde fed his guitar through an old-fashioned mantle style radio with a 3" speaker, the sound of those sizzling valves gave him the sustained reedy eastern effect he was looking for. Loyde used that strange, hypnotic guitar tone on the Hearts' version of the traditional tune 'Early in the Morning' – and in doing so, confirmed his position as the

films such as *A Break From Fighting* later show troops hanging ten at Vung Tau.

- The police drama *Homicide* becomes the third highest rating program on Australian TV, edging out competition from such overseas hits as *Peyton Place, Coronation Street* and *The Saint.*
- Holden becomes the first Australian car manufacturer to install seat belts as standard safety equipment in all of its new vehicles.
- New exhibitions at the National Gallery of Victoria include *14 Americans* (abstract watercolours by artists such as Al Held and Sam Francis), *11 Pop Artists* (including Roy Lichtenstein), *Survey* (Australian artists such as Jeffery Smart), *Emilio Greco* (sculpture) and *Two Decades of American Art* (artists such Rothko, Al Held, Jasper Johns, Jackson Pollock, Frank Stella and Andy Warhol).
- The Union of Australian Women launches a 'Boycott War Toys' campaign, forcing at least one major toy distributor to stop selling the items.
- Sydney film maker Paul Witzig releases his first surf movie *A Life in the Sun.*

- Aboriginal poet Oodgeroo (aka Kath Walker), the first Indigenous Australian to have had a collection of their work published, produces her second book of poems, *The Dawn is at Hand.*
- Peter L. Lamb produces a short documentary film about the Melbourne rock scene entitled *Approximately Panther.* Narrated by 'drunken reporter' Doug Panther, the film features interviews with local pop identities Adrian Rawlins and Lynne Randell, as well as footage of bands, venues, fashion stores and a soundtrack from the Eighteenth Century Quartet.
- *Everybody's* magazine attempts to launch its own music label, but finds radio stations reluctant to play their music for fear of promoting the publication itself. Rebranded as Spin Records, the new label brings producer and songwriter Nat Kipner together with money man Clyde Packer.
- Despite continuing to air three times a week and rate well in Melbourne, Channel 0-10 pop TV show *The Go!! Show* has its one hour format halved.
- Small, but regular anti-war protests in Sydney and Melbourne occur throughout the year, targeting US war ships, Army recruiting centres, Liberal Party offices and the homes of politicians such as Leslie Bury, the Minister of Labour and National Service. Increasingly these actions are organised by members of what will come to be known as the New Left,

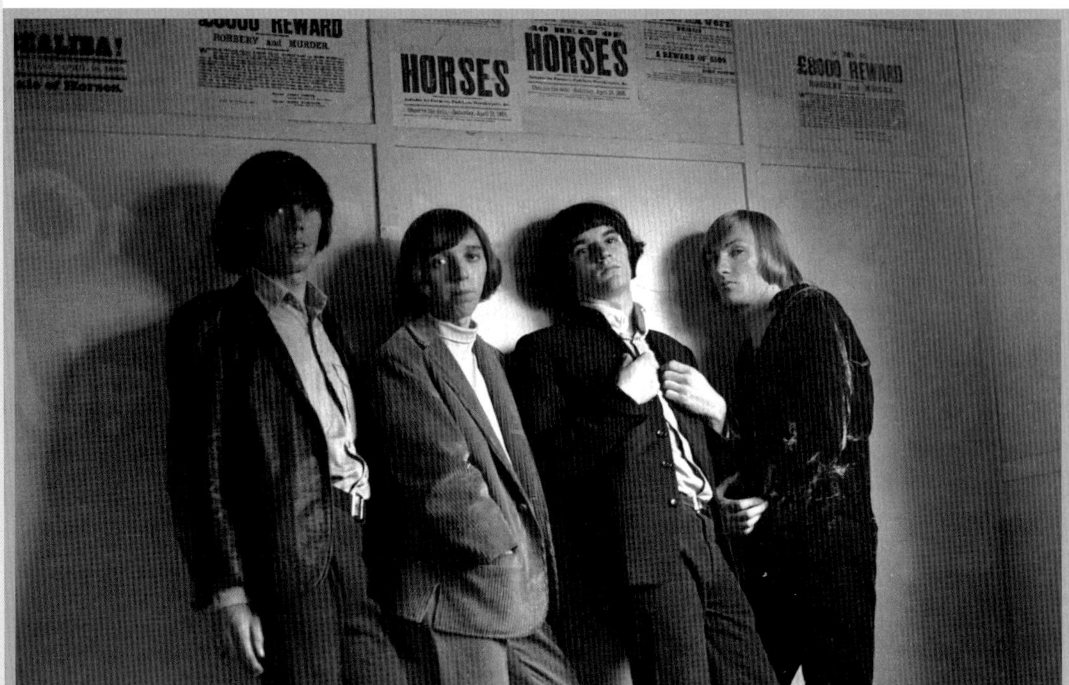

The Throb (Beard)

most advanced and adventurous guitarist in Australia. 'Early in the Morning' is a cross between a prison work-reel and a snake-charming tune. Singer Mick Hadley peppers the song with reverb-shrouded primal screams while the band support him with their deep, hypnotic *'It was urrr-lie in the morning . . .'* chant. Totally unlike any of The Purple Hearts' other 45s, 'Early in the Morning' was a #9 hit in Melbourne, #13 in the band's native Brisbane, and pretty much ignored everywhere else.

Killer Moment: 00.21, *the first time Lobby goes into his 'snake charming' riff and Mick Hadley starts his primal screaming.*

The Purple Hearts (Beard)

Jeff St John (Beard)

3. 'Eastern Dream' – Jeff St John and The Id B-side (August) Spin: EK-1446

An almost throwaway B-side to their version of Leadbelly's 'Black Girl (In the Pines)', 'Eastern Dream' (penned by Id bassist John Helman) is quite possibly Australia's first truly psychedelic record. A dinky Egyptian sounding organ line played by Ian Walsh begins the song, before the awesome cavernous voice of Jeff St John comes in to rap about a dream he had that 'Wasn't happy and it wasn't sad'. The slithery slide guitar of original Missing Link member Peter Anson balances the organ perfectly and provides even more of a Moorish atmosphere to proceedings. You can almost smell the incense and spices wafting through the desert on this one.
Killer Moment: 00.35, *the intensity with which Jeff St John says the words 'market place'.*

4. 'Every Second Day' – Bobby and Laurie Single (December) Parlophone: A-8236

In April 1966 the dynamic duo of Bobby Bright and Laurie Allen enjoyed a #1 smash with their moody version of Roger Miller's 'Hitchhiker'. They followed that up with a truly atrocious version of 'High Noon', which raced up the charts and then fell out at pretty much the same speed. But their final single of the year – an amazing self-penned blue-eyed soul track entitled 'Every Second Day' – was the creative highpoint of the duo's short, yet intensive career.

Beginning with an almost atonal guitar figure and featuring the most urgent and soulful vocals that Bobby and Laurie ever laid down, 'Every Second Day' is continuously underscored by a wailing guitar moving around within a colourfully exotic scale. Strangely, though, this excellent recording was never heard by much of the Australian public at the time of its release. Radio deejays tended to flip the single over and play the B-side – a version of Lee Hazelwood's 'First Street Blues'.
Killer Moment: 01.15, *the fuzz guitars double the clean guitars for the first time.*

5. 'Village Tapestry' – Marty Rhone B-side (September) Spin: EK-1571

Forget 'Mean Pair of Jeans' and 'Denim and Lace' – Marty Rhone – while still a teenager – made some extremely credible records in the 1960s, both with and without his backing band The Soul Agents. The self-penned 'Village Tapestry' is one that came completely out of left-field. With a gentle, almost medieval lilt, autoharps a-strumming and a charming spoken word verse – there was nothing like this released in Australia at the time. Melodic, evocative and delicate, it is a true lost gem.
Killer Moment: 01.39, *Marty steps in to tell us about how the tapestry had told of the town ravaged by the Plague.*

a predominately youthful set of activists who operate outside such traditional political organisations as the Communist Party of Australia (CPA) and the Australian Labor Party (ALP).

- The Queensland government dispenses with required public hearings to grant sand mining leases on Fraser Island.

JANUARY

- The New South Wales government sets up Australia's first full time Law Reform Commission.
- The Australian Broadcasting Commission (ABC) draws heat from the Federal government for broadcasting an interview with North Vietnamese leader Ho Chi Minh.
- The Reserve Bank becomes the first Australian organisation or business to introduce paid maternity leave.
- Having survived various obscenity cases, Sydney's satirical *Oz* magazine continues to push the boundaries by printing and selling 'I Won't Fight in Vietnam' T-shirts.

MOST 'IN' SCENE

Friday
PURPLE HEARTS
Saturday
STEVE & THE BOARD
SUNDAY AFTERNOON
60c 2-6 p.m.
THE FIVE
MOST WIGGY
BITING EYE

- Reflecting the ingrained sexism that women will increasingly resist as the decade wears on, the Victorian branch of the ALP announces it will be going all out to recruit young women to 'add glamour to the game of politics' by accompanying party notables as 'hostesses'. Proving equally enlightened, Liberal Party State President Andrew Peacock claims, 'We don't have to recruit pretty girls. We've already got them.'

5 Prison escapees Ronald Ryan and Peter Walker are returned to Melbourne after being captured in Sydney. Having escaped from Pentridge prison 17 days earlier, they face court for killing a warder and taking a prison chaplain hostage.

12 Mildura wild men The Creatures, who sport brightly dyed shoulder length hair and cruise around in heavily graffitied cars, release their first single 'Mona' on Sound 66.

14 Ballet dancer and would-be pop singer Robert Helpmann is named Australian of the Year.

20 71-year-old Sir Robert Menzies announces his decision to retire as Prime Minister after a record 16 years in the job. Harold Holt replaces him as Liberal Party leader and PM.

Great for Throwing, Burning Smells, Circle Drawings, Perry-winkling and Wheels.

"OF HOPES & DREAMS & TOMBSTONES"
by
THE
Purple Hearts
ON
SUNSHINE

Marty Rhone (Colbert)

6. 'I Can See My Love' – The In-Sect **Single (August)** **W&G: WG-S-8009**

Part psychedelia and part garage punk, 'I Can See My Love', by Adelaide group The In-Sect, is mostly just two minutes and seven seconds of absolute wild insanity. The backing track on this record was recorded at 7 inches-per-second and played back at the standard 15 i.p.s., and as a result you have a band that sounds as if they've taken a whole year's supply of speed in one hit. The already manic fuzz guitar work of Phil Wooding sounds like a swarm of mosquitoes, while Geoff Pretty's drumming sounds like one of those hyperactive mechanical bunny rabbits you see on advertisements for batteries. 'I Can See My Love' actually made #14 on the Adelaide charts, although today an original mint copy of the single can go for many hundreds of dollars.

7. 'Don't Give Me No Friction' – The Missing Links **EP Track (April)** **Philips: PE-31**

The ferocious Missing Links had used backward tapes on their first album back in 1965 – a year before *Revolver* – and on this song, from their *Unchained* EP, they predated The Velvet Underground with their primitive avant garde madness.

'Don't Give Me No Friction' was originally done by an LA band called the Green Beans, and it's a good driving pop song with rattlesnake guitar chords and an impassioned Andy James lead vocal. However, at the 2 min 15 mark, the song suddenly breaks down into Freaksville. Cacophonous peals of squealing feedback, raspy guitar scratches, caveman drums and a violent rumbling bass. Wha' happened? The 'Links decided to trash the place, that's what!
Killer Moment: 02.15, *the Links go apeshit.*

Ian D. Marks

FASHION

1966

26 Senator Dame Anabelle Rankin becomes the first woman to hold a Commonwealth portfolio when she is appointed Minister for Housing.

26 Charles Perkins and other Aboriginal activists hold a public meeting on Australia Day calling for citizenship and justice for Indigenous Australians.

26 The Beaumont children, Grant (aged 4), Anabelle (7) and Jane (9) disappear from Glenelg beach in Adelaide. Despite a massive search and rewards of up to 850 pounds they are never found.

28 Western Mining Corporation's discovery of major deposits of nickel at Kambalda, Western Australia, accelerates Australia's 'mineral boom'.

FEBRUARY

- Sydney psychedelic soul band The Id begin a residency at Rhubarbs discotheque.
- US Vice-President Hubert Humphrey visits Australia to shore up support for America's 'police action' in Vietnam.

1 Hotel closing hours are extended in Victoria, abolishing the 'six o'clock swill' and allowing people to drink until 10 pm. At the same time driving with a blood alcohol limit of greater than 0.05% becomes illegal.

• • • Paisley Pop, *Go Set* model Diana (Beard)

2 The first issue of the Melbourne based 'Teens and Twenties Newspaper' *Go Set* is launched. In its opening statement *Go Set* wears its youth based credentials on its sleeve, announcing it will be 'Going all out to capture the imagination of the movers. Every one of you cats has felt the lash of the Oldies kicking back and screaming . . . Now is the time to really break loose.'

14 Decimal currency is introduced, replacing the old system of pounds, shillings and pence with dollars and cents.

14 Following a raid on a house in Five Dock twenty people are arrested for the possession of marijuana.

15 Fresh from massive overseas success The Seekers return home for an extensive Australian tour.

16 The Rolling Stones begin their second Australian tour, playing Sydney, Melbourne and Brisbane with former New Zealanders Max Merritt and The Meteors in support.

21 Former Aztecs guitarist Tony Barber reports in his *Go Set* column that the once proud Sydney pop scene has all but collapsed in recent months, with only three teen dances still operating regularly. Meanwhile, Melbourne's combination of suburban teen dances and late night inner city discotheques establishes the city as Australia's capital of rock and pop.

The year in fashion

I was born in March 1967 in Melbourne. It was a time of great political and social change – Aborigines were given Australian citizenship, the Vietnam War raged, and Ronald Ryan was tried and became the last man hanged in Australia. However, when I look through family photographic albums, I get a different sense of time and place than these momentous events suggest. I look at the clothes and accessories that my family wore and wonder if they were typical of what everyone was wearing down the street, were they fashionable, conservative or out of date? And, what is the measure of these things, particularly in retrospect? It is interesting to consider how people construct the memory of their past, both collective and individual, and what influences those memories.

When I ask my mother's friends what they wore in the 1960s, the answers are as diverse as their social status, educational levels, work experience, marital status as their interest in fashion. Further, wider international and national social forces such as the role of the media through print media, television and film all influenced fashion in Australia during the 1960s. All these factors contributed to ideas of aspirational fashion – that clothes could create an image of oneself that could be as make believe as much as a reflection of a person's social position in the world, perceived or real.

In contrast, if I ask my friends today what they think 1960s clothes looked like, their ideas typically only reflect an English late1960s look – John Lennon glasses and Sergeant Pepper psychedelic or hippy styled clothes – which is not so much an inaccurate representation of 1960s clothes, but only a small sample of what was available in England, Europe, America and Australia from 1966 to 1970.

Miss Gerry O'Reilly (O'Reilly)

If we consider these years and focus on the major fashion cities in Australia, and then look at contemporary magazines such *Go Set* (for teenagers), *Women's Weekly* and *Flair* (for the middle classes) and *Vogue* (for the upper classes), then we can see what it might have looked like to walk down the street in Australian cities in the late 1960s.

Op Pop Dazzle

In 1964, Prue Acton opened her first clothes shop in The Block Arcade, Collins Street, Melbourne. By 1966 the shop was doing a roaring trade with girls aged fourteen to twenty four and Prue Acton appeared throughout the fashion press from *Go Set* to *Vogue*. From 1966, Acton was producing 350 designs a year, providing what became famously known as the 'Total Look'. Her shop sold everything a girl could possibly want to create an up-to-the-minute look, from dresses, trousers, tops, handbags, hats, stockings, and cosmetics.

Prue Acton was also the first Australian female fashion designer to become a brand. She marketed her daisy logo on shop bags, cosmetic containers and clothing tags, and was regularly photographed with a daisy necklace. Her shop offered an Australian adaptation of Swinging London styles, and particularly Mary Quant, Mod and Op Art looks.

Other designs that were directly exported from overseas were available in Melbourne and Sydney. Shops such as Meredith imported the latest fashions from designers and manufacturers from England, Europe and Hong Kong, selling them to an affluent middle class clientele.

In 1966, Miss Geraldine O'Reilly was a student at the Elly Lucas finishing school in Collins Street, Melbourne. During this year O'Reilly remembers wearing a handmade cream fine wool dress with a drop waist, A-line, round neck, back zip and bracelet length sleeves. With this she wore flesh coloured stockings and squarish toed slip-on brown suede shoes with a mid-sized heel. Aside from handmade clothes she made herself, O'Reilly supplemented her wardrobe from shops such as Cherry Lane, Emma, Prue Acton, Myers, Buckley and Nunn's and Georges. From 1966 she wore her red hair in a longish natural cut with a fringe, sometimes in a French roll at the back. It was not teased and full of hairspray. She wore Revlon and Helena Rubenstein make-up that consisted of a whiteish natural complexion with false eyelashes, black eyeliner and very pale pink lipstick. O'Reilly notes that petticoats or slips were commonly worn, giving skirts and dresses a more modest and even line. Convention considered it bad grooming to have one's slip showing underneath the hemline of the outer garment. O'Reilly always wore gloves, but from 1966 tended to wear fun fashion woolley hats only in winter, for warmth rather than conservative propriety. During this period, O'Reilly saw various jazz bands, such as The Red Onions, play at places such as the Chevron, Melbourne.

Mod

The English mod look translated to the Australian fashion scene as Mini dresses (hemlines well above the knee) in a shift style, sleeveless, usually in black and white, but sometimes in red, white and blue, or navy and white with geometric, linear and angular patterns.

In 1966 Yves Saint Laurent Paris collections showed an inspirational fashion adaptation of Piet Mondrian's De Stijl paintings from the early 1920s. These images of earlier twentieth century modernism became a manifestation of mid 1960s youthful visual expression. Hairstyles to match this look were similarly angular, cut originally in a bob style, but often with an angled fringe and brushed into one or multiple peaks at the nape. Notably, this bob cut was not worn in a teased bouffant manner, but was based instead around Vidal Sassoon's famous five-point geometric bob, as popularised in America from 1965 and in London with Mary Quant, who added deep cut fringes to her mod look.

It is of note that the actual mods in England during this period did not follow these mainstream fashion looks, for they were ahead of the fashion of the day. By 1966, English mod girls were sporting more cropped boyish hairstyles and they did not wear shift dresses. Instead girls who rode Vespa or Lambretta motor scooters preferred ski pants with suede jackets and perhaps a stripy top. Images of these fashions were photographed in contemporary English newspapers when mods and rockers rioted at the Clacton and Margate seaside resorts. English mod boys wore a variety of looks ranging from three button suits with side vents or a single centre vent of varying lengths, button-down collared shirts or Fred Perry tennis shirts to stovepipe trousers, bell bottoms and hipsters. Their

Go Set's Pretzel models the pop look (Beard)

28 Following ongoing disputes over costs and design, Danish designer Jørn Utzon resigns as the Chief Architect of the Sydney Opera House. Ruing what he sees as the destruction of his original design he refuses to return to Australia for 32 years.

MARCH

- Sydney filmmakers' cooperative Ubu, who go on to spearhead experimental cinema and light shows over the rest of the decade, release their pop art James Bond spoof *Blunderball*, featuring a soundtrack from Python Lee Jackson and The Id.
- Matt Taylor (later of Chain) forms pioneering blues band Bay City Union in Brisbane.
- Easybeats' manager Mike Vaughan travels to the US in an attempt to score a record deal for his young protégés. Bunkering down in a hotel room in Los Angeles he battles initial disinterest to return home triumphantly ten days later bearing a five year deal with United Artists.
- The Commonwealth Government announces it will triple the country's commitment to the undeclared war in Vietnam and raise the number of Australian troops stationed there to 4500.
- Continuing his campaign to expose the degree of censorship in Australia David Duncan publishes the second issue of *Obscenity* magazine. The first issue had castigated the role of

Customs and Excise and the Literature Censorship Boards in controlling what Australians read and view. Having been banned in Victoria and Queensland, Duncan ups the ante with his second issue by reproducing a number of extracts from banned books such as the *Kama Sutra* and the Marquis De Sade's *Juliette*, as well as humorous pieces on the 'Dirtiest Letter in the Alphabet' and 'How *Women's Weekly* is Obscene'.

- Immigration restrictions on people of 'non-European descent' are eased after pressure from home and Australia's major trading partners.
- Wild R&B act The Purple Hearts (featuring future Coloured Balls guitarist Lobby Loyde and Easybeats drummer Tony Cahill) relocate to Melbourne from Brisbane.
- Andrew Blundon and two other conscripts become the first to burn their National Service registration cards during a protest outside PM Holt's home. Under the National Service scheme, introduced by the Menzies government in 1964, all male citizens turning 20 are required to register for military conscription. Following twice-yearly registration periods, birth dates are drawn at random from the Tattersalls Lottery Barrel, with all those selected required to enrol for National Service. The chances of being drafted are approximately 12 to 1, and of being sent to Vietnam 40 to 1.

Miss Gerry O'Reilly (O'Reilly)

Go Set's Diana models Geometric Op Art (Beard)

haircuts were shortish, often with slight back-combing on the crown.

These very particular looks came to Australia with teenage English immigrants and via the international fashion press, but, significantly, they bore no relation to the notion of the Australian mod look, which had much more to do with French haute couture. This is again reflected in the popularity of the 'Pea' jacket that Yves Saint Laurent introduced in Paris in 1962, but which only became popular with Australian teenage girls in 1966. Fashionable Australian boys wearing the mod look wore four buttoned Union Jack flag jackets with high collars, emulating John Entwhistle on the Who's record cover of 1965.

These authentic or adapted mod looks in Australia in 1966 were aimed at the youth market. Women in their thirties and beyond did not wear these clothes. Indeed, some older women sported towering beehives, and wealthier, more conservative women typically cut their hair shorter or had shoulder length hair that was set at a salon. Middle and upper middle class women wore shirt dresses, twin-sets and Fletcher Jones pleated skirts to the knee or tailored capri pants during the day, sometimes with a short string of pearls. After 5 pm it was considered suitable to wear diamonds and a simple plain black dress to a cocktail party or dinner. A thirty-year-old woman might wear a velvet shift dress with short sleeves, above the knee (but certainly not too short). Much older women often wore a silk sleeveless dress in a soft feminine colour with a matching jacket with three quarter sleeves.

Despite Jean Shrimpton's appearance at the November 1965 Melbourne Cup without a hat, gloves, and hosiery, such accoutrements, especially gloves, were still considered proper for all women going into town, to luncheon, the races and charity events. Similarly, it was considered improper to go to the opera, the ballet, a symphony or a dinner dance without formal attire. Men of all ages wore dinner jackets to these events, and women often wore long dresses or skirts with silk shirts and real or faux fur stoles or jackets and long gloves.

Op and Pop

Just as the mod look was adapted to an Australian audience, so too was the English Bridget Riley inspired Op Art form. While Mondrian was admired in retrospect, the Victor Vasarely and Bridget Riley Op Art movement was contemporary with the 1960s.

In fashion terms, Op Art designs were kinetic patterns in black and white and almost fluorescent colours that lent themselves to fabric manufacture for fashion use. Many of the dress designs that featured Op Art patterns were similarly cut to mod dresses – sleeveless, with a round neck and above the knee hemlines. Often, too, these dresses had cut out designs that sometimes exposed the skin or were backed with a plastic material that added to the geometric design of the patterning on the dress.These dresses were worn with Op Art patterned hosiery or plain textured hosiery often augmented with circular patterning so that the legs appeared encased in lightweight-like lacey material. Girls also wore a variety of boots with this look – boots with Op Art patterned black and white leather, boots with cut out patterns or boots that were suede coloured.

Again, Op Art outfits were complemented with bob haircuts, sometimes cut on geometric angles like the mod looks. Girls also wore lightweight fabric, leather or synthetic material helmet styled hats, revealing the pointed angles of their bob haircuts on the jaw line, as well as angled or deep fringes.

The Op Art look lent itself to diverse accessories – angular or geometric sunglasses, fun plastic dangling earrings in colours to match the Op Art dress, often with big circular shapes, and small handbags in Op Art patterns often matching the boots being worn. These handbags were made of vinyl plastic, leather or fabric to match the dress. Handbags were also available in over-the-shoulder larger sizes. Girls at the beach could be seen in Op Art print bikinis, which were mostly structured bra tops with rather modest bottoms compared to today's standards.

Op Art fashions were not confined to women's wear. Boys could buy Op Art shirts where the shirt body would be an Op Art print with contrasting collars and cuffs. Boys tended to wear straight leg trousers with, for example, desert boots or Beatle boots featuring black leather pointy toes with a Cuban styled heel. Another advertised fashion look for boys in *Go Set*, 7 September 1966, proclaimed that the ultimate look was black and white hounds-tooth trousers worn with checkerboard windcheaters and topped off with a plastic red waist coat and Beatles cap. Earlier in the year the *Go Set* catchphrase for boys was 'If it's Op it's Top'. This idea was reflected in Op Art floral neckties with detachable cuffs and collars on shirts.

Inez and Yuk from The Clefs (Colbert)

Plastic Fantastic *Go Set* model Barb (Beard)

Students are allowed to apply for a deferral, and only Aborigines (as non citizens), absolute pacifists and those with religious objections are allowed complete exemption. Between 1965 and 1972 around 12 000 young Australians fail to register, with many more avoiding the draft by heading overseas, feigning chronic illness and, more rarely, openly resisting conscription at every turn.

- The Commonwealth Arbitration Commission hands down a decision holding that Aboriginal stockmen be granted equality in wages and conditions by December 1968.
- Anti-conscription protestors, booing and slow clapping PM Holt, disrupt the campaign launch for future Liberal leader Andrew Peacock in the safe seat of Kooyong.

1 The Easybeats, Bobby and Laurie, MPD Ltd and Normie Rowe headline the Big Show tour taking in all the major cities on the east coast of Australia.

1 Having come under the wing of Easybeats' manager Mike Vaughan, The Throb sign to Alberts Productions.

2 Three Melbourne men are arrested after being caught smoking marijuana in a car.

3 The left wing of the ALP attempts to expel Deputy Leader Gough Whitlam after he attacks them

Dazzle

During 1966 Op, Pop and Mod were not the only fashions that were available. Many other styles, such as the military look, the dolly girl and baby doll looks, the Gaucho, the vamp and Victoriana looks were also on sale. These designs will be described in further detail in a discussion of 1967 and 1968 fashion. However, it is important to recognise that many of these fashion styles lasted longer than a season, and in some cases spanned a few years. The reasons for this are multi-faceted. Principally, some fashions were better received than others and thus had a longer lifespan in the shops. Further, a person on a low income simply could not afford to constantly buy new clothes. If, for example, a dress cost $10.00 at the end of 1966, someone on shopgirl wages might be able to afford to purchase one once a month, certainly not once a week. Also, as so many mothers and daughters could sew, fashionable fabrics and dressmaking patterns would be available in stores for a longer period of time than, for example, a smaller number of manufactured finished garments in a fashion boutique. This was certainly the case in rural Victoria and New South Wales where time, cost, popularity and supply and demand were interrelated forces that made some fashion looks last longer than others.

Brigid Finlayson and Maria Sokratis

Dazzling Dolly Girl *Go Set* model Lindy (Beard)

TAHITI HUT
DISCOTHEQUE
SAT. NITE
OCTOBER 15th.
230 GLENHUNTLY ROAD, ELSTERNWICK
STEVE AND THE BOARD

for opposing the expansion of Federal aid to private schools.

13 Tony Barber, Ray Brown and Jade Hurley are loaded into a police van to escape rampaging fans after headlining an open air concert in Perth.

14 Illustrating the division in the anti-war movement, between those who favour a North Vietnamese/National Liberation Front (NLF) victory and those who simply want to see an end to Australian involvement in the war, the Socialist and Labor clubs at Sydney University begin fundraising to not only send medical aid to Vietnamese civilians, but also to the Viet Cong.

16 R&B group Mort and the Mo'Bees, who sport undertakers' outfits, win the Perth Battle of the Bands.

16 3000 attend an anti-Vietnam war rally in Sydney.

19 Kath Walker speaks out against racism at Brisbane's International Women's Day rally.

21 Overcoming resistance from the venue's Board of Trustees *The Go!! Show* spectacular kicks off at the Myer Music Bowl as part of Melbourne's annual Moomba celebrations. Braving

1966

dreary weather, an estimated 55 000 people turn out to hear sets from The Easybeats, Ian Turpie, MPD Ltd, Johnny O'Keefe, Bobby and Laurie, Lynne Randell and others.

22 The Queen and Queen Mother tour Australia.

23 After three years of operating out of the old Kings Cross Theatre, Sydney's premier beat club, Surf City, closes its doors. At its peak in 1964 the venue drew up to 5000 people a day, but with crowds dwindling and many bands moving to Melbourne it can no longer fill its massive halls.

24 Sealing their reputation as Adelaide's finest exponents of R&B, The Masters Apprentices perform four songs on Ernie Sigley's *Good Friday* TV Special.

25 The South Australian government opens Flinders University.

30 Adelaide singer-songwriter Doug Ashdown releases his first folk-tinged album *This is Doug Ashdown*.

APRIL

- Following the success of their 'If She Finds Out' single, Adelaide band The Twilights (featuring future Little River band vocalist Glenn Shorrock and Cliff Richard songwriter Terry Britten) move to Melbourne.

8 Surfers from the Pacific Femlins Surfriders Club host Australia's first all female surf competition at Manly Beach. Televised by Channel 9, the competition sees Charmaine Cornell defeat 30 others, including surf champion Midget Farelly's sister Jane, who comes in third.

12 Ubu present their *Recent Australian Films* program at the Union Theatre, Sydney University before taking it to the Australian National University (ANU) later in the month. During the screening the recently banned . . . *it droppeth as gentle rain* makes its debut alongside cartoonist Garry Shead's *Ding a Ding Day*, which chronicles the early years of *Oz* magazine.

13 On the eve of their infamous Manchester Free Trade Hall show, Bob Dylan and The Band undertake an Australian tour, encountering few complaints about their recently 'electrified' sound.

19 The first Australian conscripts, 1000 in total, leave for Vietnam. In the days leading up to their departure a number of protest rallies and candle-lit vigils are held across the nation. The largest of these sees 2000 Sydneysiders march from Martin Place to the Garden Island Naval Base, where several are arrested for attempting to chain themselves to its gates.

Go Set founder and editor Philip Frazer (Colbert)

By 1966 the new wave of youth driven rock, art and fashion had well and truly electrified the teenagers of Australia. Yet despite the growing numbers willing to lay down their money to buy records, purchase the latest threads and dance to local bands, the nation's media outlets continued to ignore or downplay the interests of youth. Stepping into the breach, to meet the needs of Australia's teenagers for the next seven years, came *Go Set* magazine. In the following interview with Iain McIntyre, *Go Set* founder Philip Frazer explains how the magazine came to play a vital role in the evolution of Australian music and culture.

How did *Go Set* magazine originally come about?

Philip Frazer: Tony Schauble and I had worked together on *Lot's Wife*, the student paper at Monash. Tony was a lot more broke than I was, and while we were on summer vacation in 1965 and looking at ways to make money, he came up with some ideas around printing. While we were working on *Lot's Wife* we had taken it through the transition to offset printing, which in those dim, dark days of the mid 1960s was a new innovation. For the first time a picture was cheaper than a 1000 words and you could use plenty of graphics.

In any event I didn't like many of his ideas until he came up with the one that we start a teenage newspaper focusing on rock 'n' roll, of which Tony knew nothing except that it was a big business in its early stages. I spent about three hours knocking out a proposal for it, including a name, which was as corny as I could come up with, combining 'Go-Go' and 'Jet-Set', two appallingly commercial terms of the time, to make *Go Set*.

We then took that to Radio 3UZ, which was the Top 40 pop station in Melbourne at the time. To our amazement their manger called us right back, and within two days we had an agreement to be advertised on 3UZ in return for a full page ad in our paper, which didn't exist yet. We then took the few ideas we had, and within a few weeks were putting out a 24 page tabloid newspaper once a week, which subsequently came out every week for seven years after that.

Which is quite amazing since as you say neither of you were huge music fans.

PF: Well Tony had heard The Beatles at parties and on the radio, but he didn't know John from Paul or The Stones from The Beatles or any of that. I was a fan, but wasn't hugely savvy about it, except that I sensed it was going to be very big, and not just commercially, but as part of a cultural shift in the making.

Inez Amaya, Ian 'Molly' Meldrum and Barry McAskill (Colbert)

Soon after we started we began attracting people who were around my age, 19, with an interest and investment in the rock scene. They ran discos or were managing bands or were way more fanatical than we were and could do the things that would make the magazine a success.

Very early on, when we were still working out of our flat, a young guy came through the door and asked what he could do and Tony said 'I don't know, but you could clean the house.' I came in and asked who he was and Tony said 'Some guy who knows a lot about the local scene.' That was Ian Meldrum. So within weeks of starting up Molly became part of the gang (laughter). He knew and cared a lot more about the venues and bands than we did, so I figured we should work with him.

Then another 19-year-old came waltzing through the door uninvited and unannounced, a woman who also seemed to know a lot about music and wanted to write about it. Tony, likewise, told me she could stick around and when I asked why he said 'Well she's got a car.' None of us did. That was Lily Brett, and along with Molly she became a key writer.

From day one we also had a local young manager Peter Rafael, who worked with Max Merritt and The Meteors, involved. He had a mate who took photos, a guy who had come out from England a few years earlier, called Colin Beard. Colin had a camera that wasn't of the highest class, so the challenge for him was to take photos in dark discos. He didn't know much about photography, but he knew about Triax film 400 ASA, and that with that you could get a decent image, even in a dark room. When he printed things out they'd come out pretty black and high contrast and that became his signature style of photography, and indeed the whole *Go Set* style.

So the whole package established itself very quickly. Within a few issues we had a style of writing, photography and management that was totally unlike anything else in existing media. Since we were making it up as we went along it was in large part just a coalescing of people who got along well with each other (laughter). There certainly wasn't any money in it in the beginning, no one got a salary.

Tell us about the focus of the magazine when it began.

PF: Early on the focus was on music, fashion and surfing – the three key areas that the new generation were into. Within the first few issues we realised our advertising base was from local

MAY

- Ubu publishes its first catalogue of films for hire. Run out of the building that houses Tula press (who will print much of Sydney's underground material in the coming years), the cooperative keeps 25% of the hiring fee to cover its costs before distributing the rest to the filmmakers involved.
- The Seaman's Union bans the provision of crews for the *Boonaroo* after it is chartered to carry supplies to the military in Vietnam.
- The Twilights win the first national Hoadley's Battle of the Sounds competition, and with it a trip to the UK.
- Having worked regularly as a band since 1958, playing musicals, nightclubs and TV spots, as well as composing hits for the likes of Col Joye, teenage vocal group The Bee Gees sign to the Spin label. Coming under the tutelage of record producer and Sydney impresario Nat Kipner, the band begin cutting demos at Ossie Byrne's Hurstville studio. Although primitive and located in the back of a butcher's shop, the studio facilities allow the trio to hone their songwriting skills, setting them up for decades of success.
- The Federal government decides against a committee recommendation to set up a new television network solely for educational purposes.

4 Sydney's legendary Missing Links break up for the last time, complaining that their management is trying to force them to sound like teenybopper Normie Rowe. Having recently released a wild album incorporating backwards masking, feedback and sound effects, members of the band now move on to play with The Richard Wright Group, The Showmen and Running Jumping Standing Still.

4 Bob Francis reports in *Go Set* that while the only regular discotheque operating in Adelaide is the Beat Basement, teen dances are continuing to draw thousands to the Octagon Theatre and Princeton Dance Hall.

5 The first Australian troops arrive in the combat zones of Vietnam.

23 Thousands rally in Sydney, and the following day in Melbourne, against the Vietnam war.

23 The Methodist Church decides at its 21st General Conference, by a vote of 132 to 18, to allow women to be ordained as Ministers.

24 Private Errol Wayne Noack becomes the first conscript to be killed in Vietnam, as well as the first National Servicemen to ever be killed on overseas duty in a time when Australia is not officially at war. His father, Walter, successfully sets a new precedent in forcing the Australian Army to return his son's body to Australia on the basis that 'He was taken from his home and sent to Vietnam whether he wanted to go or not.'

24 Having lost charismatic vocalist Ronnie Burns the previous year, Beatles imitators The Flies play

Go Set photographer Colin Beard (Beard)

Go Set ad man Terry Cleary and photographer Vera Kaas Jager (Colbert)

discos and band managers who were, for the most part, doing this stuff because they were passionate about it. One of the important things about music in Melbourne at that time was that, like *Go Set*, it was made and managed by young people themselves. We were quite happy to promote what these people were doing, because, like us, they were part of creating a new culture. In Sydney the venues tended to be controlled by old time entrepreneurs and record companies that had already covered Australian music. These were show biz professionals, whereas in Melbourne it was all going on under the radar of the established entertainment industry.

To an extent we were boring media people following the trends, but with Molly, Lily, Colin, (photographer) Vera Kaas Jager, Stephen MacLean and all the others in Melbourne, plus Greg Quill, Leo Calvo, Philip Morris and others in Sydney, we had staff who were out there every day. While we included things about overseas music, we knew there was a lot more interest in local music than you would have thought if you were just looking at the Top 40 charts. We were going out to see things live, and there were a lot of bands engaging the audience who were never heard on the radio or seen on TV.

It seems as if within a short period the paper became very popular. Who was your audience in the early stages, and where was the magazine getting out to?

PF: Well within a year we were outselling *Time* magazine. Our readers were a huge number of 13 to 19-year-olds. The high school kids of Melbourne in the first few weeks, and then within a few months we were in Sydney. By the end of 1966 we were right around the country with three different editions, one for Victoria and Tasmania, one for New South Wales and Queensland, and one for Western Australia and South Australia. Out of the 24 page tabloid paper about 20 pages were common to all editions, and then there were four pages that contained local ads, photos and content.

We also had an office in each state. In the first year I was travelling back and forth between Melbourne and Sydney because my girlfriend was up there going to the University of NSW. She was living in a group house with six boys, and what impressed me was that one of the guys was able to manage the house and get them all to pay the rent. That was David Elfick. I figured if he could

Young *Go Set* readers (Beard)

manage all that then he could manage an office, and so he became the Sydney editor of *Go Set*. David made the Sydney end a big part of the paper and had a small staff, but the other cities, Perth, Adelaide and Brisbane, were one person shows.

Unusually, for the time, we also had a number of women involved, and quite a number of our staff were gay, at a time when that word still hadn't quite emerged, but for us it was just part of life because we were of the same generation. I just looked for people who could do the job well, and whether they were straight or gay or men or women really didn't matter.

How did you promote and distribute *Go Set*?

Australia back then, and to a degree now, had an advantage for newcomers, in that most sales were via newsagents. They were the point of sale, people walked off the street and bought the thing, so your primary way of advertising what you were putting out were day bills, the posters you stick up outside the newsagents. I quickly realised you had to write them with the newsagent in mind, because you could put up some breaking group that the kids all knew, but if the newsagent didn't know them he was not going to put the poster out. We had no money to spend on promotion, but we would make up these posters and also turn up at discos with our photographers, because people would love to see photos of themselves, which we printed.

Why do you think no one else had thought about doing this kind of magazine before?

PF: The commercial publishing people had given it a bit of a shot. The newspapers would have a half page on the pop scene somewhere towards the back of the book. *Everybody's*, which was a low brow, general interest national magazine, were the only ones giving it more than a passing glance. I think the main difference in both starting the magazine and the way we did it was that we were teenagers ourselves. We were part of it, not just looking at it from the outside.

The magazine also tapped into non-musical trends such as fashion, surfing, motoring, slot cars, even hula hoops at one point.

PF: Again all of that came down to the fact that we were young. After about a year and a half we had around 30 employees around Australia, none of whom were older than 23, so we were all part of the community and reflected what was going on it.

Slot cars were a weird phenomenon whose time came and went, but while it was there we covered it. Surfing was also a new phenomenon that came to great cultural prominence in the

their last show at Pinocchio's in Melbourne.

24 The Australian branch of pharmaceutical giant Sandoz announces that due to 'The irresponsible use of the drug in the USA' it will no longer manufacture LSD for use in Australia. However, the company does offer to resume production if the Commonwealth government will take responsibility for the distribution of the drug to members of the Australian College of Psychiatrists.

24 The Sydney City Council moves to restrict the number of dances being organised by the Foundation for Aboriginal Affairs at halls in Redfern, Alexandria and Waterloo, after noise complaints and reports that police cars have been bombarded with rubbish.

25 With the overwhelming majority of Australian celebrities and pop acts avoiding any reference to politics in general, and the Vietnam war in particular, MPD Ltd take the controversial step of speaking out on the war in the pages of *Go Set*. Future ad man and 'Up There Cazaly' composer Mike Brady points to the inherent corruption involved, stating 'It seems as if both the Communists and the Americans are as much concerned with saving face and making money as they are whether its right or wrong.' Whilst saying he would serve if called up due to his 'patriotic family', Danny Finley also reveals that he 'Saw two placards on the TV coverage of an anti-Vietnam demo that appealed to me very much. One of them said in huge capital letters "Too Young To Vote – Not Too Young To Fight" and the other said on the back of a demonstrator's T-shirt "Make Love, Not War". Since I'm a practicing Christian the second one made a lot of sense.'

26 The conservative Nicklin coalition government is reelected in Queensland.

29 Harry Chan MLC becomes the Mayor of Darwin, the first Australian of Asian descent to hold such a position.

29 Following lobbying from various women's groups, the new five dollar bill becomes the first Australian currency to feature an image of a woman other than the Queen.

29 PM Holt is heckled at an election rally in Ipswich, Queensland (later Pauline Hanson's electorate) by anti-war protestors shouting 'Murderer' and 'Halt, Holt, No Conscription.'

JUNE

- Mick Lieber of Python Lee Jackson records the soundtrack for Ubu filmmaker Aggy Read's successful entry to Canada's Expo 67, *Man and His World*.
- The world's largest solar still is set up to supply water to Coober Pedy in South Australia.
- Having helped spearhead the popularity of R&B in Melbourne, the original line up of The Wild Cherries dissolves, with guitarist Malcolm McGee moving on to Python Lee Jackson and vocalist

Go Set writer Pete Steedman (Colbert)

late 1960s, and spawned its own films and publications. Because it was something that was happening more in Sydney and up the coast we realised we couldn't really keep a track of it, so after a year or so we decided to focus more on music and lifestyle.

Tell us about the advice columns.

PF: Well I looked at the British pop papers and one American publication, a dreadful magazine called *Sixteen*, and realised that teenage girls had different interests. They weren't just into the pop stars and fashion, they were also interested in talking about boyfriends and their love life, sex even. So I thought it would be a good idea to have an advice column, but there was no way we were going to have a columnist like the daily newspapers had, which was typically a mother figure, who at best was being a bit risqué and sympathetic and at worst wagging a wowser finger at everybody telling them what not to do. In the beginning we had my girlfriend at Monash writing it (laughter), but subsequently we had Wendy Saddington and Ross Wilson's wife Pat Wilson, aka Mummy Cool. I knew if we said things like 'If you're pregnant then get an abortion' that we'd get into trouble, but then who gave a damn. Parents would write in and call and give us shit, but we didn't care.

In 1967 Lily Brett and Colin Beard undertook an overseas tour that managed to put them and *Go Set* right at the heart of a number of overseas events and trends. How did this come about?

PF: As I remember it, it was through Tony. His dad was a freelance foreign journalist who sent stories back to Germany. Somehow he came into contact with BOAC, and through that Tony got them to give us some free airline tickets. This was probably the only contact that ever came through anyone's parents that did us any good (laughter). Our parents were all supportive, but none of them were rich or well positioned.

So Lily Brett, our main reporter, and Colin Beard, our photographer, got free around-the-world tickets. It was perfect timing, because the whole British pop thing was at frenzy point. We weren't able to give Colin and Lily any spending money, so they had to stay on friends' couches, but they were able to go and schmooze with all the big names in London pop. Then they went to the United States, and again happened to be there at the right time. Colin went to the Monterey Pop Festival, a seminal event almost on a par with Woodstock, and got on stage and took roll after roll of close up colour photos of Jimi Hendrix, Janis Joplin and all the rest. He had to send the rolls back to Melbourne, because he was broke and couldn't afford to develop them (laughter).

Go Set writer Lily Brett enroute to Los Angeles (Beard)

Another change from late 1967 onwards was the involvement of Ed Nimmervoll. How did he get involved, and what effect did he have on the way music was written about in *Go Set*?

PF: My memory is that he wrote a letter to the editor saying that our Top 40 charts were just a compilation of various radio station charts and that he didn't think that was a very accurate way to do it. I contacted him and he came back with a formula that to my mind was admirably thorough, complex and conscientious, so I gave him the job.

He also took the writing and reviewing a step beyond what Molly and Lily had been doing with their on the street type thing, which was a damn good thing, and he gave us something from the analytical end of the spectrum. I would have been thrilled if his dedicated, committed, local perspective had a come a year earlier, but it hadn't and that was fine.

As the decade wore on the magazine seemed to incorporate more of a serious, journalistic tone alongside incorporating the pop news and charts. Was this part of a conscious effort or just a reflection of the fact that people were taking rock music more seriously?

PF: I never sat down and said 'We've got to get more in-depth now.' It was more a reflection of the fact that I was a couple of years older and so was our community. We were growing up with our readers. By 1969 it was clear that this wasn't just a culture of pop music, it was a culture of more meaningful music and politics. Someone like myself or our readers, who had started out being 15 and excited by The Beatles, were now beyond that and interested in the lyrics of Bob Dylan or caught up in issues like the Vietnam war.

By the late 1960s the magazine had also developed a more sophisticated and psychedelic look, largely under the direction of Ian McCausland. How did he become involved?

John Bastow leaving music altogether.

1 Garage rockers The Lost Souls take out the Radio 3AK Seeker contest, winning $100 and a contract with Sunshine records.

1 Sydney discotheque Here opens with performances from The Easybeats and The Id, as well as champagne and go-go girls.

1 Melbourne pop identity and future *Countdown* host Ian 'Molly' Meldrum appears on an episode of the Australian cop show *Homicide*.

4 Riding high in the charts with their version of 'Fortune Teller', The Throb are mobbed in Hobart.

6 Troops returning from Vietnam have red paint smeared on them by anti-war protestor Nadine Johnson during a welcoming parade in Sydney.

12 Scratched, bruised and suffering from shock, teen sensation Normie Rowe is admitted to hospital after being mobbed at a wild reception at the Sydney Town Hall.

13 A fire at a Salvation Army men's hostel in Melbourne claims 29 lives.

16 Australia joins eight other countries in forming the Asian and Pacific Co-operation Council.

16 To ensure that the drug is only available for psychiatric use, the Federal Government announces that LSD will be brought under the same strict import controls affecting narcotics.

21 Federal ALP Opposition leader Arthur Calwell is shot by Peter

Kocan as he leaves an anti-war meeting held at Mosman Town Hall. Taken to hospital suffering facial injuries he rapidly recovers. Kocan is later sentenced to life imprisonment for the attempted assassination.

22 Adelaide's In Sect have three guitars stolen from their car after playing a gig at Murray Bridge.

22 In a belated attempt to bring the new generation of musicians into the fold, the Musicians' Union of Australia puts out a call offering to assist any young acts who have been ripped off by promoters.

30 During a visit to Washington PM Holt seals the Australian government's subservience to American interests. Attacking Britain and Europe for their refusal to enter or support the war in Vietnam, he declares that Australia is 'All the way with LBJ'. On the same day, following the announcement that the US had bombed Hanoi and Haiphong, eight protestors are arrested in Sydney for blockading the entry to the US consulate.

JULY

- Having lost an appeal for exemption from conscription the previous year, school teacher William White openly defies a

PF: We ran a competition in 1967 or 1968 for someone to design a front cover for *Go Set*. This was a pretty thinly disguised effort on my part to find a decent graphic artist, because up until then I'd been doing it. I knew that there were great innovations going on in design, both generally and in a psychedelic direction, and that I had neither the time nor the talent to make them happen for *Go Set*. We got something like 5000 entries, 4500 of which were better than anything I could do, and some of them were astonishingly good. In the end it came down to two entries, and Ian not only got the cover, but we also hired him to guide our graphic design.

In 1969 the magazine took an overtly political tone with Jean Gollan's series of interviews with local activists, and by 1970 you were openly supporting the Vietnam Moratorium with a peace poster competition and other initiatives. How did the readership react to this?

PF: Jean was interested in writing about what was happening politically, and I was happy to have her do so because I knew our readers would be up for it. People need to remember that the Vietnam war, which the Vietnamese call the American war, was very imminent in our lives, because they were trying to conscript us and send us off to a war that didn't make any sense.

In 1967 I'd been given an offer I couldn't refuse to leave the Medical faculty at Monash, in part because I'd been organising medical students to resist the draft. So this was part of our lives and part of a whole generational movement, which saw what our parents were doing and had done and were proposing to do as disastrous across the board. We didn't need the Marxist intellectuals to interpret this for us, we got it, we knew the war and many other things were a terrible idea.

We threw the *Go Set* office in Drummond Street, Carlton open to political groups we liked and let them use our typesetting, lay out and other support systems for free. Mainly anti-Vietnam and Moratorium groups, but we also helped people like Ross Wilson's Party Machine put their songbook together.

Judging from the interviews you ran in *Go Set*, your writers were often asking musicians to comment on issues like conscription, but in the early days very few seemed willing to do so. By 1970, however, just about everyone had an opinion on the war.

PF: Well within those four years a huge amount of things had changed. A lot of Australians and 100 000s of Vietnamese had been killed. In 1966 it was still the beginnings of an imperialist foray, but by 1970 it was a fully fledged invasion, and Australia was well and truly implicated as a lame follower of American initiatives. The war was also in the day to day headlines, which in 1966 it wasn't.

Early on, Normie Rowe, the number one solo pop star in Australia, went to Vietnam and supported the war and we didn't trash him for it, we reported it. By 1970, though, there were very few people who didn't get it. The whole country, and particularly the youth culture, had become more and more urgently upset about Australia being in Vietnam, being a lackey of the US and being run by big business people. This was a big movement and we certainly weren't leading it, but I'd like to say we were nudging it. (laughter)

What about the influence of drugs at this time? *Go Set* had talked with bands about taking speed as far back as 1966, but towards the end of the decade your stories and look reflected the fact drug use was becoming more prevalent.

PF: Once again it grew up with the magazine. When we started I'd never even smoked a joint, and was possibly behind the times, but pot use really exploded in 1967/68 and was rapidly followed by all the other drugs on the pallette at the time, the psychedelics, etc. As it became part of our lives, it became part of the magazine. We kept one eye on thc cops, but not much.

How did *Go Set*'s spin off teen magazine *Gas* come about?

PF: Well the dirty secret behind *Gas* was that in late 1968 The Monkees, the ultimate synthetic pop band out of America, were going to tour Australia. Our Sydney editor David Elfick had arranged for our photographers to get on stage and be there with the band all around the country. His idea was that we could put out a souvenir book. We were about two thirds of the way through doing this when the Monkees management got wind of it and sent us a letter saying that 'If you put this out without us owning it then you're dead meat.' (laughter)

Coincidentally, we'd advertised for an assistant art director and had decided to hire a young woman who'd come from a Melbourne ad agency. She told us that 'By the way, my ad agency have been working on creating a teenage magazine to compete with *Go Set*. It will only be sold at Shell petrol stations and will be called *Gas*.' Armed with this amazing piece of marketing intelligence I got my dad, who was a lawyer, to check that no one else had registered the business name.

We subsequently launched *Gas*, thereby killing Shell's plans, and made the first issue a special on The Monkees, thereby stopping their management from being able to sue us. So really *Gas* was a sort of bizarre response to the realities of big, bad business forces trying to push us around. The magazine proved to be very successful so we kept it up. (laughter)

Another magazine you launched out of the *Go Set* office was *Revolution*.

PF: Not long after launching *Gas* we realised that the youth culture had grown to be much more than a pop music thing, and that trying to straddle eight years of young people's lives and interests in one magazine just wasn't going to work. We started out by introducing the Core section into *Go Set* for the older, counter-cultural readers, but later realised we needed a separate publication.

In amongst putting out *Go Set* I'd also finished an honours degree in Politics at Monash, looking at theories of revolution and alienation, Marcuse and all that stuff. I was interested in the counterculture as a movement, and thought it had the potential to change society, but didn't think there was a place in *Go Set* to discuss that.

I'd brought in John Hawkes to edit *Go Set* so I could have a break, and he was interested, so the two of us plus David Elfick became the driving forces behind *Revolution*. We knew it wasn't going to make any money, but it was something we believed in.

notice to report for National Service. He later tells Greg Langley in *Decade of Dissent* that 'I was eligible for the second ballot, but knew from day one that I would not go. They were asking me to kill people, and that basically was my objection. I had other objections.
I objected to the particular war and to conscription, but mostly I objected to being asked to kill another human being. No one had refused [before] to go or had made any particular stand, and I had no idea of what to do. I just knew that I wasn't going. In the end I registered, was balloted in and then applied for an exemption.
In retrospect I would not have taken that path . . . If it was two years later [when the draft resistance movement had formed] I would have refused to register and tried to confront the system.' In the coming months further appeals are rejected resulting in White being physically removed from his classroom and suspended from work without pay.

- Perth pop singer Johnny Young tours the East Coast of Australia on the back of his Easybeats' penned hit 'Step Back'.
- The Federal government sets up the Motor Vehicle Design Committee to report on car safety standards.
- The Vince Maloney Sect breaks up, with its namesake going solo.
- Australian racing driver Jack Brabham wins the French Grand Prix in a car of his own design.

Did you encounter many problems with censorship?

PF: Well, censorship comes in many forms, and our primary problems with all the magazines were with printers and distributors. We had to battle with printers over the use of four letter words and talking about things like smoking pot. At different times we had to block out words and even change who we got to do our printing.

Most of our distributors were the establishment companies, except in Victoria, where we had grown up with a distributor who had *Go Set* and stuck with *Revolution* as well. Other than in New South Wales, where we had a friendly distributor who also did *Nation Review* and was prepared to take the hit, we encountered a lot of resistance over *Revolution*, and at times had to distribute it ourselves. We also got sued by all sorts of people, but my philosophy about being sued was always 'Know you're going to be and be ready for it.'

The most notable criminal case we faced was when the Victorian state government attacked *Go Set* for publishing Abbie Hoffman's *Steal This Book*. Hoffman was an American Yippie, a provocateur who wrote this book on how to live off this 'corrupt society' by ripping it off. It was tongue in cheek, and had things like how to avoid paying at pay toilets by sneaking under the door – pretty radical stuff. (laughter)

Anyway, we printed that and then the Victorian Attorney General launched a prosecution and I was taken to court, committed to trial and put into custody. I was later released after the cop who had me in custody, who wore a leather jacket and was trying to be a nice guy, got me out on a bond. He later turned out to be the head of the Victorian Political Squad. He spent a while trying to buddy up to me, but I don't think he learned a damn thing that helped in the cause of keeping Victoria righteous and straight. Eventually they dropped the case.

How did you eventually come to lose control of *Go Set*?

PF: Over the years *Go Set* had accumulated not some vast fortune, as some of our critics may have thought, but a vast debt to Waverly Press. We'd started the thing with absolutely no money and to their credit they had understood it had a future, but by 1970 we owed them over $100 000, which back then was a lot of money. They couldn't see us paying them off any time soon, which was true, and now here we were putting out a thing called *Revolution*.

Waverly Press, which was a family business, was then taken over by some more corporate types who essentially said 'Pay the bill or give us control of the company.' A lot of things then went down and eventually I was kicked out because I wouldn't do what they wanted me to. Around the same time Rupert Murdoch offered to buy *Go Set*, but his one condition was that I stay on. I told him I wasn't prepared to work for him and moved on to other things.

Despite the way it ended, I think the legacy of *Go Set* was that it not only helped 100 000s of young readers navigate their way through an explosive period, but also enabled a lot of immensely talented people to gain confidence in their abilities and go on to do their own things. All of these people were inspired and able to develop themselves by being part of a self-managed community.

***Go Set* limped on until 1974, but increasingly lost its focus and audience. Philip meanwhile continued to break ground with publications such as *High Times* (not to be confused with the US marijuana magazine), *Australian Rolling Stone* and *The Digger* before moving to New York in the mid 1970s. He currently edits the on-line newsletter *The Hightower Low Down*.**

- The basic wage rises by $2 after the Federal government rubber stamps the Arbitration Commission's recent recommendations.

4 Harry Vanda, guitarist of The Easybeats, is devastated when his wife, Pam, commits suicide on the eve of the band's move to the UK. In an interview with *Everybody's'* Maggie Makeig, Vanda reveals that Pam 'was subject to severe bouts of depression' and that they had been married 'on the day that [manager] Mike Vaughan discovered [the group] at a dance in Hornsby.' Vanda asserts that he had only kept the existence of his wife and child a secret to protect them from the very same press that is now hounding him day and night. Following Pam's funeral he leaves for London to hook up with the rest of the band, while his son is cared for by his grandparents in the Netherlands.

7 During a visit to London, PM Harold Holt attacks European governments and NATO members for failing to support the war in Vietnam.

9 Having collected approximately 10 000 tins of food for hunger relief in India, MPD Ltd discover that much of what they have gathered is unpalatable by Indian standards. Selling off the unwanted items at the Frankston Town Hall, the band later turn over money and powdered milk to the Indian Trade Minister and the Australian Council of Churches.

The Loved Ones

1966

10 The Easybeats experience delays enroute to London when up to 4000 fans pull down fences and invade the tarmac at Perth airport. The band members are subsequently forced to hide in a van at the end of the airstrip after a bomb threat is called in.

11 1500 people rally in Martin Place in Sydney to protest the US bombing of North Vietnam.

13 *Everybody's* reports that pop musicians around the country are finding it hard to secure accommodation due to the length of their hair. One hotel in St Kilda, The George, is hailed for bucking the trend to provide a home for members of Max Merritt and The Meteors, The Id and Running Jumping Standing Still.

13 Having scored multiple hits in Australia, Normie Rowe signs to Polydor records in the UK and Atlantic in the US.

Apex KILMORE Club

GO WOOLSHED & B-B-Q GO

SATURDAY
DECEMBER 10

CONTINUOUS MUSIC FROM 9 P.M.
BY MELBOURNE'S TWO TOP GROUPS
The Banned with their *Go-Go Girls*
& *The Tribe*

BEST GO - GO GIRL
COMPETITION
LOWDENS' WOOLSHED
FOLLOW ARROWS FROM KILMORE POST OFFICE
ALL THIS FOR ONLY $1

• • • Gerry Humphreys (Beard)

19 The newly formed Australian Artists Managers Association puts promoters on call, warning that the non-payment of musicians will result in their venues being boycotted.

20 TV channel ATN-7 airs an Easybeats special compered by Tony Worsley and Billy Thorpe.

20 Sydney pop singer Mike Furber speaks out against conscription in the pages of *Go Set*, saying 'Conscription is immoral. I believe that living in a free country means that everyone, no matter their age, is free to choose his own destiny. Conscription is therefore a lie, a mockery of our much vaunted democracy . . . you can't find an excuse for forcing a man to give up his chosen career to go into the army and fight a war in what would be one of the most dubious conflicts of all times.'

28 Over-zealous security guards at a Normie Rowe concert in Perth storm off the job after the singer kicks and pushes a bouncer to stop him from bashing a young fan.

If you needed one word to describe The Loved Ones, then that word would be 'unique'. After all, the band were a rhythm and blues group with a trad jazz background who had success in the pop charts with original songs combining baroque keyboards and catchy handclaps with raw guitars and thumping drum beats. Not to mention featuring a singer whose voice could switch between a sub-sonic guttural rumble to piercing wail within the blink of an eye. Even in the immeasurably fertile pop scene that was Australia in the mid-to-late 1960s, The Loved Ones always stood out from the rest of the deck. Everybody loved them, from their peers to punters and critics alike. And even though they only got to issue one album, *The Loved Ones' Magic Box* has never been out of print since it was first released in 1967. Ian D. Marks traces the rise and fall of one of Australia's most original bands.

In October 1965, three members of one of Melbourne's most popular trad jazz outfits decided to defect to the world of electric Rhythm and Blues. Clarinettist, vocalist and occasional violinist Gerry Humphreys (born Brian Anton Humphrys, 1941 in Battersea, England) and tuba-player Kim Lynch (born 1945) had enjoyed three years of regional success with The Red Onion Jazz Band – a band that also consisted of Brett Iggulden on cornet and saxophone, trombonist Bill Howard, Alan Browne on drums and Rainer Breit on banjo.

The Red Onions had been in heavy demand during the trad jazz boom of the early 1960s. In early 1963, the group released their first 7" EP, *An Impromptu Recital By The Amazing and Entertaining Red Onion Jazz Band* on the tiny EAST (Elwood Audio Services Transcriptions) recording label. It apparently sold well to their 'duffle coated, desert booted audience', thanks no doubt to healthy airplay on radio station 3XY's 'Jazz as You Like it' program. In December that year The Red Onion Jazz Band played at the 18th Annual Jazz Convention in Melbourne, and four tracks were recorded for a second EP. It is on this record that we first get an inkling of what would later become one of the most distinctive and exciting sounds in Australian pop: the dynamic vocals of one Gerry Humphreys.

The Red Onion Jazz Band At The 1963 Jazz Convention EP contains two vocal tracks: the bawdy sea-shanty 'Barnacle Bill', and a cookin' version of Tommy Dorsey's 'It's Tight Like That'. 'Barnacle Bill' sees Humphreys adopting an outrageously camp quasi-soprano, while the more straightforward (but equally suggestive) 12-bar 'It's Tight Like That' showcases Humphreys' outstanding multi-octave vocal leaps – a signature technique that he would later use to devastating effect on The Loved Ones' 'Everlovin' Man'. His clarinet playing, by-the-by, was none too shabby either.

In 1964, The Red Onions adopted a seventh member into the fold – a cherubic 17-year-old pianist named Ian Clyne – and that year things really moved along for the band. They signed a

The Loved Ones (Beard)

contract with the eccentric Melbourne recording label W&G and put out a well-received EP entitled *The Red Onions At Home*. Also during the year, the band got to ride atop an Egg Board float at the annual Moomba parade (dressed, appropriately enough, as roosters), as well as making an appearance on the now legendary *In Melbourne Tonight* TV show. Live, the 'Onions were a consistent draw card, attracting on one night some 2000 plus punters to a gig at the Opus discotheque in South Yarra. In early 1965, The Red Onion Jazz Band released their self-titled debut LP, with cover art supplied by tuba player Kim Lynch – a promising artist who had studied graphic art at the Royal Melbourne Institute of Technology.

Despite the Onions' apparent success within the goatee-bearded and *Gauloise* smoking world of the jazzers, it was becoming clear that music was heading in a different direction. Trad jazz was quickly becoming last-year's news, and music shops began clearing away their vast stocks of clarinets, trumpets and banjos in order to make room for the electric guitars, basses and amplifiers that all the kids wanted. Certainly three members of The Red Onions – Gerry Humphreys, Ian Clyne and Kim Lynch – were frustrated by the limitations of trad jazz; and little by little they found themselves increasingly drawn into the dark and forbidding sound of the blues.

I knew what The Red Onions were doing was old-hat when I heard this local band play the song 'Gloria' by Them. I knew that was where I wanted to go – raw and in-your-face R&B.
Gerry Humphreys in conversation with Paul Stewart, *Sunday Herald Sun*, July 2000.

Amidst this turmoil, a second Red Onions LP was recorded for W&G in August 1965, entitled *Hot Red Onions!* However, before the album even had a chance to hit the record bars, Clyne, Humphreys and Lynch had left the band. Their decision to quit was as much financial as it was musical. As Ian Clyne reflected six months later in *Go Set*, 'Let's face it, eating is just not one of those things you can give up on the spur of the moment.' The Red Onion Jazz Band continued without them however – eventually touring Europe in the '60s, '70s, '80s and '90s. The group finally came to an end in 1996 with the death of founding member Bill Howard.

Immediately after making good their defection from The Red Onions in September '65, Clyne, Lynch and Humphreys wasted no time in getting their new band together. Pianist Ian Clyne was the quickest to adapt to this new music, having previously played Rock and Roll with a band called The Vampires (who once shared the bill with US mannequin rocker Fabian). Kim Lynch had more of a challenge ahead. As he'd chosen electric bass, Lynch found that he had to adapt his oom-pah, oom-pah tuba bass-lines to fit R&B, later also admitting 'We didn't know anything about electronics or amplification . . .'

Dark-eyed Gerry Humphreys though, was a natural front man. With his exotic good looks, astonishingly broad vocal range and British accent still intact (he'd only just migrated to Australia some eight years earlier, in order to get away from an evil stepfather), Humphreys was a star just waiting to happen. The only thing was, having now ditched his trusty clarinet, he had to immediately learn blues-harp – and fast.

One local group that Gerry Humphreys and Ian Clyne had admired for some time was the purist blues outfit The Wild Cherries. The Cherries' guitarist was a handsome blond architecture student named Rob Lovett (born 1945), whom Clyne and Humphreys had come to know through the group's residency at The Fat Black Pussycat in South Yarra. An offer to join Ian and Gerry's still unnamed unit was made, and the guitarist happily accepted. Lovett also managed to supply the group with a drummer, in fellow Melbourne Uni architecture student Terry Nott. Evelyn Waugh's 1948 black comedic novel *The Loved One* provided the band's name, and barely two months after the dissolution of The Red Onions, The Loved Ones had a weekly residency at the Mad Hatter Discotheque in Little Lonsdale St, Melbourne.

With a repertoire consisting of Muddy Waters, Bo Diddley, The Rolling Stones, Howlin' Wolf, and even a few rudimentary originals, The Loved Ones began to build up a live following. Drummer Terry Nott didn't last the distance however. He was replaced in late 1965 by yet another University student: an acquaintance of Ian Clyne's named Gavin Anderson (born 1946).

1966 was a huge year for The Loved Ones. The February launch of the influential Melbourne trade paper *Go Set* coincided seamlessly with the peak of the R&B boom in Australia. And over the next twelve months, The Loved Ones, along with the ultra-hip Purple Hearts, became one of the magazine's 'darling' bands. During this time, the group also acquired a manager, Peter MacKennal, who also looked after The Groop and ran the popular Garrison discotheque in Prahran. The Loved Ones blazed a trail at all the happening venues of the time, and even had

AUGUST

- The Federal Budget sees an 18% increase in spending on arms and the military.
- Safely ensconced in London, The Easybeats hit the famous Abbey Road studios to record with their Australian producer Ted Albert. Although the band are happy with the results, United Artists are not, with the result that the band move on to work with producer Shel Talmy (The Who, Kinks and Creation).
- The Masters Apprentices tour Melbourne for the first time, impressing crowds at leading venues The Biting Eye and Thumpin' Tum.

3 The Purple Hearts admit the obvious when singer Mick Hadley details the band's amphetamine use in the pages of *Go Set*, stating emphatically 'I think drugs are necessary! I mean what do you do when you have to cram 48 hours of work into one weekend – you have to take something in order to keep awake.'

7 The biggest anti-Vietnam rally yet held in Australia takes place in Sydney on Hiroshima Day, with over 5000 gathering in Hyde Park in support of the International Days Of Protest.

17 40 Aborigines protest outside the Northern Territory Legislative Council, demanding equal pay and improved living conditions.

18 Australian troops engage and defeat Viet Cong guerillas in the battle of Long Tan, suffering 18 casualties in the process.

19 The film adaptation of John O'Grady's *They're a Weird*

Mob, which lightly satirises Australian attitudes to immigration, premieres in Sydney. The film goes on to become the highest-grossing locally-made film in Australian cinema history until the release of *Alvin Purple* in 1973.

26 The Gurindji people walk off the Wave Hill and Newcastle Waters cattle stations, demanding ownership of their traditional lands and refusing to work any longer for subsistence wages. Their actions launch a new era of struggle for Indigenous rights, and one that, for them, is ultimately successful, when they are granted land rights seven years later.

31 Sydney based record producer Nat Kipner threatens the publishers of *Go Set* and 2UW DJs Ward 'Pally' Austin and Tony McClaren with a $200 000 lawsuit over disparaging comments made about him in the paper's 17 August edition.

31 Running Jumping Standing Still vocalist and future *Sullivans* star Andy James (nee Anderson) outlines his band's obsession with noise, telling *Go Set* that 'This isn't a gimmick, although a lot of people do say we just turn on a performance, so that we can be labeled the wildest

their own fan club. They also signed with W&G's token teen label In – although the record company were at first unaware of this fact.

Ian [Clyne] scored a recording date. He told W&G that we'd be in on Tuesday, and to their surprise, The Loved Ones turned up instead of The Red Onions . . . we pulled a bit of a stunt with that. So they got a hell of a shock at W&G because they were pretty conservative.
Rob Lovett in Nigel Buesset's film *Gerry Humphreys: Loved One*, 2000.

The Loved Ones warmed up by recording a cover version of Fats Domino's 'Blueberry Hill', but for their debut single the guys decided to opt for an original number composed by Ian, Gerry and Rob at Ian Clyne's parents' living room. Rob Lovett had a chord progression and Gerry Humphreys had a couple of melody ideas, but according to Lovett, Ian Clyne provided the glue to put the whole thing together.

Ian was the person who made things work. When we wrote 'The Loved One', I had these chords and he said, 'Got anything else?' so I played these other chords and Gerry said 'Well that's two good bits but we need a chorus. And then he started singing, 'Oh baby I love you so . . .' and we said, 'Work the chords out Ian!' And then Ian later went to Kim [Lynch] and said, 'Okay this is what you're going to play.'
Rob Lovett in conversation with Ian D. Marks, May 2004.

'The Loved One' has an exuberance about it that still makes it sound fresh today. Ian Clyne had fortuitously brought along Brian Coughlan – keyboardist for Adelaide band Blues, Rags and Hollers – who loaned his 'squeaky' Farfisa organ for the recording session. Not only would this organ provide an essential component to the sound of the record, but Coughlan would also solve a potential problem regarding the song's structure. 'The Loved One' is based around a 9/8 rhythmic pattern, but drummer Gavin Anderson insisted on pounding out a straight 2/4 beat, which only met the 9/8 timing after every third bar. Brian Coughlan pointed out that such an eccentric arrangement would only confuse people wishing to dance, and suggested adding some 3/4 handclaps to tighten the song up. Not only did this suggestion solve the song's timing problem, but it also provided 'The Loved One' with a strong commercial feature – a handclap and guitar-based rhythm, as opposed to the traditional bass and drums. Kim Lynch's bass actually contributes a melodic role to 'The Loved One', while the organ alternates between violin-like percussive stabs and moist, elongated swirls. But when all is said and done, the song belongs to Gerry Humphreys. His outstanding vocals switch between rampant R&B snarling and casual conversation within a single breath. No other Australian pop vocalist had ever sung with so much confidence and attitude on their debut outing as Gerry Humphreys did on 'The Loved One'. And much of this was due to the fact that the singer was not some green 16- or 17-year-old punk, but a well-seasoned and versatile entertainer of 25. He had a unique style of internal timing as well. Rather than singing in a strict syncopated style, he tended to work around the beats.

Gerry Humphreys and Rob Lovett (Colbert)

Gerry has timing but not rhythm. The point at which he chooses to come in, is unusual – until once he does it you go okay, that's how it is. But he'd be absolutely no good in singing a rock song where you require a strict BOMP-da da-BOMP da da-BOMP. In 'The Loved One' for example, he sings 'She co-omes my way' rather than 'She-comes-my-way'. He doesn't hit the beats hard.
Rob Lovett in conversation with Ian D. Marks, May 2004.

The Loved Ones (Colbert)

'The Loved One' was released in May 1966, backed with the Ian Clyne composition 'This is Love', and soon began to sell so well that W&G actually ran out of copies. The band was then forced to take out an advertisement in *Go Set* apologising for the inconvenience. 'The Loved One' eventually peaked at #15 on the Melbourne charts and stayed on them for over four months. It wasn't until September that other states fell under the spell of the record – though when they did, it performed even better than it had done in Melbourne, hitting #1 in Sydney and Brisbane and a highly respectable #2 in Adelaide.

The middle of 1966 was a dizzying time for The Loved Ones. After a lightning tour of Sydney they returned to Melbourne where they began a relentless grind of discotheque gigs and TV appearances. Somewhere during this hectic period, they also found time to shoot a film clip for an upcoming documentary on youth culture entitled *Approximately Panther*. The film segment shows the band cheerfully miming 'The Loved One' upon a rickety looking staircase. The clip still receives the odd airing on TV, and is one of the very earliest (if not *the* earliest) rock video ever done in Australia. 'The Loved One' became a national hit again in 1987 when INXS recorded a cover version backed with an original composition entitled 'The Unloved One'.

The band's second single, the incomparable 'Everlovin' Man', was recorded in a marathon session – mainly because the band hadn't got around to writing any new songs yet – at W&G's primitive two-track studio, with Humphreys suffering a severe cold. In fact, according to the singer it was the cold that gave his voice a particular edge on the record.

The inspirational spark for 'Everlovin' Man' came about after Ian Clyne had imported a Hohner Electric Piano from Germany – one of very few models in Australia at that time. The song begins with a baroque piano figure, counter-pointed by bass, which immediately disappears as soon as the band – or more specifically Gerry Humphreys – kicks in. If Humphreys' vocal on 'The Loved One' was something wild, then his Janis Joplin-like tour de force on 'Everlovin' Man' is nothing short of magical. The song itself is actually quite formless – a scant two minutes and eight seconds existent purely upon the whim of Gerry Humphreys' vocal dynamics, and the lazy-yet-thick swing rhythm held down by the rest of the band.

The B-side 'More than Love' is a spirited blues in 'E' containing some gritty lyrics. Handclaps a la 'The Loved One' make an effective reappearance, although it's a pity that Ian Clyne's melodic piano-work is buried so low in the mix. But, for the first time on a Loved Ones record, Gerry Humphreys' newly-acquired harmonica skills (double-tracked what's more!) can be heard.

group, but that's just not true. We are sincere in our addiction to feedback and believe it gives you a release. The sound can completely capture your mind and we have seen people who were nearly hypnotised by our music. You don't just go on stage and go mad. Everything is sincere, you play and draw in the crowd with you and then comes the climax of feedback and smashing of instruments.'

SEPTEMBER

- Foreshadowing their role in providing visuals and light shows for underground events in the years to come, Ubu screen a series of their films at the Sydney University Architecture Ball.
- Anti-war activist and military veteran Les Waddington is expelled from the Returned Services League (RSL) for organising an Ex-Serviceman's Association to oppose all wars. An initial meeting of the group draws about 25 people, but its membership grows to over 500 in the coming years.
- MPD Ltd leave Australia to base themselves in the UK.

- Following an attempt by the Victorian Censor to ban *American Atrocities in Vietnam*, sales of the pamphlet skyrocket, with 30 000 copies eventually being distributed. In order to break the ban, anti-war activists regularly sell the pamphlet in the Bourke Street Mall.
- Pop group Somebody's Image, featuring Russell Morris and managed by Ian 'Molly' Meldrum, form in Melbourne.
- Following the success of *Go Set*, the proprietors of Melbourne's Albert Sebastian's discotheque launch their own magazine titled, predictably enough, *Albert Sebastian's*. Featuring a colour cover, the magazine includes interviews with local and overseas pop stars, motoring pages, advice columns and fashion tips. Although it fails to run to its proposed monthly schedule, the magazine does appear semi-regularly over the next few years, before winding up in February 1968.
- The Easybeats finish work with Shel Talmy at the Abbey Road Studios on future hits 'Friday on My Mind', 'Remember Sam', 'Made My Bed (Gonna Lie In It)' and 'Pretty Girl'.
- Graham Kennedy's *In Melbourne Tonight* begins regular transmission to Sydney, via newly laid coaxial cable, but fails to replicate its home town success.

'Everlovin' Man' b/w 'More than Love' was released toward the end of August 1966. Despite a grading of 'C' (mediocre) by *Go Set*'s 'Pop Disc Review Panel' (Note: the Beach Boys' *Pet Sounds* masterpiece 'God Only Knows' also received a 'C' that same week), the single leapt from #24 to #7 on the Melbourne 3UZ charts within just two weeks of release.

Not long after the single was issued, the band made the decision to sack their pianist, Ian Clyne. This was a potentially devastating move, as it was apparent that Clyne was clearly the best musician in the band, and his composition and arrangement skills had been crucial to the band's first two hits.

Ian [got] sick of being the only one to do any of the promotional or organising work. We were all kids, and if anyone would do it, the rest stood back. As a result, Ian was cast into the position of being the nagging parent, and became more in tune with our manager than the rest of us.
Rob Lovett in conversation with Christopher Hollow, *Rhythms* Magazine, August 2001.

I've always felt as though [sacking Clyne] was the stupidest thing that the band ever did, because he was a component of the creative circuit which consisted of all of us. It was like a little radio set where each little resistor is important, you take one out and the radio won't work – we just weren't smart enough to see that.
Kim Lynch in conversation with Jackie Vidot, *Tom Thum'*, 1992.

Ian Clyne went on to play with many top Australian bands. He formed his own group in 1967 called The Ian Clyne Group, before joining The Black Pearls and the Ram Jam Big Band. Throughout the 1970s Clyne played with such luminaries as Levi Smith's Clefs, Chain, Mighty Mouse, Cool Bananas and Renée Geyer. He later moved to Los Angeles, where he played sessions with Joni Mitchell and Deep Purple. When The Loved Ones reformed in 1987, the members unanimously petitioned for Ian Clyne to be involved.

Clyne's replacement on keyboards was Treva Richards (born Trevassa Richardson 1946) from popular Melbourne blues band The Delta Set. Little could he have realised it at the time, but Treva Richards was joining The Loved Ones at the very cusp of their ascendancy. Indeed, for a couple of months there, The Loved Ones were the biggest group in Australia.

'Everlovin' Man' hit #2 in the Melbourne charts in mid-September, and was only kept from top spot by The Beatles' 'Yellow Submarine'/'Eleanor Rigby' double-sider. Then, as 'Everlovin' Man' began to sell in other states (#3 Sydney, #5 Brisbane), it took with it the previously stagnant 'The Loved One', and soon both records were featuring in top tens all over the country. There was even some talk about a possible assault upon the United States.

By November 1966 The Loved Ones had become a truly national phenomenon. Aside from having broken out in both Melbourne and Sydney, 'The Loved One' was steadily on the rise in Brisbane, while 'Everlovin' Man' was #1 on the 6KY charts in Perth – and meanwhile, both singles were simultaneously in the Adelaide top ten. Then, in the fourth week of November, 'The Loved One' finally cracked the National top ten some six months after its initial release.

Things were getting a little out of hand for the band at this point though. Their second tour of Adelaide caused pandemonium at the airport and riots during their shows. Gigs were now being punctuated by screaming girls and stage invasions. As one member recalled, 'Suddenly we were stars and we couldn't handle it . . . everybody was saying how good we were, and I knew we weren't. We were getting worse and worse.'

During this time W&G fortuitously rush-released a self-titled four-song EP which, apart from the first two hits, featured only one previously unreleased song – 'Blueberry Hill'. Despite the fact that former pianist Ian Clyne had played on every track on the record, the EP's picture sleeve featured the post-Clyne line-up. Nevertheless, the *Blueberry Hill* EP (as it soon became known) sold well in all cities, particularly Sydney, where at one stage the band held spaces 10, 11 and 12 in the 2UW chart with their new EP, 'The Loved One' and 'Everlovin' Man' respectively. The EP peaked at #3 in Perth, #7 in Adelaide and #10 in Brisbane – yet only made it to #19 in Melbourne.

In early December, The Loved Ones were presented with a special silver disc for the being the first Australian band to have two singles in the national top ten simultaneously. But this popularity didn't necessarily translate into financial riches, with the band often having to borrow other bands' equipment!

If support band's members had day jobs they usually had these terrific amplifiers, and we'd leave our shitty amps in the car and tell them that we hadn't brought ours along.
Rob Lovett in conversation with Dean Mittelhauser, *Ram*, September 1987.

Gerry Humphreys and Ronnie Charles (Colbert)

The Loved Ones' third single, recorded in November 1966, holds the distinction of being the first original by the band not to feature the word 'love' in its title. Allegedly influenced by the high rotation of Dylan's *Blonde On Blonde* album, the discovery of marijuana and an affair that Gerry Humphreys had had with an Adelaide lady – 'Sad Dark Eyes'/'The Woman I Love' sees The Loved Ones at their most Gothic and sensual.

Beginning with a classical electric piano figure followed by a stormy piano rumble, 'Sad Dark Eyes' once again displays the majesty with which The Loved Ones could knock out a 2-minute pop song. The middle section has Rob Lovett doubling the piano with a 12-string acoustic guitar, giving it a superb harpsichord effect. Although a more restrained effort than their first two singles, 'Sad Dark Eyes', with its intense 6/8 time signature and strange descending chorus harmonies, managed to maintain a perfect three-for-three strike rate of classics. It is no surprise perhaps that Nick Cave and the Bad Seeds would later cover the song to great effect during their live shows, and that Saints founding member Ed Kuepper would see fit to record his own cello-heavy version of 'Sad Dark Eyes' in 1995.

Unfortunately, the single was poorly handled by W&G, who'd made the mistake of releasing the record just before the record presses closed down for the Christmas holidays. Despite being hard to locate in the record shops, 'Sad Dark Eyes' made #7 in Perth, #13 in Adelaide and #19 in Brisbane, but only #27 nationally, due to relatively poor showings on both the Melbourne and Sydney charts.

As 1967 loomed, the momentum for The Loved Ones didn't let up for a second. Apart from constant live work and numerous TV appearances on both *Go!!* and *Kommotion* the band set south for their first tour of Tasmania.

Extra police and security guards were needed everywhere – surrounding the stage, rescuing fainting girls, and trying to protect The Loved Ones. The climax of the evening took place when singer Gerry Humphreys had his trousers completely ripped off him by frantic girls. Lead guitarist Rob Lovett was almost dragged off the stage, and local Launceston singer Jimmy Graham was knocked unconscious and taken to hospital.
***Go Set*, January 1967.**

In April 1967, The Loved Ones released their fifth record 'A Love Like Ours'/'The Loverly Car', which made the top 40 in all cities, doing best in Adelaide (#17), and making it to #26 nationally. As with their previous releases, both sides were collaborative efforts by the whole band – a song writing approach almost unique to The Loved Ones at the time. Although it has a crisper overall sound, 'A Love Like Ours' is a weaker effort than the previous three singles. This is possibly due to the fact that The Loved Ones had enlisted an outside producer for the first time, in this case Lindsay Morehouse – house producer/engineer with W&G. Lyrically 'A Love Like Ours' is also fairly unimaginative. Gerry Humphreys' vocals are characteristically black sounding, and some of the instrumentation is tight and soulful enough, but after the brilliance of their first three singles, it was no 'Everlovin' Man' or 'Sad Dark Eyes'.

'The Loverly Car' on the other side is more interesting. Not dissimilar to something that Ray Davies might have concocted, 'The Loverly Car' is a barbed parable on the perils of cosy suburban materialism. Based upon an almost nursery rhymish melody, the song is a direct departure from anything The Loved Ones had previously attempted. Kim Lynch's former life as

4 Having scored a massive hit with their 'Hitchhiker' single earlier in the year, Bobby and Laurie launch the *Dig We Must* program on ABC TV.

4 Jack Brabham wins the Italian Grand Prix, making him the World Formula One's top driver for the third year running.

7 Works by artists Martin Sharp, Peter Kingston, Mike Glasheen, Garry Sheed and others are featured in an *Oz* magazine exhibition at the Clune Galleries in Sydney.

10 The Moods and The Purple Hearts play *Go Set* writer Lily Brett's 20th birthday bash at Sebastian's in Melbourne.

10 The Australian Council of Trade Unions (ACTU) attacks the Meat Industry Employees Union for placing a black ban on all cattle delivered from stations where the Gurindji are on strike.

17 St George defeat Balmain to win their eleventh successive Rugby League Grand Final.

20 Canberra's first late night discotheque, Chapter One, opens. Managed by Rex Bullen and future ABC journalist Paul Lyneham (both from local R&B champs The Bitter Lemons), the club's launch sees 350 pack into its basement to catch jug band Broken Things and the Jag Tamla Go-Go dancers.

22 Melbourne is hit by electricity cuts as power workers in the La Trobe Valley hold a strike in defiance of orders from the state based Trades Hall Council.

24 St Kilda overcome Collingwood to win the VFL Grand Final.

26 Having won the inaugural Hoadley's Battle of the Sounds, The Twilights leave for the UK aboard the *Castel Felice*.

28 1000 teenagers from the Yorke Peninsula sign a petition demanding Adelaide bands The Masters Apprentices and The Y?4 repeat their recent South Australian regional tour.

29 Trouser splitting Texan P.J. Proby kicks off a return tour of Australia supported by local acts Ronnie Burns, Dinah Lee, Eden Kane and Wayne Fontana. The tour proves a dismal failure, with small turn-outs leading to the cancellation of shows in Western Australia.

OCTOBER

- Women from the protest group Save Our Sons chain themselves to the gates at Richmond Barracks in Melbourne in an effort to prevent conscripts from being sent to Packapunyal for training.
- An Australian delegation attends exploratory Vietnam peace talks in Manila.

a tuba player is particularly evident on the record, as his gorgeous bass-lines would have been perfectly suited to that instrument.

Having now conquered Melbourne, Sydney, Adelaide and Hobart, The Loved Ones headed over to Perth. What followed was the most infamous period in the band's history, and one that in many ways would signal the beginning of the end.

LOVED ONES ARRESTED! CHAOS FOLLOWS PERTH INCIDENT blared the front cover of *Go Set*. The arrest in question regarded the theft of two blankets, two pillows and one lamp stand from a Kalgoorlie hotel. The Perth tour was by-all-accounts a comedy of errors.

The promoter who took The Loved Ones over to Perth still owes them $1300 dollars . . . After finishing [a] concert at Narragin, The Loved Ones were forced to leave straight away for Kalgoorlie, as it was a 500-mile trip. During this trip, the Austin Van had a smash and overturned, a new Galaxie seized and blew up. And The Loved Ones with manager Peter MacKennal had to hire a taxi, to complete the remaining 209 miles of the trip. They arrived in Kalgoorlie at 9 pm the next night, which meant they hadn't slept for two days.

As if this wasn't enough, they had trouble at the Palace Hotel were they were booked in, and after [a] disagreement with the management, were told they couldn't stay there. (Her attitude was, 'If I had have known it was a pop group, I wouldn't have accepted the bookings.') So The Loved Ones, now desperate, did their concert, which was a huge success, and then decided it would be best to go back to Perth at night as they were due to catch a plane back to Melbourne on the midday flight.

Before they left the Kalgoorlie Hotel, Gerry and Gavin took two pillows and two blankets from the hotel, as it was freezing cold in the car and they needed some sleep . . . The pillows and blankets were going to be left at 6KY radio station, who in turn would return them to Kalgoorlie.

Ian Meldrum, *Go Set*, April 1967.

On arrival at Perth airport, the promoters' cheques bounced and later both Gerry Humphreys and Gavin Anderson were arrested and jailed on charges of theft. The remaining Loved Ones eventually got back to Melbourne, but Anderson and Humphreys had to stay in Perth in order to face court the following day. The pair were found guilty and ordered to pay a fine, and in the end radio station 6KY helped pay for their fare back to Melbourne.

Gerry Humphreys (Beard)

If all of this wasn't enough, The Loved Ones then had to quickly go back to Adelaide the following Tuesday to commence an Eastern Australian tour with British bands Eric Burdon and The Animals and Dave Dee, Dozy, Beaky, Mick and Tich. And although the band went down well with all crowds, cracks were beginning to appear.

The Loved Ones had become stuck in a groove of repetition. Because of the management, because of the mode of the day in Australia – which was playing your hits over-and-over again at every performance, with no time to refresh, write new material, improvise. Or they were half-hour spots, you only had time to play six or seven numbers . . . that was it, you were out of there. The band was stagnating, frankly. And the contrast of seeing The Animals onstage playing Coltrane . . . and to see that they were involved in the events of the day, the student protests and so on . . . was a sharp contrast, a very sharp contrast. And I think it highlighted to me that the band were stagnating.

Kim Lynch in Nigel Buesset's *Gerry Humphreys: Loved One*, 2000.

Immediately after the Australian tour, Kim Lynch announced his resignation from the band. Later convicted of the possession of marijuana and amphetamines, he was still able to take up a scholarship he'd won with the National Gallery Painting School.

With Ian Clyne and now Kim Lynch gone, Gerry Humphreys was the only remaining Red Onion. Rather than search for another bass player, it was decided that Rob Lovett would switch from guitar to bass and a new guitarist would be recruited. Within just seven days of reporting the departure of Kim Lynch on their front page, *Go Set* announced that their very own reporter Brigid Monks had discovered 21-year-old Danny De Lacy, who'd recently returned to Australia after six years in the USA. According to Ian Meldrum De Lacy had played in The Sir Douglas Quintet, an American band called The Missing Links, and had done sessions for James Brown and Phil Spector, including playing on Ike and Tina Turner's wall-of-sound masterpiece 'River Deep, Mountain High'.

With the new line-up completed the band continued to tour, playing to record crowds in Adelaide before returning to Melbourne to play some of the newer 'psychedelic' clubs that were opening there. Their visual image also began to change around this time. The button-down shirts and plain coloured skivvies were replaced by beads, fringed shawls and loose fitting Asian-style tops. Gerry Humphreys had taken to wearing a floppy freak hat, and was now sporting a *Sgt. Pepper* style moustache.

After a couple of unfruitful recording sessions, The Loved Ones' fifth single 'Love Song' b/w 'Magic Box' was finally released in late July 1967. Both sides of the single are dominated by newcomer De Lacy's white-hot guitar-flourishes. 'The Magic Box' is perhaps best described as 'psychedelic soul', whilst 'Love Song' is a sweeter jazzier track. De Lacy's double-tracked lead guitar lines in 'Love Song' are melodic and sharp, although funnily enough, they are completely absent in the mono CD reissues put out by both Raven and Karussell. 'Love Song' didn't sell a great deal of copies. In fact, according to *Go Set*, Melbourne radio stations flat-out refused to play it. Ian Meldrum in one write-up claimed that this was because the song had been linked to LSD hallucinations (say, *wha'?*). In the end, 'Love Song' became the only Loved Ones single not to make the Sydney, Melbourne or Brisbane charts. It peaked at #83 nationally, due solely to its respectable showing in Adelaide (highest pos. #18; five weeks in).

By now, the sting had gone out of the pop group experience for The Loved Ones. John Phillips of the Mamas and Papas had expressed interest in producing the band in the US, but this was quashed by W&G records.

Phillips' interest disappeared when he saw the band's W&G contract. Rob Lovett says The Loved Ones' record contract bound them to Woomera Music for five years. W&G then sat on the contract, dashing his hopes of releasing the band's records in the US.
Richard Miles, *More Than a Loved One*, 1999.

It also didn't help that, despite providing the label with several national hits, W&G would not allow the band to record in state-of-the art four-track facilities. At one stage the band had even paid for their own 4-track recording in Sydney, but W&G thought the recording levels were too high and made the band rerecord the songs involved. The fact, that they'd been ripped off in Perth back in April, and were now no longer able to command the same high concert fees that they had during their hit period, also made the decision to split so much easier.

Ironically, once the band had decided to separate, W&G finally released The Loved Ones' long-overdue debut album *The Loved Ones' Magic Box. Magic Box* was not so much an album, as a collection of previously available tracks with a couple of unreleased studio warm-up numbers thrown in for good measure. Of the LP's dozen tracks, ten had previously been released in either EP or single form ('This Is Love' being the sole omission), and the other two were a couple of 12-bar numbers recorded by the Danny De Lacy line-up just prior to doing the last single. 'Shake Rattle and Roll' sounds more like the 'Three Little Bops' of Warner Brothers cartoon fame than a hip 1967 combo donned in paisley robes and purple silk finery.

On the other hand, The Loved Ones version of Muddy Waters' semi-obscure B-side 'I Want You to Love Me' is a rockin' R&B workout done very much in a 1967 vein. Danny De Lacy's clunky yet explosive electric guitar dominates the song, but he is well backed up by Gavin Anderson's rolling drums and Treva Richards' melodic boogie-woogie piano work. Gerry Humphreys' vocal performance, meanwhile, is uncharacteristically mellow.

The album's cover was very much in keeping with the times, featuring a full colour portrait

- The Bee Gees' 'Spicks and Specks' single tops the national charts, giving the band its first major Australian hit.
- Melbourne pop singer Lynne Randell leaves for the UK before moving on to the US, where she will eventually settle in Los Angeles.
- The Masters Apprentices release their debut 'Undecided'/ 'Wars or Hands of Time' single on the Astor label. The first commercially released Australian song to explicitly deal with the Vietnam war, 'Wars or Hands of Time' is in part inspired by vocalist Jim Keays' recent selection in the September conscription ballot. Had he not signed on for the Citizens' Military Force (the equivalent of today's Army Reserve), Keays may have well been sent to Vietnam, bringing the band, like so many other Australian acts, to an abrupt end.
- *They're A Weird Mob* premieres in the UK.

5 Pastor Ted Noffs announces he will set up a clinic and drop-in centre at the Wayside Chapel in Sydney's Kings Cross to provide anonymous counseling for drug users.

10 Psychiatrists from Australia and New Zealand meet in Sydney to

of the band in front of a day-glo backdrop. Drummer Gavin Anderson is at top left with a red suit on, Gerry Humphreys is standing on the right, nostrils flared, wearing his floppy hat, a purple shirt with a psychedelic tie and a wedding band on his finger. Danny De Lacy is sitting with his arms resting on the back of a wooden chair, while beneath him an unshaven Treva Richards looks ever so-slightly stoned. Commanding centre stage in the photograph, though, is Rob Lovett – resplendent in a canary yellow suit and matching granny glasses. Apparently Lovett's famous yellow suit only lasted for about three weeks.

After a week in Sydney trying to keep the damn thing clean it was ceremoniously trashed during a 12 hour psychedelic train trip back to Melbourne.
Rob Lovett in conversation with Christopher Hollow, *Rhythms Magazine*, August 2001.

After The Loved Ones split Treva Richards married in Adelaide and has remained there to this day. In 1986 he became a reigning champion on Tony Barber's *Sale of the Century* game show. Drummer Gavin Anderson moved to New York and was the only original member not to play in the band's 1987 reformation tour and subsequent live LP. Rob Lovett joined 'Australia's answer to the Walker Brothers' – namely The Virgil Brothers – who were managed by his then partner, *Go Set* journalist and future internationally acclaimed writer, Lily Brett. After the Virgil Bros, Lovett co-wrote songs for The New Seekers and Olivia Newton-John, before returning to architecture. Gerry Humphreys continued to remain a fixture on the Melbourne live circuit, becoming an MC at his own Bizaar disco. He also fronted Gerry and The Joy Boys (Mr Joyboy was a character in Evelyn Waugh's *The Loved One*), and made a couple of singles with them. In the early 1970s he returned to England where he lived until his death in 2005.

Gerry Humphreys and Danny De Lacy (Colbert)

discuss the therapeutic use of LSD.

19 Perth beat group Ray Hoff and The Offbeats relocate to Melbourne.

19 A delegation of Aboriginal leaders from Northern Victoria visit the Minister of Aboriginal Affairs, demanding they be given control of the reserves on which they are forced to live.

20 US President Lyndon Baines Johnson begins a three day tour of Eastern Australian capitals, where 100 000s line the streets to greet him in scenes reminiscent of recent Royal visits. Not all Australians are so welcoming, however, as anti-war protestors block his car in Sydney, prompting the conservative Premier Askin to order a Police Superintendent to 'run the bastards over.' Thankfully the police demur from this course of action, although they do move in to arrest, beat up and drag away demonstrators at a variety of locations across the city.

In Melbourne the next day a small band of protestors charge the President's limousine in Carlton chanting 'LBJ, How many kids did you kill today!', before tossing rotten fruit and scuffling with police. Later that day two brothers catch LBJ on a visit to Dame Mabel Brook in South Yarra, throwing paint

Sharpies, Stylists & Mods

1966

over his car windows. The brothers are later remanded in custody for three weeks and forced to undergo psychiatric testing at Pentridge Gaol before being fined $680.

A smaller protest takes place in Canberra later in the week outside LBJ's hotel. One protestor, Megan Stoyles, later makes the cover of *Time* magazine wearing a 'Make Love Not War' T-shirt.

21 Students at the Hobart Matriculation College find themselves at loggerheads after visiting Biology Professor Charles Birch disputes the resurrection of Jesus Christ. In the weeks to come some students begin wearing badges reading 'Christ Lives' whilst others announce 'Birch is Right' and call for 'Freedom of Thought'.

NOVEMBER

- The Easybeats 'Friday on My Mind' is released in Australia giving the band their second Top 10 hit (after 'Sorry') in as many months. Over the next six months the song will scale the charts in numerous countries, eventually selling well over a million copies.
- *Oz* magazine reprints a recent *Playboy* magazine interview with LSD guru Timothy Leary, in which the good doctor hypes

• • • Outside The Catcher (Colbert)

the use of acid as a tool for raised consciousness and a way for women to achieve thousands of orgasms.

- 440 Qantas pilots strike for 27 days over pay and conditions.
- Having sold more than 1000 badges reading 'Defeat US Cultural Imperialism', members of Melbourne anarchist group TREASON (The Revolutionary Emancipists Against State Oppression and Nationalism) hand out copies of their *Facts About The Anti-LBJ Demonstrations* pamphlet at Melbourne University.
- A Morgan Gallup poll held in the build-up to the Federal election finds that 63% of Australians are in favour of conscription, but only half that number think that conscripts should be sent to Vietnam.
- The constant round of gigs and promotional appearances required to maintain pop success begin to take their toll, as both Mike Furber and Johnny Young are hospitalised following physical and mental collapses.

Despite the growing influence of psychedelic culture globally, Sergeant Pepper and his kin were scorned by a large bunch of Melbourne's teens during the 1960s. For them drinking, dancing, fighting and sporting natty duds were of uppermost interest. As Tagdh Taylor relates, these were the sharpies, spawn of rocker, mod and Southern European tailors.

The original mods of late fifties London were jazz loving dandies with a taste for Continental style. By the early sixties, mod had caught on across Britain, but in a form more accessible to the average teen. Rhythm and blues, scooters and amphetamines were the order of the day. The look remained clean-cut European cool.

Melbourne in 1963 was still rocker country, but things were changing. By 1964 they were in decline. The mod aesthetic was catching on. The younger element of the rocker scene set forth in a new direction, inspired by the neat streamlined look of mod. The older blokes were too set in their ways to follow suit. The mod-style '64 Rocker' was born and soon re-christened the sharpie. And away we go.

Hair was short back 'n' sides, usually parted, cut every two weeks. The threads were swank but not foppish – trench coats, Crest-knits, pinstripe flag pants, handmade chisel toed shoes, dapper tough guy, sharp! Besides mod, the main influence was a certain kind of migrant Italian man, denizen of inner-city coffee bars, always togged just so, spiffed but macho. Sharps were nuts for Italian style, and the cult was always strongest in migrant-heavy neighbourhoods, where the tailors and shoe shops they favoured were located. Sharpie girls, or sharpie 'brushes' as they were tagged, thumbed their noses at the prevailing trends in women's fashion, favouring crisp classic simplicity – twin sets, pearls, knee length pleated skirts.

By 1966 every area of Melbourne boasted a sharp crew or three. Some were modest, under-sized mobs, content to stay put in their territory, slug it out with neighbouring teams and lord it over the local teenage populace. Others were veritable armies, journeying far and wide on search and destroy missions. It wasn't all spiffy strides.

Papers such as *The Truth* and *The Sun* were full of reports of pitched battles between sharpies and mods, most of which were more than somewhat wide of the truth. There were differences and sometimes conflict between the two groups, but the real action was elsewhere – sharp v rockers, sharp v surfies, and most commonly sharp v sharp, that is neighbourhood against neighbourhood.

Defining what the word 'mod' meant in sixties Melbourne, is a tall order indeed. When the newsmen referred to mods, they meant any youngster who wore colourful duds and sported a Beatle do, a misnomer that was greatly resented by the scores of Melbourne kids that lived by the original mod ethos.

The mod-purists/stylists listened to soul and rhythm 'n' blues, and followed local groups like The Chelsea Set and The Purple Hearts, groups that played R&B with a bit of crash-bang-wallop. Their home base was the Thumpin' Tum in Little Latrobe Street, Melbourne's most up-to-the-minute dance.

The term 'stylist' was coined in England. The mod elite adopted the label to distinguish themselves from the Johnny-come-lately variant. Melbourne's sharps and mod-purists/stylists weren't exactly brothers in arms, but they managed to co-exist without too much friction. Sharp was really just a knockabout version of English mod, and by '67/'68 there were quite a few ex-sharps in the stylist camp. As the stylist handle caught on, it too lost its original meaning, and was used to describe any kid in a Myers 'In-Gear' ensemble.

Things got doubly confusing as the original stylists/mod-purists drifted away from Italian suiting and into the more exotic togs of the psychedelic era. Mods, stylists, long-hairs, whatever-the-hells, if they had long hair and effeminate clothes sharps didn't like them, and many weren't above expressing their distaste with a smack in the mouth.

The fact that sharps were invariably on the dog-list at mod/long-hair dances didn't exactly help foster good relations between the two sides. Nor did the media. By beating up a few mod/sharp blues into a full-scale gang-war, the papers threw bucket loads of fat into the fire. But at the end of the day, belting long-hairs was just a nasty lark, there was no war. It takes two to tangle, and most of Melbourne's mods/long-hairs just weren't interested.

Sharps fought sharps, but there was rarely any deep felt enmity involved. For most it was just an exciting diversion. Most kept things relatively gentlemanlike. No kicking, no weapons, no five-on-one bashings. The point of sharp gang clashes wasn't to wipe out your opponents and

Young sharpies (Colbert)

1 Galilee wins the Melbourne Cup.

3 The Liberal Reform Group is set up by businessman Gordon Barton to oppose the Vietnam War from an otherwise socially conservative position.

13 The Easybeats make their London debut at Brian Epstein's Saville Theatre, opening for The Four Tops, Cliff Bennett and The Rebel Rousers and Bob Miller and The Millermen.

15 Normie Rowe's backing band The Playboys leave Melbourne to join the singer in London.

25 Australia receives its first satellite-transmitted TV program from the UK.

26 The Holt coalition government thrashes the ALP in the Federal election, winning it by the biggest majority ever in Australian history. Anti-war groups, who had largely pinned their hopes of success on an ALP victory, briefly falter before switching to more strident protest tactics.

29 Following the Federal elections the government decides to make an example of conscientious objector William White by dragging him from his Gladesville home to face a military court. Locked up for 21 days in Holsworthy prison, White becomes the first Australian to be jailed for draft resistance.

DECEMBER

- MPD Ltd return for a national tour following an unsuccessful series of shows in the UK.
- In the fallout from the ALP's massive election loss Gough

Whitlam narrowly defeats a vote to expel him from the party for failing to strongly support ALP leader Calwell's hard line in opposing the Vietnam War.

7 Police raid a number of houses in remote Cooktown, Queensland, after discovering an ounce and a half of marijuana and eight tabs of the hallucinogen Di-methyletriptamine (DMT) on a man returning from the local post office. During the raids they uncover 18 three foot marijuana plants as well as packets of hemp seeds. Five men and one woman, including a Latvian sculptor and a German sailor, later face court over the matter.

9 Negotiations begin over the building of a US-administered satellite spy-base at Pine Gap in the Northern Territory.

10 Melbourne police blitz chemists and clubs hoping to stamp out the illegal sale of pep pills.

10 In one of Australia's first LSD busts, a Sydney art student faces the Central Court of Petty Sessions on charges of illegally manufacturing the drug, as well as possessing marijuana he had found growing wild near Maitland. In his defence the student's lawyer tells the court that 'LSD has given him an added appreciation of his work as an artist.'

11 Acting Police Commissioner Bauer announces the formation of a Queensland Drug Squad, which will 'be on the lookout for drug passing in coffee bars and other places where teenagers frequent.'

end the war. You wanted to wreck them, but not for keeps. It was more sporting, gladiatorial. You fought for the rush and to earn a rep, and no matter who came off best you'd meet again soon for a rematch.

To pay such loving attention to the minutiae of your dress and then risk it all in backstreet punch-ons might seem a little non-compis-mentis, but it was simply a matter of devotion to the cause. A lot of sharps were apprentices in mucky, hands-on trades, but would still front up to work decked out in flags, chisels, the whole shootin' match. Being a sharpie meant you dressed right 365. Anything less would be half-stepping.

Rival gangs weren't the only callers to contend with, the police were a constant threat as well. A certain mob of city coppers prowled the suburbs in their Studdebaker Hawks, keeping an eye on the natives. Their objective was to stamp out the gangs, and by all accounts they weren't averse to pouring on the rough stuff to get a result.

Former sharps talk of a band of undercover cops called the Silent Six, who were roundly hated in sharp circles. Supposedly, their brief was to break up any group of teenagers they found loitering in the city. Their tactics are said to have included dishing out thirty-pound fines for the use of salty language, a handsome ransom in the sixties, particularly to teenage apprentices with a mania for tailored plumage.

Another method the cops are supposed to have used to rid the city of trouble making mobs was to march them down to Flinders Street Station and press gang them onto trains bound for the suburbs. Not necessarily the suburbs they hailed from, they just stuck them on the first train that pulled in!

The foremost sharpie haunt in Melbourne was The Bowl, located near Flinders street station, beneath a bowling alley at 21 Degreaves Street. The Bowl offered big name bands and a DJ spinning the kind of records sharps favoured. Sharpies liked American soul and British beat sounds, music of the R&B genus, music that led to crowded dance-floors. Big-timers such as The Easybeats, Normie Rowe, The Masters Apprentices, Max Merritt and The Meteors, Billy Thorpe and Ronnie Burns (who, according to one source, had his nose broken by a sharpie 'fan') were doing the circuit at the time, and were all well liked by the sharp crowd. Lesser known groups such as The Browns, led by legendary guitar-man Les Stacpool, were also popular. Singer John 'Swanee' Swan has said that for sheer voluminous bloodshed, Browns' gigs took the biscuit hands down.

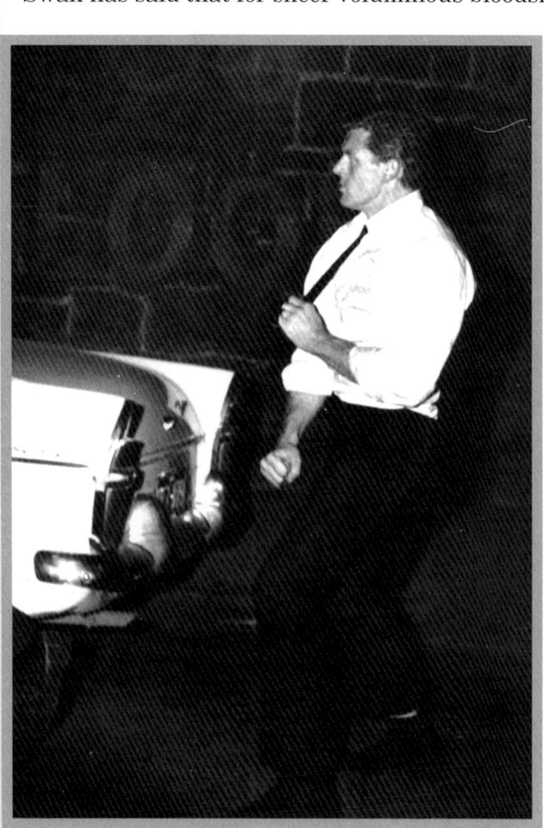

Scourge of the sharpies, bouncer Bob Jones (Colbert)

The Bowl opened in late '64 and was originally a mod dance, but by mid '65 the sharps were well and truly in residence. Like all the dancehalls, The Bowl was an all-ages, teetotal affair, but there was always alcohol in the air, as most of the clientele kicked off the evening with a spot of underage thirst quenching at Young and Jackson's.

The Bowl was a rough and rowdy joint. Brawls were common. But the atmosphere was more extrovert than threatening, the bottom line was fun, and if you got too unruly you'd have to tangle with the bouncer, Stretch, a veteran sharp street-fighter/ pugilist of colossal repute.

A rocker dance was held every Friday night above Flinders street train station in the Vic Rail ballroom, mere spitting distance from The Bowl, so if you grew tired of rug-ripping and felt like handing out some blood-shed you need only step outside. The two teams would lock horns every Friday at closing time, and the proceedings could get pretty ferocious. One ex-sharp told me of a night he was chased by a mob of rockers wielding iron baling-hooks that they'd liberated from the rail yards.

The Circle Ballroom in High Street Preston was another popular sharpie hang-out. Sunday nights at The Circle the whole scene came together, giving the youngsters a chance to rub shoulders with the older fellas. The Circle was one of the few dances the older sharps frequented; mostly they were to be found in pubs, pool-halls or at the track. Some of the older blokes were clothes conscious in the extreme, setting the pace for the lower orders. Others no longer cared and dressed decidedly un-sharp. Nobody was going to scold them for it. In general a laissez-faire attitude to matters of dress was unacceptable, but rank had its privileges. Quite a few of them had done time and some carried guns. It didn't pay to piss them off.

In late '66 a dance venue called The Catcher opened, a momentous occasion for Melbourne's teenage populace. Up till then all dances had closed at midnight, but The Catcher stayed open well into the wee small hours. The Catcher was really geared towards the long-hair crowd, but sharps were generally allowed in, and many made it their regular weekend habitat. Before The Catcher opened, the only joints still going after night's high noon were the 'sly-grogs'.

For many moons Australian drinkers suffered under laws that required pubs to close by 6 pm on weekdays, and prohibited them from opening on Sundays. These were the days of the 'six o' clock swill', when the call for last orders signalled the beginning of a tap-draining beer bacchanal.

During this time the sly-grogs thrived. The sly-grogs were pubs or private houses where the booze flowed at all hours, regardless of the law – on the sly, as it were. Sharpies were all deep drinkers. Some had a taste for rebel pharmaceuticals, Purple Hearts and the like, but they were a tiny minority; booze was the poison of choice. Most sharps were too young to pass muster at pubs, so the sly-grogs were a godsend.

Sharpie was as much a lower-middle class phenomenon as it was working class, but it was born in Melbourne's working class inner-city, and it's fair to say its mind-set was working class larrikin. The average sharp girl worked in an office, and the blokes were usually apprentices or shop assistants, a lot of them in the rag trade. But for most work was but a means to an end, keeping their pockets lined – the weekend was what really mattered.

During the week most sharps stayed in their neighbourhoods, meeting up with their mates after work. Most gangs had a coffee bar/hamburger joint that served as a meeting place cum base of operations. But on Saturday arvo the whole sharp world would be at large in the city. There were always scraps, but it wasn't all hate and war, there was a lot of brotherhood as well. The city was the place where everyone came together, and first port-of-call was always Flinders Street Station.

Sharps always travelled by train, mostly because they were too young to drive. For many who grew up in the long-hair camp, weekend train rides into the city during this period are indelibly linked in memory to the threat (real or imagined) of copping a pasting from a gang of sharps, and it was always a gang, you'd rarely see a lone sharp.

As soon as they were old enough, most sharps bought cars, and Holdens were, of course, the machine of choice. A car and licence opened the door to a whole new life. Suddenly you weren't so shackled to the neighbourhood you lived in. You could go to any part of town you fancied without having to take on the locals. You were freed from the tyranny of the last bus home. Most significantly, you could bend an elbow in any watering-hole you chose, legitimately. All this led to a lot of kids fading out of the scene.

In their late teens most sharpie blokes started feeling a yen to step out with a lady-love on their arm, rather than with a pack of mug-lair cronies in tow. The calming influence of true romance put an end to many a sharpie bash-artist's reign. Back in the sixties most folks had tied the knot by the time they were twenty-one, and the once-sharp were no exception.

The rise of Hippy played a significant role in the demise of the original sharpie scene. First off, there was flower power/psychedelia. In 1966/'67 the pop world was taking off in all manner of new directions. Eastern music and philosophy, LSD, *Tomorrow Never Knows*. '64 pop and '67 pop were horses of a very different colour. But flower power never really caught on with your common or garden Aussie teenager, at least not to the degree it did overseas. Things did change, in Melbourne dances were given new names more in keeping with the times: The Scene, a mod dance in Canterbury, became Lord Johns, The Bowl became The Trip. Musicians started to experiment more, The Purple Hearts called it a day and Lobby re-emerged with the full-blown psychedelia of The Wild Cherries. Mod/stylist garb got wilder, more colourful, more effeminate. But for every kid game enough to don a frilly shirt and beads, there were five sharpies to belt him for it.

12 Lone round-the-world yachtsman Francis Chichester arrives in Sydney in his yacht *Gypsy Moth IV*.

14 *Go Set* reports that whilst mods and sharpies have been doing battle in Melbourne, older rivalries prevail in Sydney, where 1950s style rockers have been regularly invading mod hang outs. According to police sources, gangs of up to 50 Bodgies have been hounding Beat venues with reports of 'Long haired and mod attired youths being forced to run the gauntlet of jeering Rocker-type youths.'

19 The Institute of Criminology at Sydney University releases a report indicating that there has been a significant increase in the use of marijuana use in recent years, with 57 people charged with possession in the past 15 months alone. Revealing an inability to keep up with the trends, the Institute's Professor J. Maddison comments 'There does not seem to be much doubt, as so many other studies have shown, that the use of this drug is particularly prevalent and perhaps confined to those people referred to as Beatniks, including jazz musicians, artists and fringe groups of various kinds.' In the next decade marijuana use rapidly moves from the 'fringe' to the mainstream, with 7176 cannabis offences recorded in 1975, and the estimated number of Australian smokers topping half a million.

20 The Australian government receives two resolutions from the United Nations General Assembly calling on it to grant Papua New Guinea and Nauru independence by 31 December 1968. In the case of Nauru the deadline is met by January of that year, but Papua New Guineans are forced to wait until 1975.

22 The Australian troop commitment to Vietnam is increased to 6300 men.

23 William White gains his freedom after a second application for total exemption from Military Service is granted at the Central Court of Petty Sessions in Sydney.

23 Normie Rowe returns from the UK to visit his family and play a one-off show at Adelaide's Octagon Theatre.

Iain McIntyre

Psychedelia may not have been much of a goer down-under but it set the scene for Hippy, which, in the broadest sense of the word (long haired, hooch smoking, let-it-all-hang-out rock fans), was very big indeed. By the end of the sixties Hippy was the thing, and a lot of sharp kids were growing their hair, smoking pot and bidding cheerio to the world of natty threads and blood 'n' guts street-brawls. It looked like sharp was finished, but it was just an intermission. By the early seventies it was back. And how.

The Catcher bouncers (Colbert)

Doug Parkinson of The Questions (Colbert)

1967 MUSIC

WORLD EVENTS

- Former Hollywood actor Ronald Reagan becomes Republican Governor of California.
- Yippie activists invade the New York Stock Exchange sending traders into a frenzy when they toss dollar bills onto the trading floor.
- A number of outdoor 'Be-Ins' are held in San Francisco, Berkeley, Detroit and New York, bringing together up to 10 000 hippies at a time.
- The USA, the USSR and the UK sign a trilateral treaty banning the deployment and use of nuclear weapons in space.
- Rolling Stones Keith Richards and Mick Jagger are arrested and sentenced alongside counter-cultural impresario John 'Hoppy' Hopkins for drug possession.
- Muhammed Ali is sentenced to five years in prison and stripped of his World Heavyweight title after refusing to comply with conscription.
- The Six Day War in the Middle East sees Israeli forces counter an Arab military build-up with a surprise attack on Egypt and her allies.
- The Monterey Pop Festival is held in California, featuring career making performances from Jimi Hendrix, Janis Joplin (with Big Brother and The Holding Company) and Ravi Shankar.
- Students stage a sit-in occupation of the London School of Economics.

Robert James Taylor (Colbert) • • •

The year in Australian rock music

1967 was an astounding year in Australian music. Trends seemed to come and go in less time than it took to change the batteries in your brand-new Philips 'Popmaster' transistor radio. And while '67 will always be remembered as the year of *Sgt. Pepper*, Australia still had plenty of grungy garage rock up its sleeve before the year rang itself out. In fact, four of the very best examples of Aussie '60s Punk were released in 1967: 'I Want, Need, Love You' by The Black Diamonds (January), 'Come On' by The Atlantics (March), 'By My Side' by The Elois (April), and 'Ugly Thing' by The Creatures (November).

Yet, as raw sounding as these records were, they were clearly branching out into new territories – as was *all* music in '67. Eastern-style musical scales, free-flowing middle-8 sections, blankets of fuzz guitar and exploratory echo effects were becoming de rigueur in many pop records of the year. The Bee Gees, Normie Rowe and The Playboys, The Twilights and Johnny Young all headed over to London. In The Bees Gees' case, it was for good. Meanwhile The Easybeats returned home, having cracked both the US and the UK charts.

Bobby and Laurie, MPD Ltd, The Loved Ones and The Throb all called it quits in 1967, while new bands such as Iguana, The Party Machine, Cam-Pact and The Valentines represented the new breed. Soul, blues and R&B music was still the sound of choice for punters in the clubs, but once musicians got an earful of Jimi Hendrix and Cream – things changed forever. The biggest pop story of the year however, was that of Normie Rowe being drafted into the Australian Army to fight in the Vietnam War.

International Album Releases

The Doors – *Self Titled* and *Strange Days*
The Hollies – *Butterfly*
Love – *Da Capo*
Buffalo Springfield – *Self Titled*
The Byrds – *Younger Than Yesterday*
Jefferson Airplane – *Surrealistic Pillow*
The Velvet Underground And Nico – *Self Titled*
The Grateful Dead – *Self Titled*
The Jimi Hendrix Experience – *Are You Experienced?* and *Axis: Bold as Love*
The Beatles – *Sgt. Pepper's Lonely Hearts Club Band*
The Kinks – *Something Else*
The Easybeats – *Good Friday* (UK/US)
Incredible String Band – *5000 Spirits or the Layers of The Onion*
The Small Faces – *Self Titled*
The Yardbirds – *Little Games*
The Beach Boys – *Pet Sounds*
Tim Buckley – *Goodbye And Hello*
Cream – *Disraeli Gears*
The Rolling Stones – *Their Satanic Majesties Request*
The Who – *The Who Sell Out*
Love – *Forever Changes*

The Charts

Melbourne

On the strength of the year's number one hits, one could be forgiven for thinking that Melbourne was strictly 'Squaresville' in 1967. The only Australian #1 of the entire year was 'Georgy Girl' by The Seekers, which topped the charts for three weeks over March–April. Otherwise (aside from The Beatles' 'Strawberry Fields'/'Penny Lane' double-sider and Procol Harum's 'A Whiter Shade

- Massive anti-Vietnam marches are held in America and Europe.
- Richard Neville and Martin Sharp launch the UK version of *Oz* magazine, rapidly establishing it as a leading voice of the British counter-culture.

AUSTRALIAN EVENTS

- Paul Witzig's second surf film, *Hot Generation*, opens, featuring narration from Sydney DJ Tom Johnson and a soundtrack from Newcastle's Sunsets.
- South Australia introduces 10 pm hotel closing time.
- Australia Square in Sydney opens, featuring a design by architect Harry Seidler.
- Truffauts's *Fahrenheit 451* opens in Australian cinemas.
- Architect Morrice Shaw designs the Cottlesbridge House at Cottlesbridge, Victoria using curvilinear forms and tradition building construction methods such as rammed earth.
- The Commonwealth Censor cuts or bans 38 overseas films including Godard's *Une Femme Marie*, Le Roi Jones' *The Dutchman* and an adaptation of James Joyce's *Ulysses*.
- Nat Young appears in a 13 part ABC TV series entitled *Let's Go Surfing*. Demonstrating the moves that have delivered him the World Championship, Young teaches the youth of Australia to 'take off', 'trim the wave', 'nose dive' and 'cutback'.

- Tired of being reined in by the conservative state based Trades Hall Council, 27 'rebel' Victorian trade unions break away to set up their own organising base.
- Construction begins on the Harold Holt Memorial Swimming Centre in Glen Iris to the Brutalist design of Kevin Borland and Daryl Jackson.
- New Australian TV series include *Adventure Island* (ABC), *Bellbird* (ABC), *Contrabandits* (ABC), *Divorce Court* (HSV-7) and *Hunter* (Channel-9).
- The Victorian *Jury Act* grants women the right to voluntarily serve as jurors.
- Enrico Taglietti designs the Conference Centre at the Associated Chamber of Manufacturers of Australia in Barton, ACT, using a pool as a water-filled roof for an underground conference space.
- *Georgy Girl* open in Australian cinemas.
- Hurstbridge High student Fabian Douglas is suspended from school for refusing to cut his hair. With the support of State Labor Opposition Leader Clyde Holding, his father unsuccessfully attempts to petition the UN over the matter, later telling *Broadside* magazine that his son 'showed definite temperamental changes for the worse' whenever his hair is cut, as he 'associates long hair with all the good things he knows.'

The Groop (Colbert)

of Pale'), it was either middle-of-the-road ballads, commercial flower power or novelty songs that made it to the top spot. Tom Jones' 'Green Green Grass of Home', Frank and Nancy Sinatra's 'Somethin' Stupid', 'The Last Waltz' and 'Release Me' by Englebert Humperdinck, 'This is My Song' (shared by Petula Clark and Harry Secombe), Lulu's 'To Sir With Love' and 'Snoopy vs the Red Baron' by The Royal Guardsmen were some of the biggest hits in Melbourne. The biggest overseas smash of them all was Scott McKenzie's 'San Francisco (Be Sure to Wear Flowers in Your Hair)', which held the Melbourne #1 spot for eight weeks from August to October.

As far as local acts go, The Cherokees made #3 with the call-and-response 'Minnie the Moocher', while The Vibrants did well with 'Something About You Baby' (which also peaked at #3). Eventual Battle of the Sounds winners The Groop had the city's 20th biggest hit of the year with 'Woman You're Breaking Me', which peaked at #4 and spent 19 weeks in the charts.

Sydney

The Harbour City fell for The Monkees in a big way. The Pre-Fab Four scored no less than *nine* hits there in '67, including *Theme from the Monkees* EP and 'I'm a Believer'/'I'm Not Your Stepping Stone', which both hit #1 – plus a further FIVE top 10 entries. The band's token English member, Davy Jones, had two solo top 5 hits as well, with 'Theme for a New Love' and 'Dream Girl' making it 11 Monkees-related hits for the year all-up.

As with Melbourne, Sydney saw MOR, novelty songs and commercial flower power tracks consistently topping the charts – although Sydney did have the good taste to send The Rolling Stones to the top with 'Ruby Tuesday'/'Let's Spend the Night Together' and The Small Faces with their phase-fest 'Itchycoo Park'.

1967 wasn't a great year for local acts in Sydney. Apart from The Seekers – whose 'Georgy Girl' was the second biggest hit of the year (#1 for three weeks) – the only other Aussie bands to make a big dent were The Masters Apprentices, who made #3 with 'Undecided' and #5 with 'Living in a Child's Dream', and The Executives, whose 'My Aim is to Please You' and 'Sit Down, I Think I Love You' made #5 and #4 respectively.

Adelaide

No less than *seven* Australian acts had #1 hits in Adelaide during 1967 (eight, if you include the Bee Gees with 'Massachusetts'). 'Buried and Dead' and 'Living in a Child's Dream' by The Masters Apprentices, and 'Cathy Come Home'/'The Way They Play' by fellow local heroes The Twilights all hit top spot – as did The Groop with 'Woman You're Breaking Me'. But the two biggest Australian hits of the year were 'What's Wrong With the Way I Live' by The Twilights (highest pos. #2; 17 weeks in the top 40) and The Masters Apprentices' debut double-sider 'Undecided'/'Wars or Hands of Time' (highest pos. #4; 16 weeks in). 'Sadie (The Cleaning Lady)' by Johnny Farnham spent the last six weeks of 1967 atop the Adelaide charts.

When it came to overseas acts, Adelaide once again embraced radical new overseas sounds before the other states did. 'When I was Young' and 'San Franciscan Nights' by The Animals were two massive #1 hits there and nowhere else. And what about The Jimi Hendrix Experience? 'Hey Joe' made #1 in Adelaide in May, yet it didn't even *chart* in Sydney or Brisbane. Hendrix followed it up with three more top ten hits for the year: 'Purple Haze' (#7), 'The Wind Cries Mary' (#3) and 'The Burning of the Midnight Lamp' (#9). Adelaide caught onto Cream months before other states did as well.

The 1967 *Go Set* Pop Poll Winners (as voted by the readers of *Go Set*)

Top Male Singers:	1966 Result
Ronnie Burns: Gold	2nd
Normie Rowe: Silver	1st
Johnny Young: Bronze	6th

Top Female Singers:	1966 Result
Lynne Randell: Gold	1st
Bev Harrell: Silver	–
Cheryl Gray: Bronze	–

Top Groups:	1966 Result
The Easybeats: Gold	1st
The Twilights: Silver	2nd
The Groop: Bronze	–

1967 Hoadley's Battle of the Sounds Winners

The Groop: Gold
The Questions: Silver
The Flamingoes: Bronze

Ronnie Burns (Colbert)

The Sonic Landscape

The Small Faces' massive hit single 'Itchycoo Park' introduced a sensational new sound effect known as 'phasing'. The effect was not entirely new, it must be said – the song 'Hurt' by US artist Timi Yuro featured phasing on it back in 1961 – but when tape operator George Chkiantz phased Kenney Jones' drums on 'Itchycoo Park' in 1967, it was exactly the right effect at exactly the right time.

Phasing – or 'flanging', as it is also known – is achieved when you play two identical recordings simultaneously; but ever so slightly out-of-phase with each other. The resultant sound is a vast liquid 'whooshing' effect – sort of like an aeroplane flying over your head while you're standing underwater. Creating this effect was a complicated process. It involved making duplicate copies of a backing track, wheeling in two tape machines to play the track simultaneously, while somebody controlled the speed of one of the machines by manipulating the tape with their finger. This simultaneous dual recording was then recorded onto a *third* machine. Once done, the phased section from the third machine would then be physically cut and spliced

JANUARY

- During the January/February National Service registration period, draft resisters Michael Matteson, Chris Campbell and Errol Heldzingen become the first Australians to refuse to comply with conscription at any level.
- Perth pop group The Valentines, featuring future AC/DC vocalist Bon Scott and journalist Vince Lovegrove, play their biggest show yet, before 3000 at a Legacy concert in the Supreme Court Gardens.

1 30 Commonwealth police officers raid 12 houses in Sydney, after three Australians, two of them former New South Wales police officers, are arrested in New York as part of a heroin smuggling operation.

3 Melbourne band MPD Ltd's clothes, including Mike Brady's best Carnaby Street suit, are stolen from the back room of Geelong's mod tavern.

9 The Playboy club reopens as the Winston Charles, Melbourne's first fully licensed disco. Open from 7 pm to 1 am seven days a week, the venue is modelled on D'Arthurs of New York.

11 *Go Set* magazine announces that pop duo Bobby and Laurie have split up.

11 The NSW *Poisons Bill* is passed, making it unlawful to be in possession of 'prescribed, restricted substances' such as barbiturates, narcotics and amphetamines. The Bill also gives the police easier access to warrants, allowing them to search people as well as premises where illicit drugs are believed to be used or stored. Under the legislation doctors are however still allowed to prescribe certain drugs, including heroin, to registered addicts.

13 The Australian unemployment rate hits 1.9%, the highest in 4 years.

14 The Victorian state government announces it is gearing up to impose tougher regulations on the unauthorised possession and use of LSD, barbiturates and sedatives.

16 Melbourne pop group MPD Ltd split up

18 Marshall Ky, the Premier of South Vietnam, visits Australia for five days meeting opposition from anti-war activists wherever he goes.

18 Robert Vaughn (aka Napoleon Solo of *The Man From UNCLE*) tours Australia with fellow cast member David McCallum. Whilst in Sydney, Vaughn makes his position on the Vietnam war clear, stating 'I am totally opposed to US involvement in Vietnam, not just the bombing of the North.'

21 Melbourne 'baroque 'n' roll' group Eighteenth Century Quartet play their final gig at Angelsea, Victoria. Members Keith Glass and John Pugh go on to play with Cam-Pact whilst Hans Poulsen establishes himself as a solo singer-songwriter.

23 In a big month for Melbourne based acts, R&B act The Purple

back onto the main master tape. Complicated? You bet! (Producers these days can achieve the same effect by simply double-clicking a mouse.)

Locally, Festival records were the first to get onto the phasing bandwagon. 'And Things Unsaid' by Doug Parkinson and The Questions (October) is the earliest Australian recording to feature the effect – drummer/producer Bill Flemming tastefully applied it to his drums in certain sections of the song. But it was Pat Aulton who first used phasing as an entity, almost an instrument in its own right, in The Wild Cherries' second single 'That's Life' (released in November).

The other major revolution regarding the sound of Australian records during 1967 was the fact that an unprecedented amount of local artists had travelled to the UK. The London recordings of acts such as Johnny Young, The Easybeats, Lynne Randell, The Twilights and Normie Rowe and The Playboys featured stately new flavourings such as harpsichords, full string sections and lush multi-overdubbed harmonies. Things had definitely shifted up a notch.

1967 Top 30 Psychedelic Pselections

Title – Artist	Status (release date)	Label: Cat. No
1. 'Living in a Child's Dream' – The Masters Apprentices	**Single (August)**	**Astor: A-7081**

'When I first saw the lyrics to "Living in a Child's Dream" I said, "I'm not going to sing that!" But that was in 1966 when we were still all bluesy.' – vocalist Jim Keays.

Written by rhythm guitarist Mick Bower, 'Living in a Child's Dream' – by accident more than design – became Australia's first ever flower-pop record. The song itself is extremely melodic, if not especially psychedelic, and the production (assisted by Ian Meldrum, by the way) is fairly straightforward and gimmick-free. But it is the evocative lyrics and magnificent counterpoint guitar lines that elevate 'Living in a Child's Dream' into perfect-pop-song territory. This is a wondrous summer of love gem recorded in the middle of a chilly Melbourne winter.

Killer Moment: 00.28, '*. . . see the clown who makes the children laugh, as he spins around and shows them all his tricks.' Pop music seldom gets better than that.*

The Masters Apprentices (Colbert)

2. 'Black Sheep R.I.P.'/'Sad' – The Playboys **A/B-side (August)** **Sunshine: QK-1872**

After Normie Rowe failed to become the mega-star in Britain that he was back here, his backing group The Playboys decided to stay on in the Old Dart for a while and try their luck. The band managed to get themselves signed for one single with ex-Rolling Stones manager Andrew Loog-Oldham's Immediate record label – and the resultant 45 was a two-song corker!

'Black Sheep R.I.P.' is a trippy re-writing of the traditional 'Baa-Baa Black Sheep' nursery rhyme, augmented by military beats, stately organ lines and fine harmonies, before signing off with a surprise 'rave-up' ending. On the B-side 'Sad', The Playboys pulled out all the psychedelic stops. Bassist Brian Peacock (ex-NZ Librettos) wrote both sides of the single and had a great ear for the dreamy pop sound that was enveloping the British scene at the time of this release. Pop art feedback-soaked guitars courtesy of Mick Rodgers, bizarre time signature changes and lush multi-layered harmonies make 'Sad' a freakbeat/psychedelic treasure.

Killer Moment ('Sad'): 01.54, *that stray feedback squeal.*

The Playboys (Colbert)

3. 'That's Life' – The Wild Cherries
Single (November) Festival: FK-2052

Not to be confused with the Frank Sinatra hit of the same name, 'That's Life' is a Lobby Loyde original, played with Sherman Tank aplomb by the loud 'n' legendary Wild Cherries. 'That's Life' has a certain intangible Australian quality about it – and it's not just the reference to Melbourne in the second verse either (*'Melbourne is a big big city, so it looks like I'll have to stay'*) – it's more to do with the record's uncanny combination of toughness and beauty. The track contains an arsenal of explosive special effects (phased feedback, oceans of reverb), but they are never overused. If anything they tend to support the music rather than threaten to overtake it. The record was produced by the great Pat Aulton, which probably had something to do with it. 'That's Life' was a substantial hit for the band too, it made #5 in Melbourne and #29 nationally.

Killer Moment: 01.25, *Lobby's first phased aeroplane power-chord. WOW!*

4. 'Style of Love' – The Hergs B-side (December) Parlophone: A-8272

This is a psychedelic record in the sense that it features quasi-raga guitar figures, references to 'Frisco', 'pot' and 'hash' – and too much weirdness to possibly ignore. But the attitude and snarl behind 'Style of Love' is pure 1977 London punk. The Hergs were an obscure Adelaide band and 'Style of Love' was the B-side of their idiosyncratic version of Vince Taylor's 'Cadillac' (the same song that the Clash did on *London Calling*). Incredibly, The Hergs' version of 'Cadillac' hit #5 on the mainstream Adelaide charts, but 'Style of Love' is a different animal altogether.

Kicking off with a dismembered guitar intro, followed by a claustrophobic main riff the song then adds some sneering Johnny Rotten-ish vocals intoning the nihilistic lyrics *'Switched-on the anti-social light, life and death is so small/ There must be an exit to this world, if love be in us all.'* But it's the third verse where things get *really* interesting: *'Hate burning in my soul, for pain we've found a cure/ Pot and hash, keep us loving, the love bus took me on a tour.'* This would have to be the first blatant drug reference in an Australian rock song ever! Onya Hergs!

Killer Moment: 02.45, *the song suddenly collapses into drunken raga with extraneous background chatter and squealing feedback.*

5. 'Cathy Come Home'/'The Way They Play' – The Twilights A/B-side (November) Columbia: DO-5030

During The Twilights' British sojourn (courtesy of Hoadley's confectionary and the Sitmar cruise ship line), guitarist Terry Britten had bought himself a sitar – and when the band got home, he proved that he was not afraid to use it. Aside from bringing it out on stage for 'Within You

Hearts issue a press statement announcing that they feel they are stagnating musically and have decided to break up.

24 Legendary Australian rocker Johnny O'Keefe is signed up to compere Channel 10's new pop show *Where The Action Is*.

24 The Big Show tour, featuring Roy Orbison, The Walker Brothers and The Yardbirds, tours Australia with supports from Johnny Young and The Mixtures. As part of The Yardbirds set, guitarist Jimmy Page pulls out a violin bow to perform a 10 minute deconstruction of the blues standard 'I'm a Man'. After the show a custom-made Gibson Les Paul, loaned to Page for the tour by Keith Richards, is stolen, as well as a Fender guitar belonging to Mixtures guitarist Laurie Arthur.

26 Hundreds of anti-war activists meet in Sydney over the Australia Day weekend to plan civil disobedience for the coming year.

29 Dave Panther of *Go Set* and R&B act The Wild Colonials is badly injured when his car hits a tree en route to Melbourne.

FEBRUARY

- The Bee Gees leave Sydney to return to their native England, where the three brothers sign up to Robert Stigwood's NEMS organisation within weeks of their arrival. Preparing to play live, they add guitarist Vince Melouney (aka Maloney) and drummer Colin Petersen (who had starred in the film *Smiley* as a child) to their line-up.
- Royal Australian navy divers attached to the US Navy begin operating in waters off North Vietnam.

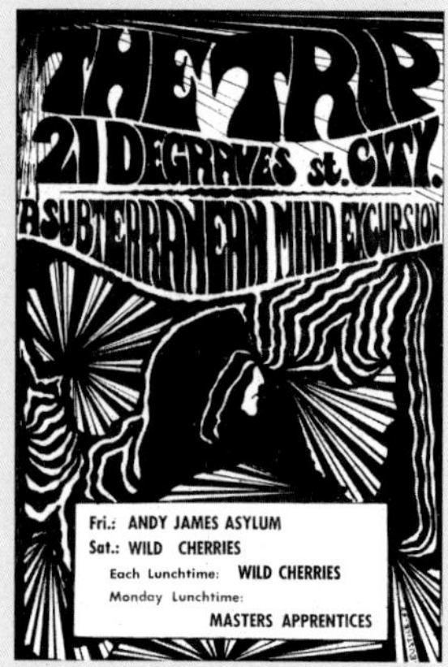

- The Masters Apprentices relocate from Adelaide to Melbourne.

1 Billy Thorpe takes off for the Gold Coast leaving the remaining members of The Aztecs to founder in Sydney after their *It's All Happening* TV show is axed.

3 Ronald Ryan becomes the last person to be executed in Australia when he is hung at Pentridge prison for the killing of a warder during a prison escape in December 1965. Spurning public protest, conservative Victorian Premier Henry Bolte holds firm in refusing to spare Ryan. On the night of the execution hundreds marching outside the prison are set upon by police, and 90 are arrested.

6 The Melbourne City Council's Building Committee decides to allow the Thumpin' Tum and Catcher discotheques to continue trading, despite receiving a series of noise complaints.

6 Demonstrating their versatility, Sydney soul belters The Id compose over 40 minutes of instrumental music for Bob Evans' surf movie *High On A Cool Wave*.

7 One of Australia's worst bushfires claims 59 lives, 1500 vehicles and 1300 houses when it comes within two kilometres of Hobart.

Without You' when the band performed the entire *Sgt. Pepper's Lonely Hearts Club Band* album live, he used it on both sides of their first Australian-made single for 1967.

'Cathy Come Home' was inspired by a gritty kitchen sink telemovie of the same name, and is one of the standout tracks of The Twilights none-too-shabby career. With the band's customary harmonies in full-flight, some sharp guitar motifs, fluttery drums, sitar glissando's and a melody to die for – 'Cathy Come Home' is first-rate freakbeat. 'The Way They Play' on the other side is only marginally less sublime. With the sitar taking more of a central role, and despite the slightly square lyrics, 'The Way They Play' is further proof that Terry Britten was beginning to establish himself as a songwriter of the highest order.
Killer Moment ('Cathy Come Home'): 00.23, *the sitar says hello.*

6. 'Magic Eyes'/'And I Heard the Fire Sing' – The James Taylor Move **A/B-side (August)** **Festival: FK-1892**

This band had nothing to do with any American singer-songwriter, but everything to do with a first-rate bunch of Adelaide musicians who'd been assembled by a canny discotheque owner in order to cash in on the current acid rock boom, as personified by The Jimi Hendrix Experience and Cream. Their first single, 'Magic Eyes', was a catchy bit of loping pop with a snappy *'La la-la-la. La la-la-la . . .'* vocal hook and an excellent vocal performance by Robert J. Taylor. 'Magic Eyes' was a #10 hit in Adelaide and made #15 in Melbourne. But the single's real gem lies on the flip-side.

Kevin Peek and Kevin Spencer (drummer) of The James Taylor Move (Colbert)

To say that 'And I Heard the Fire Sing' is a direct Hendrix rip-off (think 'Purple Haze' meets 'Foxy Lady' with a 'Hey Joe' bassline) would be stating the bleeding obvious. But what saves this song from being in any way mediocre is the fact that The James Taylor Move's guitarist just happened to be a fellow called Kevin Peek – best known as the electric guitarist with the globally successful classical supergroup Sky. Peek manages to match the intensity of Hendrix when he fires off flurries of manic notes in the lead guitar sections of the song. The complete lack of studio trickery on the record is another plus as well, in fact, I'd lay odds-on that the whole thing was done in one take, no overdubs.

7. 'Every Christian Lion Hearted Man Will Show You'/ 'Epitaph to Mr Simons, Sir' – Johnny Young **A/B-side (November)** **Clarion: MCK-2080**

While admittedly not nearly as good as the The Bee Gees' original, Johnny Young's version of 'Every Christian Lion Hearted Man Will Show You' is still an impressive record. While The Bee Gees' version is full of angry monks spouting Latin and creaking iron gates hidden within dank castle walls, Johnny Young lets plenty of sunshine and fresh air in, so as not to frighten off the kids. Though I must say, those angry monks do turn up at the 01.35 mark of the song just to keep an eye on things.

Young's self-penned B-side 'Epitaph to Mr Simons Sir' is just plain odd. It sounds like an opening production number to a Swinging London TV variety show (imagine a troupe of dolly-birds swirling Union Jack umbrellas about in front of men in bowler hats and pinstripe suits waiting for a big red double-decker bus; it's that kind of vibe). The song tells the story of a man who sets out on the bus to the Sandown Park greyhound track one Sunday morning, yawns several times, goes to the races, sees a young girl who 'blows his mind' and then promptly dies. I think. And Johnny Young constantly does these weird yelps that make the whole song even weirder.
Killer Moment ('Epitaph to Mr Simons, Sir'): 01.33, *Johnny Young gets on the Sandown Park PA and does a bizarre commentary.*

8. 'Time Will Come'/'Social Cell' – The Tol-Puddle Martyrs **A/B-side (October)** **Spiral: KJ-1937**

'Seems like man can't trust his kind today/ Love has died and death is here to stay . . . Time will come and death will pave the way' – 'Time Will Come' (Peter J. Rechter).

'Every day you see it, it happens everywhere/ Man will use his brother, and still he doesn't care . . . Everyone's in a social cell, and fighting for his share . . .' – 'Social Cell' (Peter J. Rechter).

Remarkably bleak lyrics for songs penned in 1967, and that is what makes this single so special. The Tol-Puddle Martyrs hailed from the regional Victorian city of Bendigo and were originally known as Peter and the Silhouettes. As the Tol-Puddle Martyrs, they released two singles and this was their first. Both sides are eerie, dark and brooding with a tight rhythm section holding down the bottom, harsh fuzz guitar smothering the middle and – in the case of 'Time Will Come' – piercing organ lines cutting through the top. But it is vocalist/organist Peter Rechter's cynical, dissatisfied lyrics that really take centre stage here. Unique stuff.

Killer Moment ('Time Will Come'): 02.02, *guitarist Kevin Clancy's control of feedback in the guitar solo. Sensational.*

The Tol-Puddle Martyrs (Rechter)

9. 'Going Home' – Normie Rowe **Single (March)** **Sunshine:QK-1731**

While he's not generally known as being a psychedelic performer Normie Rowe did make a few slightly *out-there* recordings in his time – the best being the Graham Gouldman-penned 'Going Home', which perhaps not surprisingly, became Normie's first single *not* to make the Melbourne top 10. *Going Home* was produced by former Yardbirds manager Giorgio Gomelski in London during Rowe's time there when he was attempting to crack the English market.

The record features discordant swirly violins, eerie flutes and weird false starts at the beginning of each new verse whilst the song itself is melodic in an almost Gene Pitney-ish vein. The reverb is overblown and there is even the odd bit of psychedelic poetry hidden within the lyrics (*'In my mind, I see the stalks of corn, stand dewy in the dawn . . .'*). A top track.

10. 'Carousel of Love' – Peter Best **B-side (November)** **Columbia: DO-5039**

One suspects that future jingle writer Peter Best (remember 'Care For Kids'? That was him) had totally immersed himself in the newly released *Sgt. Pepper* album before creating the bizarre carnivalesque 'Carousel of Love'. Featuring a twangy sitar, real-live carnival noises, slurpy strings and absurd time-changes – 'Carousel of Love' is 1 minute 47 seconds of pure joyful madness.

Killer Moment: 01.01, *those stabbing violins come in.*

11. 'And Things Unsaid' – The Questions **Single (October)** **Festival: FK-2026**

The Doug Parkinson-penned 'And Things Unsaid' is a classy piece of work. It goes without saying that the vocal performance is first-rate – Parkinson is one of those 'could sing the phone book and it'd be worth hearing' singers – and The Questions contained some of the best musicians in the country. Billy Green coats this track with a caramel-smooth Indian-influenced fuzz guitar line, while veteran session drummer Bill Flemming (who had the good sense to add a nice smidgin of phasing on his skins in certain sections of the song) and bassist Duncan McGuire combine to lay a solid bedrock. It has been said that 'And Things Unsaid' was inspired by US psychedelic-symphonic rock band Vanilla Fudge, but this is hard to believe, since the

7 Aboriginal author and inventor David Unaipon dies. His achievements are later commemorated by the national David Unaipon Award for Aboriginal writers, and by his portrait, featured on one side of the $50 note.

8 Edward Gough Whitlam supplants Arthur Calwell as the leader of the Federal Australian Labor Party. He immediately dampens down his predecessor's hard line on Vietnam, saying that if elected he would withdraw Australian forces to 'holding areas', rather than immediately pull them out.

8 The first issue of *Drift*, a Sydney based 'magazine for young moderns', is launched at Beethoven's Discotheque with The Unknown Blues playing to assembled guests, including members of The Yardbirds. The magazine is owned, written and laid out by a team of workers aged under 21, and includes features on local rock and pop acts, surf reports, a disco guide and an anti-corruption column entitled 'The Angry Eye'.

15 The poetry and folk den Cafe Des Artists is closed down by the Cronulla council, after it receives a petition from local shopkeepers complaining about noise.

16 The Loved Ones are mobbed in Western Australia and their return to Melbourne delayed by bomb threats called in to the Perth airport.

17 Normie Rowe and The Playboys tour the UK as part of a package tour with The Troggs, Gene Pitney, The Loot and Sounds Incorporated.

26 Film-makers cooperative Ubu hosts a night of *Experimental*

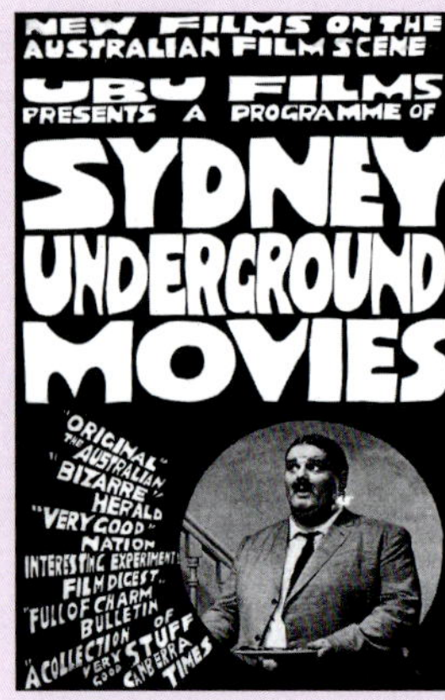

Films and Underground Movies at the Anzac Auditorium in Sydney. On the morning of the event the *Sunday Mirror* beats up the appearance of Michael Boddy, star of ABC TV's *Crackerjack* children's show, alongside naked women in David Perry's *The Tribulations of Mr Dupont Nomore*. An unrepentant Boddy responds to the paper's moralising by declaring 'This film gave me a great deal of acting freedom. Dancing with naked girls was no problem – in fact I quite enjoyed it.'

MARCH

- The Seaman's Union refuses to transport armaments and other military goods to South Vietnam, forcing the Australian navy to take over supply duties.
- The Gurindji people occupy part of the Wave Hill station as part of their demands for compensation for decades of low wages. The Aboriginal Rights Council unsuccessfully appeals to the United Nations for support.
- Outraged at their University's decision to award 'Hanging Premier' Henry Bolte an honorary degree, students at Monash prevent him from entering the campus.

Normie Rowe (Colbert)

single was released around about the time that Vanilla Fudge were first being signed by Atlantic Records; months before they even made their first record! Due respect to Mr Parkinson, please.

Killer Moment: 02.13, *keyboardist Rory Thomas lets fly with his first of three scorching Hammond Organ swells during the fadeout.*

The Questions (Colbert)

12. 'But One Day' – The Masters Apprentices — LP Track — Astor: ALP-1025

Obviously Yardbirds inspired (think 'Still I'm Sad'), the Mick Bower original 'But One Day' is garage-raga at its absolute best. With a suitably droney, Tandoori-flavoured main guitar figure and Gregorian-chant vocals that sound less like a chapter of monks than a bunch of snotty Adelaide kids, 'But One Day' is a terrific track, because despite its would-be pretensions, it ends up sounding exactly like The Masters Apprentices. Listen out for Mick Bower's magnificently chiming rhythm guitar playing.

Killer Moment: 02.25, *the reverse tape outro.*

13. 'Dapper Dan' – Vyt and The World — B-side (October) — CBS: BA-221456

Possibly more freakbeat than psychedelic, 'Dapper Dan' is a jerky English-sounding tune with an insistent *'Tell-me, tell-me, tell-me, tell-me where are you?'* refrain, some great vocal percussion tricks and moody chord changes. Vyt and The World are something of a mystery group. They apparently came from regional New South Wales and had the Bee Gees sing back-up on one of their records. That's about all we know about 'em, except that they made three other singles for CBS.

14. 'Woman You're Breaking Me' – The Groop — Single (June) — CBS: BA-221406

A driving organ-infused slice of classic pop with more hooks than you'd find in a hardware shop. 'Woman You're Breaking Me' was one of The Groop's first attempts at writing an original tune and its sizeable chart success certainly inspired keyboardist/vocalist Brian Cadd to keep plugging away at the craft. The most psychedelic moments of the song come about in the section just after the first chorus and in a mad echo/reverb rush at the very end.

Killer Moment: 00.38, *everything suddenly goes exotic and Middle-Eastern in the blink of an eye.*

1 The Angry Eye reports in *Drift* that Sydney police have been regularly raiding local discotheques and leaning on club managers for money. In some cases patrons have been bundled out of shows and roughed up for no other reason than having long hair.

1 The Bentbeaks debut single 'Caught Red Handed' is banned by Melbourne radio, due to supposedly lewd references.

1 Normie Rowe tells *Go Set* that his recent tour of Scotland was 'Just like Australia. The girls were screaming, trying to pull us off stage, grab our hair, it was really wild.'

8 La Trobe University, Victoria's third university, is opened at Bundoora by Premier Bolte.

12 Despite the Trustees of the Myer Music Bowl declaring they would no longer allow the use of the venue for Melbourne's Moomba pop concert, the event goes ahead with 200 000 crowding in to see The Seekers.

13 Record floods devastate northern Queensland.

15 The 2UW Spectacular at Sydney's Trocadero sees 2500 turn up to hear sets from The Loved Ones, Lynne Randell and Ray Hoff and The Offbeats.

17 The Honeysuckle Creek space tracking station opens near Canberra.

20 Sydney discotheque Rhubarbs is forced to close in North Sydney after shows are marred by fights between patrons and bouncers. The venue had only recently relaunched itself with a party featuring The Id and Python Lee Jackson, after being shut down earlier in the year due to noise complaints.

25 The Bee Gees make their UK debut over the Easter Weekend, supporting Gerry and The Pacemakers and Fats Domino at London's Saville Theatre.

25 Having released two Bee Gees compositions as singles earlier in the year ('Exit Stage Right' and 'Coalman'), Ronnie Burns headlines the Sydney Easter Show with Johnny Young, causing riotous scenes. Making their debut as the pair's backing band, as well as playing in their own right, are The Dave Miller Set, whose namesake had previously fronted his very own Byrds in New Zealand.

25 Following the death of a Carlton man from an overdose of the painkiller Pethedine, the head of Melbourne's two man drug squad reveals that break-ins at chemists have doubled in Victoria since 1965, with overall dug charges increasing from 101 to 137 in the past year. He also names Carlton, St Kilda and South Yarra as being Melbourne's main 'drug spots', with the majority of dealers still in their teens.

31 The SEACOM cable is finished, linking Australian telecommunications with South East Asia.

31 The *Age* reports that 'Beatniks thinking they can substitute banana peels for marijuana or LSD should think again',

15. 'Take A Trip' – Gift of Love **B-side (November)** **Ramrod: RS-1002**

Gift of Love was a pseudonym for The Atlantics, and this one-off single on their own Ramrod label is a surf instrumental with a violent psychedelic undertow. The thundering drums – so evident on The Atlantics' early recordings – are present here; however a whirling organ and the Fuzz Guitar from Hell take the place of twangy Fender Stratocasters.
Killer Moment: 00.02, *the Fuzz Guitar from Hell violently explodes into life.*

16. 'House of Bamboo' – Peter Wright **Single (October)** **Festival: FK-1973**

By the time of this release, Peter Wright had already made two singles on two different labels, and they were tepid at best. 'House of Bamboo' was a self-penned number, and judging by his flexible vocal performance, Wright was a big fan of the Platters and Jackie Wilson. Indeed this track is a particularly weird one. Wright is singing with the earnestness of a well-seasoned cabaret singer, yet the group behind him (a combo called Chapter III) sound cool and grungy as fuck. This is one strictly schizophrenic hunk of wax, and all the better for it.
Killer Moment: 02.01, *that lonely buzz-saw guitar riff followed by one of best drum rolls ever.*

17. 'Krome Plated Yabbie' – The Wild Cherries **Single (August)** **Festival: FK-1879**

The Wild Cherries' first single, and one of the most stunningly original Oz debut releases ever. Disjointed, dynamic, demented and dazzling; the cryptically named 'Krome Plated Yabbie' is a mini-epic which still manages to clock in at under three minutes.
Killer Moment: 01.35, *Lobby Loyde's orchestral 'Beck's Bolero' style guitar solo.*

18. 'Still I Can Go On' – The James Taylor Move **B-side (October)** **Festival: FK-2025**

The B-side to their second and final single, 'Still I Can Go On' is a raga rock piece *par excellence*. Is it a rewrite of The Yardbirds' 'Over Under Sideways Down'? – well, possibly. But Kevin Peek's single-string Moorish guitar playing is brilliant, backed by a single continuous drone chord played throughout the whole song by organist Allan Tarney.

19. 'The Loverly Car' – The Loved Ones **B-side (April)** **In: IN-S-8066**

This B-side to 'A Love Like Ours' is a gentle yet blackly humorous parable to the perils of materialism. With a nursery rhyme melody, twinkling piano and some lyrical bass playing; 'The Loverly Car' follows the adventures of the hard-working, church-going 'Little Tiny Man' and his newly acquired vehicle.
Killer Moment: 01.45, *we learn the sad fate of 'Little Tiny Man'.*

20. 'Green Mansions (The Residence of Simon Grae)' – Marty Rhone **Single (November)** **Spin: LK-2053**

A mournful, eerie track, written by Marty Rhone and filled with death and loneliness. Pat Aulton's spiky string arrangement and Rhone's compelling vocal performance combine to create a totally original piece of work.

21. 'Annabelle Lee'/'Seems More Important To Me' – The Groop **A/B-side (November)** **CBS: BA-221457**

Another double-sided nugget. The A-side 'Annabelle Lee', written by Brian Cadd and Max Ross – whose stellar bass-playing absolutely *makes* the song – sounds uncannily like The Twilights, and why not? The Twilights won the 1966 'Battle of the Sounds' and in '67 it was The Groop's turn. Perhaps appropriately then, it only charted in Adelaide (highest pos. #29). 'Seems More Important to Me' is more deliberately left-field with its whimsical merry-go-round verses and rocky chorus – though this was to be the side that charted in The Groop's home town of Melbourne (#19 for 7 weeks).

22. 'Craise Finton Kirk (Royal Academy of Arts)' – Johnny Young **Single (August)** **Clarion: MCK-1954**

Recorded in England during Johnny Young's first sojourn there and written by Barry and Robin Gibb, 'Craise Finton Kirk' is a jaunty and very very English baroque pop tune with flourishing harpsichords and Young's ever-affable voice floating above the distinctive harmonies of the brothers' Gibb.

23. 'Come in You'll get Pneumonia' – The Easybeats **B-side (December)** **Parlophone: E-8277**

The B-side to The Easybeats' minor hit 'The Music Goes Round My Head' (#33 nationally) 'Come in You'll get Pneumonia' starts off sounding like a George Harrison outtake with its mystical sounding (and phased) vocals and a bongo tabla thumping away in the background. Admittedly, the song goes downhill once the lame chorus kicks in, but the first 40 seconds are worth the price of admission.

24. 'Magic Box' – The Loved Ones **Single (July)** **In: IN-S-8093**

This was The Loved Ones' final single and their poorest effort chartwise, but that doesn't mean that this song was a dud. Far from it. 'Magic Box' is a sweltering slice of up tempo psychedelic go-go music, with Treva Richards absolutely blitzing the Hammond organ and lead guitarist Danny De Lacy riffin' up a storm. 'Magic Box' sounds like those radio tunes you see groovy teenagers frugging to in 1960s sit-coms before an irate parent comes along and abruptly switches the radio OFF.

25. 'Imagine This' – The Iguana **Single (October)** **Festival: FK-2007**

Debut single for this Melbourne quintet who made a name for themselves at suburban dances with their tight harmonies. 'Imagine This' was a complex, adventurous piece of work, penned by guitarist brothers Gary and Clive Littlewood and produced by Pat Aulton.
Killer Moment: 02.45, *that luscious B major a-cappella chord which ends the song.*

26. 'Tell Me Love' – Marty Rhone
B-side (May) **Spin: EK-1790**

Marty Rhone seemed to have a natural affinity with traditional folk melodies – 'Tell Me Love' is a lilting air in 3/4 time originally done by US band Gentle Soul. Rhone's version contains some superb dramatic pauses and a monster drum sound. Not surprisingly, the producer of this fine piece was the venerable Patrick Aulton.

Marty Rhone (Colbert)

27. 'Not This Time' – The Black Diamonds
B-side (March) **Festival: FK-1693**

A sumptuous power-pop tune with soaring harmonies and a driving beat, The Black Diamonds' guitarist Alan Oloman wrote 'Not This Time' as a warning to a drug-addled friend (*'You're high and then you're down/ Your clouded mind is spinning 'round . . .'*). The 12-string he plays on the record was actually a home-made job, which could only play open chords. Fortunately though, every chord on 'Not This Time' chimes like a bell. And yes, Pat Aulton was responsible for this record's production.
Killer Moment: 00.39, *harmonies that burst out of the chorus like a sunflower.*

28. 'Why? Why? Why?' – The Dave Miller Set **Single (November)** **Spin: LK-2064**

Superior cover version of a Paul Revere and the Raiders album track, 'Why? Why? Why?' shifts between Moorish verses and strong choruses, featuring Dave Miller's rich baritone at its best.

29. 'Upstairs, Downstairs' – Jon **Single (February)** **Leedon: LK-1662**

A tense, breathless song with driving brass-lines and some Vanda and Young-ish *'Na-na-na-na-na-na's'* – 'Upstairs, Downstairs' was written by Barry Gibb and it is possibly a recycled Bee Gees

as Californian tests have proven they have no narcotic effect whatsoever.

APRIL

- The Sydney-based Vietnam Action Campaign begins publishing a regular magazine, *Vietnam Action*, distributing up to 20 000 copies per issue.
- Royal Australian Air Force (RAAF) planes begin bombing raids in Vietnam.
- The Bolte government is re-elected in Victoria with a 44 seat majority.
- The Australian branch of *Oz* magazine publishes its '*Oz* on LSD' issue.
- Proving hugely popular as the years go by, live talk-back radio premieres on 2SM in Sydney and 3AW in Melbourne.
- Students hold sit-ins at Sydney University opposing exorbitant library fines. 1000 later march on the Vice Chancellor's office, after student activist and future Marxist historian Humphrey McQueen is expelled for handing out leaflets publicising the protests.

4 Sydney based R&B act Phil Jones and The Unknown Blues shoot a film clip for their single 'If I Had a Ticket' and promote the single with 5000 stickers reading 'Buy a Ticket Today'.

10 Long-running current affairs program *This Day Tonight* is launched on ABC TV.

12 Australia's Roman Catholic Bishops come out in opposition to Australian involvement in the Vietnam war.

14 Within three months of arriving in the UK, The Bee Gees score their first international hit with the haunting 'New York Mining Disaster – 1941'.

15 ATV-0 broadcasts the first colour TV program in Australia with its coverage of the Pakenham race meet.

16 Sydney anarchists The Push host a party for visiting American Poet Kenneth Rexroth. The event later becomes the basis for a Frank Moorhouse story and Michael Thornhill film.

17 The Australian Destroyer HMAS *Hobart* shells North Vietnamese oil installations, lorry parks and radar defences near Dong Hoi.

18 The Animals, The Loved Ones and Dave Dee, Dozy, Beaky, Mick and Tich play two nights at Festival Hall in Melbourne as part of their East Coast tour. The second show is marred by walk offs by the latter, over the quality of sound, and The Animals, due to their drummer Barry Jenkins being left behind at their hotel.

Things only get worse when Animals tour manager Terry McVay and Jenkins are arrested outside a party in Toorak later that night. Taken to the local police station the two are bashed, with McVay later telling *Drift* magazine 'Upon leaving [the party] I was tripped by a policeman and thrown into a police wagon. Barry and I were then driven to the watch house. There I was charged, I still don't know what with. They then took off my jacket, my shirts, my boots and my belt, which they classified as an offensive weapon. To prove it he whacked me over the ear with it . . . Four policemen started to hit me, one walked out because he could not stand it . . . At six o'clock my solicitor arrived and authorised my release and I was taken to

Jon Blanchfield (Colbert)

demo with Jon Blanchfield replacing the original lead vocal. It made #32 in the Brisbane charts.

30. 'Sitting by a Tree' – The Escorts

B-side (October) **Sunshine: QK-1998**

Whimsical piece of nonsense written by Marty Rhone and recorded by formidable Brisbane back-up group The Escorts. *'Do the ants want my leg or do they want the tree?'* I've often asked the same question myself.

Honorable Mention

'Hey, Hey, Hey' – Bobby James Syndicate

Single (May) **Go!!: G-S-5054**

Okay, we're *really* pushing it to be labelling this 'psychedelic', but 'Hey, Hey, Hey' is just such a groovy, non-stop piece of exuberant beat music that it's impossible to ignore it. The final single ever on the iconic Go!! label, 'Hey, Hey, Hey' – by well-seasoned discotheque band The Bobby James Syndicate – has it all, from dive-bombing fuzz guitars, throbbing bass and shrill organ lines to imaginative tempo changes and Gregorian chant-inspired vocals.

Choice Australian Albums of 1967

	Artist	Title	Label: Cat. No
1.	The Loved Ones	*Magic Box*	W&G: 25/5127
2.	The Masters Apprentices	*The Masters Apprentices*	Astor: ALP-1025
3.	The Allusions	*The Allusions*	Parlophone: PSCO-7540
4.	The In-Sect	*In-Sect-A-sides*	W&G: 25/5045

Ian D. Marks

FASHION 1967

the aeroplane. Paul and Barry Ryan's road manager had to carry me to and from the plane.' Despite releasing a press statement and photos of the injuries, the band's plight fails to make it into any of Australia's mainstream newspapers.

21 After an informal poll carried out at various Sydney night spots, *Drift* concludes that amphetamines remain the drug of choice amongst Sydney's band goers. Methedrine, Benedrine, Dexedrine, Ritalin and Driamyl are apparently easily obtained from dealers and 'certain chemists' by those wishing to 'loosen up and stay awake for the weekend.'

29 A majority vote against a referendum proposal to create a new state in northern New South Wales.

MAY

- A Morgan Gallup poll finds that 62% of Australians are in favour of remaining in Vietnam, 24% against and 14% undecided.
- Ill-health forces Masters Apprentices lead guitarist Rick Morrison to leave the band, after he collapses on stage during a gig at The Catcher in Melbourne.
- A number of films made by members of the Ubu cooperative are declared 'obscene' and refused registration by the Commonwealth Censor R.J. Prowse. Normally Prowse

• • • Go Set model Lindy (Beard)

only deals with imported films, but as under Victorian law filmmakers must have their product approved by the Commonwealth authorities, Ubu are now prevented from screening the films in that state.

- Bassist Kim Lynch leaves The Loved Ones.
- To help promote their second single 'Buried and Dead', The Masters Apprentices shoot one of Australia's first promotional video clips.

1 Vaccination against polio begins across Australia with the introduction of the Sabin oral vaccine.

3 At the end of the Big Show tour, Animals singer Eric Burdon expresses his growing dissatisfaction with playing to teen audiences who 'are only interested in the clothes you wear and don't listen to the music.'

7 Pete 'Stripes' Langham opens his Art Nouveau Bazaar in Melbourne, catering to the psychedelic set and specialising in 'flowery shirts for fellas', 'Dragon Slayer' PVC mini skirts, wide belts, Tiffany lamps and massive ties.

8 Aboriginal activist Pastor Doug Nicholls speaks out against the whipping of young Aboriginal boys in Pingelly, Western Australia.

9 An American tourist in Sydney is busted for importing 237 lollies laced with LSD.

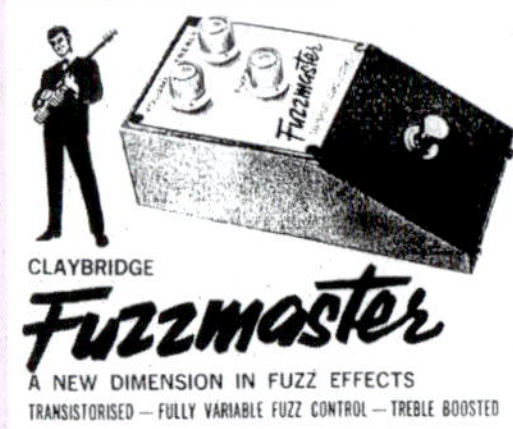

The year in fashion

Three generations of day wear (Finlayson)

Lindy models the Tweed Look. (Beard)

GROOVY

As with 1966, mainstream men's and women's fashion during 1967 was inherently conservative. It was still commonplace for women to wear dresses and skirts rather than trousers in public. Miss Robin Rogers from Adelaide recalls that she wore trousers at home only during the mid 1960s and always wore skirts and dresses out – never mind that the hem lengths on these skirts and dresses were extraordinarily short. Rogers completed a sewing course during 1966, and as a consequence made many of the dresses she wore during 1967.

Rogers recalls that her favourite dresses during 1967 included a limey yellow sleeveless mini dress worn with matching limey yellow shoes, a pink and white gingham mini dress with small covered buttons and pink shoes, and a pale blue and white gingham mini dress with matching pale blue shoes. It would appear that it was both the fashion of the time as well as a conservative convention that 'proper' grooming involved matching outfits and accessories. In the October 1967 issue of *Vogue Australia*, Clark's shoes advertised their Skyline range, which consisted of different coloured women's shoes that were low heeled and sling backed with a range of different shoe fronts. These were available for $9.99.

Miss Elisabeth White was an English literature student at the University of Melbourne during 1967, and says that she was very visible on campus because of the fact she wore trousers or culottes. This was not so much as an anti-fashion statement, as it was a necessary practicality as she rode a Vespa 150 scooter to university. She remembers being asked by an overseas student if he could take a photograph of her with her scooter, because it was so unusual at the time to see a woman both in trousers and riding a scooter. Elisabeth said her scooter riding attire consisted of wool or tweedy trousers, usually made by her mother with fabric purchased from a draper in High Street, Preston, topped off with a brown suede jacket and desert boots. She said she seldom wore make-up and wore her curly hair cut quite short. By contrast, she vividly remembers ex – St Catherine's School girls on campus wearing beautifully tailored navy or camel coats, the finest quality wool twin sets, pearls and their hair in immaculately set bobs, just above the shoulder.

In March 1967, *Go Set* noted 'the theme for winter '67 – colours burning bright, clear, in burgundies, wines – the deep rich shades of red; from shiny patent leather shoes to Zhivago – inspired coats with fur trimmings – the Russian look is catching on fast.' During this year White went to a wedding at the Southern Cross Hotel Ballroom, and her mother made her a Vogue pattern claret coloured velvet dress with an intricate rope detail on both the sleeves and the floor length hem, which she wore with Mary Jane styled shoes featuring a small heel. She hardly ever wore jewellery, but with her best dress she wore a pair of Mexican silver clip-on earrings. Mexican inspired fashions were also noted in January 1967, when *Go Set* described 'the

Go Set model Diana in pants set (Beard)

10 ATV-7 runs a prime time program entitled *As Dreams are Made on*, documenting the effects of LSD on two young Australians. According to the Sydney *Sun* 'The young woman said she had a good trip imagining she was 10 years old . . . she believed a pipe protruding from the water was an entrance into the earth through which she could see. The young man however was undergoing some of the most terrifying moments of his life as he had a vision of hell. He kept saying "I don't understand it. Everything's nothing."'

10 Normie Rowe's backing band The Playboys sign to Rolling Stones manager Andrew Loog-Oldham's Immediate label, recording their 'Sad'/'Baa Baa Black Sheep' single in London.

16 Liberal politicians call for a new inquiry into the sinking of the Australian Naval ship *Voyager* in 1964.

16 Animal rights campaigner Walter Hoysted hits the streets of Melbourne denouncing the whipping of horses at race tracks around Australia. Driving in a van adorned with slogans and statistics, Hoysted travels from Hawthorn to Mentone in an attempt to recruit supporters for his cause.

18 The Victorian government orders an inquiry into the Catholic Morning Star Training Home for Boys, after a number of runaways confront a magistrate with allegations of abuse and torture.

20 The Reverend Ted Noffs announces plans for his Wayside Chapel in Kings Cross to set up medical facilities for drug addicts, and calls for better education on the issue in schools.

21 Ubu presents a program of *Sydney Underground Movies* at Melbourne's Dendy Cinema. Challenging local authorities, they show a number of recently banned films.

25 A seven year dispute over the future of Lake Pedder kicks off when the Tasmanian government seeks approval from Federal parliament to build a $100 million hydro-electric scheme. Whilst offering a source of renewable energy, the scheme angers locals and conservationists, as the damming of the Gordon River will drown an area that has been a national park since 1955.

26 A ruling by Victorian Justice Menhennit in an abortion case sets out that abortion is lawful in Victoria if a doctor believes that the procedure is 'necessary to preserve the woman from a serious danger to her life or her physical and mental health which the continuance of the pregnancy would avail.' Although abortion clinics continue to be harassed by police, the decision lays open the way to safe, affordable and accessible terminations in the future, albeit under continuing restrictions.

27 A Commonwealth referendum allowing the Federal government to pass laws concerning Aborigines and for them to be counted in the census is passed by a record majority of 90.8%. A second referendum proposing to abolish the link between the size of the House of Representatives and the Senate is rejected.

28 Perth pop singer Johnny Young leaves for the UK after

Primitive' look as 'a collection of wild swirls, patterns and colours with just a touch of Mexico.'

Like White, Miss Kate Harman, a Melbourne teenager in 1967, wore clip-on earrings and said that 'nice girls' did not have their ears pierced – indeed she did not have her ears pierced until she was 30, such was the implication of pierced ears amongst the middle classes. White never did have her ears pierced.

Miss Harman, like White, had a lot of her clothes made by her mother. Harman said her favourite fashion shops in Melbourne were at the new Chadstone Shopping Centre, Sportsgirl in Collins Street and Myers in Bourke Street, as well as Mr. John and House of Merivale. Harman wore a rather spectacular Op Art outfit in 1967, which consisted of a short black linen split tunic top with white linen hotpants. Her make-up comprised of a pale foundation with accentuated eyes with black eyeliner, black false eyelashes and a very pale pink lipstick.

This make-up style was extremely popular throughout the mid to late 1960s, and was not just localised to Melbourne. Miss Robin Rogers from Adelaide also wore this make-up *sans* the false eye lashes. Both girls wore Max Factor make-up.

Both girls also used hair pieces, known as wiglets, which added height to the crown of the head. Rogers said she used to have her wiglet set at the hairdressers before she went out – even to a football match! Sometimes it was set into a smooth bob shape and sometimes it was set into ringlets that fell glamorously around the back of her head. Wiglets were commonly held in place with a comb and disguised with a flat bow. In June 1967 *Go Set* reported that wigs were fashionable and could be set at the hairdressers in any number of styles.

Men's fashion was, like women's fashion, both conservative as well as contemporary. Mr Robin Grove was a senior tutor in the English Department at the University of Melbourne during 1967 and bought his clothes in small menswear shops in Carlton, Buckley and Nunn's in Melbourne as well as at Pittard's in Ballarat, where his family lived. During this period, he wore plain or checked shirts, fine knitted sweaters, straight legged trousers and a pale caramel coloured wide corduroy jacket. His shoes were lace up brogues with punched leather decoration.

In May 1967 *Go Set* describes the 'military' look as being fashionable for both men and women, with jackets featuring epaulettes, pleated pockets and saddle stitching. Cuban heeled Beatle boots were still popular and the 'Dandy' look was also appearing, featuring patterned shirts, paisley coats and cravats.

The Military Look at The Catcher (Colbert)

Go Set also noted in June that 'the world seems to be going hippy', and by September protest buttons and badges with suitably anti-establishment slogans had become fashion statements. Popular slogans included 'Ban the Bra', 'Draft beer not boys' and 'Make Love Not War', as well as apolitical messages including 'Pity the Hippies', 'Groovy' and 'Let Them Swing'.

Mr Jim Jonas of Adelaide was a young draftsman who was contracted to work in Hobart, Tasmania from 1967 until September 1968. During this time in Tasmania he remembers always wearing a tie to work, but noticed an 'outlandishly dressed group of people hanging out in Hobart looking like Jimi Hendrix', with colourful outfits, flared trousers, beads and 'Ban the Bomb' badges. Jonas remembers during this time in Hobart that he learned how to play the guitar and saw bands such as The Loved Ones, The Twilights and The Easybeats. He says he was not a fashion follower, but dressed rather conservatively, with short parted hair.

Brigid Finlayson and Maria Sokratis

The Wild Cherries

1967

headlining a huge outdoor concert in Melbourne.

29 Five dollar notes come into circulation.

JUNE

- Having signed to United Artists for £80 000, the *Bee Gees First* album is released in the UK.
- The Masters Apprentices release their self titled debut album, featuring photos of the band decked out in all their psychedelic sartorial splendour. Thanks to the release of the album and the success of Mick Bower composition 'Living In A Child's Dream', the band rapidly become one of the nation's top acts.
- Jeff St John quits The Id to start up a new band Yama (Hindu for firstmen), who release one single 'Nothing Comes Easy' before breaking up when the singer enters hospital for surgery on his legs. In the meantime The Id continue to play, dropping their brass section and opting for a more experimental sound.

• • • The Wild Cherries (Beard)

1 Donald Dunstan becomes Premier of South Australia upon the retirement of Frank Walsh. Famous for his campy safari suits, he quickly moves to institute a series of reforms that will see Adelaide become Australia's most progressive state, as homosexuality is legalised and women's rights locked in over the coming years.

2 The first colour television signal from overseas is received at a satellite tracking station at Cooby Creek, Queensland.

2 22-year-old Adelaide MP Andrew Jones releases a single 'recorded by the youth of Australia, on behalf of the youth of Australia', attacking communism and lauding the heroism of Australian soldiers at Gallipoli, Korea and Tobruk. Despite plenty of hype, the conservative politician's effort fails to enter the Top 40.

5 The Conciliation and Arbitration Commission replaces the 'basic wage' with a legally enforceable minimum 'total' wage based on the overall amount of money needed to survive.

5 American folk trio Peter, Paul and Mary tour Australia.

14 New Zealand's La De Das help relaunch the Sydney Bowl as the Op Pop discotheque.

14 Normie Rowe appears as part of an Australian display at Canada's 67 Expo.

16 New Zealand pop crooner Rim D. Paul is dropped from Sydney TV show *Blind Date* after its producer discovers he is a Maori. Commenting on the matter, Paul tells *Drift* 'I just laughed when I heard about it, but you multiply an instance like that and it is not funny anymore.

Playing inner city venues such as The Thumpin' Tum and The Fat Black Pussycat, the original Wild Cherries were the one of the first bands to bring the new wave of R&B oriented Rock 'n' Roll to Australia in 1964. Constantly evolving, the band's early line up had collapsed by mid 1966, but reformed later in the year as a soul influenced psychedelic unit. With fellow R&B pioneer and Purple Hearts guitarist Lobby Loyde joining the band in January 1967, The Wild Cherries were now set to explore the outer reaches of contemporary rock, as Lobby recalled in conversation with Iain McIntyre.

Lobby Loyde in The Purple Hearts (Beard)

Keith Barber at Black & Blue (Colbert)

How did you come to join The Wild Cherries after playing in The Purple Hearts?

Lobby Loyde: The two bands used to play together and were so diametrically opposed that they admired each other. The Wild Cherries admired the Spartan attitude of The Purple Hearts and The Purple Hearts admired the weird edge that the Cherries had. There were all sorts of line up changes going on with (drummer) Tony Cahill leaving the Hearts to join The Easybeats and (guitarist) Malcolm McGee leaving the Cherries to move to Sydney and form Python Lee Jackson. I wanted to move on because I knew that Mick Hadley (singer) and Bob Dames (bass) of The Purple Hearts were such blues purists that they were never going to move away from that. I loved that spunky R&B stuff too, but now wanted to do originals. The Wild Cherries were really creative, so I jumped at the chance to play with them.

Tell us about the line up of The Wild Cherries you joined.

LL: They were a great bunch of guys to play with because they really wanted to go into unusual things. The drummer Keith Barber was an incredible guy with a great feel. Being an Englishman, he'd listened to a lot of European music and was always pushing the band in a new direction, to move the music on. He was a powerful force in the band.

Les Gilbert (keyboards) was one of those piano eisteddfod children, one of those golden haired genii. When I first saw The Wild Cherries he had a cello which he'd chopped down and turned into some kind of weird bass guitar with piano strings for strings so it would be deep and butch. He was pretty well off tap. He had a weird keyboard and built the Leslie himself by chopping up the old Hammond to make it lighter to carry around. He also made his own rotating speaker.

When I first joined Peter Eddy was on bass. He was inclined towards jazz fusion and crossed that with a lot of the San Francisco sounds like Big Brother and The Holding Company and The Grateful Dead.

John Phillips took over on bass when Peter left. He'd come through Running

Jumping Standing Still who were pretty wild in that they were carrying on the legacy of The Missing Links. He had a much more aggressive approach and added a new dimension to the band.

Danny Robinson was just a fabulous singer. I've never heard anyone quite like the bugger, he was so different, so unique. He was another child prodigy with a huge range. Classically trained, a great double bass player and a fair hand at most instruments he also studied music at Melbourne University. He did a lot of compounded, compositional stuff.

Danny Robinson (Beard)

So what were the things that were influencing the band at this point?

LL: Psychedelia itself was an interesting subject musically because it meant you could improvise most of the time. All you had to do was write a loose framework for a song or take anybody's song, it didn't matter if it was 'Three Blind Mice', and you could turn it into a ten minute epic. That was the big appeal.

I was classically trained as well. I had started playing piano when I was four years old, but once I heard Chuck Berry I was a dead man and had to get a guitar or die. But still that training sticks in your mind and I'd already been exposed to fair amount of Arabic and Indian music. I love that stuff. In my mind it correlates to the original Irish fiddle playing, which turned into Appalachian folk music in America. They're all fairly improvised, energetic types of music.

So the influence of psychedelia was to let you take rock music in new directions?

LL: Yes, because these were all new horizons. Things were pretty bloody straight at that time too. Most Aussie bands, if they weren't doing careful covers, were doing fairly careful self write jobs that were verging on the worst part of the Top 5 in England and America. No one seemed to be able to write any decent rock in this country at that time, and those that were were relegated to the underground for their damn life.

Les Gilbert (Colbert)

All of the band's single releases were original songs. Was this the case with your live set too?

LL: Live we jammed on anything and everything. There was a fair bit of original stuff, but if anyone in the audience called out a song we'd have a go and extend it out. We'd take Wilson Pickett songs, which were three minutes long, and twenty minutes later we'd still be doing it, but it would be so different it would be hard to remember what we'd started with. So even if they were covers they were originals.

Danny also had a real thing for soul music, so all the B-sides of the band's singles were soul, blues things because Danny loved to sing it. While we did a few of those songs live, they weren't

I have heard that they have also booked Ja-ar (another Maori pop singer) for the show. This is even more amusing when you know that they asked my agent if I was darker than him. I guess he passed the whiteness test.' Other Australian programs prove to be less racist, as Paul subsequently makes appearances on *Bandstand, Where the Action Is, Saturday Date* and *Kommotion.*

22 The Australian Tourist Commission holds its first meeting in Sydney.

22 Students demonstrate in North Melbourne in support of Aboriginal land rights.

22 3AK DJ Lionel Yorke is busted in Toorak for speeding.

24 On their way to a gig in Morwell Max Merritt and The Meteors' van collides head-on with a truck. Only bassist John 'Yuk' Harrison, who had been sitting in the back with the band's equipment, escapes unhurt. Singer/guitarist Max sustains severe head injuries, saxophonist Bob Birtle's leg is badly broken, and drummer Stewie Spears suffers multiple serious injuries when his legs are crushed, both arms are broken and the tips of several fingers cut off. As a result of his injuries, Max loses his right eye and his face is badly scarred, Bob is left with a permanent limp and Stewie never regains full mobility.

25 Sydney's gang wars escalate with the murder of leading underworld figure Richard Gabriel Reilly.

29 Holding firm after being out on strike for more than six months, the Gurindji people march on Government House in Darwin.

JULY

- During the July to August registration period 17 draft resisters publicly refuse to sign up for conscription.
- Ubu film maker Garry Shead's *Give Me Your Hand* documents his fiancée American folksinger Odetta performing her songs at Spectrum Film Studios and the La Perouse Aboriginal settlement.
- The Bee Gees play their first tour of the US, meeting Otis Redding and appearing on Dick Clark's *Bandstand* TV show.
- A national four digit postcode is introduced.
- The Ubu film cooperative's appeal against the banning of a number of their films fails, with Commonwealth Appeal Censor Colin Campbell stating that they are 'not fit to be shown on a lavatory wall.'

1 Key Melbourne rock venue The Biting Eye is relaunched as Ginza, featuring a psychedelic light show and underground movies.

1 New Zealand's La De Das return to Sydney with a flurry of TV, radio and concert appearances and the release of their 'Hey Baby'/'Other Love' single.

6 Despite it still being legal to possess LSD in New South Wales, the state government threatens Billy Thorpe with jail if he goes ahead with plans to take the drug and report on it to the media.

the band's main fare. It was the psychedelic edge that the audience came for. We could play to teenyboppers, uni students and desperate psychedelically influenced hippies and had a fair chance of communicating to all of them.

Where did the band mainly play?

LL: Well there were still plenty of gigs available. You could do five shows on a Saturday night, no problem. I just liked the inner city clubs. The suburban dances could be great, but you could get down and dirty in the inner city. We'd go on at The Catcher from about 2 am to 5 am and they'd have to shoot us to get us off stage. We'd have these notorious jams that would go on until they sent the bouncers in.

Danny Robinson and Lobby Loyde at The Catcher (Colbert)

The Catcher was enormous. It had three floors and from 8 pm to 2 am it was chockers to the roof, you could barely breathe in the joint. After that it would thin out by about a third so you probably still had up to 1000 in there by 3 or 4 am. Of course, by the time we finished playing it would be down to a couple of people asleep on the floor and a few unconscious on the couches (laughter).

The worst shows were at Drive-in theatres. They were bloody awful. They'd be out in the suburbs on a Sunday afternoon and the local belligerents would turn out. Those were some pretty uncomfortable gigs (laughter). Drive-ins were everywhere, but they weren't making any money so they'd put on gigs, sporting events, etc. None of them knew anything about running gigs, and they certainly didn't know anything about PAs or security and crowd control. No one ever attacked the bands, but we spent most of our time providing a soundtrack for brawls.

Did you play many high school shows?

LL: A lot, surprisingly enough. We'd play in the school canteen or the hall or whatever and the kids would just push the teachers into the background. The music teachers would think we were interesting, although way too loud, and we'd often have principals going red in the face with anger over the volume. I loved those gigs, though, because the kids were open to things and often way more hip than anyone else.

The band also toured Sydney a lot.

LL: We liked it up there. The Sydney crowd was very interesting. Psychedelia had slowly kicked off there and started to really happen. A lot of people in Melbourne talked about Sydney as this kind of uncouth place, but I found the psychedelic crew up there were way harder and more bizarre. They would accept stranger music than the pricks in Melbourne ever did.

Sydney had a true underground and Suzie Wong's was the gig of gigs. It was the home of all the weird stuff. The Missing Links had played there (in 1965) back when they were recording *Hey Momma* backwards and all that. The Id were also amazing. Jeff St John was at his best when the band were doing psychedelic stuff.

When The Wild Cherries went up Sydney had The Nutwood Rug Band and all the basis of what was to come, like Tully and Tamam Shud, was beginning to come together. Nutwood Rug had a really warm, rich sound and were young Americans who had bolted to Australia to escape the Vietnam War and conscription. They brought with them a bin style PA with horns, which was the first one of those I ever saw. They were unusual for the time, in that they were deeply into the whole North American hippy thing, these guys were virtually snorting Echinacea and dispensing patchouli oil to the crowd (laughter). They were very stoned guys.

It seems as if in Melbourne that a lot of the psychedelic influence in music came from emulating overseas records, whereas in Sydney it genuinely evolved from drug use and musical experimentation.

LL: Absolutely, and that difference played a big role in the demise of The Purple Hearts. Every time we went to Sydney (in 1966) to play I'd fall into the bad company of all these musicians who were playing jazz and the early sounds of the Sydney underground. They'd pass you silly cigarettes and pieces of blotting paper and say 'Try this man!' and I started to drift in a psychedelic direction. The last six months or so of The Purple Hearts was like counting beans for me.

I think what made Melbourne straighter was that it had massive quantities of venues and people were being paid okay money. Once you got out of the hands of the promoters and into the outer suburbs and the inner city clubs they'd pay you decent money if you could pull a crowd. Even if you were just being paid a fixed scale you could play so many shows that you'd still have enough to eat and buy strings.

In Sydney there were bugger all gigs and they were all in the inner city. There was ferocious competition for those few gigs. Bands got way more butch and took more risks to show that they were worth coming to listen to. In Melbourne there were a lot of show bands playing covers and shitty pop-rock who would have given up if they were in Sydney because the money wasn't there.

Sydney also had a massive audience of black and white American soldiers on leave from Vietnam. These guys would play you music from around the world and also demanded a lot more from the bands they saw.

Tell us about the rehearsal space where you lived with Keith Barber.

LL: That was in South Melbourne and we used the main room as a painting room where we were slowly muralising the whole joint with elaborate paintings. Keith and I lived there so we spent our whole life in the rehearsal room writing music. It was a drop-in space for lots of other musos, so we used to jam with them and it's good for you to jam a lot. Anyone down from Sydney would drop in and jam, so we got to play with all the crazies. Shane Duncan, who played with Jeff St John, came down for a day and stayed for a month. He took us to areas we'd never been before.

All that playing meant that no matter what The Wild Cherries were doing, Keith and I could head out on a well laid out tangent. Les could improvise on anything, he wouldn't need the chords, he'd just hear it and away he'd go. Dan would spend half his time just making noises, letting great big beautiful notes go.

The Wild Cherries signed to Festival Records not long after you joined the band . . .

LL: Pat Aulton, who had produced The Purple Hearts' singles, came and saw us in Sydney. He was blown away and said 'C'Mon, let's get into the studio boys.' He was the one who really got us onto the label.

People used to put poo on the old Festival studios because they only had a four track recorder with a couple of mono machines, but everything in the place was valve, so it had a warm sound and a bit of an edge to it because valves distort. A lot of the Melbourne recordings of the time were too clean and clinical, they sounded like The Shadows to me.

The record companies were always pressuring you to have a hit. For us 'Krome Plated Yabbie' and 'That's Life' were bloody commercial. They were still a bit bent so far as Australian

LOBBY LOYDE
now has vacancies for a few more serious pupils
LEARNING ADVANCED BLUES GUITAR
enquire **26 2279**

8 John Newcombe wins the Men's Singles tennis title at Wimbeldon.

9 Sydney's first Happening is held at the Paddington Town Hall, bringing together 400 members of Sydney's burgeoning film, music and arts underground.

12 The new Australian drama series *You Can't See Around Corners*, starring Ken Shorter as a draft dodger and Rowena Wallace as his girlfriend, premieres on TV. The opening episode causes a sensation because of a love scene in which Shorter runs his hand up Wallace's thigh.

12 Normie Rowe arrives back in Australia to be met by hundreds of screaming girls at Sydney airport. Over the next 11 weeks he tours the country, showcasing the abilities of new Playboys members Mick Rodgers and Trevor Griffin.

14 Having lost their residency at Sydney's Here discotheque after disagreements over the level of volume, The Id announce they will be starting their own venue.

16 Ubu present a program of *Recent Australian Movies* at the Union theatre in Sydney, launching Kit Guyatt and Chris Cordeaux's anti-war film *Vietnam Report*. The program tours Melbourne and Canberra during September.

18 Two teams of art students are given five hours each to give a Morris Minor a 'pop art' makeover on Don Lane's *Tonight Show*.

19 Former Loved One bassist Kim Lynch is convicted at the South Melbourne Court of Petty Sessions for the possession of Methedrine and Indian hemp.

20 Conservative students from Wollongong complain to the local paper that their more radical counterparts are growing marijuana at the Wollongong University College, as well as making regular trips down to Sydney to buy LSD.

22 The BBC World Service runs a story on the Sydney disco scene as part of its *Outlook* program.

22 The Aboriginal film actor Robert Tudawali dies in Darwin at the age of 36 from burns received in a fire.

30 A new security team hired by Sydney's Jungle discotheque proves overly aggressive, terrorising crowds to the point where the club is forced to close through lack of patronage.

30 The La Mama theatre opens in Carlton, Melbourne. At a time when the production of plays written by Australians is almost non-existent La Mama's non-profit organisation allows directors, writers and actors a vital space for airing new and experimental works. Founder Betty Burstall later recalls in *La Mama: Story of A Theatre* that 'I got the idea for La Mama when we went to New York in the sixties. We were poor. It was impossible to go to the theatre, but there were places where you paid 50 cents for a cup of coffee, and if you felt like it you put some money in a straw hat . . . It was very immediate and exciting and when I came back to Melbourne I wanted to keep going, but such

records went at the time, but it was a struggle to even get those things recorded. Pat Aulton was great to work with, though, because he was a musician himself and secretly liked the fact we were slipping off to the dark side. If you suggested something to Pat he'd get onto it whereas most of the engineers and producers of the time wouldn't listen to you at all. They'd say 'What do you want to do that crap for?', which is not what you want to hear just before a session starts. (laughter) They weren't interested in making Australian music, they just wanted to copy what was happening overseas.

Nevertheless, you managed to get some interesting sounds, including the use of feedback and phasing, on the A-sides of your singles. You might not have taken it as far as you wanted to . . .

LL: But with Pat we took it as far as we could. To get the phasing we used dual recorders. You'd put the guitar solo on one track to get it in stereo with all the reverbs and then put it on the other recorder at the same time. Then when you ran the recorders, instead of synching them you'd put a line on them and set them both at that interval, but as they both started you put your finger on one. As they caught up they'd go through all the phase angles and make the sound. When they did catch up you'd put your finger down again or grab it and make it go a little bit faster so you'd get the metallic flanging sound. You were phasing below and flanging above. We used a combination of both of those sounds.

Lobby Loyde recording on bass (Colbert)

What were the other sounds you'd try and capture?

LL: Our favourite trick was to use a little transistor radio as a pre-amp to make things dirty. We'd also push all the valve circuits as hard as we could. I had a Maestro fuzz-tone, which I'd had before The Purple Hearts days, and also a very early American Wow (later Wah) pedal. Chet Akins had invented them back in the 1950s. He made some crazy stuff like the Talking Guitar Bag, the Wow pedal, the fuzz tone and the little octave divider they used to call the Mu-tron. He was a very square jazz guitarist who told everyone the fuzz-tone was to make guitars sound like a sweet violin or a banjo and a Wow pedal was so you could move it a little bit to find a different tone control. All of his devices had little diagrams of how you could set them and there was bugger all fuzz or any of that. He never envisaged people jumping up and down on the Wow pedals or turning up the fuzz-tones so that the tone sounded like shit (laughter).

How long would it take to get the sounds you wanted?

LL: Frigging hours (laughter). You were putting together little tiny bits of the record at a time. It wasn't easy. We'd spend hours getting all the backing down, though, and then Danny would step in and do his vocals in one take. Pat would sing with us too. If you listen to 'Krome Plated Yabbie' there are some pretty elaborate harmonies on that. The rest of us would put our wobbly bits on the side, but the really good parts are Danny and Pat.

Why did you end up writing all the singles?

LL: I was the only one who would actually sit down and put those things together. The band's music was much more spontaneous than the singles would suggest, and if the others had had their way we would have just gone in, jammed and used the best bits. I would have loved to do that too, but we were never going to get that out of a record company in Australia at that time. So it was left to me to knock up a shape, give it some riffs and licks and then sit down with Dan to work out a simple story line. We knocked up all of the singles in a very short time.

How much time were you allowed in the studio?

LL: More than in The Purple Hearts. With that band we had a Saturday afternoon from 2–6 pm and managed to record the first three singles. We went home and that was it. We didn't need to record again because for the next two years they were still putting out the songs (laughter).

With The Wild Cherries we got a whole day! (laughter) We'd get in at 8 am in the morning and record until 10 pm. We'd throw the B-sides down like going for a walk in the park because they were just little soul songs for Dan. The rest of the day would be spent on the A-side, because we'd try them lots of different ways – fast, slow, medium, butch, light, we'd try it all.

The record company only ever liked the B-sides. We never got to make an album because the record company thought it would be full of feedback and crap, which it would have been (laughter).

The Wild Cherries live on stage (Beard)

Apparently in 1968 PAs and amplifiers suddenly got a lot bigger.

LL: They got bloody big (laughter). It was good really because most of the PAs in the venues were pretty rotten. You'd have to walk out in front of the stage to hear anything the singer was doing. When the big bins and PAs came through you finally got a bit more control over the sound and could even have fold back. (laughter) It was an exciting time because for the first time you could hear everybody on stage.

John Phillips worked at (Australia amp manufacturer) Strauss, so when he joined all these big amps came in with him. They were into bands having some input, so I'd take down things like a circuit I'd found in an old book from an amp that was used for early radio broadcasts. We'd push everything as far as we could. I had speakers that could take 300 watts in the days when English Celestions could only take 30 watts. The Strauss amps were killers, they were beasts, but the company couldn't capture an overseas market and went bust in the end.

In 1968 your stint with The Wild Cherries came to an end as one by one the members dropped out.

LL: As time went on we just fell apart and became a proxy soul band that did the odd good, out there thing. There was also a bit of the old discomfort between people. Les had always been artist

a place didn't exist. So I talked around a bit, to a few actors and writers and directors, to sound them out about doing their own stuff.' Playwright Jack Hibberd, whose play *Three Old Friends* is one of the first to be presented, also recalls 'I felt there was a desperate need in Melbourne for a permanent venue for alternative and experimental theatre. And what better place than Carlton with its strong sense of community and rich melting-pot of types?'

AUGUST

- The Australian government approves the Leave-In-Australia scheme for US and Australian troops. The presence of soldiers on 'Rest and Recreation' in Sydney proves a boon not only for local night clubs and brothels, but also for musicians such as Billy Thorpe who are turned on to the new, heavier sounds coming out of North America. The visiting Americans also provide a pipeline for the importation of heroin and other hard drugs into Australia's capital cities, laying the foundations for the massive Asian-Australian drug trade of the 1970s and beyond.
- The 0-10 Network axes both of its popular music programs *The Go!! Show* and *Kommotion*.
- Teens demonstrate in the streets of London over a decision by the UK government to deport Bee Gees members Vince Melouney and Colin Petersen. Following a series of court challenges, protests and threats to leave the country the band prevails, with the pair being granted long term working visas.

- The La De Das make their first trip to Melbourne, playing gigs at The Catcher, Berties and Thumpin' Tum.
- American R&B pioneer Ray Charles tours the east coast of Australia.
- Barry Oakley's *Witzenhausen Where Are You?* debuts at La Mama.
- The Society for the Cultivation of Revolution Everywhere (SCREW), later known as Resistance, opens the Third World radical bookshop in Sydney, selling posters, records, badges, books and political magazines.

2 Vibrants singer Rupert Perry priggishly hits out at the use of LSD, telling *Everybody's* that 'I know of numerous instances where artists depend on drugs. They convince themselves that drugs actually help them play better music.'

2 ABC TV's new drama serial *Bellbird* premieres. Set in a fictional Victorian country town, the show soon becomes Australia's most popular drama series, drawing 1.2 million viewers nightly by 1969.

13 5000 march from Hyde Park to Rushcutters Bay in Sydney, where they meet another 2500 people to protest against the US bombing of North Vietnam. The next day 10 people are arrested in a sit-in action outside the US consulate.

18 Large protests in Canberra call for justice for Indigenous Australians and the withdrawal of troops from Vietnam.

27 The Ram Jam Big Band lose all their equipment and stage outfits in a fire at Adelaide's 20+ Club.

Lobby Loyde with The Aztecs, 1969 (Newhill)

and he's pretty famous around the world now for doing displays and installations in museums and things. He was working with fibreglass and ceramics and putting spinning colour wheels in front of projectors and wanted to do more and more of that stuff. Danny meanwhile had succumbed to some of the evils of the world and was starting not to give a rat's butt about life and John Phillips wanted to go off and join a pop band.

None of that was where I wanted to go, so as people dropped out I formed a band with Big Goose (Barry Sullivan) and Little Goose (Barry Harvey) plus Matt Taylor from Bay City Union who sang for a while. At the same time I was jamming with old Thorpie (Billy Thorpe), who I'd been mates with since I was a kid, as well as Jimmy Thompson who I'd always admired as a drummer. We had a few jams and they asked me to come and tour Brisbane with them and I became part of The Aztecs. Meanwhile Big Goose and Little Goose and the rest of the guys linked up with Phil Manning and became Chain, taking over where Wendy Saddington had left off.

What was it like playing with The Aztecs?

LL: Well Bill and Jimmy had been playing around with rock 'n' roll and R&B for a while, but Bill had never really played that kind of music before. He'd done 'Over The Rainbow' and all that, and when he had done R&B he'd played the worst elements of it. However, whatever was going he was keeping up with it. If Jimi Hendrix had have shot off his willy and hung by his testicles from the light bulb while he played guitar with his bum, then Bill would have had a go at it. Bill's no schmuck, but he always wanted to make it.

With the core line up of Paul Wheeler playing bass, Jimmy playing drums and Piggy playing organ, it was an exciting band to play in. It got a bit overbearing after a while, though. Bill's a great guy, but you wouldn't want to marry him (laughter). Also he could see which way the pub rock industry was going. The venues wanted straight rock 'n' roll and if you played anything too long or too weird that was it.

In my heart I had another vision. I could never get over The Wild Cherries, and I kind of got sick of twelve bar blues after a while. I love twelve bar blues, but I prefer listening to them to playing them. It was hard to get away from the psychedelic, experimental stuff once I played it. Songs that I later did with the Coloured Balls like 'G.O.D.' went back to things I'd explored in The Wild Cherries days.

After leaving The Aztecs in 1970 Lobby reappropriated The Wild Cherries name to release the 'I am The Sea'/'Daily Planet' single on Havoc Records, before recording his first solo album *Plays With George Guitar* for Infinity. In 1972 he formed the legendary Coloured Balls, releasing the *Ball Power, Heavy Metal Kid* and *First Supper Last* albums, as well as a solo work entitled *Obsecration*. Heading off to the UK in 1976, he began working as a producer, and upon his return to Australia cut a series of classic albums with X, The Sunny Boys and Painters and Dockers, as well as recording a live album of his own with Southern Electric. More recent years have seen Lobby occasionally playing with the reformed Coloured Balls and Purple Hearts, as well as with Melbourne bands Fish Tree Mother and Blacksmith Hopkins.

27 The Love In coffee lounge opens in Carlton, replete with psychedelic decor and a 'head shop' selling posters, beads and hippy gear.

28 New South Wales Education Board members meet with the NSW Drug squad after it is revealed that a teacher had given two teenage students LSD and subsequently evaded arrest because he had not distributed or sold the drug in a public place.

29 A benefit is held at the Maccabean hall in Sydney to raise money to help members of The Id defend themselves against charges over the possession of marijuana.

SEPTEMBER

- The Masters Apprentices suffer a major blow when songwriter Mick Bower collapses due to a nervous breakdown. Hospitalised during a tour of Tasmania, he returns to Adelaide where he continues to write music, but does not play live again until the late 1970s.
- The Bee Gees' second UK single, 'Massachusetts', becomes a worldwide hit, selling over five million copies.
- HMAS *Perth* is hit by NLF shore batteries while pursuing enemy patrol boats off the coast of South Vietnam.
- Controversy breaks out when the extent to which Federal politicians have been rorting VIP jet flights is leaked to the media.
- Ubu establishes itself as a business, offering their films and light shows, including coloured

1967

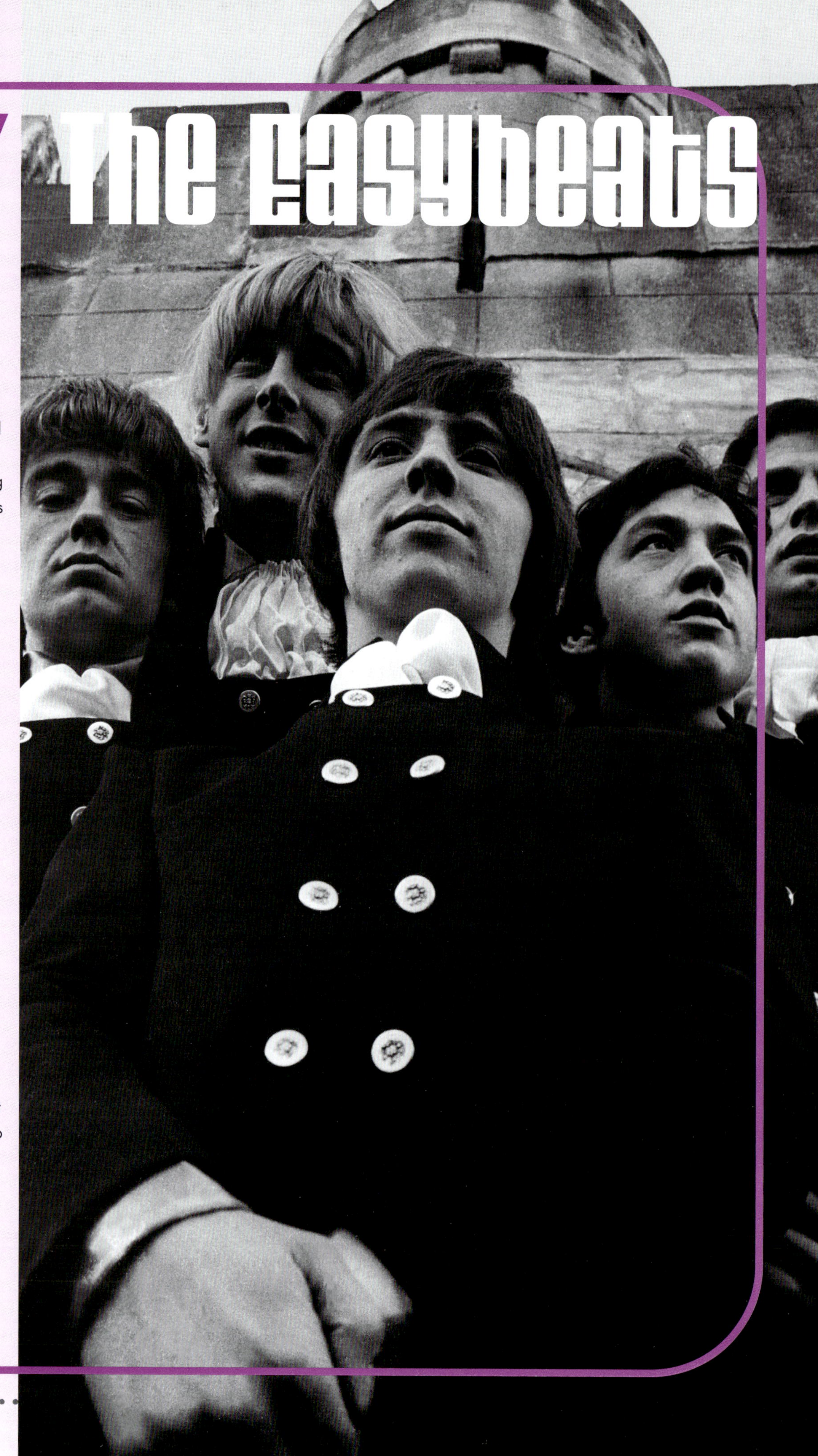

lights, slides and oils, for use at parties, promotional events and concerts.

- Radical activists and academics set up the Free University at Sydney. Modelled on a similar effort in New York, the staff and students study together with no fees, exams or degrees. Peaking in 1969, the organisation draws in hundreds of participants before fizzling out three years later.

1 The Commonwealth *Trades Practices Act* comes into force, regulating business competition in Australia.

1 The Customs Department announces it is introducing stringent regulations regarding the importation of ingredients used in the manufacture of LSD.

2 Ubu Films publishes its *Handmade Film Manifesto*, declaring 'Let no one say anymore that they can't raise enough money to make a film – any film scrap can be turned into hand made film at no cost.'

4 *AM*, a new half-hour morning current affairs magazine, premieres on ABC Radio 2.

6 The Commonwealth government limits the ability of Australians to appeal to the British Privy Council, thereby making the High Court of Australia the final court of Appeal in the land.

6 The Cellblock Theatre at East Sydney Technical College hosts Clem Gorman's *Explosion*

The Easybeats in London (Beard) • • •

Originally formed at the Villawood Migrant Hostel in 1964, The Easybeats brought together recent arrivals Harry Vanda (guitar), Dick Diamonde (bass) and George Young (guitar) with Stevie Wright (vocals) and Snowy Fleet (drums). Spotted by real estate agent Mike Vaughan at Sydney's Beatle Village, the band signed to Albert Productions and were rushed into the studio in early 1965 to record a number of songs, including their first hit 'For My Woman'. Within months the band had stormed the Australian charts, scoring numerous Top Ten hits over the next two years and releasing three albums in the process.

Having inked a worldwide recording deal with United Artists, the band headed to London in mid 1966. Initially daunted by the talent surrounding them, the newly prominent song writing duo of Vanda and Young redoubled their efforts, recording with Shel Talmy and scoring a massive worldwide hit with the anthemic 'Friday on My Mind'. However, as Paul Culnane and Iain McIntyre relate, whilst 1967 was to see the band reach the peak of its success, it also saw the first in a series of missteps that would eventually bring about their demise.

Having stormed the international charts with 'Friday on My Mind', The Easybeats faced new challenges in 1967, not least those posed by the wave of musical experimentalism that was sweeping their snappy brand of power pop aside. Operating under pressure to follow up their recent hit, the band increasingly retreated from live performance to focus on studio work. Moving away from the relatively cohesive sound of the first three albums, Vanda and Young furiously churned out songs in a variety of styles, often with erratic results.

Cracks in the friendships that had bound the five members together also began to emerge. Vanda and Young, flush with the success of one of their first collaborations, increasingly focused on writing together, while Stevie, suffering from writer's block, found what few ideas he had to offer unwanted, or dismissed as outdated. Boredom soon kicked in as, along with Snowy and Dick, he now found himself with long days to kill in a city where he was an unknown with few friends. Adding to the come-down from the very recent heady days of Australian fame was the fact that Stevie and Dick, never the best of the friends, intensified their bickering over a myriad of petty matters.

Management also began to prove a problem for the band as Mike Vaughan, like many managers of the era, adopted the dictum that 'any publicity is good publicity.' Attempting to capitalise on the success of 'Friday on My Mind', he put the band through a series of silly and demeaning PR and publicity stunts, many of which they later repudiated.

The most serious problem for The Easybeats, however, remained musical. After the Christmas euphoria of a Top 10 hit came the New Year headache of finding a suitable follow-up. This was a crucial moment in their career, and it's arguable that this is when it all began to unravel. Although there was an obvious, gold-plated contender in the superb 'Pretty Girl' (a track recorded alongside 'Friday' during their September 1966 Abbey Rd sessions), the song was inexplicably passed over and relegated to the B-side of a later single. Instead, the band's label opted for a new Vanda-Young track, 'Who'll be the One You Love', which had been written in haste and was clearly not in the same league as 'Friday'. Indeed, George later dismissed it as 'crap'. It was released in March in the UK and flopped. Ominously, UA didn't even bother to release it in America.

Meanwhile, the preceding months had been used to record tracks for their new album with Shel Talmy. By all accounts this was not a happy working relationship. The track 'Do You Have a Soul?' was supposedly written about the American, as was the Who's 'Waltz for a Pig', and this would be the last time he worked with the band.

In April 'Who'll be the One You Love' was released in Australia, and predictably went Top 20, whilst the disappointment of the new single was relieved by news that 'Friday' was now Top 20 in America. In the same month the band also began their first, hugely successful tour of Europe, which would become their most loyal market outside Australia, supporting The Rolling Stones. 'Easy-fever' hit the continent, as Harry was feted as royalty in Holland, while the band witnessed scenes of pandemonium after 13 000 gathered at Schweeat airport to greet them and their somewhat better-known companions. A show in Dortmund also introduced the band to European style pandemonium, with Easybeats manager Mike Vaughan telling *Everybody's*, 'When the fans tried to rush the stage the police put on knuckle dusters, tied on rubber truncheons and hit out. I saw one boy knocked over and kicked in the mouth.'

At the end of the European tour the group made a triumphant return to Australia, arriving

Factory. Billed as an 'assault on the senses', it features music from The Id, a psychedelic light show and sponsorship from 'head shop' the Pothole.

6 According to a three day investigation by the *Canberra Times*, two Sydney LSD dealers have set up shop in the nation's capital, selling 100 microgram doses to students and public servants for up to $1.50.

7 Following months of painstaking research, *Film Digest* reveals that 12 films have been banned and 53 cut by the Commonwealth Censor's Office in the past two years. Films receiving unwelcome edits from the secretive censors include *One Million Years BC*, *Blow Up*, *A Fistful Of Dollars*, *Scorpio Rising*, *The Wild Angels* and *Alfie*.

9 Moves by the Queensland government to effectively ban public demonstrations are challenged by a march of over 4000. The protest is brutally broken up by police, who arrest 114 people.

9 The Commonwealth government announces the establishment of the Office of Aboriginal Affairs.

16 The US spy base at North West Cape is declared operational.

16 South Sydney defeat Canterbury-Bankstown in the NSW Rugby League Grand Final.

17 PM Holt announces that Australia will increase its military aid to South Vietnam by another 1700 troops.

20 Normie Rowe is called up for national service during the September intake. In the following months he affirms his willingness to serve in Vietnam, telling *Go Set* magazine that communism must be defeated in that country.

20 The Presbyterian Assembly calls on the Commonwealth Government to initiate peace talks in Vietnam.

21 The Victorian Housewives Association attacks the ABC for putting 'too much emphasis on sex' in its TV programs.

23 Richmond beat Geelong to win the VFL Grand Final.

25 Having recruited Rick Harrison (ex The Others) to fill the place of guitarist Mick Bower, The Masters Apprentices experience more dramas when drummer Stephen Hopgood is bashed and taken to hospital after leaving a Melbourne dance.

25 Johnny Young and *Go Set* scribe Lily Brett return home from the UK. In the months to come Young admits on air, in an interview with 6PR's Keith MacGowan, that he took LSD whilst in the UK, rueing it as a 'silly thing to do.'

29 Australia's only national pop radio show, *Sunday Club*, is replaced on ABC National with a BBC program.

30 Initiating a Federal Government drive against drugs, the Commonwealth Minister of Health announces amendments to the Poisons and Dangerous Drugs Ordinance, imposing fines of up to $1000 and sentences of up to three years in prison for the use, sale or manufacture of LSD in the Australian Capital Territory.

Harry Vanda (Beard)

on 13 May for a national tour. Greeted by thousands of screaming fans waving banners at Sydney's Kingsford Smith airport, Dick Diamonde stunned both fans and band mates by fainting, but he soon recovered and the tour got underway. Supported by The Twilights (also just back from London), Ronnie Burns, Larry's Rebels and a selection of local supports in each city, the band received a tumultuous welcome around the country, climaxing with two rapturously received shows at the Sydney Stadium. Three tracks from a Melbourne live show on 21 May released on the *Live: Studio and Stage* collection indicate just how popular the band was as their renditions of 'Sorry', 'I'll Make You Happy' and 'In My Book' are all but drowned out by teenage screaming. As a testament to the band's skill, they remain tight and energetic throughout, despite the fact it is unlikely they could have possibly heard anything they were playing.

The tour also planted the band squarely in the eyes of the nation's media, with newspapers across the country hailing their success. Whilst most writers sensationally focused on the group's rabid fans, with headlines such as 'The Torment of the Teens', others were astute enough to note both the band's cultural significance and their prodigious skills. Writing in the *Sydney Morning Herald*, social commentator Craig McGregor credited the band's rise as 'Partly through sheer vitality and especially the infectious dynamism of lead singer Stevie Wright, but partly also through the musical sophistication [of the band] which could be discerned through the barrage of screams which greeted them last night.'

Although effectively sidelined as a creative force within the band Stevie Wright, as McGregor's review indicates, reaffirmed his supremacy in the eyes of the Australian public, garnering most of the press and audience's attention. Given the opportunity to perform older songs he had co-written, such as 'Women', Stevie gave the crowd his all. Stoking up the affections of the hordes of teenage girls around the country, he also promised a kiss and a cuddle to any of those daring, or foolhardy enough, to succeed in breaking through the wall of security to reach him.

In summing up the tour George later recalled it as 'probably the highpoint of the group's career . . . we didn't come back with any of the standard excuses for failure.' The band was given a civic reception at the Sydney Town Hall, hosted by Lord Mayor John Armstrong, and Sydney tabloid *The Daily Mirror* ran a week-long series on them entitled 'The Million Dollar Story'. Unfortunately, this attracted the interest of the taxation authorities, who began inquiries into the band's financial affairs, which was ironic, as the five members of this 'million dollar' group were still on a piddling $10/week allowance!

The tour concluded in Perth, but after this triumphant homecoming came yet another disappointment. The frantic Australian tours of 1966 and the trip to England had kept Snowy Fleet away from home for long periods, and by his own admission he had been experiencing growing anxiety over the separation from his wife and daughter. His wife Maureen, who had gone to London to be with him, was not allowed to return to Australia for the 1967 tour, and he had not seen his 5-year-old daughter Mandy – left in the care of her grandparents – for almost 12 months. Reunited with his daughter in Perth, he made the difficult decision to leave the group. Maureen returned home and the Fleet family settled in Perth, where Snowy became a successful builder.

In an article published in *Everybody's* magazine some months later, Snowy also revealed that the pressures of fame and the changing nature of the music scene had taken its toll. In conversation with Maggie Makeig he admitted that 'The strain of pretending to be single brought me to the point of collapse in London . . . By the time we left Germany on The Rolling Stones tour, I knew quite definitely I had to pack it in. When we were in Germany we were surrounded by all these wild, funny-looking people with long hair, charging around, taking drugs, the whole business. I used to think "What if my daughter Mandy were to see me on TV? What would she think?"'

Back in London, the group spent June and July regrouping and recording. Seeking a replacement for Snowy, they auditioned 60 drummers with the guernsey eventually going to Tony Cahill, former drummer with Brisbane R&B legends The Purple Hearts. While Cahill was being recruited, The Easybeats – plus session drummer Freddie Smith and renowned session keyboardist Nicky Hopkins – went into the fabled Olympic Studios in Barnes, London (where Jimi Hendrix, The Move, The Small Faces, Traffic, Family and The Rolling Stones cut many of their seminal late '60s tracks) to record their next LP, produced by Shel Talmy's erstwhile engineer, the now legendary Glyn Johns.

This should have been the breakthrough they needed, and contained some of their best

OCTOBER

- *Cinema Papers* is launched at La Trobe University in an attempt to champion local approaches to cinema and highlight the growing Australian film industry.

3 A Melbourne youth is freed by police after being caught selling methedrine at The Catcher.

3 Tasmanian police announce that they are interviewing a number of people in relation to LSD sales in Hobart.

4 The first US military personnel arrive in Sydney under the Leave-In-Australia program.

4 The host of TV show *Beauty and the Beast* and naval veteran of both the Korean and Second World wars, Stuart Wagstaff, speaks out against the Vietnam War, stating 'I don't think we should be involved. I feel we should be encouraging the Vietnamese to stabilise themselves rather than disrupting the countryside and supporting the bombing of the North.'

7 The Melbourne *Truth* lives up to its reputation for sensationalism by dubiously claiming that LSD is easier to buy than cigarettes at some local schools.

According to a conveniently unnamed school boy source, 'Blokes are getting LSD from pen pals in the States. They make big spending money selling the acid to kids in discos and after school hang-outs. I know of a uni student who impregnates sugar lumps with acid. He and his mates then go around to dances and pop the sugar into girls' coffees without them knowing it. The girls become easy targets for the night.'

11 *Honi Soit* editor Keith Windschuttle (who later in life moves to the far right as a denier of Aboriginal genocide) is reprimanded by Sydney University for publishing instructions on the manufacture of LSD. Criticising recent New South Wales legislation against the use of the drug, Windschuttle tells the *Sydney Morning Herald* 'Were LSD difficult to produce, like heroin, the main effect of the government legislation would be to pass the trade over to Sydney's gangsters. [They] are trying to move into the acid scene. They are charging $10 for 100 micrograms up at the Cross. The normal uni price, when there is any charge at all, is $1 for 100.' Windschuttle's predictions prove prescient, as despite ever increasing police powers, organised crime comes to control much of the drugs trade by the mid 1970s.

13 Having won the Western Australian final of Hoadley's Battle of the Sounds and made a good showing in the national finals, The Valentines decide to move to Melbourne. Initially

George Young (Beard)

Snowy Fleet and Friends (Beard)

material to date, but even though a complete entire album was recorded, sequenced, mastered, titled (*Good Times*), and a cover prepared, it was never released. The band had become involved in a complicated contractual wrangle, with five companies claiming rights over their work. The immediate result was that Albert Productions, who had been footing most of the bills, now closed their chequebook. With both Johns and Olympic unpaid, the record stayed in the can and only two cuts – the magnificent title track 'Good Times' and the psychedelic gem 'Land Of Make Believe' managed to emerge many months later. The remaining tracks languished for another decade until Raven Records released them on the 1977 LP *The Shame Just Drained*.

In June, UA released the superlative psychedelic rocker 'Heaven and Hell'. It was The Easybeats' last Talmy-produced single, with Nicky Hopkins prominent on harpsichord, and featured some great bass playing by Dick. Backed with the wonderful 'Pretty Girl', it became another Top 20 hit in Australia, and by rights should have been a double-sided hit for them worldwide. For a while it looked set to restore their chart fortunes, especially in the US, but once again bad luck intervened. Just as it entered the charts, the single was banned by various US radio stations, due to the lines 'Hell is finding your face has gone red, Discovering someone else in your bed.' Also playing a role in the song's failure was the fact that in a country still possessing its fair share of hellfire and brimstone preachers, the title did not play well with radio, particularly in the Southern states. The band rapidly rushed out a new version changing the offending line to 'Discovering her love has gone dead', but by this point they had missed the boat.

Based on the success of 'Friday', Vanda and Young had naturally enough continued to mine what they saw as a winning formula, packing remarkable musical and lyrical innovation into a concise single format (what George later called their 'three minute operas'). When they saw one of their best efforts fail they effectively gave up trying. They began making music primarily to please themselves, and according to George a lot of similar material was shelved. Their fortunes were further hindered by consistently poor timing and choice of material by United Artists, and by a lack of direction and support from both label and management. From this point on, according to George 'the rot set in'. The outcome was doubly lamentable – abandoning any pretence of 'commerciality', the group went on to produce some of their most outstanding material over the next year, but sadly many of the tracks were only ever cut as demos, and the public never got to hear them until many years later.

In July the Talmy-produced *Good Friday* LP was finally released in the UK and US, but was

managed by former Loved One Gerry Humphreys, the band begins a hard slog of country touring, travelling around in a garishly painted Kombi van.

14 The Masters Apprentices play a free outdoor concert in Hyde Park, Sydney, as part of the Waratah Spring Festival. Attended by an estimated 50 000 frantic fans, the concert quickly degenerates into a near riot, forcing police to stop the band's performance after a few songs when the surging crowd threatens to demolish the makeshift stage. As the band is hustled away, one of two limousines hired to carry them is overturned and wrecked. That evening they headline the more sedate UNSW Living in a Child's Dream Ball in suburban Ashfield.

14 Village Drive-in theatres in Melbourne offer free 'scare pills' to moviegoers viewing the horror film *Theatre of Death*. According to cinema advertising the pills have 'No medicinal value, but we believe sucking a sweet calms the nerves quite considerably.'

22 10 000 march in Sydney in support of anti-Vietnam protests at the Pentagon in Washington.

25 The Playboys announce they are quitting as Normie Rowe's backing band to become Procession. The band had planned to wait until their Australian and New Zealand touring commitments were over, but changed their minds following a fight with Rowe at Melbourne's Pinocchio's disco.

28 Former Prime Minister Sir Robert Menzies attacks the ABC after *This Day Tonight* cuts an extensive interview with him down to 2.20 minutes in order to make way for a 13 minute segment on anti-war protests.

28 New pop show *Uptight!* starts on Channel 0.

29 Fashion designer Prue Acton leaves Australia to try her luck in New York.

NOVEMBER

- Direct telephone dialling between Australian cities on the east coast becomes possible, with the opening of automatic trunk switch centres in Sydney, Launceston, Canberra, Newcastle and Geelong.
- Greg MacGillivray and Jim Freeman's *Free and Easy* makes its premiere in Sydney. Sporting influences from experimental film and the American West Coast music scene, the film heralds a shift in the sophistication of surf movies, as the makers utilise dual narration, hand held camera work and colour filters.
- The Bee Gees record their eccentric *Cucumber Castle* film in London with the aid of comedian Spike Milligan.

1 Having recovered from their recent car crash, Max Merritt and The Meteors play a week long stint at Melbourne's Winston Charles.

1 A Canberra university student is fined $150 for sending LSD to a friend through the post.

2 The Victorian Legislative Assembly approves changes to the *Poisons Act*, imposing a maximum fine of $4000 and/or 10 years in jail for the possession and sale of LSD and other hallucinogens. During parliamentary debate, the Deputy Leader of the Opposition

held off in Australia until some time later, and eventually released in an altered form. Featuring, predictably enough, 'Friday on My Mind', the album collected together a number of the band's most powerful, catchy pop classics, including 'Pretty Girl', 'Made My Bed (Gonna Lie In It)', 'Remember Sam' and 'Happy is the Man'. Topped off with a sublime freakbeat take on 'See Line Woman', the album was only let down by the inclusion of unnecessary and somewhat ordinary covers of 'River Deep, Mountain High' and 'Hound Dog'.

July also saw the first of three compositions written for Perth bubblegum act The Valentines (featuring future AC/DC singer Bon Scott) released on Clarion Records back in Australia. Having penned the highly successful 'Step Back' for another West Australian performer, Johnny Young, in 1966, the band had whipped off the track 'She Said' for The Valentines during their recent Australian tour. Little more than a throwaway, the single failed to make much of an impact outside of the band's hometown, but nevertheless launched a relationship that would prove more successful in years to come.

In August The Easybeats first American tour saw them put on a mismatched bill supporting Gene Pitney and The Buckinghams. They got off to a shaky start, due to injury and illness, but soon won hearts and minds, just as they had in Europe. In New York Australian expatriate rock critic Lillian Roxon took them under her wing, showing them the sights and introducing Stevie to Andy Warhol. While in town they also cut a new track, 'Falling off the Edge of the World', which was subsequently rush-released in the US. Despite failing to enter the charts, the song was highly praised – and frequently played – by Lou Reed who, no doubt introduced to it by fellow Factory cohort Roxon, reportedly described the song as 'one of the most beautiful records ever made'.

The next single, released in November, was 'The Music Goes Round My Head'. Inspired by Vanda and Young's discovery of bluebeat (the ska precursor which also inspired McCartney's 'Ob-la-di, ob-la-da'), they cut two versions – one fast and one slow, but UA oddly chose the slower, less commercial version, and it barely scraped into the Australian charts. The single was also noteworthy for being the first official Vanda and Young production. They had kept their eyes and ears wide open during earlier sessions and, within a year of arriving in the UK, were producing themselves, with superb results.

During early 1968 the Vanda/Young team scaled new heights, with a string of superb singles. In March they released the epic 'Hello How Are You?', which briefly took them back into the UK Top 20. The song had been an attempt to emulate the 'big ballad' style of singers like Tom Jones and Englebert Humperdinck. It's a fine song, and although, in typical fashion,

The Easybeats (Beard)

Stevie Wright (Beard)

Mr Wilkes calls for the Victorian Drug Squad to be expanded to match the NSW squad of 30.

3 Red Handed wins the Melbourne Cup.

8 The Victoria and Alberts disco opens in Spring Street, Melbourne, with a party drawing over 1000 guests.

15 Promoter Ivan Dayman's Bowl venue in Melbourne is relaunched as The Trip with a show headlined by The Masters Apprentices and The Wild Cherries.

16 Over 60 Law students sitting their final exams at Melbourne University have their copies of the *Rules of the Supreme Court* confiscated when it becomes known that many have inserted 'cheat sheets' into the guide's pages.

17 Ubu's Albie Thoms writes and directs the 'Just For Kicks' episode of ABC TV crime show *Contrabandits*, in which an underground filmmaker is unfairly harassed by police. Drug references are rife throughout, and a number of Ubu regulars appear as frolicking hippies during an outdoor scene shot in Paddington.

18 Students at Maribyrnong High school in Melbourne hoist a girl's bra up the school flagpole during end of year celebrations. The previous night students had daubed the school with graffiti, and when ordered to clean it up by teachers they respond by throwing flour bombs. The police are eventually called in to quell the disturbances, but are initially thwarted when students lock the school's gates.

19 Australia launches its first satellite, WRESAT 1, from the Woomera rocket range.

20 Marking a break with the Empire's economy, the Australian government ends the fixed rate of exchange between the Australian dollar and the British pound sterling.

22 American expatriate acid rockers Nutwood Rug set up a 'collective community dwelling place' 50 miles north of Sydney.

25 In the Federal election for the half Senate the conservative Democratic Labor Party (DLP) wins four seats, giving it the balance of power.

25 The Melbourne *Truth* runs another dubious LSD expose, in which their intrepid reporter is taken on a wild goose chase by 'former pop singer Paul', before scoring a tab of acid in a Carlton club.

29 The 3XY Happening at Melbourne's Velodrome draws 3000 to hear sets from The Twilights, Groove, Masters Apprentices, Vibrants and others.

Harry Vanda (Beard)

Young later dismissed it as 'cornball schmaltz shit', it obviously influenced some listeners, as the first line of Jeff Lynne's 1974 ELO hit 'Telephone Line' is undoubtedly a direct quote from The Easybeats' epic.

'Hello' was backed by the even grander 'Come in You'll get Pneumonia', which had been the B-side of 'The Music Goes Round My Head' when it was released in Australia back in December '67. 'Come in' was a truly amazing production, featuring arrangements from Bill Sheppherd (Bee Gees), backing vocals by Olivia Newton-John and Pat Carroll (then working as a duo in London), and saxophone by George's older brother Alex, who was then playing in British band Grapefruit.

In June a second United Artists LP *Vigil* was released in the UK. The album was a curious mixture of styles, combining straight ahead rock with mini-epics like 'Hello' and 'Come in' and a couple of odd covers of 'Hit the Road Jack' and 'Can't Take My Eyes off You'. The album also included the far superior UK re-recording of 'Falling', as well as two escapees from the doomed Glyn Johns LP, 'Land Of Make Believe' and 'Good Times', which were paired on 45 in Australia in July, and reached #22 in August. 'Land of Make Believe' was coupled with a (Beatles-inspired) B-side 'We All Live Happily' for June release in the UK, and 'Good Times' was finally released there in September, backed by an instrumental version of the track 'Lay Me Down and Die'.

'Good Times' deserves special mention, as it is one of the greatest rock singles ever recorded. Why this track was not a smash hit at the time is hard to explain. Looking back years later, Young suggested that 'Good Times' should have been the follow-up to 'Friday on My Mind', and it's hard to argue with him. 'Good Times' is gutsy, hard-driving rock 'n' roll, highlighted by Nicky Hopkins' tasty piano, a terrific guitar solo from Harry, and a knockout chorus, with blistering backing vocals courtesy of the band's new friend, Small Faces' singer Steve Marriott. The famous anecdote associated with the song is that Paul McCartney heard it on his car radio one day while driving on the motorway, and immediately pulled over to phone the BBC to ask that it be replayed. In spite of such accolades, the single was ignored by British radio and failed to chart.

On 7 July The Easybeats featured in an all-star line-up at what must have been a truly incredible concert, Sounds '68, at the Royal Albert Hall. Topping the bill were co-headliners The Move and The Byrds (featuring Gram Parsons). Other supports included the Bonzo Dog Doo Dah Band, Joe Cocker and the Alan Brown Set.

Through late 1968, the formerly tight-knit band drifted further apart. Drugs were a factor, along with the growing independence of the Vanda/Young axis. By this time the duo were working substantially on their own, and between them they could now play almost any instrument they needed. They were writing prolifically, but were reluctant to do more than a few gigs per month, and so the band only came together for the occasional show or demo sessions at Central Sound studios in Denmark St.

In October, *Vigil* was released in an altered form in Australia and the USA, where it was retitled *Falling Off the Edge of the World*. In November the band's label and management showed their increasing disregard for both the band's career and their fans by releasing the instrumental track 'Lay Me Down and Die' in Australia.

On a more positive note, the year saw yet more Vanda-Young compositions released back in Australia. Having given Wollongong band Reverend Black and The Rockin' Vicars the largely forgettable 'Down to the Last 500', the pair handed The Valentines one of the their most majestic creations. 'Peculiar Hole in the Sky', with its thunderous horns, massed studio effects and obtuse lyrics, was a bonafide psychedelic classic. Although it failed to hit the charts, the song helped propel The Valentines into the upper echelons of the Australian pop scene. Now based in Melbourne, the band followed up with two more Vanda-Young compositions, the bubblegum 'My Old Man's a Groovy Old Man' and flipside 'Ebeneezer', scoring their first Top 40 hit the following year.

In early 1969 Harry and George took over a flat in Moscow Road that had previously been used as a jingle studio for pirate radio stations. With modifications it became a 4-track home studio, and Vanda and Young began churning out demos, working mostly on their own. One of the only official recordings they made – which proved to be the last Easybeats single – was the powerful 'St Louis', which was both fitting farewell and a pointer of things to come. 'St Louis', and its B-side 'Rock and Roll Boogie', were produced in April at Olympic Studios by Ray Singer, who had made a name for himself with Peter Sarstedt's 'Where Do You Go To My Lovely'. An odd choice on the face of it, but he did a good job. The single was issued in June in the UK and USA, and ironically began to chart in the States just as the band completed what would prove to be their final tour.

In August 'St Louis' was released in Australia, along with an album released on the band's new label Polydor Records. *Friends* was not an Easybeats album at all, with the only true

Stevie Wright with *Go Set* writer Lily Brett (Beard)

DECEMBER

- Dr Kandy's Third Eye begins playing around Sydney. Featuring former pop star (Little) Gulliver Smith on vocals and Id member Ian Walsh on keyboards, the band builds a reputation for weirdness, thanks to its psychedelic light show and acid rock sound.
- Exploiting his links to The Beatles to the hilt, Transcendental Meditation master the Maharishi Mahesh Yogi tours Australia, lecturing crowds and demonstrating meditation practices to skeptical journalists.

7 Legendary Sydney beat club Suzie Wong's is redecorated and relaunched as The Flower Pot, with Wright of Waye and Python Lee Jackson playing the opening night.

7 Bruce Petty's anti-war film *Hearts and Minds* receives an 'Honorable Mention' at the Australian Film Industry (AFI) awards in Melbourne.

10 The Twilights, Questions, Somebody's Image and Ronnie Burns play the 2UW Christmas Special at the Sydney Trocadero.

15 The Vibe discotheque opens in Sydney. Boasting decor designed by Architecture lecturer Michael Day, it features regular residencies from The Sect and Nutwood Rug.

17 Prime Minister Harold Holt disappears while swimming in heavy seas off Cheviot Beach near Portsea, Victoria. His body is never recovered, prompting a variety of bizarre theories on his disappearance, ranging from murder to kidnapping by Chinese agents.

17 Procession make their live debut before a crowd of 1300 at the Victoria and Alberts disco in Melbourne. Featuring three members of The Playboys (Brian Peacock, Mick Rodgers and Trevor Griffin), plus former Librettos' drummer Craig Collinge, the band incorporate film and sound effects into a polished performance. The band record an *Uptight* TV special soon after, featuring a 40 piece chorus backing them on their debut single 'Anthem'.

22 Representatives of 26 nations, including President Johnson of the US, attend the Holt memorial service in Melbourne. Whilst in the country, Johnson uses the opportunity to lobby for increased Australian involvement in Vietnam.

24 The Groop play their last show at a Sandringham dance before heading to the UK a fortnight later.

27 With the arrival of a third Infantry Battalion, total Australia troop numbers in Vietnam now exceed 8000 men.

Iain McIntyre

The Easybeats (Beard)

Easybeats tracks being 'St Louis' and 'Rock and Roll Boogie'. The rest of the album's tracks were merely Vanda and Young Moscow Road demos, intended for other artists. Other than the single tracks and the album's title song, the overall quality was well below par, with its release creating further disillusionment amongst the band. *Friends* was also issued in the UK in October, and in November in the US on Motown's Rare Earth label.

In September the band completed a short European tour before reluctantly accepting the offer of a five-week Australian jaunt. It was to prove a considerable come-down from the heady days of their '67 tour. The group, worn out and at odds with their management, saw the tour as a last-ditch attempt to bail themselves out of their mounting pool of debts. Again the victims of bad timing, they found themselves, having reverted to 'no frills' rock 'n' roll, out of favour with Australian audiences preoccupied with the burgeoning progressive rock and soul scenes.

The situation was further complicated by Parlophone's unwelcome release of 'Peculiar Hole in the Sky' as a single, presumably to cash in on the tour. Although a fine piece of work in its own right, it was released against the band's wishes. Originally intended simply as a demo for The Valentines, it flopped, which was no surprise for a slice of pure psychedelia by then about two years old.

The band made a valedictory TV appearance on the ATN-7 *Easybeats Special* before giving their final live performances in Sydney, at the Trocadero and Caesar's Disco, in October. The tour over, The Easybeats drifted apart. Although there was no official announcement, it was obvious the band was finished, and after one last gathering, for Dick Diamonde's wedding in early 1970, they went their separate ways.

Following the break up of the band Dick Diamonde retired from the music scene altogether, whilst Tony Cahill returned to England to join Python Lee Jackson. Stevie Wright stayed in Australia, forming a short-lived and none-too-successful band called Rachette, but soon regained the spotlight and earned acclaim for his electrifying performance in the role of Simon Zealotes in the Australian production of *Jesus Christ Superstar*. Vanda and Young, who had been left shouldering an $85 000 debt from The Easybeats, returned to England in early 1970, where they worked for several years, producing and recording under a variety of pseudonyms. Eventually returning to Australia in 1974, they immediately oversaw Stevie Wright's solo career, writing and producing the massively successful 'Evie (Pts 1, 2 and 3)', and his acclaimed 'comeback' LP *Hard Road*. From this point on, operating from the inner sanctum of Alberts Studios in Pyrmont, they became a major force in Australian music, producing a string of classic rock and pop albums and singles for John Paul Young, Bobbi Marchini, Ray Burgess, William Shakespeare, Cheetah, Rose Tattoo, The Angels and the first six albums by AC/DC.

Part Three
1968

John 'Yuk' Harrison of Max Merritt and The Meteors (Colbert)

1968 MUSIC

WORLD EVENTS

- A general strike paralyses France during May as tens of thousands of students and workers battle police.
- Soviet troops invade Czechoslovakia to crush the 'Prague Spring' reform movement.
- US troop numbers in Vietnam top half a million.
- Pope Paul places a ban on contraception.
- US President Johnson announces he will not seek or accept presidential re-nomination.
- Police and students clash outside the US embassy in Grosvenor Square, London.
- The Society for Cutting Up Men (SCUM) founder Valerie Solanas shoots Andy Warhol in New York.
- North Korea seizes US Navy ship *Pueblo*, holding the 83 sailors on board as spies.
- Yippies and anti-war protestors clash with police in Chicago during the US Democratic Party convention.
- Civil Rights leader Martin Luther King and Senator Robert Kennedy are both assassinated in the US.
- Students are shot and killed during protests at the Olympic Games in Mexico.
- Richard Nixon is elected US President.

Procession (Beard) • • •

The year in Australian rock music

1968 was a transitional year for rock music all round. In the wake of *Sgt. Pepper's Lonely Hearts Club Band* and the Monterey Pop Festival things were beginning to disperse in all directions. Judging by the Australian charts, it seemed that record buyers had shunned rock altogether and decided to opt for the safety of middle-of-the-road schmaltz. But, as we all know, the charts never tell anything near the real story. Even so, Australian rock artists were seemingly caught on the hop during this year.

The beat boom had long gone bust, that much is for certain. Good time R&B was now replaced by a heavier, more earnest form of blues that had more to do with musical prowess than dancing. Soul was still very popular in the live clubs, although the original black artists were not selling a single unit in this country. The success of The Monkees and the new phenomenon of producer-driven bubblegum pop created a massive gulf between the 'serious' and the 'popular' bands around town. Likewise, the rift between Melbourne and Sydney radio stations was still a talking point, with Sydney stations often refusing to play Melbourne-made records and Melbourne stations overlooking a lot of Sydney-based product. Nevertheless, the music scene was healthy and vibrant in all the Australian cities, and plenty of interesting records were made during 1968.

The Hoadley's Battle of the Sounds doubled its prize money from $1000 to $2000. Winners still received a return ticket to the UK on the Sitmar Cruise Ship line plus Maton guitar equipment and other goodies. 1968's winners were The Groove who'd had two big hits with cover versions of The Isley Brothers' 'Simon Says' and Sam Cooke's 'Soothe Me'. Formed by Twilights manager Gary Spry, The Groove's highly polished combination of soul and bubblegum music was very much the sound of commercial Australian pop in this year.

One of the most hyped Australian bands of '68 was Normie Rowe's former backing group The Playboys, who had only recently renamed themselves Procession. Procession's first single, 'Anthem', was the first ever acapella Oz pop record, their second single, 'Listen', was the first single to be recorded locally on an eight-track machine, and their album *Live At Sebastian's* was the first Australian live debut album release. Yet despite an unprecedented promotional push from *Go Set* and weekly spots on the new TV show *Uptight*, Procession failed to click with audiences in any significant way. Meanwhile The Twilights were at their creative peak, yet this immediately coincided with their descent as a popular singles act. The Easybeats had been writing and recording increasingly complex tunes in England, and their big orchestral ballad 'Hello How Are You?' actually did better on the UK charts (#20) than it did in Australia (#34). The Masters Apprentices – despite constant line-up and style changes – continued their rise, to becoming one of the biggest bands in the country, but they were still some months away from becoming a powerhouse. Everything was in disarray.

International Album Releases

The Byrds – *The Notorious Byrds Brothers* and *Sweetheart Of The Rodeo*
Leonard Cohen – *Songs Of Leonard Cohen*
Joni Mitchell – *Joni Mitchell*
The Move – *The Move*
Simon and Garfunkel – *Bookends*
Fairport Convention – *Fairport Convention*
Pink Floyd – *A Saucerful of Secrets*
The Small Faces – *Ogden's Nut Gone Flake*
The Buffalo Springfield – *Last Time Around*
Jeff Beck – *Truth*
Cream – *Wheels Of Fire*
The Moody Blues – *In Search of the Lost Chord*
Jefferson Airplane – *Crown Of Creation*
The Zombies – *Odessey and Oracle*

- Riots break out in Derry after police suppress the nascent movement for civil rights in Northern Ireland.

AUSTRALIAN EVENTS

- Australia's population reaches 12 million.
- The fluoridation of water begins in New South Wales.
- The first section of Melbourne's Tullamarine freeway is opened.
- New Australian TV productions include *Skippy* (Channel 9), *Motel* (ATN-7), *The Battlers* (Channel 7) and *Vega Four* (ABC).
- Exhibitions at the National Gallery of Victoria include *Marcel Duchamp*, *Contemporary Nordic Art*, *Design in Scandinavia*, *Belvedere Op Art* and *The Field*.
- Australia's first Kentucky Fried Chicken franchise opens at Guildford, New South Wales.
- The Australian Broadcasting Control Board introduces minimum quotas, stipulating that at least 18 hours of local content must be shown on prime time TV each month.
- The first Australian exhibition of sculpture, *Form In Action*, to travel overseas tours New Zealand.
- *The Graduate* and *To Sir, With Love* open in Australian cinemas.

- The Government announces that Australia will adopt the European PAL colour TV standard, instead of the American NTSC system, although it will be seven years before colour TV is finally introduced.
- The Museum of Modern Art, Heide 2, designed by architects McGlashan and Everist, is awarded the Royal Australian Institute of Architects (RAIA) Victorian Chapter Bronze Medal. Phillip Goad later describes the plan and section of Heide 2 as a 'sophisticated de-Stijl composition.'
- The President of the Melbourne Viaduct Theatre is taken to court over the performance of *When Did You Last See My Mother?*, a light comedy dealing with homosexuality, but wins the day when it is revealed that the police have mistakenly charged him with blasphemy rather than obscenity.
- Female workers covered by the 1967 Commonwealth Hostels' Award briefly gain wage parity with their male counterparts, before an appeal by the Commonwealth Government sees the decision overturned.
- Shops in Tasmania begin 24hr/7day a week shopping.

JANUARY

- The Australia Council for the Arts is established to finance the Arts and advise the Government on related matters.
- Uniform Australian censorship laws take effect, with the creation of the National Literature Board of Review.

The Jimi Hendrix Experience – *Electric Ladyland*
The Band – *Music From Big Pink*
The Beatles – *The Beatles (The White Album)*
The Kinks – *The Village Green Preservation Society*
John Lennon/Yoko Ono – *Unfinished Music No. 1: Two Virgins*
The Rolling Stones – *Beggars Banquet*

The Charts

Melbourne

Did I say *1967* was Squaresville in Melbourne? Well the city of gardens totally out-squared itself in 1968 – seldom has a bigger load of shockers ever topped the charts. Johnny Farnham earned the biggest Australian-made hit of the year with 'Sadie (The Cleaning Lady)' – and that was relatively hip compared to some of the other songs that aced the top 40. 'Love is Blue (L'amour est Bleu)' by Paul Mauriat and his Orchestra, 'The Impossible Dream' by Jim Nabors, 'Honey' by Bobby Goldsboro, 'Judy in Disguise (with Glasses)' by John Fred and his Playboy Band and 'Dear Heart' by Mike Preston were big smashes in the early part of the year. Then Canadian band The Irish Rovers hogged the #1 spot for two entire months between June and August with 'The Unicorn' (shared with The Bachelors) and then 'The Orange and the Green'/'Whiskey on a Sunday'. The Beatles held a mortgage on the top spot from October 1968 until February 1969 with their 'Hey Jude'/'Revolution' double-sider and this 18 week consecutive run at #1 remains a Melbourne chart record to this day.

The satirical skiffle song 'Melborn and Sideny' by The Idlers Five (#1 for two weeks during March) was the only Australian composition to make the year's top 50. An *annus horribilus* for Australian music on the Melbourne charts indeed.

Johnny Farnham (Beard)

Sydney

MOR schlock was also the order of the day in Sydney during 1968. 'Love is Blue (L'amour est Bleu)' was the biggest hit of the year there, although no less than FOUR artists shared chart honours with that particular piece of music. Versions by Paul Mauriat and his Orchestra, Al Martino, Cheryl Kennedy and Jeff Beck all registered on the Sydney charts. Some other, slightly more interesting records, to fare well in the city were 'Macarthur Park' by Richard Harris, 'Classical Gas' by Mason Williams, 'To Sir With Love' by Lulu, 'This Guy's in Love with You' by Herb Alpert and Vanilla Fudge's heavy version of 'You Keep Me Hangin' on' – which became the third biggest hit of the year. The only Australian composition to make any reasonable impact at all on the Sydney charts was The Easybeats's 'Land of Make Believe'/'Good Times' double-sider (highest position #13; 13 weeks in).

Adelaide

While Adelaide was following the same MOR path as everyone else in Australia chart-wise, the crow-eaters at least had the good taste to send a couple of killer tracks to #1. 'Lazy Sunday' by The Small Faces and 'White Room' by Cream were both chart-toppers in the city of churches and nowhere else. Aussie songstress Bev Harrell also scored an ace with 'Mon Pere' – a song that didn't even make the top 40 in Melbourne or Sydney. The fabulous Masters Apprentices had the 38th biggest chart hit of the year with 'Elevator Driver' (highest position #6; 16 weeks in).

The 1968 *Go Set* Pop Poll Winners (as voted by the readers of *Go Set*)

Top Male Singers:	1967	1966
Normie Rowe: Gold	2nd	1st
Johnny Farnham: Silver	–	–
Ronnie Burns: Bronze	1st	2nd

Top Female Singers:	1967	1966
Bev Harrell: Gold	2nd	–
Lynne Randell: Silver	1st	1st
Dinah Lee: Bronze	4th	2nd

Top Groups:	1967	1966
The Twilights: Gold	2nd	2nd
The Masters Apprentices: Silver	5th	–
The Groove: Bronze	–	

1968 Hoadley's Battle of the Sounds Winners

The Groove: Gold
The Masters Apprentices: Silver
Doug Parkinson In Focus: Bronze

Dinah Lee (Colbert)

The Groove (Colbert)

The Sonic Landscape

For guitarists, the new must-have accessory was the wah-wah pedal (or 'wow-wow' as they were advertised during this first year). Wah-wah pedals (sort of like an accelerator or sewing machine pedal in design) create a distinctive 'crying' or 'talking' effect when they are pressed or depressed by the foot. The effect is achieved because the unit converts the guitar's input signal into one

- Postal strikes halt the delivery of mail across Australia.
- Various anti-conscription groups meet in Brisbane to coordinate coming protests.
- The Sydney underground paper *Chaos* is published.
- During the National Service registration period anti-war activists hold 'Fill in a falsie' parties, signing up such luminaries as Mickey Mouse, Robert Menzies and Malcolm Fraser for conscription.
- In yet another reshuffle, Masters Apprentices lead singer Jim Keays sacks half the band, bringing former Missing Links and Running Jumping Standing Still guitarist Doug Ford and drummer Colin Burgess into the fold.

1 Following a long struggle, female teachers in Victoria are granted equal pay, although their wage increase is staggered over a three year period.

3 4000 teens attend the 3XY Happening, held at the Melbourne Velodrome in Swan Street, Richmond, to see The Wild Cherries, Max Merritt and The Meteors, The Chelsea Set, The Groop, Laurie Allen, Somebody's Image and Ronnie Burns.

4 The search for the body of Harold Holt ends without success.

5 The Vibe discotheque opens in Sydney, with The Sect and Nutwood Rug playing its launch.

9 John Gorton defeats Paul Hasluck in the race for the leadership of the Federal Liberal Party and is appointed Prime Minister the following day.

12 Sydney police begin regularly searching US servicemen after ten soldiers on leave from Vietnam are arrested for the possession of marijuana.

15 The Who, The Small Faces and Paul Jones arrive in Australia to undertake their notorious Big Show tour. Ian McLagan of The Small Faces kicks things off in style by abusing journalists after they bring up the topic of his recent UK drug bust. Over the coming weeks the tour visits Brisbane, Sydney, Melbourne and Adelaide, giving local acts such as Doug Parkinson In Focus a chance to play before massive crowds.

15 The first Australian soldier since the Korean War faces a court martial for murder following the killing of a Lieutenant Brigadier in a grenade attack on his sleeping pit. Whilst such 'fragging' attacks on officers become widespread in the US military they remain relatively unknown amongst Australia's smaller forces.

single frequency, and the pedal then works as a simple 'tone' control – sweeping through that frequency's entire tonal range as the pedal goes up and down. Excellent examples of this sound include 'White Room' by Cream and 'Voodoo Chile (Slight Return)' by The Jimi Hendrix Experience.

Another effect that was gaining in popularity was the use of the Hammond organ's distinctive 'Leslie' speakers. The Leslie speaker is a unique piece of equipment consisting of a rotating horn contained within a wooden cabinet. This rotating action is responsible for the rich wavering sound of Hammond organs, but by 1968 artists had discovered that Leslie speakers were also trippily effective on vocals, guitars and anything else that made a noise.

Amplification had surged ahead as well. Marshall stacks had finally arrived in Australia, and guitarists such as Terry Britten of The Twilights, Kevin Peek of The James Taylor Move and Doug Ford of Running Jumping Standing Still (and later The Masters Apprentices) were using 200 watt Marshall rigs on stage. Lobby Loyde of The Wild Cherries was one step ahead of everyone (of course); he had the local Strauss company custom build a 300 watt monster for him – which he still managed to blow up! Gone were the days of entire bands (vocals included) plugging into a solitary 15 watt Goldentone amp.

The biggest news on the Australian recording front in Australia in 1968 was the fact that Bill Armstrong in Melbourne had gone and invested in a Scully eight-track recording machine. Many of Australia's best studios were still only coming to grips with four-track units, so Armstrong had certainly gained the march on the rest of the country in terms of technology. The first single to be recorded on Armstrong's magical eight-track was Procession's 'Listen' and there was plenty of publicity surrounding this event – *Go Set* published shots of the band earnestly discussing important matters around the recording desk with engineer Roger Savage. When you consider that the beatified *Sgt. Pepper* of only twelve months hence had been recorded on mere four-track technology, this was a big step for the local music industry.

1968 Top 33⅓ Psychedelic Pselections

Title – Artist	Status (release date)	Label: Cat. No
1. 'Love Machine' – Pastoral Symphony	Single (May)	Festival: FK-2343

The band Pastoral Symphony did not exist, but were a studio project put together by British producer Jimmy Stewart and local entrepreneur/doctor/shyster Geoffrey Edelston. The musical clout that made up the basis of Pastoral Symphony was a more-than-impressive bunch of musicians armed with a top notch song. The Twilights provided the musical backing, while Johnny Hawker provided the brass and string arrangements. Terry Walker of The Strangers sang lead and members of The Groop provided harmonies.

'Love Machine' is a pompous, over inflated psychedelic balloon, but it totally works. Extreme phasing and gimmicky sound effects kick in from the very first note and don't stop until the end. The lyrics are as subtle as napalm (*'When this ride is at its end, I promise we'll be more than friends . . . My machine is guaranteed, to satisfy your every need'*). The song hit #10 in Melbourne, #14 in Sydney and #6 in Brisbane.

There is a funny twist to the story of Pastoral Symphony. Manager Geoffrey Edelston and producer Jimmy Stewart were all ready to form a 'real' version of the group to begin performing live around Australia, but were pipped to the post by a decidedly amateur (and obviously canny) bunch of musicians in Melbourne, who had legally registered the name before the pair had a chance to.

Killer Moment: 01.07, *that trippy* 'come and fly . . .' *break between the first chorus and the second verse.*

2. 'Drawing Room' – Cam-Pact	B-side (May)	Festival: FK-2364

'Drawing Room' is a sensuous, distinctively Melbourne song, originally done by 'Baroque' band Eighteenth Century Quartet in 1966 as the B-side to their second and final single on the Go!! label. The 18CQ version is quite stilted and muted, though not without its charm – particularly in the seductive vocal performance by composer Keith Glass and the nice amount of atmospheric reverb on the guitars.

Once Glass had formed his next group Cam-Pact, he decided to re-record 'Drawing Room' for the B-side of their second single 'I'm Your Puppet' – only this time, it was anything BUT muted.

New guitarist Chris Stockley's thrashy rhythm guitar was let loose, there are sweeping strings flowing everywhere, thundering drums added and finally, an industrial-strength dose of phasing for the coda.
Killer Moment: 01.41, *those delicate pizzicato strings followed by the industrial-strength phasing.*

Chris Stockley of Cam-Pact (Colbert)

3. 'Moving in a Circle' – The Executives
B-side (March) Festival: FK-2179

The Executives were an ultra-professional, ultra-slick, sophisticated pop unit who enjoyed plenty of chart success, particularly in Sydney, with cover versions of overseas numbers. But their most astonishing recording ever was an original composition penned by guitarist Dudley Hood and singer Carole King. 'Moving in a Circle' was originally issued as a B-side to their fairy-floss version of Cynthia Mann and Barry Weil's 'It's a Happening World', and might as well have been from another planet.

Haunting, sweet, creepy and utterly beautiful in equal measures, 'Moving in a Circle' begins with a distant piano thumping out a wonky merry-go-round melody, before the voice of Carole King comes in chiming like a crystal bell. The band is so crisp and tight, and King's voice so simply immaculate, that everything sounds gorgeous. Then all of a sudden, things start to fall apart with spooky backward tapes and layers of murky reverb. Cue-in once again the merry-go-round piano, and it starts all over again. Bizarre.
Killer Moment: 00.56, *things suddenly get very strange.*

The Executives (Colbert)

17 Following their massive success in the UK and at home, The Seekers are named Australians of the Year.

22 Three Victorian state school teachers leave for India to become the first Australians to study Transcendental Meditation with the Maharishi Mahesh Yogi.

27 70 remand prisoners at Pentridge jail begin a hunger strike.

28 Sydney film makers co-op Ubu host a night of *Sydney Underground Movies* at the Avalon Cinema.

28 The Big Show tour entourage is removed by police from a plane in Melbourne following an allegation by a flight attendant that she was abused by Who guitarist Pete Townshend. A storm of media controversy ensues as the bands are threatened with deportation.

30 A 12 mile fishing limit around Australia is introduced.

31 Nauru receives independence from Australia.

31 The Tet Offensive begins, with attacks on 100s of military bases across South Vietnam during the traditional Tet holiday period. Despite Viet Cong losses of up to 30 000, the offensive marks a turning point in the war, as both the troops on the ground and the citizens at home in the US and Australia realise that the war may be unwinnable.

FEBRUARY

- The Sydney leg of the Big Show sees yet more disasters for UK act The Small Faces, as the Stadium's revolving stage breaks down, allowing only a quarter of the audience to see the band. At one point in proceedings singer Steve Marriott threatens to call off the show, telling coin throwers that he will 'belt them around the bloody ears.'
- A meeting at La Mama theatre in Melbourne sees the establishment of the Draft Resisters Movement (DRM). Echoing the stiffening trend in resistance to the war, the organisation's slogan is 'Wreck conscription, not oppose it.' Advocating non compliance to the point of assisting draft resisters to go underground, the DRM and other anti-war groups set up safe houses and new identities for those who wish to avoid jail. At the same time the group sets out to expose the government's inability to catch draft resisters by organising surprise appearances for them at rallies and on TV.
- Having topped the European and American charts with a string of hits including 'World', 'Holiday' and 'Words' The Bee Gees release their second UK album, *Horizontal*.

4. 'Comin' on Down' – The Twilights **Single (August)** **Parlophone: A-8448**

On their return from England in late 1967, The Twilights built an incredible live reputation through being able to reproduce *Sgt. Pepper's Lonely Hearts Club Band* in its entirety on stage. They later did the same thing with The Small Faces' *Odgen's Nut Gone Flake* set, as well as complex numbers by the likes of Cream, The Move, Traffic and more. This practice of dismantling sophisticated pop music to its very core and then reconstructing it on stage helped Twilights' guitarist Terry Britten to develop a prodigious understanding of the mechanics of pop song writing. Between 1967–68 he was overflowing with creativity.

At a scant two-and-a-quarter minutes long, 'Comin' on Down' is a tight psychedelic operetta with a lyric line dealing with impending nuclear doom. And no half-measures with phasing either – the band track is phased for the entire song! There's even a post-apocalyptic infant singing 'All Things Bright and Beautiful' at the very end. Yup, in terms of psychedelic-value-per-second, 'Comin' on Down' would be up there with the best of 'em.

Killer Moment: 01.38, *a brilliantly cynical line: 'People in the pop world were complaining, 'cos the deadly fallout kept away the crowds.'*

The Twilights (Newhill)

5. 'I Had a Dream' – Doug Parkinson In Focus
Single (May) Festival: FK-2389

A startlingly uncommercial choice as a single and no wonder it flopped – but boy is this good! 'I Had a Dream' (written by guitarist Billy Green) shifts from '50s style doo-wop, to raunchy blues rock, fuzzed out soundgasms – and finally a spacey echo-laden outro. This track has it all, including the dark chocolate vocals of Doug Parkinson. I'd love to know what they were taking before having this particular dream – and more importantly, could I get some too?

Killer Moment: 01.02, *the first fuzz-drenched soundgasm kicks in.*

Billy Green of In Focus (Newhill)

6. 'Peculiar Hole in the Sky' – The Valentines
Single (July) Clarion: MCK-2441

After the massive international success of 'Friday on my Mind', The Easybeats' songwriting duo – Harry Vanda and George Young – began to see themselves as writers rather than performers. And, like The Beatles and Brian Wilson before them, Vanda and Young were planning to shun the live concert stage in favour of the soundproofed sanctuary of a recording studio. One of the first tracks that V&Y wrote for an outside group was 'She Said', for West Australian band The Valentines (featuring Bon Scott on vocals). A year later, the pair presented The Valentines with the decidedly more psychedelic 'Peculiar Hole in the Sky'.

With reverse-tape cymbals, a magnificent horn arrangement and existentialist lyrics about God looking down with bemusement at the mankind he created on 'The day of the clay', 'Peculiar Hole in the Sky' is a masterful piece of work. Bon Scott's vocals are strong and soulful and the band plays with a tangible electric energy.

Killer Moment: 00.35, *the carnival comes to town.*

The Valentines (Colbert)

7. 'Elevator Driver'/'Theme for a Social Climber' –
The Masters Apprentices A/B-side (February) Astor: A-7087

The unfortunate departure of songwriter Mick Bower from The Masters Apprentices saw the band temporarily without an internal source of original material, so their manager turned towards Brian Cadd (known in those days as Brian Caine) from The Groop. A few days later, a tape arrived at Masters Apprentices HQ containing a song by Cadd and bandmate Max Ross entitled 'Silver People'. Vocalist Jim Keays recalled in his autobiography *His Master's Voice* that he and the band radically rearranged 'Silver People' and renamed it 'Elevator Driver'. To be honest, Keays deserves a medal just for being able to wrap his tongue around such clumsy psychedelic lines as, *'Colours tinge but gold prevails, coloured ships with silver sails . . . Rosellas sail the amber skies, polka-dotted butterflies . . .'*

'Elevator Driver' was an unashamed attempt at jumping on the psychedelic bandwagon, and it was totally successful. Featuring trippy echo-rushes, jerky time changes and several strong

- Teen dances at Baulkham Hills and Mosman in Sydney close after raids by police.
- Lacking financial support from their label Astor, The Masters Apprentices finance their own film clip for new single 'Elevator Driver'.
- Having been inducted into the Army, Normie Rowe plays irregular dates around Australia with a shorn head and new backing band, Nature's Own. During one concert at the Melbourne Town Hall fans break through a police cordon to invade the stage. Following the ensuing fracas Rowe is taken to hospital, but suffers no permanent injuries.

1 Australian troops come under heavy attack in Nui Dat.

2 The first Commonwealth–State government conference on censorship is held in Hobart.

3 Sydney rockers the Barrington Davis Powerpact announce they are changing their name to Mecca before kicking off a promotional tour for Smirnoff vodka.

7 Sydney pop singer Mike Furber leaves the Sunshine label and sacks his manager after he refuses to allow him to end a punishing schedule of touring in order to concentrate on recording.

8 Anti-conscriptionists protest outside the Swan Hill Army Depot.

8 Having completed a three month tour of military bases and been trapped in fighting in the Cholon suburb of Saigon, Melbourne based girl group The Pussycats are finally able to leave Vietnam. Complaining that assurances by promoters to keep them out of combat zones had been broken one member states that the four piece had seen 'people killed and fighting' both before and after the Tet Offensive.

12 PM Gorton rules out any further increase in Australia's troop commitment in Vietnam.

13 Three men posing as agents from the Official Receiver in Bankruptcy rob Billy Thorpe of $5000 worth of property. Arriving in dust coats at Thorpe's home the men present Aztecs bass player David MacTaggart with a list of goods police believe had been compiled from newspaper reports. Thorpe, who had been made bankrupt over a $333.70 debt, loses two guitar amps, 20 suits, two guitars, a $600 tape recorder, a fur coat and various personal items.

13 Melbourne fashion designer Peter Langham is fined $300 in

The Masters Apprentices live (Beard)

hooks, its chart success (#6 Adelaide, #15 Melbourne) kept the band soldiering on during a difficult period, until the arrival of guitarist Doug Ford ushered in a new era by providing Jim Keays with a songwriting partner.

For the flip-side, a Mick Bower composition from the band's self-titled debut of a year ago was chosen, and it's a thoroughly melodic and underrated little gem. Anchored by a snare drum pattern borrowed from The Yardbirds' 'Evil Hearted You', 'Theme for a Social Climber' is classic Bowerpop with colourful guitar trills aplenty, and a tasty little bit of reverse-tape at the end, just to round things off.

Killer Moment ('Elevator Driver'): 00.50, *that* 'Elevator Dri-vah-ah-ah-AH-AH!' *echo rush.*

8. 'King of the Mountain'/'Tea and Sympathy (Don't You Worry)' – The Proclamation **A/B-side (August)** **Clarion: MCK-2432**

Perth group The Proclamation was formed by guitarist Tony Sommers, who had previously played with both Johnny Young and Kompany and The Masters Apprentices. Sommers wrote both sides of this single, and judging by these two fine songs he had a good grasp of quirky pop songwriting.

The A-side 'King of the Mountain', with its dramatic *'I-am-the-king-of-the-mountain / Living-so-high-in-the-air . . .'* chorus, is the pick of the two. 'King of the Mountain' was one of the first songs to be recorded on Clarion label owner Martin Clarke's newly acquired four-track machine. 'Tea and Sympathy (Don't You Worry)' is a quaint and very British sounding tune about a schoolboy who shares a cup of tea and biscuits with the lonely old lady from Number Three.

Killer Moment ('King of the Mountain'): 00.41, *the organ gets snaky.*

9. 'Blue Roundabout' – The Twilights **LP Track (October)** **Columbia: SECO-7870**

Drawn from their ambitious *Once Upon a Twilight* LP, 'Blue Roundabout' leaves no psychedelic pstone unturned. Featuring a feedback intro, vocals fed through a rotating Leslie speaker cabinet, a searing guitar break and bursts of heavily echoed harmonies that come in like sunbeams the song veers between ever changing time signatures (including, of course, the now obligatory 'carnival' bit).

Killer Moment: 00.34, *John Bywaters' single-note staccato bass fill.*

10. 'Sun God' – The Wright of Waye **Single (January)** **Philips: BF-362**

The Wright of Waye evolved from wildly-kitted R&B band The Richard Wright Group, which in turn had mutated from the outrageous Missing Links – the common factor being guitarist John

Jones. 'Sun God' is a powerfully bombastic piece – not unlike the Doors in some ways – with deep chanting vocals adding a certain macho menace to the song. The guitars, meanwhile, sound as if they're emerging from some subterranean gravel pit. The single's other side 'The Dollar Song' is depressingly cheerful by comparison.

11. 'I Can't Help Thinking of You' – The Bucket **Single (December)** **Festival: FK-2683**

Somewhere between leaving The Masters Apprentices and removing himself from pop music altogether, Mick Bower found time to pen one last piece of psychedelic joy. 'I Can't Help Thinking of You', by Adelaide group The Bucket (surely one of the worst band names ever), would not have been out of place on the Pretty Things' *S.F. Sorrow* LP – as it features a similarly dreamy vocal quality and lyrical wah-wah guitar work.

12. 'Brass Bird' – Lloyd's World **Single (July)** **Festival: FK-2433**

A luscious pop track with phasing galore and a mini-freakout guitar break in the middle, the stately 'Brass Bird' was written by the band's guitarist, Colin Stead. Lloyd's World were a teenage Sydney quartet who were apparently connected with Robert Stigwood via their pals in The Bee Gees. However, when they travelled to England to meet up with him, he wouldn't answer the phone (bastard!), and the band split up soon afterwards.

Killer Moment: 01.40, *Ow!*

13. 'Penelope Play'/'You Can't do it Alone' – Wright of Waye **A/B-side (November)** **Natec: VSM-004**

Girls' names from the Victorian-era, such as Penelope and Emily, lent themselves well to psychedelic songs – and these girls often found themselves feyly prancing about in somebody's garden or else tripping through enchanted woods. 'Penelope Play' by The Wright of Waye is no exception to this rule, as the authoritative voice of John Jones urges Penelope to come and play in the garden '. . .*where the golden daffodil says "I beg your pardon"* . . .' Psych-pop by numbers really, but cute just the same.

The B-side 'You Can't do it Alone' is a lot more seductive and groovy. A pair of piercing fuzz guitars slice through the drummer's bubblegum beat like razor blades through a marshmallow, while Jones wolverine voice whispers hornily over the top. 'You Can't do it Alone' is just too cool for school.

Killer Moment ('You Can't do it Alone'): 01.56, *the guitarist goes into auto-raga when he is asked to* 'Make music with the lead guitar'.

14. 'What a Silly Thing to Do' – The Twilights **B-side (May)** **Columbia: DO-8361**

A sneak preview from their yet-to-be-released *Once Upon a Twilight* album, 'What a Silly Thing to Do' was the B-side to The Twilights' breezy single 'Always' (#5 Adelaide; #17 Brisbane). Featuring a bright acoustic guitars and mandolins, heavily reverbed percussion and an organ put through both a Leslie speaker AND a wah-wah pedal, 'What a Silly Thing to Do' is further proof that Terry Britten and The Twilights were in a league of their own.

15. 'Belinda'/'Elizabeth Bridge' – The Puppy **A/B-side (November)** **Natec: NSM-003**

The Puppy were a Sydney quintet about whom very little is known. They made one single on the small Natec label, which contained two original compositions. 'Belinda' is a jaunty 2/4 number with plenty of lush phased bits and a nice jangly guitar underneath. 'Elizabeth Bridge' is moodier and more dynamic, yet with a certain naïvety and earnestness about it. Both are great examples of grass-roots Australian psychedelia, 1968 style.

16. 'Tiny Timothy' – Vyt and The World **Single (April)** **CBS: BA-221501**

A melancholy little song about a polio-stricken boy who *'lives in a world of giants . . . concealed peeping through blinds'*. Written by singer Vyt and guitarist Chris Eggleton, the sparkling vocal harmonies on this track are up there with the Hollies, and the production is top-notch as well. The Eggleton-penned B-side 'Silhouette of a Shapely Miss' isn't bad either.

Killer Moment: 01.23, 'I'm a groovy, groovy boy!' *Heart-melting stuff.*

a Prahran Court for the possession of marijuana.

19 The Questions and Ronnie Burns play the Major Broadcasting Network of Australia's annual trade fair at the University of NSW. Later that night The Twilights take out the organisation's Best Group award, whilst Mick Bower of The Masters Apprentices wins the Best Australian Composition gong for 'Living in a Child's Dream'.

21 Johnny Farnham weeps upon receiving a Gold Disc for 'Sadie' at an EMI reception.

21 Doug Parkinson puts a new spin on the recent Big Show aeroplane controversy telling *Everybody's* that one of the bands' managers was abused by a hostess, whilst another hostess offered to give Pete Townshend a coffee 'right in his face.'

24 The conservative Askin government is re-elected in New South Wales.

25 80 Australian soldiers are wounded and 20 killed in operations following the Tet Offensive.

27 Lionel Rose defeats 'Fighting' Masahiko Harada in Japan to win the World Bantam-weight boxing title. He is subsequently voted ABC sportsman of the year.

28 The Australian Bob Dylan Appreciation Society is founded.

MARCH

- The Factory discotheque opens in Blacktown Sydney, boasting a light show designed by Ubu member Aggy Read.
- Returning from overseas, American comedian and late night TV presenter Don Lane is charged with the possession of cannabis. Successfully claiming that the drugs were planted in his flat, he is eventually cleared on all charges.
- In a sign of the growing power of pop, the Ram Jam Big Band are added to the line up of the 1968 Adelaide Festival of the Arts.
- A number of anti-war activists are arrested during a sit-in at the Commonwealth government offices in Melbourne. Two are subsequently beaten and charged with 'offensive behaviour.'

1 Sydney light show artist Ellis D. Fogg smashes a piano on campus lawns during the University of NSW's orientation day. Later in the month he presents a one act play, *Out of the Frying Pan*, at various venues along with his *Canon Montessori's Suggestion* revue.

2 The Liberal-Country party coalition ties with Labor in the South Australian election, with each party winning 19 seats a piece.

2 Phil Jones and The Unknown Blues cancel shows at Warrimoo and Hornsby after their drummer and guitarist are injured in a car accident.

3 Foco nights begin at the Brisbane Trades Hall, with the Students for a Democratic

17. 'Ride the Wind Away' – Nonesuch | **Single (October)** | **Philips: BF-408**

Nonesuch was a recording pseudonym for child prodigy/producer/composer/orchestra leader Sven Libaek, in that there was 'none such band' – it was all him. Geddit? 'Ride the Wind Away' was a song that he'd originally written and recorded for a TV documentary, and afterwards thought it might be worth releasing it as a single in its own right.

'Ride the Wind Away' is a bizarre blend of cabaret, fuzz punk and hard-core spaced-out psychedelia. The session vocalist sounds uncannily like Doug Parkinson, and apart from the vicious fuzz guitar growling away underneath, you'd almost guess that this was going to be a big TV production number replete with flashy satin shirts, velvet bow ties and shiny shoes. But then the song breaks off into a swirly waltz, Libaek sets the echo chamber to '11', lets loose with some turbo jet aeroplane phasing – and nothing is ever the same again.

Killer Moment: 01.12, *cue in the waltz section and the phasing and echo chamber set to '11'.*

18. 'See See What I See' – Chapter III | **B-side (November)** | **Festival: FK-2566**

Toowoomba band Chapter III were responsible for providing the backing on Peter Wright's masterful 'House of Bamboo', but here they are on their own – and how! 'See See What I See' is a velvet smooth psychedelic soul number with dynamics aplenty and some great noodling interplay between the guitar, bass and organ. This band obviously loved to jam.

19. 'Picture of A Girl'/'Gained for a Fall' – The 1863 Establishment | **A/B-side (November)** | **Spin: EK-2615**

Both sides of this very classy double-sider were penned by guitarist Ray Nancarrow and singer guitarist Jimmy Cerezo (who'd previously played in Tony Worsley's Bluejays, The Pleazers and Grandma's Tonic). 'Picture of a Girl' is a pleasant pop number with some colourful organ playing by Dennis Warner and a couple of interesting musical interludes. 'Gained for a Fall' is more raw and upbeat, with some splashy guitar chords and an absolutely *crackling* rhythm section.

Killer Moment ('Picture of a Girl'): 01.36, *a Spaghetti Western guitar comes out of nowhere!*

20. 'Land of Make Believe' – The Easybeats | **Single (July)** | **Parlophone: A-8406**

A somewhat twee attempt by The Easybeats to get into the spirit of sunshine and flowers, 'Land of Make Believe' still has much going for it with melodic 'dinka-dinka' guitars a la 'Friday on My Mind', Tony Cahill's phenomenal drumming, and Harry Vanda and George Young's superb understanding of chord patterns and dramatic pauses.

21. 'Sebastapol Street' – Procession | **LP track (November)** | **Festival: SFL-33-091**

The highlight of Procession's UK-made second album. From the opening *'See my lane'* chant, to the clattering freakout at the end, 'Sebastapol Street' is the musical equivalent of a locomotive hurtling at full-pelt through the countryside. Trevor Griffin's Hammond organ work is white-hot, Craig Collinge's drums are simply out of control, and guitarist Mick Rodgers plays some searing lead guitar toward the close.

22. 'Sipping at the Vine of Days' – Geoff Oakes and The Reprieve | **B-side (November)** | **Natec: NSM-005**

A real oddity this one. Geoff Oakes was possibly a nightclub singer in Sydney, and this, his one solitary single, is a strange hybrid of jazz, soul, gospel and cabaret. 'Sipping at the Vine of Days' is a simmering soul toon with honking saxophones and some fine girl singers filling out the background. It is not even remotely psychedelic, until the middle-eight section of the song when, instead of a guitar solo, a big creaking door opens and all these loud echoey party people come in to have a bit of giggle and a yak before the door slams and the song continues on as if nothing ever happened. Odd.

Killer Moment: 01.00, *enter the echoey party people.*

23. 'Hurt, Love and Fire' – Chris Malcolm | **Single (October)** | **Ramrod: RS-1010**

Seething psych-fuzz workout by Sydney artist Chris Malcolm with back-up provided by none other than the incomparable Atlantics. The only thing wrong with 'Hurt, Love and Fire' is that it abruptly ends just as it begins to get really interesting.

24. 'Sunshine People' – The Iguana
Single (August) Festival: FK-2473

Melbourne band The Iguana released this gentle little paean to the hippy style of life (*'They were sitting in a circle, everybody holding hands . . .'*) as a follow-up to their highly successful cover version of the 5th Dimension's 'California My Way'. 'Sunshine People' was written by a *true* hippy in Hans Poulsen, and the band's vocal harmonies on this record are simply breathtaking.

25. 'You'd Better Get Going Now'/ 'Three Jolly Little Dwarfs' – The Zoot
A/B-side (August) Columbia: DO-8438

The debut single by Adelaide's Zoot, which made #15 in their hometown. The formulaic bubble gum of 'You'd Better Get Going Now' (written by Jackie Lomax) features a menacing fuzz riff and a few clever production effects here and there. Far better is the B-side – a frantic cover of the Tomorrow album track 'Three Jolly Little Dwarfs' – led by Steve Stone's liquid wah-wah guitar lines and Daryl Cotton's boyish vocals.

Daryl Cotton of The Zoot (Newhill)

26. 'Age of Consent'/'Picadilly Pages' – Ronnie Burns
A/B-side (December) Spin: EK-2550

If Terry Britten hadn't already established himself as a songwriter *par excellence* with The Twilights, then his achingly beautiful 'Age of Consent' for heart throb Ronnie Burns firmly put a big rubber 'Approved' stamp on his ability. Okay it's not psychedelic, not even remotely, but just listen to those gorgeous melting strings! The B-side 'Picadilly Pages', with its twinkling harpsichords and Handel-riffing oboe has enough Beatles/Kinks quirky Englishness about it to comfortably fit into this list. Ronnie Burns even pinches his nose for a Rudy Vallee megaphone effect on the chorus. 'Age of Consent' was a well deserved top ten hit in Melbourne (#10) and Brisbane (#7), although it only made #27 in Sydney.

Ronnie Burns (Beard)

27. 'The Lonely Heart's Club Christmas Party' – The Love Machine
B-side (September) Festival: FK-2526

Like Pastoral Symphony, The Love Machine was a studio project – and like Pastoral Symphony they had a connection with Dr Geoffrey Edelston. However, rather than being an amalgamation of various bands, Love Machine were an actual working unit – namely, Tymepiece (formerly known as The Black Diamonds). 'The Lonely Heart's Club Christmas Party' was the B-side to a cover version of 'The Lion Sleeps Tonight', which actually charted well (#4 Brisbane; #9 Sydney). It's a deliberate piece of silliness – co-written by producer Pat Aulton – with a rather cute waltz section in the middle.

Society (SDS) attempting to bring together the pop and political with folk acts, lectures, poetry and a residency from former Purple Heart Mick Hadley's Coloured Balls. The nights prove popular, pulling crowds of up to 2500.

3 A former kitchen supervisor recently sacked by the Northern Territory government calls for a full inquiry into the administration of government run Aboriginal Settlements. Claiming he was treated like a 'mongrel dog' and sacked for refusing to give white administrators the best cuts of meat Barrie Foster also alleges widespread corruption by staff who have 'forgotten that their job is to look after the aborigines – all they worry about is looking after themselves.'

12 UK film *The War Game* opens at Melbourne's Grosvenor Theatre, after the ABC refuses to air the anti-nuclear drama on the grounds that it is 'too horrible for general release.'

14 The Australian Army confirms that one of its officers has been involved in the torture of Vietnamese prisoners.

15 The final issue of Sydney's *Drift* magazine is published.

16 The Questions find themselves in court fighting over ownership of their name, after drummer

Bill Flemming decides he can no longer work with the rest of the band. After a brief stint playing as The Other Questions Doug Parkinson (vocals) and Billy Green (guitar) adopt In Focus as their new moniker.

17 Thanks to the state's electoral gerrymander, Liberal leader Steele Hall becomes Premier of South Australia, with only 43% of the vote, after the independent speaker puts his weight behind the Liberals.

17 Ubu presents a night of *Hand Made Films* at the Union Theatre, Sydney.

18 Kevin Peek, guitarist for The James Taylor Move and later Sky, is overcome and taken to hospital after fellow band Larry's Rebels set off smoke bombs and orange flares during a show at Melbourne's Opus disco. In a bad week for musicians, The Masters Apprentices' Doug Ford is king hit in Wagga Wagga, whilst members of pop act The Town Criers are bashed at a gig in Anglesea.

19 The hype kicks in for Melbourne psychedelic-soul band Cam-Pact when they are mobbed by teenage fans during a gig at 10th Avenue.

20 New trading laws in Melbourne are introduced, requiring venues to shut by 2 am Sunday morning. Offenders are

28. 'Gotta Stop Lying' – The Wild Cherries **Single (April)** **Festival: FK-2258**

Not as experimental as their earlier singles, 'Gotta Stop Lying' by Melbourne's Wild Cherries is still a quality piece of work. Lobby Loyde's guitar blisters away, Les Gilbert's Hammond organ slooshes all over the place and Danny Robinson's simply astounding voice seals the deal. Listen out for drummer Keith Barber's bizarre double kick drum patterns.

29. 'I Gotta Know What You're Like' – Tymepiece **B-side (August)** **Festival: FK-2258**

'The Bird in the Tree' was the first single by the newly named Tymepiece, and it's a pleasant enough acoustic number with flutes and congas fluttering away, but far more interesting is the B-side 'I Gotta Know What You're Like'. Led by Alan Oloman's scathing wah-wah guitar and Glenn Bland's sweetly soulful vocals, the band settle into a fine groove on this one. Producer Pat Aulton earned himself a writing credit on both sides of this single.

30. 'Mary Go Round' – Steve and Stevie **B-side (November)** **Festival: FK-2636**

Before Tin Tin, Stephen Groves (ex-Kinetics) and Steve Kipner (ex-Steve and The Board) were known as Steve and Stevie (*not* their choice of a name it must be said). Steve and Stevie released one Nat Kipner-produced album on the UK Toast label, and 'Mary Go Round' (released in Australia as the B-side to 'Remains to Be Seen') was the pick of the litter. Dripping with strings 'n' brass and the lighter-than-air harmonies of both Steves, the song goes into a mandatory carousel section in the middle, before fading out with some megaphone carnival noises.

Procession (Beard)

31. 'Listen' – Procession **Single (April)** **Festival: FK-2247**

The first Australian-made pop record to be recorded on eight-track technology. 'Listen' uses the medium to good effect, particularly in its use of whispers and subtly atmospheric backing instruments, even if the vocalist does occasionally sound as if he's trying to win a Steve Marriott sound-alike competition.

32.'Engagement Party'/'Mr John' – Nineteen 87 **A/B-side (June)** **Parlophone: A-8366**

A two-minute nine-second aural invitation to celebrate the engagement of Mr and Mrs J. Burke's daughter to the Postmaster's son, 'Engagement Party', written by former Last Straws member Phillip Quirk, has a nice village green atmosphere to it, and even managed to sneak into the lower reaches of the Melbourne charts (#43, 3 weeks in). The B-side 'Mr John', with its stately horns and inventive time-signature changes, is even better.

33. 'Let's Get Together' – The Dave Miller Set **Single (September)** **Spin: EK-2550**

A cover of the Youngbloods' hit, and a far more upbeat and colourful version than the original, with John Robinson's sitar taking centre-stage. The great thing about Robinson's sitar playing here is that he doesn't limit himself to just single note runs (as many Western rock guitarists often did) – there are several glorious *glissandos* thrown in to lift the mood and the atmosphere. Production was handled by the venerable Pat Aulton.

34. 'Sunshine and I Feel Fine' – Ram Jam Big Band **Single (January)** **Spin: EK-2125**

Written by former Loved Ones keyboardist Ian Clyne, 'Sunshine and I Feel Fine' by the formidable Ram Jam Big Band is a glorious flower pop song with brilliant horn and vocal arrangements. The fact that it peaked at #8 in Melbourne and didn't even chart in Sydney is a telling example of the radio rift that was going on between the two cities.

35. 'Shoeshine Boy' – The Affair **Single (July)** **Festival: FK-2450**

The Affair were a highly polished Sydney discotheque act who would go on to win a trip to England as the best vocal group at the 1969 Hoadley's Battle of the Sounds. The melancholy wah-wah psychedelia of 'Shoeshine Boy' (a cover of a Lemon Pipers album track) is very classy, although lacking a little in the emotion department. Yet another fine Pat Aulton production.

Honorable Mention

Adreneline and Richard – Pip Proud **Album (September)** **Polydor: LPHM-108**

The most unusual album release in Australia during the year of 1968 was undoubtedly *Adreneline and Richard* by 21-year-old Sydney poet Phillip 'Pip' Proud. Originally pressed in a limited quantity a year earlier (with a couple of different tracks) under the name of *De Da De Dum*, *Adreneline and Richard* is a singularly eccentric and indescribable piece of work, consisting of Proud mumbling stream-of-conscious free verse over idiosyncratic guitar playing.

Depending on your point of view, Pip Proud was either a pop primitive with a unique poetic vision or an untalented fraud. Certainly he scores a perfect ten out of ten for sheer individuality.

Choice Australian Albums of 1968

	Artist	Title	Release date	Label: Cat. No
1.	The Twilights	*Once Upon a Twilight*	June	Columbia: SECO-7870
2.	The Easybeats	*Vigil*	October	Parlophone: PMCO-7551
3.	Procession	*Procession*	November	Festival: SFL-33-091
4.	Johnny Young	*Surprises*	March	Clarion: MCL-32752
5.	Procession	*Live At Sebastian's*	July	Festival: FL-32-903

Ian D. Marks

threatened with a $500 fine or up to 6 months in prison. Theatres and drive-ins are permitted to open after 8.30 pm on a Sunday night, but discotheques and dances are not accorded the same privilege.

20 Following the successful screening of Ubu's *Sydney Underground Movies* in Brisbane, Foco hire a light show for their weekly disco.

23 The Brand government is reelected in Western Australia.

24 Police raid eight discotheques in Melbourne after they flaunt new Sunday trading rules.

25 30 anti-war activists travel to Holsworthy prison to protest the imprisonment of draft resister Denis O'Donnell. A number are arrested during a sit-in outside the prison gates.

27 A Larry Rebels' performance is halted during a lunch time gig at Melbourne's Trip, and the band fired for playing too loud.

30 Arthur Penn's groundbreaking *Bonnie and Clyde* opens in Australian cinemas.

30 Revealing his love for the quality press, Victorian Premier Henry Bolte demands a Parliamentary

1968 FASHION

Inquiry into recent revelations by the *Truth* concerning Easter antics at Monash University. Having been chased off campus after snapping a few shots of students pelting a mock Jesus with flour bombs, hacks from the paper are apoplectic in their attacks on the university. Sensing an opportunity to have a go at his harshest critics, Bolte holds a press conference to announce the Inquiry and condemn the student hi-jinks as 'an act of sacrilege.'

APRIL

- Sydney Underground magazine *Lucifer* is launched with an ambitious circulation of 5000. A member of the US-based Underground Press Syndicate, the extensively illustrated journal features articles on alchemy, the psychedelic drug STP, flying saucers, Australian experimental theatre and more.
- Crowning their meteoric rise to success, The Bee Gees perform a special concert at London's Albert Hall, backed by the Royal Air Force Apprentice Band, a 60 piece orchestra and a 40 piece choir.
- A flurry of media condemnation follows the distribution of copies of the anti-war poem 'The Ballad of Ho Cheng' in Victorian high schools.

Robin Rogers wearing conservative work wear (Rogers)

The year in fashion

Bonnie and Clyde

With the release of the film *Bonnie and Clyde*, a 1930s Chicago gangster look became the height of fashion for both women and men. This look permeated the fashion press. In January 1968, *Go Set* described the gangster look as striped suits, huge lapels, dark coloured shirts with light ties. With this look, and in general, men were clean shaven with neither whiskers nor moustaches.

Girls wore ties, too, as well as romantic 1930s inspired blouses with lace trims, and *Go Set* reported that black dresses with white collars and cuffs were considered the latest look at English discos and dances. As the gangster look was favoured by the young, sewing patterns reflected this, as seen in the *Butterick* pattern book of November 1968, which shows a pattern (#4762) for a Misses one piece mini dress with a pleated drop waist (a la 1930s), with a wide belt worn on the hips and wide cuffs in contrasting material and colour.

Gerry O'Reilly met her future husband, Peter Gerner, during this year, and remembers that he was cleanly shaven, but that his hair was the length of a grown out college cut. O'Reilly, who was busy modelling during the year, says her hairstyle was basically the same as during 1966 and 1967. It is interesting to note that women's hairstyles generally did not change substantially during the late 1960s, and the same can be said for make-up. O'Reilly, Kate Harman and Robin Rogers were all still wearing a light coloured and lightly applied foundation, black eyeliner, black mascara (or false eye lashes) and pale pink lipstick. This lack of change is born out in the press of the time, with *Australian Women's Weekly*, *Flair*, *Woman's Own*, *Go Set* and others all showing pictures of women's hair and make-up that could easily have been photographed in the two or so previous years.

Budget buying

In the 16 October issue of the *Australian Women's Weekly*, an article appeared recommending dresses for budget conscious women. These dresses ranged in styles from mini shirt dresses to A-line shift style dresses, but what made them affordable was the material of which they were made – terylene viscose, nylon and crimpelene. Synthetic fabrics were considered the very latest in modern technology, and were comparatively inexpensive with natural fibres such as cotton and wool. They were also practical, as they could be washed in the washing machine, hung up to dry and left unironed.

All manner of dresses, tops, trousers, jackets and coats were being made out of these man-made fibres, which were available Australia-wide in large department stores and small boutiques. One of the most popular items of the day was women's sleepwear made of Bri-Nylon. These women's nightdresses were typically sleeveless, and came with a matching house coat/dressing gown in a typically short dolly girl style with clouds of Bri-Nylon giving the outfit an ethereal quality.

Lindy models a modest floral bikini (Beard)

- Health problems continue to plague The Masters Apprentices, with bassist Gavin Webb leaving the band due to persistent stomach ulcers. Switching rhythm guitarist Peter Tilbrook to bass and bringing in former Bay City Union guitarist and future Little River Band/Johnny Farnham manager Glenn Wheatley to fill his slot, the band signs on with manager Daryl Sambell.
- Having released their second single 'Hope'/'Havin' a Party' on Spin Records, The Dave Miller Set sign a deal with AMCO jeans, giving them free clothes in return for playing promotional sets around Sydney's shopping centres.
- 1000 march across the Sydney Harbour Bridge to protest against visiting US Secretary of State Dean Rusk.

1 American Christian evangelist Billy Graham begins his second tour of Australia.

3 Wollongong's Reverend Black and The Rockin' Vicars release an Easybeats composition 'Down to The Last 500' on

There does not seem to have been a class distinction between wealthier and less wealthy women's sleepwear. All seemed pleased with Bri-Nylon.

Swimsuits were made of both natural and man-made fibres. Women's bathers were rather modest compared to today's standards. One of the popular brands of girl's swimsuits was Sandy Shaw (no relation to the singer), and over the summer of 1968 and 1969 many Australian beaches would have exhibited endless examples of colourful Sandy Shaw bikinis. On 1 January 1969, *Go Set* mentioned that Sandy Shaw bikinis were available from 'all swinging stores' in Australia's major cities.

One-piece bathers were available in 1968 in black and white Op Art patterns or colourful floral patterns, featured in the October *Australian Women's Weekly* as 'Art Nouveau'. Bikinis during this period consisted of modest sized bra tops and pants, sometimes with a boy leg – the pants were never high cut as we find in swimsuit legs today. The bra tops were almost always made with a fitted bra inside the external layer of fashion fabric. Sometimes bikinis were made out of a cotton material, and one-piece suits were usually made of a synthetic stretchy material that allowed for ease of dressing. Sometimes one piece bathers had elasticised sides giving a smocked look, again aiding ease of dressing.

Knitting and Crocheting

As so many women made their own clothes, they and their mothers, aunts and grandmothers were often accomplished knitters. Miss Elisabeth White of Melbourne remembers that throughout the 1960s her mother hand-knitted her jumpers and cardigans. Similarly, Miss

A Thumpin' Tum staffer shows off an extraordinarily short hemline (Newhill)

Sunshine records. The label plays down the band's moniker, billing them as R. Black and The Rockin' V's, after copping flak from the Sydney media. One unhappy pop DJ, 2UW's Phil Hunter, is quoted as saying 'I'm not a square and I dig all the good gimmicks, but not this. Things like this should be left alone.' In spite of, or perhaps thanks to, the controversy, the band pulls in crowds of up to 600 at Sydney's Op Pop disco.

12 Following a six year dispute over whether their members should be subject to an industry award the Victorian Trades Hall Council backed Mannequins and Models Guild of Australia and the conservative, anti-union Australian Institute of Professional Models agree to work together as the state government has announced it will be setting up a wages board within the year. Playing down fears of wage cuts the Minister for Industry and Labour Relations points out that 'The fact that wages have fixed minimum rates of pay for musicians and actors has not precluded the top ranks from negotiating contracts for whatever fees they can command.'

Robin Rogers' aunt hand crocheted a dress for her that is reminiscent of one of the dresses the character, Miss Pamela Dare, wore in the film of the period, *To Sir, With Love*. Rogers' dress was white, sleeveless, V-neck and mini. Like Dare's dress, Rogers' dress had a tied wool drawstring waist.

The 1968, *Woman's Own Supplement*, 'Knitting for the Life You Lead', provided patterns for home knitters to make an A-line, short sleeved, round neck, zip fronted knitted dress in white wool with striped contrasting wool bands. In May 1968, *Go Set* described hand crocheted dresses as the height of fashion, suggesting 'be daring – wear it unlined or be modest and wear it with a slip'. Rogers blushingly remembers wearing her dress without a slip. Indeed, modesty seemed to bare no relation to women's hem lengths during 1968. Hems on both skirts and dresses were extraordinarily short.

Patons was the leading knitting pattern and wool supplier for women during the late 1960s (and beyond). They produced knitting patterns for English designers such as Mary Quant and Jean Muir and Australian designers such as Prue Acton, Norma Tullo and Kenneth Pirrie. In the late 1960s these designer knitting pattern booklets cost 50–60 cents, and the availability of European designer patterns for both knitting and sewing meant that Australian women had immediate access to the latest overseas fashion trends.

Military, Frontier and Maternity Looks

During 1968 various other fashion styles were popular. The military look survived from 1966, with its characteristic stand up collars, epaulettes, brass buttons and saddle stitching. In 1968, Butterick offered a sewing pattern (#4542) described as a 'trim military pant dress' for little misses. In retrospect, it seems rather incongruous that at the very time that the news press was filled with the Vietnam War articles and anti-war protest badges were being worn by students, fashion did not reject a military image.

In September 1968, *Go Set* documented the arrival of the 'frontier look', which consisted of suede and leather fringed jackets. Miss Gerry O'Reilly wore at this time an A-line brown suede panelled mini skirt with a thin matching suede belt on the hips and a suede vest. She also wore a fur coat of rabbit skin with a contrasting collar. When she went skiing that winter she wore a Cossack hat, which reflected the popularity of the film *Dr Zhivago*.

During 1968, Miss Elisabeth White bought a dark blue leather coat that went to just below the knee, while at the same time Mrs Joy Cassidy wore a more conservative camel hair coat. Cassidy was pregnant during 1968, and her maternity wear consisted of dresses that were not too mini and somewhat fitted. She remembers that she went to hospital in July 1968 wearing a white paisley viyella dress trimmed with a tiny tan and green ruffle around the neck and long sleeves. Her most glamorous maternity dress was bought for a wedding she attended. The dress was an A-line layered silk and organza to the knee in a pale cornflower blue with ruffles down the sleeves and high neck. She wore many of her maternity dresses with flesh coloured stockings and a pair of plain court shoes with a small heel.

Brigid Finlayson and Maria Sokratis

Audience members at the Thumpin' Tum model the frontier look (Colbert)

17 Emulating their hero Jimi Hendrix, New Zealand bad boys Compulsion burn their guitars during a show in Melbourne.

18 Members of the Australian Nazi Party are beaten up at Sydney's Domain when they arrive dressed in full SS regalia to deliver a series of racist soap box speeches. Set upon by youths, the would be storm-troopers are rescued by the police, who send six anti-fascists to hospital.

20 Aborigines protest after being refused service in Darwin pubs.

23 Australia's first liver transplant operation is performed at Sydney Hospital.

24 *Everybody's*, the first mainstream magazine in Australia to embrace 60s pop culture, is renamed *EBs* and refloated as a glossy, largely colour newspaper featuring pull out posters.

27 18 anti-conscription protestors are arrested for trespass in the lobby of the Federal Parliament in Canberra.

30 Jim Cairns narrowly loses a challenge to Gough Whitlam for the leadership of the Federal ALP.

MAY

- Australia sends an envoy to Paris to take part in Vietnam peace talks.

1968

The Twilights

- The Queensland government bans lime mining on the Great Barrier Reef.
- Conscientious objector and future *Wonder World* host Simon Townsend is locked up and put on bread and water rations at Ingleburn Army Camp for refusing to follow orders.
- Sydney experimental film maker Garry Shead's documentary *Da De De Dum* about 'pop primitive' Pip Proud is completed. Financed by stockbroker patron Michael Hobb's the film features Proud, accompanied by 'constant companion Alison', singing his wispy tunes in a variety of locations.
- Sydney University's Commem ball is hosted on a floating stage at Luna Park, replete with bands and a psychedelic light show.
- The Virgil Brothers, featuring Rob Lovett (ex Loved Ones), Mal McGee (ex Python Lee Jackson) and Peter Doyle, are formed as Australia's answer to The Walker Brothers.

1 Linda McGill, using a special cage to protect her from sharks, becomes the first person to swim across Port Phillip Bay.

5 Three Australian journalists are killed by the Viet Cong in Saigon, while one other survives the attack.

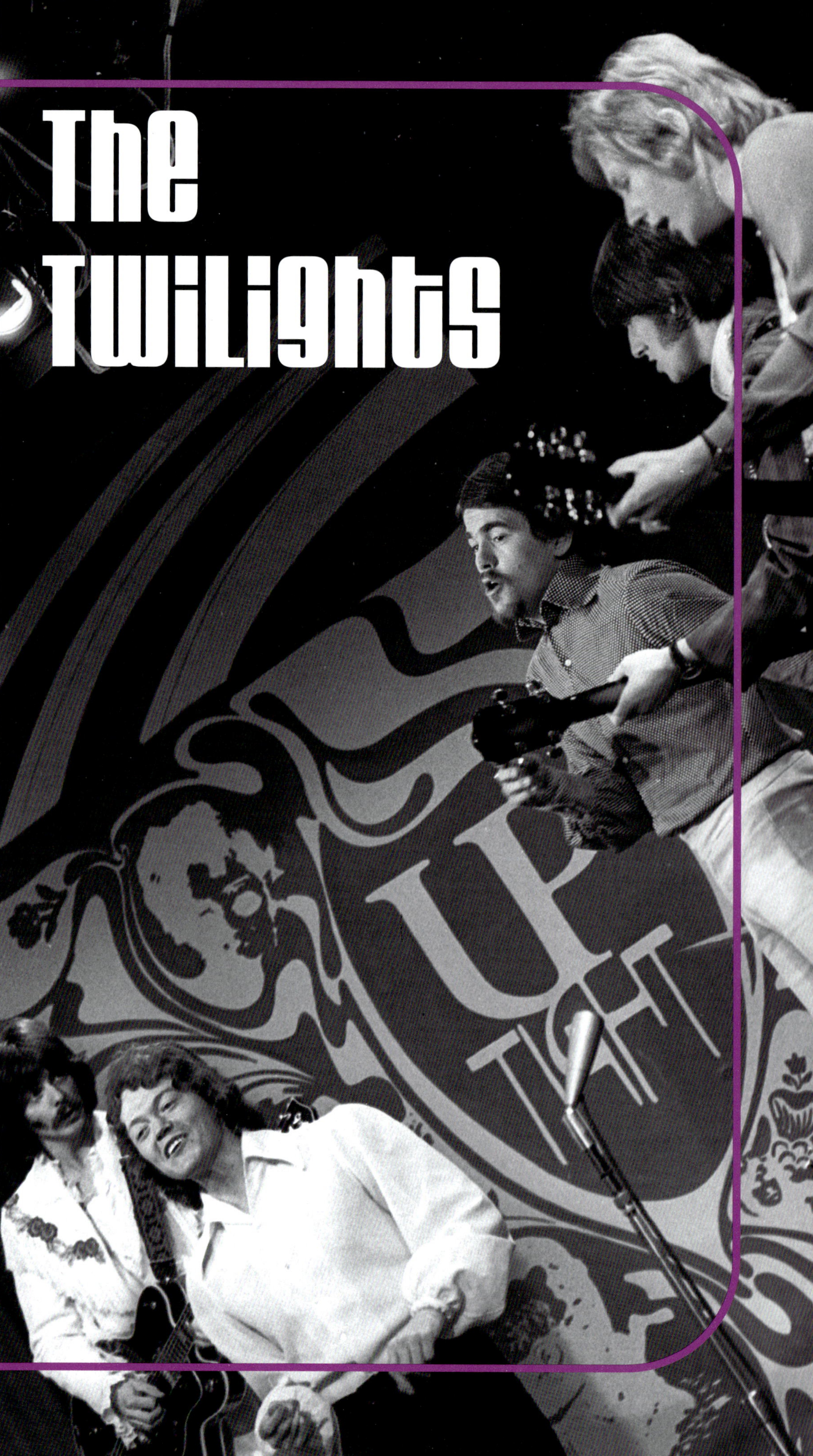

The Twilights live on *Uptight* (Beard)

Hailing from the suburbs of Adelaide, The Twilights attracted early attention up and down the east coast of Australia for their high energy stage show and ability to replicate Beatles hits at will. Featuring the talents of (future Little River Band) vocalist Glenn Shorrock and songwriter/guitarist Terry Britten, the band scored their first big hit with a cover of 'Needle in a Haystack' in 1966. Taking out that year's Hoadley's Battle of the Sounds competition, they travelled to the UK, playing Liverpool's Cavern Club and recording for EMI.

Unable to crack the highly competitive British music scene, they returned to Australia in 1967. Having been exposed to the experimental sounds and styles of London at its psychedelic peak, the band stunned crowds with a series of startlingly original songs and outlandish outfits.

It was 1968, however, that was to be a watershed year for The Twilights, arguably the premier Australian group of the time. The year started optimistically for the band with the chart success of 'Cathy Come Home', and continued with an invitation from the Seven Network to develop a weekly half-hour television sit-com series based loosely along the lines of *The Monkees* or *A Hard Day's Night*. Paul Culnane relates the unlikely series of events that were to follow.

The Twilights and Mary Hardy (Beard)

From the beginning *Go Set* magazine documented the pilot of *Once Upon a Twilight*, as the band's show was to be titled, with photos of the group on location around Melbourne. The shots showed various Twilights lounging about with their proposed co-stars, the late comedienne Mary Hardy (from the *Mavis Bramston Show*) and pop star Ronnie Burns. The images augured well for the program, and its projected debut in late '68 was highly anticipated.

When Screen Sound Australia (aka the National Film and Sound Archive, based in Canberra) screened the pilot in 2003 as part of its brilliant Spinning Around pop exhibition, audiences were uniformly bemused. There was much laughter, but for all the wrong reasons. Only one episode, the pilot, was ever made, and it's little wonder that the General Motors-Holden's motor company withdrew its sponsorship in 1968.

Scripted by the illustrious team of Peter Homeword and John Vandenbeld, the flimsiest of plots sees Mary Hardy, as agent for EIGT (Entertainment In Good Taste), make her 'first professional mistake' by mixing up a couple of bookings. Instead of the concert pianist hired to back young singer Alphonse (aka Ronnie Burns), six smartly-attired Twilights inadvertently show up

6 Left wing folk icon Pete Seeger kicks off his Australian tour with two shows at the Sydney Town Hall.

8 James Taylor Move guitarist Kevin Peek leaves the band to try his luck as a session player and songwriter in the UK.

8 Ubu hosts *Film Experimental* at Australia Square, featuring recent films from Churchill Fellowship recipient Frank Eidlitz.

10 Prince Philip begins a month long visit to Australia.

11 The Mother, Monkey and Child disco opens in Sydney, offering free Chinese food and coffee as part of its $2 entry fee.

12 The Twilights, La De Das and Mecca headline a huge show at Sydney's Trocadero.

13 A North Vietnamese attack on an Australia Fire Support Base in Vietnam ends with 11 Australians killed and 25 wounded.

13 A young woman is arrested in North Melbourne for disrupting a seminar on Vietnam held by the ultra-conservative Democratic Labor Party (DLP).

14 Haile Selassie, Emperor of Ethiopia and Rastafarian spiritual figurehead, arrives in Australia for a five day visit.

15 The Northern Territory member in the House of Representatives is granted full voting rights.

15 La De Das guitarist Kevin Borich is reported to have followed The Twilights' Terry Britten in adding sitar to the band's line up.

15 Australia's first live album is released with Procession's *Live At Sebastian's*.

15 *EBs* looks at the 'Underground Youthquake', profiling such movers and shakers as graphic designer Bob Smith, film maker David Perry, producer Martin Sanderson and artist Sweeny Reid.

16 Bruce Petty's anti-war film *Hearts and Minds* premieres at Sydney's Wintergarden Theatre after being rejected by Australian TV.

17 Off duty soldiers scuffle with anti-war protestors in Canberra, pulling down banners from a Trade Union bus in the process. During the week of action protestors also hold a demonstration outside Federal Parliament and a sit-in at the Prime Minister's Lodge.

21 The Prime Minister of India, Indira Gandhi, begins a six day visit to Australia. Coinciding with her visit, a series of Sound of the Sitar concerts see sitarist Nikhil Banerjee and tabla player Mahapurnish Misra tour the east coast of Australia.

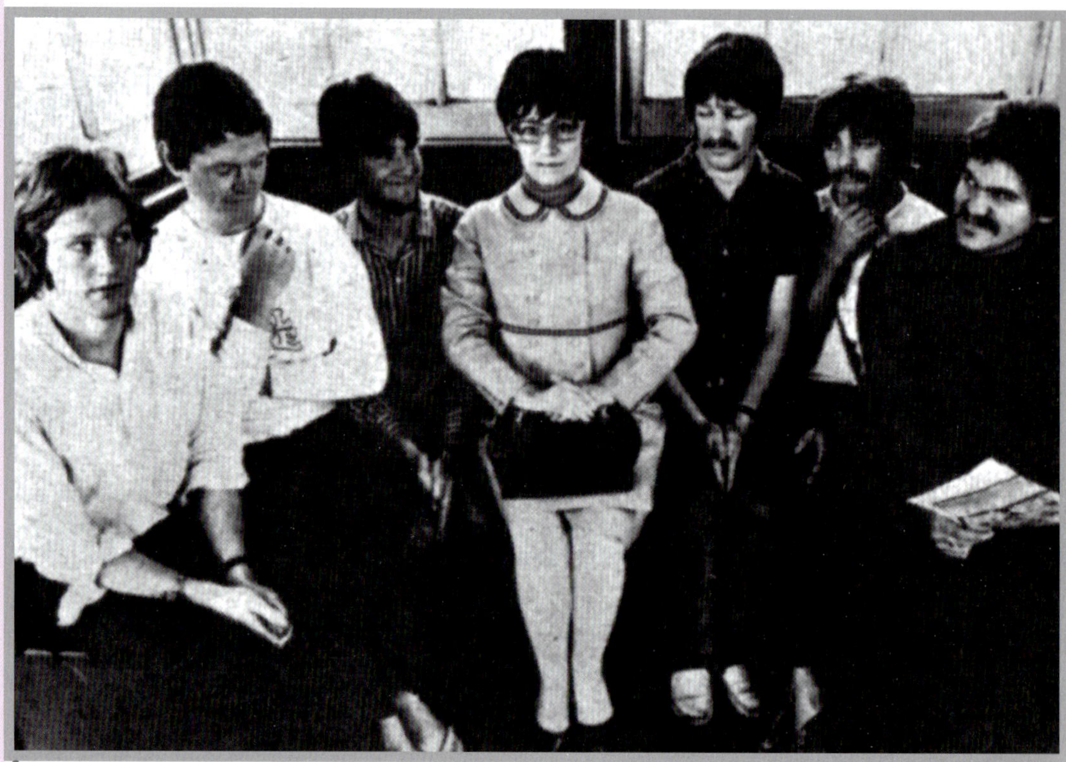

A scene from *Once Upon A Twilight* (Beard)

for the decidedly genteel Gumnut Gully Ladies' Auxiliary Concert. They win over the crowd of elderly matrons, however, and as The Twilights Chamber Sextet they back Ronnie/Alphonse on a string-embellished ditty called 'In the Morning', transforming the nerdy novice into a bona fide pop star.

The pilot starts off promisingly enough, with a rickety title sequence featuring the *Once Upon A Twilight* theme. Things quickly deteriorate, however, and here's where the fun really begins. I can fully imagine viewers, even in the late sixties, grimacing and muttering 'uh-oh' as they witnessed wooden 'acting' contributions from the six musicians (Glenn Shorrock, Terry Britten, Paddy McCartney, Peter Brideoake, John Bywaters and Laurie Pryor). Every 'groovy' filmic cliché in the book is employed repetitively, including fast-cut chop-frame comedy edits, fish-eye lenses, fast motion soft-focus shots and Abba-style changing-focus facial profiles.

Only when the group mimes to its contemporaneous hit 'Cathy Come Home' late in the program are the effects used effectively. With deftly-cut shots of their 12-string Rickenbackers and Edwardian finery, this scene makes a lovely denouement to possibly the tackiest piece of celluloid made in the name of Australian entertainment. A brief snippet of the sequence can be found on the *Long Way to the Top* DVD.

If there is any legitimate humour in the show, it is certainly not abundant. A measure of the wit employed can be seen when Laurie Pryor declares 'Hey hey we're The Twilights'. It is a delight, though, to see Hardy hamming it up in classic style, frugging to the group's 'You Got Soul', and subtly reprising (although most would have missed its significance, I suspect) Judy Garland's iconic pose from *A Star is Born*.

The film is also notable for its period touches and nostalgic scenes. Much of it was shot in the band's manager Gary Spry's ornate pre-eminent Melbourne disco, Victoria and Alberts (aka Berties). There is also the obligatory *Hard Day's Night* style chase scene, filmed outside the Melbourne Town Hall, with girls going ape-shit, as was their wont.

Although the TV show deservedly died a quick death, the project helped to propel work on what was to become The Twilights' zenith, as the soundtrack to the show took on a life of its own. A long gestation period, interspersed with the band's most concentrated regime of live touring yet, resulted in one of the finest albums of the era, *Once Upon a Twilight*.

The record, while showcasing Peter Brideoake's plaintive cello and horn-embellished 'Tomorrow is Today' and Laurie Pryor's raucously daft comedy turn 'The Cocky Song', is essentially Terry Britten's own. As the main songwriter he provided lush settings for Glenn Shorrock (the title track, 'Found To Be Thrown Away' and 'Paternosta Row') and delicate arrangements for Paddy McCartney's sweet lilt ('Bessemae'). Terry also made his own mark with lead vocals and solo instrumentation on cuts like 'Mr Nice' and 'Devendra' – the latter featuring an arrangement of Indian string and percussive sounds not far removed from his hero George Harrison's 'Within You Without You'. Elsewhere brass sections, string quartets, Clapton-esque wah-wah, feedback, Keith Moon-ish drum patterns, backward masking, stereo panning and Leslie-d vocal effects decorate a suite of generally spirited and captivating pop songs.

Terry Britten (Colbert)

Once Upon a Twilight was initially pressed in mono only, as the stereo mix commissioned in America was delayed when a US release failed to eventuate. When it finally arrived, the stereo version of the album was slightly disappointing with its thin, murky mix, but it did highlight the dense layers of overdubs, sound effects and studio trickery the group and producer David MacKay had meticulously laboured over. Completing the package was another typically innovative touch: a gatefold pop-up 3D cover depicting the six lads frolicking with lusty wenches around a medieval castle!

Oddly enough to consider now, the album was regarded by some critics as past its use-by-date at the time of its release. The considerable time-lapse between the album's conception and its eventual release certainly didn't do the band many favours, but 30-odd years later it sounds as fresh and fine and seminal to this writer's ears as, dare I say it?, *Ogden's Nut Gone Flake* – an album The Twilights were known to perform in its entirety in concert (something The Small Faces – godblessem – could never have done with their limited live chops).

Concurrent with the release of the album came the group's eleventh single. 'Always', recorded during the same sessions, is a sumptuous ballad featuring a rich mix of acoustic guitars, flute embellishments and Terry's haunting lead vocal. However, the lacklustre reception to

The Twilights and John McMahon (Colbert)

28 Vice king Joe Borg is killed by a car bomb in Bondi, bringing Sydney's gang wars to a close. In the wake of the killing, organised crime groups, some later linked to the Liberal Party and Premier Askin, reorganise the prostitution and gambling trade, allowing them to focus on New South Wales' growing drug market.

29 Former Four Corners camera man Peter Bray puts together psychedelic act The 1863 Establishment while working with an independent film company in Brisbane.

JUNE

- The New Theatre's production of Jean Claude van Itallie's *America Hurrah* is banned in New South Wales, thanks to a scene in which two giant dolls copulate and write obscenities on a wall. In response to the ban, the troupe rewrites the offending section to parody censorship before holding a special, free public performance of the complete work at the Teacher's Federation Theatre in Sydney. On the night over 3000 turn up to protest censorship, while members of the 500 strong audience later tackle police to prevent them from arresting actors. Whilst the play's run comes to an end in Sydney,

the furor sees NSW authorities back off from banning other controversial works such as *The Boys in The Band* and *Hair*.

- The Masters Apprentices' song writing team of Doug Ford and Jim Keays release their first composition in the form of the single 'Brigette'. Featuring strings arranged by John Farrar, guitarist for Melbourne pop act The Strangers and future songwriter for Olivia Newton-John, the single barely scrapes into the Top 40.

5 Procession sign to Philips-Mercury and prepare to depart for the UK.

14 After a court martial and three civil court cases, Simon Townsend is finally granted exemption from National Service.

17 The Seekers split up in the UK.

18 Sydney's Warringah Expressway opens.

19 The Groop tour Germany.

19 90 anti-war protestors barricade themselves into the seventh floor of the Commonwealth Offices in Sydney before being dragged out by police. Hours later a separate protest takes place outside in Martin Place, where more than 100 people hold a 24 hour vigil in support of Aboriginal land rights.

19 Anti-conscriptionists march on Pentridge Gaol to protest the imprisonment of Bill Currie for draft resistance.

19 The Victorian state government moves to amend the new Liquor Control Act to prevent people from consuming alcohol in milk bars.

Terry Britten and Glenn Shorrock (Colbert)

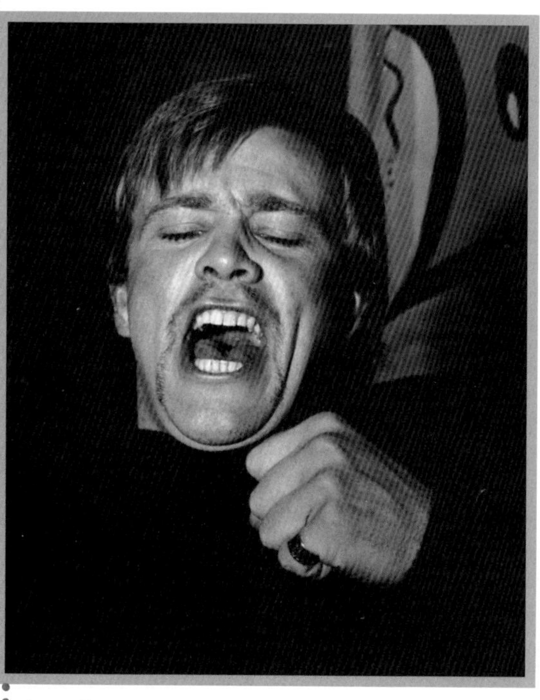

Clem 'Paddy' McCartney (Colbert)

The Twilights' second album and new single begged the question: how much longer could they sustain the momentum?

Nevertheless, 1968 was still the band's year in terms of live performances. Melbourne was 'theirs' as they dominated the city's thriving dance and disco circuit. Popular venues such as Sebastian's, Bertie's, Pinocchio's, Catcher, The Thumpin' Tum and Opus played host to the most polished stage shows yet witnessed by Australian audiences. With their enormous Marshall amplifiers, impeccable presentation and tight professionalism, the boys could do no wrong. Sprinkled among a grab-bag of their own songs and funkified Motown and soul classics, came assertively powerful cover versions of such numbers as Cream's 'Sunshine Of Your Love', Traffic's 'Dear Mr Fantasy', Hendrix's 'Purple Haze' and The Move's 'Night of Fear'.

It should also be noted that a Twilights show at the time would not have been complete without the prominent comedy/slapstick element. Egged on by the sardonic wit of John Bywaters, Shorrock was frequently prone to adopting his alter-ego 'Superdroop', dressing in a most disreputable super-hero jumpsuit (or a ridiculous but scary gorilla outfit on occasions), to taunt the audience with puerile gags, sometimes swinging precariously on a trapeze over the crowd!

Remaining busy at Armstrong's studios recording with long time producer MacKay, the group released the double-A-side, 'Tell Me Goodbye'/'Comin' On Down' in August 1968. The former was a distinctively catchy singalong with a wicked tremolo guitar figure from Terry, while the cosmic, slightly confusing flip seemed to be about the apocalypse or something – only Britten knows for sure. It was a fine single, but criminally ignored by the public. By this time the band was beginning to outgrow the audience that had so hungrily supported them only months before. They had achieved much in their short time together, and according to some observers had simply lost interest, become complacent and were merely going through the motions. Spry had quit as manager mid-year and internal divisions and petty power struggles had begun to surface.

November 1968 saw the release of the group's swansong, this time produced by the up and coming Howard Gable. 'Sand in the Sandwiches' attempted a jaunty, frivolous 'let's all head off for the beach' theme, but fell short of target, coming across as somewhat stilted and forced. The B-side, by contrast, shoe-horned just about every vital strength the band had into an absolutely exhilarating 2 minutes, 48 seconds. Led by Pryor's ferocious tom-tom fills, heavily compressed handclaps, boisterous 'Hey!' call-and-response vocal chants and yet another idiosyncratic Britten

The Twilights (Newhill)

solo, 'Lotus' was a solid affirmation of The Twilights' outstanding musical skills. Yet again though, airplay and sales reception were comparatively pitiful.

Preparations for a return foray to the UK were thwarted late in 1968 when Laurie Pryor declined to participate and resigned from the group. Disappointed and dejected the group decided to cut its losses and disband, announcing a series of final live appearances.

The Twilights gave their last concert performance at Bertie's disco, Melbourne, in January 1969. Emotions were bittersweet. As you would expect, they took the roof off the place and left the audience gobsmacked. But at that moment Australia had lost one of the finest bands to emerge from the fertile '60s beat boom, and would never see its like again.

Following the break up of The Twilights, Glenn Shorrock went into band management, before joining Axiom and then the Little River Band. Terry Britten eventually headed to the UK to play with Quartet and Homer and establish himself as a songwriter for the likes of Tina Turner, Cliff Richard and Michael Jackson. Laurie Pryor played drums with Chain and Healing Force, while Peter Brideoake turned his hand to classical composing and TV soundtrack work, before going on to teach music at Adelaide University. The remaining former Twilights, Paddy McCartney and John Bywaters, seem to have disappeared altogether from the pop scene, presumably returning to 'normal' lives back in Adelaide.

22 Australia's tabloid media respond with typical hysteria to their discovery that local radicals have been reprinting the US draft dodging manual *How Not to Join the Army*. The Third World Bookshop and the home of Sydney activists Mari and Bob Gould are raided four days later, but thanks to an anonymous tip off the raids are turned into an anti-conscription media event.

24 The *National Service Act* is toughened to impose a two year non-military prison term for draft resistance.

24 Managers and members of The Twilights, Wild Cherries, Groove, Masters Apprentices and others march from Albert Park to the John Batman Inn to protest against the unscrupulous practices of promoters in docking band's pay and falsely advertising line-ups. Wild Cherries guitarist Lobby Loyde carries a placard reading 'I spend more on booze than they do on bands.' A boycott placed against the Opus nightclub due to the cancellation of gigs for the Ram Jam Big Band is ended when the venue finally coughs up compensation in the hope of avoiding further bad publicity.

25 British comedian Tony Hancock commits suicide in Sydney.

25 A policeman dies of a heart attack during an anti-war sit-in at the Commonwealth Offices in Martin Place, Sydney.

1968

26 In a sign of things to come, pop promoter Dr Geoffrey Edelston's business folds without warning, leaving a number of Melbourne bands out of pocket and out of work.

29 Victorian police arrest Frances Newhill and force her to spend a four day stint at the Fairlea Women's Prison after she refuses to pay a fine for 'wilfully obstructing traffic' during a recent protest at the Prime Minister's Lodge.

JULY

- Australia signs the Treaty on the Non-Proliferation of Nuclear Weapons.
- Tougher safety design standards for cars are adopted by all states.
- Rod Laver wins the Men's Singles Titles at Wimbledon.
- The Bee Gees kick off their second US tour with a headlining performance at the Hollywood Bowl.
- A major epidemic of Hong Kong flu spreads across Australia.

2 Police bash anti-war protestors outside the Commonwealth Offices in Sydney breaking up an attempt to blockade a meeting of the Federal Cabinet. During the ruckus a police inspector snatches an ABC reporter's microphone and a *Herald* journalist's arm is injured when police smash his tape recorder.

Juno Gemes

Juno Gemes in 1968 (*Everybody's*)

During the 1960s many young Australian artists and musicians travelled to London to take part in the momentous cultural changes occurring there, as well as to try their luck in the 'Old Dart'. Whilst figures such as Germaine Greer, Martin Sharp and Richard Neville have been widely acknowledged for their role in the creation of the British Underground scene, many others have simply passed under the radar. One such person is performance artist and photographer Juno Gemes, who discussed with Iain McIntyre her experiences amongst Europe's avant garde, as well as the creation of the seminal performance space at 10 Cunningham Street, Sydney.

Tell us a bit about your background and how it led up to you working in performance art.

Juno: I'm Hungarian born and come from a theatrical, culturally significant family. My great aunt was the head of the National Theatre in Hungary. My uncle was the owner of the main evening newspaper in Budapest and private secretary to the last free Prime Minister of Hungary. I don't know if that counted for much, but by the time I was 17 I was tremendously interested in theatre and very aware that the only culture we have in Australia is the culture we make. There was absolutely nothing here in terms of theatre in the mid 1960s except very poor productions of American and English plays.

Juno Gemes in 1965 (Gemes)

I spent a year at Sydney University where I got involved in the Drama Society, the Ubu Roi plays and the general intellectual ferment, which went on in the Union Foyer. I discovered it was a waste of time for me academically to be there, so I went to the National Institute for Dramatic Arts (NIDA) to do a director's course. This was an extraordinarily optimistic gesture for a woman in the 1960s, since there were only two women in the world who were running theatre companies at that time – Joan Littlewood and Helena Weil.

I attempted to set fire to the final exam paper, but [the academic] John Clarke believed in me. He knew what kind of a firebrand I was and told me I could just ignore the questions on the page and write about what I thought Australian theatre should be. I passed the exam with a distinction. My production of Edward Albee's *Zoo Story* was transferred to play in a theatre in town. I used to joke that I was afflicted with a disease called optimism. I really believed that art could change the way people think and perceive as what is possible.

Not long after that I got together with Jim Sharman, who was in the year behind me at NIDA. We created a performance entitled *Terror Australis* at the Jane Street Theatre in 1965 or '66. It was one of the first attempts to deal honestly with Australian history, and indeed was a seminal moment in the evolution of Australian theatre. It was a collaborative venture because we were very much into this theatre form where everybody contributes and discusses what the piece is really about. Helen Moorse and Garry Macdonald were among the actors in this piece.

From there I worked on various events. There was a place up in Newport called Serendipity, which was owned by John Bull, where I was already directing fairly free form performance events with poets and dancers. I was uninterested in anything other than that which would reflect our own experience.

Where did you first go when you left Australia for Europe in 1964–65?

Juno: Unlike most people I didn't follow the trajectory straight to England. I went to a university in Perugia to learn Italian, but became bored with that pretty quickly. I decided I would learn Italian by simply living there. Having heard that *The Festival of Two Worlds* was happening at

3 An Ubu performance during the Combined University's Ski Ball at the Roundhouse, Sydney, marks the first use of overhead projectors in an Australian light show.

3 Finally losing its circulation war with *Go Set*, *EBs/Everybody's* magazine folds.

4 Mounted police clash with 1500 demonstrators outside the US consulate in St Kilda Road, Melbourne, after members of the crowd smash windows and attempt to pull down and burn the American flag. When the protestors head down to the Russell St lock-up to bail out the 50 or so people arrested, they are again charged and beaten by mounted police. Meanwhile, in Sydney, protestors occupy the Liberal Party's headquarters in Ash Street.

9 50 protestors in Hobart are dragged out of the offices of the Department of Labour and National Service during a protest against conscription.

12 In dismissing a case against the use of indecent language by an anti-war protestor Victorian Stipendary Magistrate K. Hudspeth rules that the word 'bastard' has become

'acceptable in Australian society'. During the court proceedings police bashfully hand over a sheet of paper carrying the word, for fear of uttering it themselves, whilst the plaintiff, a post-graduate student at La Trobe University, illustrates its commonplace use by quoting lines from Shakespeare, Milton and the Australian author Patrick White.

13 1100 march through Melbourne in support of Aboriginal rights.

The light-tower at London's 14 Hour Technicolor Dream (Unknown)

A flour bombed crowd at the 14 Hour Technicolor Dream (Unknown)

A spotlight at the 14 Hour Technicolor Dream (Unknown)

Crowds at the 14 Hour Technicolor Dream explore the Alexandra Palace (Unknown)

Juno Gemes in Spoleto, Italy (Gemes)

Spoleto, I raced over there and demanded to see the director, who was Juan Carlo Menotti. His secretary rang him in Rome saying 'There is this most enthusiastic young theatre woman who is demanding to see you.' He said 'Okay, send her down to Rome, I have to see her.'

I'll never forget meeting him. Here was this distinguished composer, musician and the director of the best Arts Festival I have ever attended to this day. Menotti explained 'My Festival brings together artists from different mediums who would normally never work together. Of course you must come work with me, this is how the young like you will learn from the best artists in the world today.' He was incredibly encouraging, and in no time I was back at Spoleto working as an assistant to some of the major directors of the day.

One of the directors I worked with was John Cox, who invited me later to come and work on a touring event in Great Britain called *The Great African Dance Gala*, which involved tribal peoples from all over Africa performing across England in venues like the Albert Hall. I went over there and did the tour. I was particularly managing the dancers and musicians from Sierra Leone.

So already at the age of 22 the key influences in my life – the interest in ceremonial performance, the leaning towards traditional knowledge and the idea of bringing different art forms together – all these things were already happening for me.

How did you come in contact with the British psychedelic scene?

Juno: Well by this point (1966) you'd have to have been blind, deaf and dumb not to know that there was something happening in England. I was staying in Chelsea and mooching around when a friend suggested I go up to Indica Bookshop. I went there and met up with Jim Haynes, who was an American entrepreneur behind [seminal UK underground paper] *International Times*. I told him my story and he asked me to come along and see a dress rehearsal of Rick Billington production of Brecht's *Threepenny Opera*. We sat through that and then he looked at me and said 'This is not what you want is it?' and I said, 'No.' So he said, 'I know what you want' and took me down to UFO.

UFO was really the central meeting place of the British underground. It was a vast cavernous club off Tottenham Court Road, which started at 8 pm and finished at dawn the next morning. UFO house bands were Pink Floyd, The Soft Machine and The Crazy World of Arthur Brown.

Jim Haines introduced me to John 'Hoppy' Hopkins and Joe Boyd, who ran the venue, as well as Jim Curtis of the London Filmmakers Cooperative. Jim Haines mentioned my interest in Happenings, and they immediately offered me the job of organising some weekly events there.

Shortly after that I met up with Charles Marovitz, an American director, and he had this idea we should run a serial called *The Plight of The Erogenous at UFO*. This was a play on sexual freedom and I would go out and find strippers and other people to take part in the piece. The performance required nude performance, a sequence of rehearsed movements through dry ice, and projection. David Curtis would project experimental films onto the performers and audience while Mark Boyle, a painter and a light show pioneer, projected the most beautiful light shows onto a screen and the performers as well, using oil paint moving microcosmically on water. The performance had very little text. It was light, movement and film coordinated with Pink Floyd usually playing in the background. UFO was a place where people took acid, and it was our task to provide them with a stimulating and beautiful experience. I worked there for around six months.

I also began to field other ideas with people. Most memorably around this time Hoppy and

Joe Boyd decided to hold the *14 Hour Technicolor Dream* at Alexander Palace. The idea of this was to bring people together for a superb 14 hour trip to see just how many of us there really were in the English Underground. It also became a show of strength to the establishment forces, many of who were very hostile to us. We said 'Let's see how many people there are who are thinking the way we are, how many with the same vision, how big a cultural movement this is?' And there were over 20 thousand people who came to this seminal event.

There was a ground crew of only half a dozen people, and the bands who played included most of the major English Underground bands of the time, including The Soft Machine, Pink Floyd and The Pretty Things. As the event began we wondered how we would all get through so Hoppy pulled out a trip and that's what we did. (laughter) Hoppy asked me to look after the bands – be stage manager for the running order for one of the three stages. Everything was organised, but when I went downstairs all these band managers starting lobbying me about this band not being able to play after that one and all of that crap. (laughter) I was already off on my trip and I just started rolling around with laughter thinking 'These stupid pricks, what are they on about? Who gives us a damn? All this ego strutting, game playing and posturing!' It just seemed absurd to me.

I told them this and said 'I'm not going to spend the next 14 hours listening to this. Here's the running order, you guys can sort it out yourselves!' They were astonished, no one had called them on this before. Then I went back over to the performance part of the event and had a very nice time. There weren't many women around in the scene at that time, but those of us who were there were fearless.

How did your collaboration with Yoko Ono come about?

Juno: While I was working at UFO I got a call from Tim Rudnick, who was making a film with Yoko. He said 'Juno why don't you come over here to Mayfair? We want to get your ass on film.' So I headed over to this grand, but mostly empty pad in Belgravia to be part of *Bottoms*. I was ushered into this room with the Duchess of Argyle, one of The Who and all of these people from the underground. Eventually my name was called and you entered another room, where there was this beautiful wooden circular disc on the ground with a piece on wood attached to the marble fireplace for you to hold and a circle beneath your feet. After dropping your daks behind a Japanese screen, you stepped onto this wooden structure. By the time you went on everyone had had a few joints and Tim fixed the cine camera frame tightly onto your bottom as you walked. Yoko stood there all dressed in black talking softly in a very Zen way.

Afterwards, as she and I struck up a conversation, she told me about how the film would show how all humanity was in fact one family. All differences are irrelevant when you focus on a person's bottom. She loved the tone of my voice and asked me to call up people and get them to come and be in the film. I agreed to because I liked her. She had immense strength and originality and spoke like Haiku poems. It might have been the dope (laughter), but her voice was very particular and precise to me.

Not long after, she called me up and invited me to move in to her place in Regent Park, and said I could have the gallery to sleep in. I was quite happy in the World's End, but she snookered me over there. Then she asked me to do this performance piece with her called *The Scream at The Perfumed Garden*. She said 'You'll have to be a performer in this and I'll bandage you from head to toe.' I said 'Well what do you do?' and she said 'I'll scream for about an hour.' It was all about women's pain.

We did that piece at the Perfumed Garden and it took hours. (laughter) I was wearing a leotard and she bandaged me so that all that was showing were my lips and my eyes. Yoko started with a low moan and it built into this excruciating wail right from her solar plexus. The extraordinary thing is that the audience cheered. The more painful she got the more they cheered. We thought that was pretty disturbing.

Soon after, Joan Littlewood lent us the Stratford East Theatre for a Performance Art Festival. I worked up a piece with Australian actor Lawrence Bourke called *The Truth About Love*. I filled this store dummy's stomach with raw meat. Lawrence had to disembowel her while reciting Shakespearean love sonnets with mock tenderness to the dummy. Once again you had this stoned audience packed to the rafters, which shows you how popular these events were, and as he started to cut her, once again there was all this cheering. 'Yeah cool man, go for it, groovy.' Once again I thought 'What? (laughter) This isn't the effect I wanted to have. I'm talking about

14 500 people, mainly high school students, attend a Vietnam Teach-in at the Greek Atlas Club in Oxford Street, Sydney.

16 The Party Machine's drummer Peter Curtain is put out of action for a few weeks following a car crash on Toorak Road, which destroys the band's van and much of their equipment.

17 Masters Apprentices' front man Jim Keays creates a furore in the Melbourne press by confirming in a *Go Set* interview that, yes, Australia's teenage girls do have sex with pop stars. Speaking with Lily Brett Keays complains of no longer having any private life since he and the rest of the group have 'about 20 girls a day come to our home. On Sundays it averages 50. It's hard to tell their ages because they can make themselves look anything . . . The public are very naïve and narrow minded. They think we're corrupt, dirty and to blame! I just wish a few adults could come on tour with us.

They'd see exactly what their precious good girls get up to. They would be shocked out of their minds!'

30 Australia draws the Fourth cricket Test in Leeds to retain the Ashes.

31 A large demonstration is held outside the Vestey corporation's Sydney offices in support of the continuing strike by Gurindji stockmen.

AUGUST

- Annoyed at the loss of the band to EMI, Astor release one last Masters Apprentices single, the ageing 'But One Day'. The band immediately implore their fans not to buy the release and it subsequently fails to reach the charts.
- Victorian police raid the Contact Theatre in Melbourne seizing a roneo-ed copy of the play *The Beard* and charging the owner of the script, who is later fined $100, with the 'making of an obscene article'.
- A march comprising over 100 Sydney leftists protests against the Soviet invasion of Czechoslovakia. Soon after the Communist Party of Australia makes a major break with its past, criticising many of the dictatorial aspects of the Soviet Union and taking the party in an independent direction.
- David Williamson's first play, *The Indecent Exposure of Anthony East*, runs for three performances at Melbourne University.

2 Joh Bjelke-Petersen is elected leader of the Queensland

the violence men do to women', but no one got that except a few women who came and talked to me afterwards.

Tell us about performing with The Soft Machine.

Juno: After the Stratford East I joined Mark Boyle and The Soft Machine in the South of France. We had been picked up by Jean Jacque Le Belle who ran the Festival de Livre (Festival of Freedom), which was held annually in a circus tent outside of St Tropez.

We devised a performance piece to perform by the swimming pool in the villa where we were staying. I was sequencing events in a collaborative way, but never told people what to do, it was more about co-ordinating and facilitating.

We decided that at sunset the audience could enter, but that the price of admission would be their clothes. We made huge vats of paint for the shy or the tribally minded, and people could paint themselves up however they wanted to. 500 people came in and some got really into it. The Soft Machine were also naked, apart from their instruments, and as they started to play various events were performed in the water. We made this circular hoop that we covered with cloth dipped in kerosene, and as the sun rose the next morning we encouraged people to chant Ohm, set this thing on fire, and the sun rose through the hoop of fire as everyone chanted. It was a very beautiful new ritual.

How did you come in contact with The Living Theatre?

Juno: When I came back to London with the gang Jim Haynes from the *International Times* asked me to cover an Experimental Theatre Festival happening in Belgrade. I had written various reviews for *IT*, but I was such an idealist that I never signed my pieces.

So I went across to Belgrade and encountered the Living Theatre. Well . . . They were something else. (laughter) They were very confrontational and boy did they have a lot of dope. This guy Rufus would open his jacket and he had everything, opium, hashish, you name it, everything.

I remember there was one main piece that they asked me to be in. For the opening of the Festival the Mayor gave a party at the Town Hall for all the participants. The Living Theatre decided to do this event as a performance. We were to dress in black, walk in casually, take up a position as a statue, and not move for two hours. On the night the other people attending were beside themselves, it totally freaked some of them out. It was a clever strategy, because it made usual social intercourse impossible. It was impossible to pretend that we weren't there and it was impossible to interact with us because we wouldn't respond. They tried to laugh at us, they tried to rant and rave at us, they tried all sorts of things, but eventually I think the party packed up pretty fast.

This event was seen to be a form of sabotage, but the Living Theatre just wanted to make people think and feel about their social interactions. They were more confrontational than what I was used to, as I was more into the kind of thing where you structure something and then let it go. When you do that you have an interesting mix between an already determined meaning and an additional layer of meaning that happens through spontaneous interchange. They invited me to come to Turkey, but it was a bit heavy duty for me, you never had any privacy. If you were in it they demanded your attention in every way.

Another group in Belgrade were Gerry Grotowski's Theatre Laboratorium. Once I saw their performance of *Apocalypse* I was gone, I thought that was the most powerful theatre I had ever seen. The Theatre Laboratorium people had a very monastic approach to what they did. They had a lot in common with the Living Theatre in that they were a dedicated group who lived in order to create and perform, but Theatre Laboratorium adopted a different way of performing. They looked and explored inwards towards ceremony and ritual. Their main thing was to apply a systematic disciplinary approach to becoming a vehicle for what needed to be said. Their theatre pieces were collaboratively created, sometimes taking up to eight years to develop. The performances were powerfully truthful, abstract and strangely precise.

I spoke to Grotowski about studying with him and said 'Yes that is possible, I am based in Krakow, and you are welcome, but you realise that the only way you can stay with me is to get a scholarship from the Polish government in Warsaw. You will have to meet with the Minister of Culture every day. He is an absolute moron who knows nothing about culture, but he is a good party member. You will have to overlook all that and be polite and answer his questions every day for a month. If you survive all that without going nuts or losing interest he will give you a scholarship, as I will recommend you. It will be a good test for you. You need to think very carefully about this as we are talking about the next five years of your life.'

So I went to Poland. First of all I spent a month with Grotowski as a guest student at The Theatre Laboratorium, attending daily classes and workshops. Then I went to Warsaw where I embarked on this process of seeing the Minister every day. Grotowski also put me in touch with playwrights, performance artists, musicians and intellectuals. These artists existed in an underground where people met in secrecy, behind closed doors, because anything out of step with the state was fiercely repressed. All these tremendously creative and brilliant people were constantly planning, and in the time that I was there, I didn't see a performance. I just saw the material.

With all of this happening how did you come to return to Australia?

Juno: I got his letter from Martin Sanderson who had gotten together with my father Alex to work out a way to lure me home. In two separate letters they said there were a whole group of artists in Sydney who knew what I had been doing overseas and who really wanted to work with me. It occurred to me that perhaps now I could carry on the kind of work I was doing in Europe in Sydney. When I left there was nobody doing this kind of work so I thought I'd check it out.

I arrived back via India and had this huge log of beautiful grass in my bag. I arrived at Customs, at four am, and the guy at Customs said 'You wouldn't have anything in that bag would you?' 'Naaaa.' I flashed him my killer smile and walked straight on through. (laughter)

I went straight to Underwood Street where my friend Annette Gale had rented a flat for the both of us. Within 24 hours I had a flat full of 30 artists from different mediums saying 'We know about the stuff you have been doing in England, tell us more because we want to do similar stuff here. We have our own ideas and we are ready to do it now.' I thought that it was fabulous that it had all come together so quickly.

Juno Gemes (*Everybody's*)

The people who were there that night became the basis of 10 Cunningham Street. They included Martin Sanderson, a Cambridge Scholar and playwright, Brian Thompson, a theatre designer coming out of architecture, James Rickertson, Andre St Claire, actor Gillian Jones and video wiz Stephen Jones. Johnny Allen, who edited the theatre magazine *Masque*, and filmmaker Mick Glasheen, who had been working for the Buckminster Fuller World Design Science Decade from Darlinghurst, were also there, as well as Peter Kingston and Tom Barber.

Others who became involved included David Humphries, who was a painter/performer and Laurel Fox, who was a situationalist performer, as was Julia Sale. Clemency Brown, who was a feminist painter, carpenter and filmmaker, was part of the gang, as were Adrian Rawlins, our music guru, and Jacky Joy Jacobson, a cab driver from the Bronx who was our in-house genius electrical engineer. Jacky was a large man who lived on hamburgers, and he could make anything you envisioned from single frame lens for time-lapse film cameras to geodesic light structures for kinetic light shows.

From that night it was clear that we needed a place to perform. Soon we found a huge magic empty three-storey warehouse at 10 Cunningham Street in a lane behind Chequers, the society nightclub in Goulburn Street in the city. We rented it for six months with some money that was lent to us. For the next three months we set about preparing it for the public.

On the top floor Mick Glasheen, Johnny Allen, and Jack Jacobson decided to build a geodesic spider out of light bulbs. There were five thousand light bulbs in this geodesic dome light

Country Party, replacing the recently deceased Jack Pizzey as Premier six days later.

2 Students attending an anti-war meeting at Sydney University notice a pair of plains-clothes Special Branch police monitoring them from a Morris Minor. Letting down the tires of the car and covering it with stickers, hundreds of students hold the occupants captive for hours, demanding they hand over their notes and camera. The car is only dumped on Parramatta Road after the Acting Metropolitan Superintendent of Police steps in to sign a statement reading 'State police will not attend student meetings on the campus nor will they take tape recordings or short-hand notes at such meetings'.

7 Adelaide loses two major band venues when Opus closes its doors and Sergeant Pepper's burns down.

7 ABC TV premieres a new show *Now Time*, focusing on the London music and fashion scene.

9 Ubu's *Liquid Light Show* at St Aloysius College and the *Trip Without Glue* night at the Briar's Club in Sydney feature the first Australian use of warm oils and Jumbo strobes in a light show.

14 Adelaide's The Zoot, who feature the talents of future Little River Band songwriter/vocalist Beeb Birtles, move to Melbourne.

15 The new National Library of Australia building is opened in Canberra by PM Gorton.

16 The Commonwealth government admits that, despite comprising only a tiny proportion of the overall population, Aboriginal infants make up 10% of all infant deaths in Australia.

16 Clerics from a variety of Christian denominations march in Melbourne against the Vietnam war.

20 The $14 million National Gallery of Victoria and the first stage of the Victorian Arts Centre are opened in Melbourne.

29 The Queensland tram and bus strike comes to an end after 29 days.

SEPTEMBER

- Sydney's *Ubunews* upgrades from a newsletter to a fully fledged Underground paper, featuring articles and multi-coloured illustrations.
- Federal MP Don Griffiths attacks the Foco nights in Parliament, claiming Brisbane's youth are being 'corrupted by the most evil and repugnant night-spot in Australia.' Club numbers subsequently drop off as attempts by Foco to counter media attacks, through press statements and 'Foco Lives' stickers, fail to prevent parents from banning their children from attending.
- Having scored chart success with their single 'Temptation 'Bout to get Me' (later released on Motown's 'White' label Rare Earth), vocal group The Virgil Brothers replace Malcolm McGee with former Wild Cherries vocalist Danny Robinson.

1 Melbourne police attend the screening of Ubu's

structure and when your foot fell on the ground it would echo your movements in light on the floor. Countless hours and weeks went into creating this amazing structure. It was also linked to the stage where The Id, Tully and Tamam Shud would later play all night.

The second floor was given over to Brian Thompson. Martin Sanderson also had an environmental artist friend called Geoffrey, who built surreal sculptures out of wood. Downstairs Laurel Fox wanted to do a live-in piece. She said 'I want to get rid of the division between art and life. I just want a bedroom suite and I'm going to live publicly in that space for 4 weeks.' My dad, who owned Berryman and Co., lent her a birds eye maple bedroom suite, which we placed in the loading bay as a discreet space. Laurel, dressed head to foot in silver, conducted her life as a performance piece in this setting for a month.

How did The Human Body performance group come together?

Juno: It was put together by myself, Clem Gorman and Johnny Allen as an experimental performance group. A whole lot of other people came in, including Gillian Jones, Andre St Claire, James Rickertson, David Humphries, Stephen Jones, Johnny Allen, Johnny Bell, Adrian Rawlins, Clemency Brown, Dickie Weight, Tom Barber, Michael Glasheen, Jacky Joy Jacobson and Jack Myer.

What we would do is devise performance pieces. Somebody would come forward with an idea, and then we would work on it for several months. One of the first major pieces we performed at the PACT theatre was called *The Human Body Eats a Peach*. Kenny Implosions made us some inflatable plastic structures that went all the way up the stage and underneath the auditorium. At the end of the piece everybody got pushed together as the whole floor space beneath the actors and audience inflated to about two feet high.

We were asking what was the nature and structure of language? How did it evolve and how does it function? We created this sound loop including gurgling baby noises, the notation of time passing . . . 'at the third stroke it will be.' Then you heard accumulative abstract sounds. As this happened you had people building these structures out of six 2x4 wooden beams bolted together until eventually they were imprisoned by the structure they had built. They were absolutely still inside this structure for quite some time. This was quite confronting for the audience, as the performers were still and staring straight ahead. Then somebody had the great idea to turn the structure into a toy, and it became this huge seesaw with about 30 people on it going one way or another.

It was quite a long piece, well over an hour and a half I think. Mick made a film loop that was projected onto the inflatable structure. It would take us at least six weeks to work up a piece like that.

Tell us about what was happening at 10 Cunningham Street at this time.

Juno: The Human Body used to rehearse there. We would have workshops in which people would lead each other through plastics and various exercises. These were mainly for the group, but the group was open to artists in any media. During these sessions we would work up our performance pieces. There was also quite a lot of discussion.

On the top floor Jacky Joy Jacobson, Mick Glasheen, Johnny Allen and Tom Barber designed and welded the structure for the geodesic light show over a period of months. Brian Thomson painted on all the three walls on the ground floor a design using words and abstract patterns, which previewed his later work as a stage designer.

10 Cunningham St had a lot of different names. At one point it was called FART (Factory of Art Research Technology), that was Johnny Allen's name for it. Then Martin Sanderson and Brian Thompson came up with The Powerhouse and designed a poster for it as The Powerhouse – The House of Happenings.

We all wanted a revolutionary experience. We wanted to create a revolutionary underground that would make people think for themselves. We opposed the Vietnam war, the war based economies. We would hold up our own ideals. There was no need for divisive competition. We could make the World Work for Everyone on the Planet.

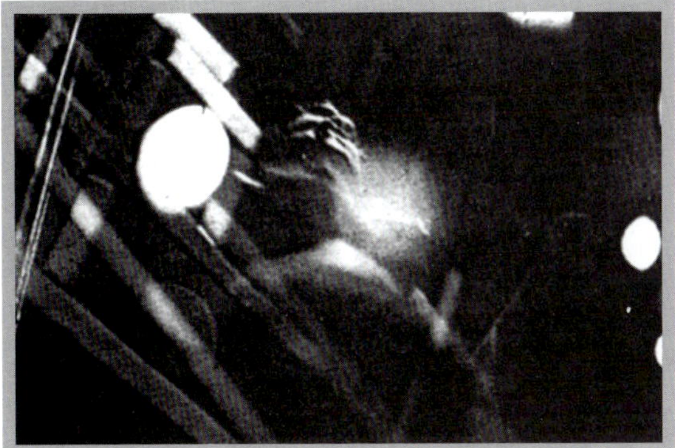

A performance at 10 Cunningham Street (*Bulletin*)

We loathed and rejected racism, the White Australia policy and were against everything that Menzies stood for. We wanted to create a truly Australian culture.

At this time 10 Cunningham St was the heart of the underground in Sydney. I don't think anyone would dispute that. The press were confounded as to whether to review this as theatre or as art? Some arts writers like Daniel Thomas, who was the senior art critic for the *Sydney Morning Herald*, and Lesley Walford, arts writer, wrote about events there, and regarded us as an Australian Avant Garde. Sandra Hall wrote about events at Cunningham Street for the *Bulletin*. We were interviewed on ABC TV for various arts programmes. There was quite a lot of bewildered media coverage.

Out of the six months lease, we only performed for three months, because it took three months to get all three areas ready. After that the Human Body started getting invitations from other states. La Mama invited us down to Melbourne to perform, so a group of us went down and devised a performance for them. Then Tribe in Brisbane invited us to come up, so we went up and devised a performance for them. We were now operating on a national circuit of the Australian underground. Finally we were invited to take part in a Festival of Happenings in New York by a friend of Daniel Thomas.

Can you describe what would happen there over a weekend?

Juno: There would be different events on each of the three levels. We were very bad at taking money at the door, and people often paid with hashish. I would organise people to be on the door and ten minutes later see them doing something else. (laughter)

The top floor was for the bands and the geodesic, kenetic light show and the second level was environmental art and performance. The Human Body could perform on the second or first floor. On the first floor Laurel Fox's live-in piece continued at whatever stage she was at with it. There could be poetry readings or a staged argument exploring an idea . . . Someone would take position A, and someone would take position B, and they would sometimes not even direct the argument at each other.

People would move through the floors. Events would go on for a duration and then they would go upstairs to see what was happening up there. Aggy Reid and Albie Thoms from The Filmmakers Co-op sometimes came and projected film onto Human Body Performances. Roger Foley (aka Ellis D. Fogg) one time added a light show. The Human Body performed another piece called *Ceremonies*, devised by Clem Gorman. We explored and devised our own ceremonies. Usually the visitors would all end up upstairs listening to the music and looking at the light shows late into the night. The Id were our house band.

Dancers at 10 Cunningham Street (*Bulletin*)

Underground '68 program at the Dendy Cinema to prevent the group from screening any banned films.

3 The Zoot launch their 'Think Pink' publicity campaign decking out Berties Disco in pink and giving away pink champagne and pink carnations to journalists. In keeping with the new image, the band adopt matching pink suits, pink guitars, and even dye singer Daryl Cotton's Afghan Hound pink.

5 Rural affairs program *A Big Country* premieres on ABC TV.

9 A massive haul of hashish is impounded in Western Australia from the Danish freighter *Mads Skou*.

9 Anti-war group High School Students Against the War in Vietnam (HSSAWV) publish the first issue of *Student Underground*. The magazine proves to be a hit, with its print run rising from 6000 to 26 000 within a year, but not surprisingly is frowned on by educational authorities. The Director of Education, Sydney Metropolitan Western Directorate, bizarrely attacks the publication as 'a serious threat to students studying for their examinations', whilst the Principal of Fort Boys High emphatically states 'We will restrict publication – this goes without saying. We work for Her Majesty and anything of a controversial nature – anything not instructional – has to receive Education Department approval.' Such official approval is not forthcoming, but irregardless the magazine goes on to be distributed to 100 schools throughout New South Wales, spawning a number of school specific papers including *Super Rat, Yellow Subterranean, Bleah* and *Out of Apathy*.

Meanwhile, down in Melbourne, Students In Dissent keep themselves busy undermining the authorities with their *Tabloid Underground*, whilst the production of individual school papers such as *Ubique Underground, Fallout, Tirade* and the ambitiously named *Pravda* sees students reprimanded and on occasions even expelled for their efforts.

9 Mine workers at Groote Eyland go on strike during a visit by Prime Minister Gorton.

14 Aboriginal activists Pastor Doug Nicholls and Charles Perkins are refused service at the Cairns' Crown Hotel.

16 Unions call on the Federal government to prevent students from working for the security services following the revelation by a former Queensland University student that he was only one of six spies working on campus for Brisbane's Special Branch.

Adrian Rawlins (*Go Set*)

The weekend events were very popular and the place was often packed. We also had a stellar audience of fellow artists. Martin Sharp was there all the time, Peter Weir, Peter Wright, Peter Kingston, Brett Whiteley, Johnny Bell, everybody from everywhere wanted to know what the hell was going on.

How much of a role were drugs playing?

Juno: There were a lot of drugs available in Sydney by this point, and Cunningham Street would reek of hashish on the weekends. We were very lucky, however, in that we knew our dealers and we knew who made the acid we were taking. For some reason we were never busted.

The Human Body performed a lot on acid. People might like to snigger at that, but it takes real courage to explore yourself that far in public. We were after a visionary experience and we were after sharing that visionary experience. The aim of all of this was to inspire and to liberate.

Unfortunately people didn't always pick up on what we trying to do. In a lot of ways that was fine, we weren't pushing a message, the audience was free to interpret things for themselves. Other times I wondered why we were pushing ourselves, taking such risks. Once Martin Sharp and Johnny Bell came up to me and said 'That was amazing, far out, but what was it all about?' I began to wonder that if they weren't getting it, then who was?

Although you got some press for your involvement in the underground at this time very few other women did. Who were some of those that you worked with?

Juno Gemes running a light show in 1969 (*Bulletin*)

Juno: The women artists were few. Clem Brown was a feminist painter, she made a film called *Toby Icarus Aged Two*. She was one of the first women in our group to have a child. What is it for a woman artist to have a child? One of the ways that you deal with it is that your child and your relationship with your child becomes part of your subject matter. That's what Clem did in her excellent film.

Gillian Jones was a fabulously inventive and courageous actor then, as she is now. Laurel Fox was inventive and wry. Jennie Little was a fabulous singer, she had a great voice and was exploring different types of music from all over the world including Jacques Brel, Brecht, the music of resistance. Tina Date was a fantastic folk singer. Julia Sayles was interesting. An enigma, she just turned up and made things, chairs with feathers, objects.

The reason why I got so much attention is because I made things happen. I brought people from many different mediums together, and with Martin Sanderson, created a dynamic space where artists in all media could perform and exhibit with far greater freedom than had existed before. My concern was not only with creating my own work, but with creating the possibility to create for many other innovative artists.

Tell us about Adrian Rawlins.

Juno: I don't know that Adrian Rawlins was ever given enough credit. He was a follower of Meher Baba, a people loving gay guy who loved music and musicians as a medium for the Divine, in the Sufic sense. He was a great catalyst who encouraged the creativity of others. He could recognise new talent. He worked with entrepeneurs who brought out international musicians here and MCed shows to make money, but what he really was interested in was encouraging, discovering and bringing together musicians. He also loved the poet John Shaw Neilson. He wrote and published poetry and music reviews and was a living encyclopaedia of music.

His great love was Bob Dylan. Adrian always had this way of getting backstage, and he managed it when Bob did his gig at the Stadium. He then took Dylan out to the Blue Mountains where they took acid. Dylan always met up with Adrian when he toured for decades after that. Adrian knew most of the Rock 'n Roll players who toured.

How did Cunningham Street come to an end?

Juno: After six months the people who owned Chequers, the City Fathers, the police, and all the powers in the city wanted us closed down. On the weekend there were hundreds of young people milling around 10 Cunningham St and it wasn't what the people who ran Chequers wanted to see. They kept sending around people from the council and the health department to hassle us, and of course we hadn't done all that much to the building in terms of putting in the required number of toilets and all that. We put them off for as long as we could, but we realised that they were making a concerted effort now to close us down. Word had come down from on high and putting in a few extra toilets or whatever was not going to stop them from getting rid of us.

N.A.S.U. PRESENTS

ALEXANDER NEVSKY'S HOMECOMING

A THEATRICAL EVENT AND LIGHTSHOW WITH TULLY
CELLBLOCK THEATRE APRIL 11-12 AT 8 P.M.

PRICE $1.50
N.A.S.U. MEMBERS $1.00

We decided to move on, but The Human Body continued to perform, putting on events such as *Ceremonies*, and going up the coast to do a series of shows. Perhaps because we put such little effort into documenting our work, Cunningham Street has never received full acknowledgement for what it achieved. In many ways it was the catalyst and the model for much of what came later in terms of performance art and multimedia work in a living, collaborative artists space. The Yellow House grew directly out of what we had done at 10 Cunningham Street.

We brought together art forms in an environmental way, within a three storey building. This was news in the Australian art world, but because we were so into the moment, creating work that was immediate, and also non materialist, we didn't create anything which could be bought or sold. We didn't really document what we were doing and you don't leave an obvious legacy when you work that way. However, 10 Cunningham Street made a strong mark on all who took part in it and those who experienced it. It was a seminal event in Sydney's Underground Culture. People still come up to me thirty years later to tell me that being at 10 Cunningham Street changed their lives.

In 1969 Juno returned to the UK where she continued her work in the underground, before coming back to Sydney in 1971 to help found The Yellow House multimedia space and work on the film *Uluru*. In 1972 she began to study photography, the medium she has primarily worked in since. Today Juno continues to exhibit widely around Australia and information on her current work can be found at www.junogemes.com.

20 1000 demonstrators march from Hyde Park in Sydney to the US Consulate, before visiting the Chevron Hotel in Kings Cross to hand out anti-war material to US and Australian troops on R&R.

21 South Sydney beat Manly-Warringah in the Rugby League Final.

28 Carlton defeat Essendon in the VFL grand final before a record MCG crowd of 116 828.

OCTOBER

- Melbourne postman John Zarb becomes the first person to be sentenced under the amended National Service Act spending over a year in Melbourne's Pentridge jail. Interviewed by *Go Set* in 1969, he recalls prison concerts by The Zoot and Masters Apprentices, and regular protests by unions and anti-conscriptionists as being the only bright spots of his stay.
- The Frankston home of *In Melbourne Tonight* star Graham Kennedy is severely damaged by fire.

1 Technicians at the ACT space tracking station go on strike over wages.

1 New South Wales school-teachers go on strike for the first time ever.

2 Students at Melbourne University raise enough money to buy the Gurindji strikers a truck.

3 The anti-war multi-media event *Arts Vietnam* is held at the Paddington Town hall in Sydney, with performances from The Id, Nutwood Rug, Pip Proud, Stray Wild Dogs and others.

1968

5 Experimental films hit the countryside with a program of Ubu films shown in Cootamundra, NSW.

6 The Commonwealth Censor upholds the ban on Ubu member David Perry's *A Sketch on Abigayl's Belly*.

7 The Australian Council for Civil Liberties is founded.

8 The West Australian town of Meckering is levelled by an earthquake whose tremors are felt as far away as Perth.

8 After conducting extensive investigations students at the University of Tasmania confront an ASIO agent, dubbed 'M', forcing him to leave the campus for fear of having his identity publicly revealed.

10 The Minister for the Interior announces that he is about to introduce changes to allow the showing of films in the ACT before 8 pm on a Sunday.

16 1967's Battle of the Sounds winners The Groop return from the UK after experiencing problems with their record label CBS.

16 35-year-old Irish anarchist William Dwyer faces Paddington Court on charges of possessing and selling hundreds of tabs of LSD. An obvious target for the police, Dwyer is later sentenced to 18 months prison before being deported.

Tamam Shud

Tamam Shud's final line-up (Falzon)

By 1968 Sydney had developed a genuine counter-culture with a number of political, drug and surfing subcultures all interacting to bring forth an 'underground' scene that boasted a look and perspective on life and art that was largely all its own. Whilst Melbourne continued to offer the most work for bands, its scene remained largely teen and Top 40 oriented, whilst in Sydney musical chops and the ability to compose original songs became increasingly paramount. Bands elsewhere in Australia may have adopted psychedelic accoutrements and sounds because they were popular overseas, but in Sydney LSD and marijuana became an integral part of the musical experience for both inner city audiences and musicians. A rejection of mainstream values also brought together members of the New Left, artists and musicians in ways that the rest of the country would not experience until the 1970s.

Alongside acts such as The Id, Dr Kandy's Third Eye (featuring psychedelicised former teen star Little Gulliver Smith) and American expatriates Nutwood Rug, Tamam Shud formed part of the vanguard of Sydney's late 1960s acid rock scene. Iain McIntyre traces the roots of the band from their days as Newcastle surf instrumentalists through to their evolution into the acoustic folk act Albatross, while Nick Black and Melthoid provide quotes from the band's mainstay Lindsay Bjerre.

Before the beat explosion of 1964/'65 brought the music of The Beatles and The Rolling Stones to these shores, the aim of just about every young Australian guitarist was to emulate the feats of Hank Marvin and The Shadows. Instrumental music reigned across the country, with nary a rock 'n' roll vocalist left in sight as youths grooved to twangy surf stompers from Scarborough to Sorrento. Little surprise, then, that the members of Tamam Shud, many of whom would remain surfers throughout their career, would make their beginnings in a small instrumental unit named after a Shadows song, operating out of the coastal New South Wales city of Newcastle.

Originally named The Strangers and featuring a line-up comprised of Dannie Davidson (drums), Zac Zytnik (guitar), Ernie Connell (bass) and Lindsay Bjerre (guitar), the band came together in 1964. Having been gazumped to their name by a popular Melbourne pop unit, they switched to The Four Strangers to release a one-off single 'The Rip'/'Pearl Diver' for Astor. For a time vocalist Gary Johns joined the band, but following his departure they opted to remain a four piece with Bjerre out front.

Unlike in Melbourne and the other capital cities, regional Newcastle had few teen dances or unlicensed discotheques, meaning the band's playing schedule largely revolved around a circuit of local pubs and clubs. Despite the fact that most of the band were under the legal drinking age, this placed few obstacles in their way.

Lindsay Bjerre: I started out quite young at 15 with The Strangers and stuck it out with the same guys for about six years. We were in Newcastle at the time, where we surfed with the Merriweather Boardriders Club. We played all the pubs and clubs, which was very lucrative because we could get four or five nights' work a week, which we did for years on top of our day jobs. Pubs in New South Wales closed at 10 pm, so there would be a night's gigging and then you got home early. When we came down to Sydney to play Surf City we did late shifts after Max Merritt or Billy Thorpe. We had to play until midnight, and would be exhausted (laughter). We were under age, but if you were an entertainer you were allowed to be in there. No one ever asked us anything, and we certainly drank (laughter).

Deciding that The Four Strangers sounded 'pretty naff', the band ran a contest on local radio opting for the title of The Sunsets. Whilst the name certainly matched their lifestyle, it was perhaps an odd choice, given that their music during 1965, in keeping with their contemporaries, saw them dump the instrumentals in favour of a gutsy, R&B vocal sound. Over the next few years the band, like Sydneysiders The Atlantics, would find themselves stretched between the old and the new, often paying the price in terms of hipness and commercial credibility.

Tamam Shud's first line-up. L–R: Lindsay Bjerre, Dannie Davidson, Zac Zytnik, Peter Barron (Stacey)

In an article published in *Tharunka* in 1970, Kenneth Maddock notes that 'Dwyer took acid seriously as a means by which the right sort of person could have psychologically strengthening experiences . . . Peddling acid was a way of helping people to enjoy and improve themselves despite the law. He was never interested in merely making a lot of money quickly. He was interested in making money because he wanted to fund anarchist propaganda.'

16 Melbourne high school student Michael Eidelson speaks out in the local media over his recent suspension for distributing the student underground newspaper *SS Sentinel*.

17 A petition by 70 doctors forces the Medical Defence association to hold a meeting to consider offering legal aid to members charged over abortion related offences.

22 The Federal government announces that Aboriginal stockmen in the Northern Territory and Aborigines employed in settlements and on government projects will be paid full wages from 1 December. No mention of providing compensation for years of 'stolen wages' is made, however.

23 Australia's first open heart surgery transplant operation is successfully completed.

25 Swimmer Michael Wenden wins the 200m freestyle, taking the Australian gold medal tally at the Mexico Olympics to five.

26 Radio 3XY sponsors the *Roof Top Happening* at the Big W department store in Melbourne, featuring local acts Johnny Young, The Virgil Brothers and The Browns.

28 The Department of the Post-Master General ends twice daily postal deliveries.

29 Huge bushfires race through the Blue Mountains, coming close to Wollongong, destroying hundreds of properties and killing three firefighters.

31 The RSL proposes that student activists be expelled from university if they are convicted of criminal acts.

NOVEMBER

- The Federal government announces it will provide up to $1000 a year tertiary study grants for Indigenous Australians.
- John Romeril's *A Nameless Concern* premieres at La Mama.
- Bob Evans' surf movie *The Way We Like It* is hailed internationally for its mesmerising slow motion camera work and Tamam Shud soundtrack. Others, however, condemn the film maker's collusion with the apartheid regime in filming footage in South Africa.
- Having spent most of the year preparing to record their *Happy Prince* concept album, NZ expatriates The La De Das find their plans scotched when Adelaide label Sweet Peach drops the band from their roster.

3 Ubu host the *First Intergalactic Lightshow Festival* at the

Bjerre: We started doing surf soundtracks in the mid 1960s, and eventually did six over the years. These were great fun and a fantastic opportunity, but in other ways trapped us in the past in many people's eyes, with Molly Meldrum being particularly scathing in *Go Set*. All of this was hard because live and on our singles we were very much a band in the inner city mould, playing the music of The Beatles and The Stones, but thanks to our name and the soundtrack work, we got stuck with the surf tag.

Recording two entire soundtracks in quick succession for Paul Witzig's and Bob Evans' *Life In The Sun* and *Hot Generation*, the band set themselves in good stead for the improvisational work that would come to dominate their sound in future years. By the end of 1966, The Sunsets had also released two R&B flavoured singles for Festival, including the gutsy 'Sad & Lonely', which features some premier falsetto work from Bjerre, and the pulsating 'Hot Generation'. With the singles doing well in Newcastle and their status as the city's top act well and truly cemented, the band decided to try their luck in Sydney, predictably enough settling near the ocean.

Bjerre: We initially started out on the Southern Beaches, and lived around Coogee for six months before moving to the North Shore in the heady days of the late 1960s. In 1966 and 1967 there was still a fair bit of violence around. In Manly it was mainly between the surfers and the clubbies, the straighter guys who were in surf lifesaving clubs. In the mid 1960s sharpies didn't really exist in New South Wales in the way they did in Melbourne, but rockers would come down on the weekends and fight with surfers on the beaches. While we were still in Newcastle the rockers took us under their arms, funnily enough. If anyone tried to hassle us for being surfies they would take them apart (laughter). As the decade progressed all that stuff died out.

1967 was to see major changes for the band, as early in the year, whilst playing a three month residency at Digby Wolfe's club in Surfers Paradise, they were turned onto LSD. Introduced to the psychedelic sounds coming out of America's west coast scene, they rapidly ditched their former set of pop standards in favour of elongated, free jazz influenced, rock workouts. Perturbed by the changes he was witnessing in his former pals, the relatively straight Eric Connell quit the music scene to be replaced by fellow 'head' and Manly resident Peter Barron. Barron was a relative newcomer to the bass, but quickly adopted a free flowing style that set him in good stead, as Bjerre switched to acoustic guitar and the band created their own unique brand of progressive rock.

Bjerre: Tamam Shud were quite synonymous with the drug and alternative lifestyle. I remember that Channel 7 ran a news item where they listed us as one of the bands to keep your children away from, because they could be exposed to drugs. In reality we were a bit aimless, but as the revolution happened, in which the bands were no longer the nice boys next door and became anti-government, we got caught up in it. I put very political and environmental lyrics into everything I wrote. Drugs were just part of the general counter-cultural revolution. You did everything your parents didn't do. Their thing was alcohol and clubs and we were anti all that.

The changes occurring within the band and the music scene around them necessitated a further name change, and this time around they were well in keeping with the times in adopting Tamam Shud. A derivation of the old Persian phrase *Taman Shud*, meaning 'the very end' Bjerre holds that the name was drawn from the *Rubaiyat* of Omar Kahn. It is worth noting, however, that this particular spelling of the phrase was also used by Marvel Comics' Stan Lee to close each issue of *Strange Tales*, featuring the mystical Dr Strange, that he worked on.

Tamam Shud live at the *First Intergalactic Lightshow* concert (Bulletin)

Bjerre: One time I was interviewed on *GTK* in Waverly Cemetery talking about my views. The name Tamam Shud comes from the old

Persian and means the 'ultimate end', so they stuck me in front of a headstone (laughter).

From late 1967 through 1969 the band played continuously appearing everywhere from surf shops to cinemas, even performing a set at the Sydney Opera House for the launch of Craig McGregor's *In The Making*. They also became regulars at various Happenings hosted at venues across Sydney. Playing events at Paddington Town Hall, 10 Cunningham Street and the AMP Pavillion, the band appeared alongside psychedelic light shows, art installations and theatrical works. With all of this abetted by heavy drug use, audiences generally chose to lie back and soak in the ambience rather than dance. Appearing at events such as the First Intergalactic Lightshow, The Great Happening and The Underground Dance, Tamam Shud built a core inner city following, whilst also occasionally playing to crowds of surfers nearer their Northern Beaches home. Although generally well accepted by coastal audiences, they could still run into trouble, such as on one occasion when a benefit for the Coogee Boardriders Club was shut down by a hall manager who found the band to be 'the ultimate in depravity.'

Tamam Shud live at the Greek Theatre (Bulletin)

For the most part, though, the band's continuing connection to surf culture was to prove more of a boon in the late 1960s than it had earlier in the decade. An approach by Paul Witzig to provide the soundtrack for his latest film *Evolution* led to their first album and, for an Australian band, a rare deal with overseas label CBS. Jamming in the studio, alongside members of fellow underground act Tully, to film footage projected on to the studio wall, the band's soundtrack, in keeping with surf movies themselves, had now moved on from the relatively straightforward instrumentals of the past to reflect contemporary, quirky psychedelic rock. Upon the film's release the band recreated their efforts, reproducing the soundtrack live for the film's premiere in mid 1969.

Bjerre: I've always liked a stripped back approach to music making, and that album had a real 'I don't give a shit who likes it, here it is' feel. The soundtrack featured ourselves plus Richard Lockwood and Michael Carlos from Tully on clarinet, keyboards and all that. Paul Witzig had booked us into the studio to provide the music for the surf film *Evolution*, and when that was done we still had a couple of hours paid for, so Paul said 'Go in there and record whatever you like.' We set up and just played what we would normally do at a gig. It has always been a bone of contention, but my understanding was that our payment for doing the soundtrack was that studio time, and subsequently when the film went well, CBS picked up our recordings and put them out.

Bearing little relationship, beyond three songs, to the film itself, and dispensing with Lockwood and Carlos' contributions, Tamam Shud's debut was released in 1968. As rough and ready as its two and half hour recording schedule would suggest, the album represents a prime slice of Australian psychedelia. From the raucous, funky opener 'Music Train' onwards, the band retain a sound that is all their own, avoiding the fate of other contemporary Australian acts in never becoming repetitive or formulaic. Although, in keeping with new ethos of contemporary rock, the band favoured the long playing format over singles, they nevertheless also released the upbeat 'Lady Sunshine' from the album, a track Bjerre would return to in later years.

Bjerre: I always thought 'Lady Sunshine' had the potential to be huge . . . By the late 1970s I was in my late twenties and decided to have a crack at the mainstream. In truth I lost my way a bit, because I've always been left of centre. After I had a hit with (1977's) 'She Taught Me How to Love

THE FIRST INTERGALACTIC FESTIVAL LIGHTSHOW CONCERT FEATURING THE ID AND THE NUTWOOD RUG CELL BLOCK THEATRE NOV 3RD 7.30

Cellblock Theatre, Sydney, featuring music from The Id and Nutwood Rug.

4 A 22 year old student is sentenced to one month's prison for 'having published and distributed an obscene article' after he hands out over 1000 copies of the underground newspaper *Laissez-Faire* at Melbourne University.

5 Rain Lover wins the Melbourne Cup.

6 Joining a number of Melbourne venues that have recently undergone psychedelic makeovers, The Catcher reopens as Cathedral.

11 Cam-Pact tour Queensland, playing Festival Hall and the Brisbane Children's Show.

12 The Zoot are lucky to survive a crash when their van is hit by a car running a red light. Their psychedelically adorned vehicle is written off and band member Roger Hicks hospitalised.

13 US youth exploitation film *Wild in the Streets* opens in Australia.

15 The National Trust of Australia launches its Keep Australia Beautiful anti-litter campaign at Government House, Melbourne.

17 Radio 3XY and Channel 0's *Uptight* hold a Happening at the Melbourne Velodrome, featuring The Twilights, Masters

Apprentices, Johnny Young and The Zoot.

21 ALP leader Gough Whitlam introduces an Adulthood Bill into Federal Parliament calling for the voting age to be reduced to 18, a reform that does not occur for another four years.

24 The London to Sydney car marathon begins.

27 A Party Machine gig at the Melbourne Nurse's Home is cancelled due to adverse publicity arising from the banning of their songbook for obscenity.

DECEMBER

- Tasmania abolishes capital punishment.
- Ubu film maker Albie Thoms writes and directs an episode of *Skippy the Bush Kangaroo.*
- The Dave Miller Set's third single 'Get Together'/'Bread and Butter Day' makes the charts in Fiji after the band plays a series of shows in Suva.
- Hooking up with Adrian Rawlins in Sydney The La De Das unexpectedly find their *Happy Prince* album back on track, as the Melbourne writer helps convince EMI and Essex Publishing to sign on for the project.
- Bee Gees guitarist Vince Melouney announces he is leaving the band.

Tim Gaze (Falzon)

Again', I redid 'Lady Sunshine', but it didn't prove to be much of a follow up (laughter).

Towards the end of 1969 lead guitarist Zac Zytnik moved on to play country rock with Bootleg, before eventually joining one of the many line-ups of Blackfeather. With plenty of touring work on offer, the band began auditioning new guitarists. Initially unable to secure a player who could combine muscularity with finesse, they were soon to receive a call that would unearth a hitherto unknown Australian talent.

Bjerre: Tim Gaze was only 15 when he joined us. We were trying out really seasoned people to replace Zac. I spoke to him on the phone and told the other boys 'I've got a 15 year old kid coming up who's got a speaker cabinet with chicken wire on the front of it, but I've got a vibe that he's really going to be something.' They looked at me as if I'd lost the plot. He arrived and pulled out his seedy looking gear and after the boys asked him what he knew, we started jamming on Cream and Hendrix, and I stopped playing because there was no room for me (laughter). He was so good and we just wound up jamming for hours. By the time he was 16 the trade papers had named him as the best guitarist in the country.

With Gaze allowing the band to scale new heights, Tamam Shud quickly resumed playing live, although following a disastrous double booking which saw them miss out on the Ourimbah Pop Pilgrimage, they now dispensed with the use of a regular agent. Following on the creative success of their debut album, they headed into Sydney's United Sound Studio to record the concept album *The Goolutionites and The Real People*. Ostensibly built around environmental themes, the album also explored the acid experience.

Bjerre: Many of my songs sound very happy or positive, but they were also very sarcastic. One unrecorded song, 'The Air's so Thick I Lost My Way Home', was very venomous. The second album *The Goolutionites and The Real People* was a lot darker than how it sounded, and as well as being environmentally themed was about the LSD experience in its extremes and opposites. The track 'Heaven is Closed' is a good description of that acid state; one minute it's flowers and bells, the next its terrifying. Kevin Platt contributed some lyrics to the album. He was a well known surfing identity, and his parents owned a surf shop and Platt's surfwear was very well known in the Northern Beaches in particular. Kevin also wrote a lot of poetry and told me I could use any of his material as lyrics.

Released by Warner Brothers in October 1970 Tamam Shud's second album featured far higher sound quality than its predecessor, and Gaze's guitar work undoubtedly raised the overall bar so far as the band's playing was concerned. The band could be found at the height of their powers on 'The Goolutionites', in which they move from the plaintive melancholy of 'Part One' to the screaming solos of 'Part Two'.

Despite receiving critical raves, the album and single 'Stand In The Sunlight' (previously recorded for the surf film *The Way We Like It*) failed to trouble the charts and tensions within the band came to a head, with Davidson leaving the band shortly after its release, citing disagreements over royalties, and Gaze quitting over lifestyle issues. By this point the evolution of the 'soul surfer' was well and truly underway, with many board riders embracing spiritual consciousness, environmentalism and psychedelic drug use. In keeping with this, champion surfers such as Nat Young increasingly turned their back on the competitive circuit, choosing to live in rural retreats where the focus was on communing with nature rather than battling to overcome it. Bjerre and Barron were apparently largely in accordance with these trends, whereas the teenage Gaze was more intent on partying. Speaking to *Go Set* in July 1970, Gaze said 'Peter and Lindsay have their own scene. They're into surfing and living outside Sydney. They are crazy about their diet and hate discos and all that side of the pop scene. I'm different. I like smoking fags and eating meat pies and spending my nights at discos listening to other bands.'

Peter Barron and Lindsay Bjerre (Falzon)

With the band split down the middle, Tamam Shud continued to play, opting for a jazz influenced sound and recruiting Kevin Sinnot on drums and Kevin Stephenson on reeds. Gaze and Davidson meanwhile formed Kahvas Jute, alongside guitarist Dennis Wilson (ex Mecca) and journeyman bass player Bob Daisley (who would go on to play with Rainbow, Ozzy Osbourne and Gary Moore). Releasing their debut album *Wide Open* on Infinity in January 1971, the band betrayed a heavy blues rock influence, not least on Cream influenced songs such as 'Odyssey' and 'She's So Hard To Shake'. Despite boasting impressive musicianship, particularly in the interplay of Wilson and Gaze's guitars, the LP, as with many progressive releases of the time, tended to focus heavily on soloing to the detriment of many songs' overall feel and balance. Nevertheless, the band's album and live show proved popular both in Australia and overseas, and *Wide Open* has remained in print to this day.

Within months, Gaze had apparently put his lifestyle differences aside, returning to Tamam Shud as the rest of Kahvas Jute prepared to move to London. In further line-up changes, Sinot exited and Stephenson was replaced by Richard Lockwood, while 18-year-old drummer Nigel Macara came in from Gaze's old high school band, Stonehenge. Touring the country throughout 1971, the band's lineup continued to expand, eventually settling as a six piece with Larry Dureya on percussion. On occassions jazz pianist Bobby Gebert would also be drafted in to create a very full sound and stage.

Bjerre: Tim came back when Kahvas Jute didn't work out, and then one day when we were all living in a place in Newport, Richard Lockwood from Tully came in as a horn player. We didn't say no to anybody. Larry, the conga player just turned up one day as well and that was it.

Surf soundtrack work came the band's way once more in late 1971, with them contributing extended, largely improvisational pieces to Alby Fanzon's epochal soul surfer film *Morning of the Earth*. Recording at Melbourne's Channel 9 studios, Tamam Shud were originally slated to provide all the music for the film, but politics were to see producer G. Wayne Thomas take the reins, with only three of the band's tracks eventually released on the *Morning of the Earth* album. Adding insult to injury, Gaze's vocals (Bjerre had chronic throat trouble on the day) on 'First Things First' were later wiped and replaced with Broderick Smith's, a fact the band only discovered at the premiere of the film!

Bjerre: When we reformed for the Long Way To The Top tour in 2002, we decided to do some of our stuff from *Morning of the Earth*, since our work on that was probably what we were best known for. However, we decided to introduce our segment with the chorus, and some of Thomas's title track so people would know where this music had come from. In the end we only had five minutes on stage each night anyway which was bit weird for a band like us (laughter).

- Anti-war activists are arrested in Melbourne for distributing *Don't Register* pamphlets. Two are charged under the Crimes Act with 'incitement' and the rest under a Melbourne City Council By-Law that prohibits the handing out of printed matter.
- In a final reshuffle, The Masters Apprentices' bassist Peter Tilbrook quits the band to form Paradise in Adelaide. Glenn Wheatley shifts to bass and the band's classic line up is completed.
- Long term Trotskyists Nick Origlass and Issy Wyner are elected to the Balmain Council on the non-ALP Balmain Leichardt Labor Party ticket. Origlass proves a popular councillor, going on to be independent Mayor from 1971 to 1973, and remaining a thorn in the side of developers for decades to come.

1 Melbourne's 10th Avenue discotheque is taken over by promoter Eddie Floyd, who reopens it as Campus to cater for 'guys with long hair.'

4 Melbourne's Marquis discotheque is set alight by unknown arsonists two nights running.

5 Texas oil troubleshooter Paul 'Red' Adair arrives at Lakes

Entrance to deal with a huge gas fire on Esso-BHP's $10 million Marlin Bass Strait gas and oil platform.

8 A battle between conservationists and the RSL over the fate of 80-year-old elm trees near the Shrine of Remembrance in Melbourne comes to an end when the City of Melbourne removes eight of them.

13 The Id and Tamam Shud play Ubu's *Underground Dance* at the Paddington Town Hall, Sydney.

14 A proposal to construct the Wrest Point casino is passed by referendum in Tasmania.

19 Breathalysers are first used in New South Wales to combat drink driving.

26 The first of many summer Beach Stomps sponsored by 3XY kicks off at Lorne Beach with sets from Cam-Pact and the Virgil Brothers.

31 Following a number of brawls on the beachfront the previous summer police beef up their numbers setting up road blocks along the Mornington Peninsula to turn away carloads of youths during New Years Eve celebrations.

Iain McIntyre

Larry Dureya and Tim Gaze in the studio (Falzon)

With the *Morning of the Earth* album soundtrack going gold, Tamam Shud decided to release the *Bali Waters* EP in mid 1972, featuring one track from the film and two songs, 'Got a Feeling'/'My Father Told Me', which already been released as a single earlier in the year. Although Thomas' production had created their slickest recordings yet the single had not sold well although the EP fared somewhat better reaching the charts in New South Wales.

The band continued to tour heavily throughout this period and their ability to mix easy going, pastoral pieces with quirky hard rock is borne out on the *Live In Concert: July 2, 1972* CD. Released by Canetoad Records in 2003 the album features 15 songs, almost all of them otherwise unreleased Bjerre originals. Consisting of a cassette recording made by audience member and surf rock writer Stephen McParland the sound is relatively rough, but surprisingly even, recalling the lo-fi feel of the band's first album. Playing before a sedate, but clearly appreciative crowd at the Mona Vale Memorial Hall the highlights of the sextet's set include the Gaze original 'Bow Wow', the gentle 'I Turned Around to Find My Father Gone' and the hard hitting, guitar driven 'Morning Song'.

Despite possessing more than a few albums worth of new material the *Bali Waters* EP was to be Tamam Shud's final release for over 20 years as internal tensions and the departure of Dureya, to the imaginatively named Duck, saw them play a final swag of shows in August 1972. Bjerre and Barron decided to buck the prevailing trend towards pub rock and formed the lilting, acoustic Albatross whilst Lockwood returned to Tully. Gaze and Macara remained together, playing with various groups, before eventually joining up with Spectrum's Mike Rudd and Bill Putt to form Ariel in 1974.

Bjerre: Eventually I got tired of the whole thing. Up to that point sound systems and running a band wasn't such a big production with roadies and trucks and everything. This was before the hire thing took off, and I could see that there was more and more pressure on us to keep upgrading to bigger gear, and as an underground band we didn't have the big bucks coming in. I wanted to simplify things and kick back so just Peter and I formed Albatross as an acoustic band to avoid the big multi-stack amps and things.

After Albatross and the mainstream success of 'She Taught Me How to Love Again' Lindsay Bjerre turned to punk in the late 1970s and 1980s, playing with bands such as Shu-Shu and A Portable Beach. In 1995 Tamam Shud reformed briefly to release the single 'Stay' and album *Permanent Culture* on Polydor, before reforming once again in 2002 for *The Long Way To The Top* tour.

Part Four 1969

Max Merritt (Colbert)

1969 MUSIC

WORLD

- The US begins a phased withdrawal of troops from Vietnam, while simultaneously increasing the number of bombing missions over North Vietnam and Cambodia.
- US astronaut Neil Armstrong becomes the first person to walk on the moon.
- British soldiers are sent in to occupy Belfast following sectarian rioting.
- Massive famine breaks out in Biafra.
- Heralding the rise of the Gay Liberation movement, days of rioting kick off in New York following a police raid on the Stonewall Inn.
- French film directors establish the Cannes Film Festival.
- The Woodstock music festival takes place, drawing 100 000s to Yasgur's farm for 3 days of 'peace, love and music.'
- Three months after Woodstock a Rolling Stones concert at the Altamont Speedway sees Hells Angels terrify and beat the assembled crowd, killing one audience member in the process.
- Richard Milhous Nixon is inaugurated as the 38th President of the United States.
- Yasser Arafat becomes leader of the Palestinian Liberation Organisation (PLO).

Bon Scott (Newhill) • • •

The year in Australian rock music

1969 was the year of 'The Real Thing' – the zenith of Australian psychedelia – and 'Mr Guy Fawkes' by The Dave Miller Set, which wasn't that far behind. From this moment on, psychedelic music in Australia (i.e. experimental music that was still a bit of fun) tapered off, to be replaced by something that would later become known as 'Progressive Rock' (i.e. experimental music that took itself very seriously indeed).

The ongoing 'Soul vs Bubblegum' music war made news in *Go Set* during '69, as both styles of music hit their respective peaks. On the soul side you had Doug Parkinson In Focus, Max Merritt and The Meteors, Wendy Saddington and Chain and Jeff St John and Copperwine, up against lighter more commercial acts such as Flying Circus, The Zoot, The Town Criers, The Valentines and The New Dream. But in reality there was no war to speak of. The heavier, more serious outfits were about to have their day in the sun, as albums began to sell in greater quantities than ever before, while the more commercial pop groups would always continue to sell singles to their own predominantly younger audience.

Bon Scott with The Valentines (Newhill)

While some pop records were sounding frothier than ever, big-riffing overseas bands – particularly Led Zeppelin – were encouraging guitarists to crank up louder and louder. The newly revamped Masters Apprentices, with the dynamic Doug Ford on guitar, released three singles in succession that all featured big distorted guitar riffs as their main feature; namely 'Merry Go Round' (February), '5:10 Man' (July) and 'Think About Tomorrow Today' (December). But many guitarists in 1969 decided *not* to plug into a 200 watt Marshall rig, stomp onto a Big Muff distortion pedal and cause plaster to flake from the walls – they were happier to gently pick and strum on an old acoustic, or even twang away on a pedal steel. Brian Cadd and Don Mudie of The Groop, along with former Twilights singer Glenn Shorrock, took their major inspiration from The Band to form the rootsy 'supergroup' Axiom. Their very American, but extremely accomplished 'Arkansas Grass' was a huge hit at the end of 1969, and it would herald in a more grass-roots and timeless approach to music making. Both Cadd and Shorrock would enjoy plenty of American success in the 1970s.

The most talked about Australian LP release for the year was *The Happy Prince* by former New Zealand band The La De Das – a concept album based on the Oscar Wilde children's fable, which took years to come together and nearly a month to record. Despite the hype, *The Happy Prince* was musically quite unexciting and just a little too earnest. It flopped. On the other hand, *Evolution* by Tamam Shud – recorded in a mere two and a half hours and receiving virtually no press – remains *the* pioneering Australian progressive rock album of the late 1960s.

International Album Releases

The Beatles – *Yellow Submarine*
Santana – *Santana*
The Band – *The Band*

- A massive demonstration in New York sees 250 000 people mobilise against the Vietnam War.
- The Manson Family wreak havoc through the Hollywood Hills, murdering Sharon Tate and six others.
- John Lennon returns his MBE award to the Queen in protest against 'Vietnam, Biafra, and *Cold Turkey* slipping down the charts.'

AUSTRALIAN EVENTS

- South Australia becomes the first state to reform its abortion laws, making the procedure, subject to certain qualifications, legal.
- The Commonwealth Government declares the Coral Sea Australian territory.
- The Federal Narcotics Bureau is established.
- New Australian TV productions this year include *Division Four* (GTV-9), *GTK* (ABC), *Delta* (ABC) and *Freddy Bear's Breakfast A-Go-Go* (ATV-0).
- *Romeo and Juliet*, *Up The Junction* and Kubrick's *2001 – A Space Odyssey* open in Australian cinemas.
- Exhibitions held at the National Gallery of Victoria include *Art of the Space Art*, *Three Trends in Contemporary French Art* and *Christo-Woolworks*.
- The Czech Consul-General in Sydney defects to Australia.

- Robert J. Hawke is elected President of the Australian Council of Trade Unions (ACTU).
- An Aboriginal delegation presents the U.N. Secretary-General with a statement on the shocking living conditions of Indigenous Australians.
- Frank Moorhouse publishes his first collection of stories, *Futility And Other Animals*.
- Cam-Pact bassist Chris Lofven begins work on his experimental film *Part One: 806*, which he completes two years later. Building on his film clip work for the likes of The Vibrants the film features footage of hippy life in Carlton as well as music and appearances from the likes of Cam-Pact, Spectrum, Daddy Cool, The Sons of the Vegetal Mother, The Captain Matchbox Whoopee Band and others.
- Adelaide anti-war activist Bob Hall threatens to publicly immolate his dog Pluto, pointing out that while some would decry the burning of a dog in Australia, many continue to ignore the burning of children in Vietnam.
- Caroline Jones becomes the first female reporter to appear on Australian TV when she joins the ABC's *This Day Tonight* team.
- The lesbian rights organisation The Daughters of Bilitis, modelled after the US group of the same name, is set up in Melbourne.
- Local productions make up half of the Top 10 rating TV shows, with *Homicide* returning to top spot and *Division Four*, *Showcase 69*, *Riptide*, *New Faces* and Channel 9

Axiom (Beard)

The Beatles – *Abbey Road*
Van Morrison – *Astral Weeks*
Deep Purple – *Deep Purple*
The Jefferson Airplane – *Volunteers*
John Lennon/Yoko Ono – *Wedding Album*
The Rolling Stones – *Let it Bleed*
King Crimson – *In the Court of the Crimson King*
The Kinks – *Arthur*
Blind Faith – *Blind Faith*
Nick Drake – *Five Leaves Left*
Led Zeppelin – *Led Zeppelin*
Neil Young – *Neil Young*
MC5 – *Kick Out the Jams*
The Temptations – *Cloud Nine*
The Velvet Underground – *The Velvet Underground*
Leonard Cohen – *Songs From a Room*
Bob Dylan – *Nashville Skyline*
The Flying Burrito Brothers – *The Gilded Palace of Sin*
Joni Mitchell – *Clouds*
Joe Cocker – *With a Little Help From My Friends*
Crosby, Stills & Nash – *Crosby, Stills & Nash*
Jeff Beck – *Beck-Ola*
The Doors – *The Soft Parade*
Fairport Convention – *Unhalfbricking*
The Who – *Tommy*

The Charts

Melbourne

1969 was a year of wall-to-wall classics on the Melbourne charts. Elvis Presley came back in a big way with three quality #1 smashes: 'Edge of Reality' (March), 'In the Ghetto' (August) and 'Suspicious Minds' (December). The Beatles equalled this feat with three aces of their own: 'Hey

Jude'/'Revolution', 'Get Back'/'Don't Let Me Down' and 'The Ballad of John and Yoko' (in which the word 'Christ' was edited out for radio). Meanwhile, 'Ob-la-di, ob-la-da' (which only reached #2) stayed in the charts for 20 weeks, becoming the eighth biggest Melbourne chart hit of the year. 'Something'/'Come Together' was another #2 hit for the Fab Four later in the year.

The Rolling Stones were back in town with 'Honky Tonk Woman' (#1 for two weeks during July), while Simon and Garfunkel topped the charts with a four-year-old song, 'Sounds of Silence', thanks to the success of the film *The Graduate*. In September Roy Orbison had his first #1 for five years with 'Penny Arcade'. Tammy Wynette's iconic 'Stand By Your Man' (March) was another Melbourne chart topper, as was Peter Sarstedt's clever 'Where Do You Go To My Lovely' (April) and 'My Sentimental Friend' by Herman's Hermits (August). A new group from San Francisco, namely Creedence Clearwater Revival, had two big #3 hits – 'Proud Mary' and 'Bad Moon Rising' – but the biggest international hit on the Melbourne charts for 1969 was 'Hair' by The Cowsills (#1 for two weeks; 26 weeks in).

In a year full of so many overseas classics, three of the top four biggest hits for the year were by Australian artists. The biggest Melbourne hit for 1969 was 'The Real Thing' by Russell Morris (#1 for three weeks, 26 weeks in). Morris also scored a #2 double-sided hit with 'Part Three: Into Paper Walls'/'The Girl That I Love'. The third biggest Melbourne hit was Johnny Farnham's cover of Harry Nilsson's 'One' (shared on some chart listings with Three Dog Night). The fourth biggest hit of 1969 was 'Picking Up Pebbles' by Melbourne cabaret singer Matt Flinders.

Johnny Farnham (Newhill)

The expatriate Bee Gees cracked their first #1 (for four weeks during February) with the mournful 'I Started a Joke'. Other big Australian-made Melbourne hits during 1969 include 'Funny Man' (#4) and 'The Star' (#3) by *Uptight* host Ross D. Wyllie. 'Timothy' (#6) and 'Boom Bang-a-Bang' (#9) by Anne Hawker and 'Real True Lovin'' (#8) by Anne and Johnny Hawker also did well, as did The Valentines with 'My Old Man's a Groovy Old Man' (#4). The evergreen Kamahl had his one and only Melbourne top ten hit with 'Sounds of Goodbye' (#5). The Masters Apprentices had two hits: 'Linda Linda'/'Merry Go Round' (#16) and '5:10 Man' (#3), and Battle of the Sounds winners Doug Parkinson In Focus enjoyed some major success with 'Dear Prudence' (#2) and 'Without You'/'Hair' (#3).

News also proving hugely popular.

- Melbourne vocal group The Virgil Brothers relocate to London.
- Despite fierce opposition from the Coalition government, women working in the meat industry receive equal pay under the 1969 Commonwealth Meat Industry Award. Although this only affects 10% of women covered by Federal Awards, it helps set the standard for the eventual granting of equal pay in 1974.

JANUARY

- Anti-conscription activists launch a major 'Don't Register' campaign during the January–February registration period.
- Having been in the Army for close to a year, Normie Rowe is sent to Vietnam.
- Rail strikes break out across Australia as drivers and construction workers push for better wages and conditions.
- Having released their third album *Idea* the previous year, The Bee Gees reach the apogee of their 1960s song writing with the double album *Odessa*. Recorded in the US and UK the album is originally envisaged as a concept piece, but with the brothers Gibb unable to agree on its direction, it finishes as a mixture of styles spanning novelty songs, psychedelic ballads and country rock.

1 Abortion activist Beatrice Faust claims that over 100 000 illegal abortions are performed in Australia each year.

4 A party is held at Paddington Town Hall to welcome back *Oz* artist Martin Sharp. The Id perform at the event, alongside a stunning new acid rock band named Tully who feature three former members of popular club act Levi Smith's Clefs.

8 Bushfires burn large areas of Victoria, killing 23 people.

16 The world premiere of *You Can't See Around Corners* breaks box office records in Western Australia. The film is an adaptation of the 1967 TV update of Jon Cleary's novel in which a Newtown conscript goes AWOL from the Army after inadvertently killing a girl in a Kings Cross club.

18 Ubu hold a party for hippy tennis player Ray Moore. In return Moore promises to wear a 'Turn on with Ubu' T-Shirt during his Australian Open matches.

26 Peter Clifton's *In The Summer Time* premieres at the Palais Theatre in St Kilda. Featuring footage of The Beatles, Rolling Stones, Bee Gees, Easybeats and 40 others, the film is accompanied by a live set from The Groop.

FEBRUARY

- *Oz* magazine ceases publication in Australia. Editor Richard Walsh, however, continues to use the name for a muckraking subscriber-only newsletter that variously takes aim at corrupt politicians, the 'loony' left and Sydney gangsters.
- Members of radical theatre group Tribe appear in Barry McKimm's *Saturday* at La Mama

Sydney

As with Melbourne, 'The Real Thing' (#1 for two weeks; 21 weeks in) was the biggest hit for 1969. The follow-up 'Part Three: Into Paper Walls'/'The Girl That I Love' also did particularly well staying at #1 for three weeks in October and becoming the city's fourth biggest chart hit of the year. Some Sydney chart-toppers that didn't achieve the same feat in Melbourne include 'Star Crossed Lovers' by Neil Sedaka (#1 for five weeks over January–February), 'In the Year 2525 (Exordium and Terminus)' by Zager and Evans (August), 'Aquarius'/'Let the Sunshine In (Medley)' by The 5th Dimension (May), 'I'll Never Fall in Love Again' by Bobbie Gentry (November) and 'Something'/'Come Together' (December) by The Beatles. The two longest lasting #1 Sydney hits of '69 were The Beatles' 'Ob-la-di, ob-la-da'/'While My Guitar Gently Weeps' (eight weeks from February to April) and Roy Orbison's 'Penny Arcade' (six weeks at #1).

Locally, the bubblegum band Flying Circus had three top ten hits in Sydney during 1969 with 'Hayride' (#3), 'La La' (#5) and 'Run, Run, Run' (#9). The sublime 'Mr Guy Fawkes' by The Dave Miller Set (#7; 18 weeks in) was the fifth biggest Australian-made Sydney hit of the year, yet didn't even register on the Melbourne charts due to the inter-city radio rift.

Adelaide

'Adam and Eve' by Buzz Cason and Canned Heat's 'Goin' Up the Country' were the first two #1 hits in Adelaide for 1969. Aussie acts didn't fare nearly as well here as they did in Melbourne and Sydney, with the only two Australian records to make it to #1: 'Dear Prudence' by Doug Parkinson In Focus and 'La La' by Flying Circus. 'The Real Thing' and 'Part Three: Into Paper Walls'/'The Girl That I Love' both made #3, while local heroes The Masters Apprentices scored two big hits with '5:10 Man' (#2) and 'Think About Tomorrow Today' (#3).

The Masters Apprentices (Beard)

Brisbane

Brisbane saw an astonishing 36 different records top the charts during 1969, some of which were unique to this city. For instance, The Doors had their only ever Australian #1 hit in Brisbane with 'Touch Me' (March), and Neil Diamond had his first of many with 'Sweet Caroline' (October). Russell Morris enjoyed #1s with both 'The Real Thing' and the 'Part Three: Into Paper Walls'/'The Girl That I Love' double-sider. In fact, the latter was the biggest hit of the year in Brisbane, outdoing 'The Real Thing', which was fifth biggest. Other Aussie-made 1969 #1s in Brisbane included '5:10 Man' by The Masters Apprentices, 'Hayride' by Flying Circus, 'The Star' by Ross D. Wyllie and 'Arkansas Grass' by Axiom.

The 1969 *Go Set* Pop Poll Winners (as voted by the readers of *Go Set*)

Top Male Singers:	1968	1967
Russell Morris: Gold	–	–
Johnny Farnham: Silver	2nd	–
Ronnie Burns: Bronze	3rd	1st

Top Girl Singers:	1968	1967
Allison Durbin: Gold	–	–
Anne Hawker: Silver	–	–
Bev Harrell: Bronze	1st	2nd

Top Groups:	1968	1967
The Zoot: Gold	–	–
The Masters Apprentices: Silver	2nd	5th
The Avengers (Aust): Bronze	–	–

Hoadley's Battle of the Sounds Winners

Doug Parkinson In Focus: Gold
Aesop's Fables: Silver
The Valentines: Bronze

Beeb Birtles of The Zoot (Newhill)

The Sonic Landscape

Stereo was finally becoming a reality on Australian 45s, if only just. In July, RCA issued Kevin McCann's 'I've Got You On My Mind' b/w 'The Skeleton on the Roundabout' in stereo, and this was possibly Australia's first ever single release in that particular format. Pirana's 'Here It Comes Again' is often cited as the first Australian stereo single, but it didn't come out until May 1971 – nearly two years after the Kevin McCann 45.

1969 Top 30 Psychedelic Pselections

Title – Artist	Status (release date)	Label: Cat. No
1. **'The Real Thing' – Russell Morris**	**Single (March)**	**Columbia: DO-8710**

What can I say about 'The Real Thing' other than it's the complete psychedelic package – from its flanged finger-picking intro to its '*Sieg Heil!*' and atomic bomb climax. The secret of this song's longevity and success has much to do with the fact that it is repetitious, but constantly shifting and evolving at exactly the same time – much like the best elements of latter day house and techno music. 'The Real Thing' is completely danceable, make no mistake – it really cooks. And of course there is all that glorious phasing, that complex yet melodic main guitar figure, the horny backing vocals of Maureen Elkner, plus Adolf and the Hitler Youth Choir, and finally, The Bomb – which was surely the only logical way to end the song, after all. Johnny Young's lyrics: *'There's a meaning there, but the meaning there, does it really mean a thing?/ Come and see the real thing . . .'* also perfectly tapped into the questioning of the times.

Killer Moment: 04.15, *that Satanic 'Ha-ha-ha-ha-ha ha-haaah!'.*

Russell Morris (Newhill)

Theatre in Melbourne. Famous for nudity, 'dropping acid in communal houses in Toorak' and confrontational performances, the troupe had first come together the previous year during a series of acting workshops run by Doug Anders.

- Having been sacked from Caesar's discotheque for playing music that was too 'difficult to dance to', Tully find a home at the Adam's Apple disco in Oxford Street, Sydney.
- After a year spent convalescing, Jeff St John unveils his new band Copperwine during a series of low key gigs in Perth. Often confined to a wheelchair, the singer uses the vehicle as a stage prop, pointing out that 'With crutches, your hands are always full. The wheelchair allows me to move around onstage and be self-sufficient.'

2 The Twilights perform their final show before 5000 at the Trocadero in Sydney alongside The Groove, The Dave Miller Set, The La De Das, Heart 'n' Soul, and Clapham Junction.

3 Lionel Rose is declared Boxer of the Year by the US based World Boxing Association.

7 Nine are killed when the *Southern Aurora* ploughs into a freight train at Violet Town following the death of its driver from a heart attack.

7 Defying a ban on further shows at the Paddington Town Hall, Ubu moves its latest dance, retitled *Underground at the Showground*, to the A.M.P. Pavilion in the Sydney Showground. 1500 witness sets

from The Nutwood Rug Band and Tully, and a second successful show with the bands is held a fortnight later.

12 Singer Pip Proud is banned from a NSW public library for refusing to wear shoes.

18 Bee Gee Maurice Gibb marries UK singing star Lulu in London.

19 The Northern Territory legislature tightens up its drug laws, increasing penalties for the possession of marijuana.

26 Jimi Hendrix inspired act Compulsion split up.

26 Brisbane's Foco group announce they are ending their weekly Happenings.

28 Victoria introduces 'P' plates for probationary drivers.

MARCH

- Graham Kennedy wins his fourth Gold Logie at the annual TV Week Logie Awards.
- Amidst fraternal squabbling Bee Gee Robin Gibb announces he is leaving the band to pursue a solo career. He goes on to score a UK hit in the form of 'Saved by the Bell' and records a pair of bizarre albums, including the much sought after *Robin's Reign*.
- Tim Burstall's *Two Thousand Weeks*, featuring several

2. 'Mr Guy Fawkes' – The Dave Miller Set — Single (July) — Spin: EK-3160

If it wasn't for 'The Real Thing' then 'Mr Guy Fawkes' would most likely be seen as the ultimate Australian psychedelic record. The song isn't an Australian composition, but if you've heard the original (by Irish band Eire Apparent, written by guitarist Michael Cox), then you'd appreciate that The Dave Miller Set remake is an improvement at every step of the journey. Singer Dave Miller had taped a copy of the nine-minute Eire Apparent original on his trusty reel-to-reel and, armed with a pair of scissors and a roll of sticky tape, physically trimmed the song down to half its original length. Miller, and DMS bassist Leith Corbett then rearranged the song for the band and presented it to producer Pat Aulton ('Australia's equivalent of George Martin' – Dave Miller).

Those familiar with the legend of Guy Fawkes will know that he and a bunch of others were hatching a plan to blow up the English House of Parliament on 5 November 1605. In real life, the Gunpowder Plot was foiled, but in the song, Mr Guy Fawkes got to do his deed (*'He's got one love and she is dynamite . . .'*), and it is heralded by a huge explosion, followed by a lonely post-apocalyptic reflection featuring a tin can vocal effect. With silky violins and mournful cellos filling out the background, and phasing aplenty to create an other worldly effect, 'Mr Guy Fawkes' is an astounding achievement – especially when you consider that it was recorded on a four-track machine ('The Real Thing' had the luxury of eight tracks).

However, far from being impressed with such artistry, the suits at the Festival recording company said that 'Mr Guy Fawkes' was the worst record they'd ever heard, and that had they'd known that their money was going to be wasted on such rubbish then they wouldn't have let it go ahead. Fortunately, it was too late for them to withdraw the single from release and it became a well-deserved smash.

Killer Moment: 02.56, *the 'cello that underscores Dave Miller's lonely post-apocalyptic tin-can vocals – chilling!*

3. 'Light Shades of Dark (Pts 1 and 2)' – The Atlantics — A/B-side (September — Ramrod: RS-1017

Despite being remembered for all eternity as a surf instrumental group, The Atlantics were actually a fine barometer of '60s musical trends – they had a crack at all sorts of styles and always did so with absolute integrity and individuality. Not only that, but they were also a pioneering 'indie' band, in the sense that they self-financed and produced their own records under their own label – an extremely brave and radical step for Australian bands in those days.

The group's sixth and final single on Ramrod was a ten-minute epic that stretched over both sides of the 45 rpm record. 'Light Shades of Dark' is supreme heavy psychedelia comparable to anything else released at the time, featuring creamy sustained wah-wah guitars, stately organ, menacing fuzz bass, intense vocals, a drum solo that totally WORKS and brilliant music-making all round. 'Light Shades of Dark' (note the LSD reference in the title initials) was written and sung by organist/guitarist Jim Skiathidis, who by now was going under the pseudonym Jim Addams, and is the sound of a band at the absolute top of their game. A sensational swansong for a sensational band.

Killer Moment (Part 2): 01.59, *the Fuzz Bass vs Drums battle begins.*

4. 'Part Three: Into Paper Walls' – Russell Morris — Single (July) — Columbia: DO-8828

Not many people realise that 'The Real Thing' had a sequel, and one that was just as grandiose and innovative as its bigger and more famous counterpart. Firstly, it is important to explain the significance of 'Part Three' in this song's title. 'The Real Thing', at some six and a half minutes, was considered outrageously long for a debut single back in 1969. To appease radio disc jockeys the label listed the song as 'The Real Thing: Parts 1 and 2', and even put a random gap in the middle of the grooves to make it look as if it was two songs, not just one. Nevertheless, every station played the entire song anyway. Once the song became a massive hit, EMI were not scared to put out a 7 minute 'Part Three' follow-up, although Johnny Young's highly commercial ballad 'The Girl That I Love', on the other side, ended up getting the majority of airplay.

'Part Three: Into Paper Walls' begins with a phased atomic bomb and then switches to main piano figure of 'The Real Thing'. Russell Morris then goes on about nothing being real and *'seeing a picture in my mind'* and colours this and colours that. Ian Meldrum's production is slicker and more measured than that on 'The Real Thing' – the horn arrangements, in particular,

are superb. There are lashings of flanging and phasing, some searing guitar work, and a stunning symphonic build up and climax. The best way to experience 'Part Three: Into Paper Walls' is to play it back-to-back with 'The Real Thing' – and you'll have yourself 13 minutes of 100% primo psychedelia.
Killer Moment: 04.57, *that funky guitar followed by Russell Morris singing through a telephone receiver.*

5. 'Lady Sunshine' – Tamam Shud **Single (February)** **CBS: BA-221706**

Tamam Shud are synonymous with the surfing culture of the New South Wales northern beaches. So much so, that in late 1968 surf filmmaker Paul Witzig paid for the recording of the band's first album *Evolution*, in return for being able to use four tracks for his film of the same name. The resultant album was recorded in some two and a half hours, and on less than flash equipment, and is a genuine rough diamond. The band's musical chemistry is almost telepathic at times, with Tamam Shud somehow managing to create a sound that is crunchingly heavy, yet gentle and delicate at exactly the same time. The album's choicest cut, 'Lady Sunshine', was remixed into mono for release as a single in February 1969, and is a perfect introduction to the unique sound of the 'Shud.
Killer Moment: 00.46, *the first chorus kicks in.*

6. 'Unforgotten Dreams' – King Fox **Single (September)** **Du Monde: SDM-307**

This is garage punk psychedelia at its best, done by a bunch of 15 to 16 year old rich kids from Vaucluse. And in case you didn't know it, the singer of King Fox was Billy Field of *Bad Habits* fame, although you'd never pick it from the record.

'Unforgotten Dreams' began life as a demo tape that the band had made with fledgling DuMonde label boss Martin Erdman on his primitive Revox reel-to-reel tape machine at 7 inches per second, as opposed to the standard 15 inches per second. Erdman wasn't able to afford many blank tapes, so by recording at half-speed his tapes would last twice as long. The only trouble is that at 7 i.p.s. the sound quality tends to lose brightness.

Irregardless, the raw intensity of the backing track, with its dominant metallic fuzz tone guitar, turned out so well that Erdman decided to keep it and record vocals (and the golden flute of Paul Radcliffe) over the top, instead of redoing the whole thing in the studio proper. And thus, a lo-fi classic was born.

There is a certain naïve honesty about 'Unforgotten Dreams'. The lyrics are your typical teenage love-lorn drivel, but it's genuine and the musicianship is rough yet heartfelt, with a coda that is particularly spectacular. The band's home town took to 'Unforgotten Dreams' in a big way, as the single peaked at #8 on the Sydney charts and stayed in the top 40 for over four months.
Killer Moment: 03.05, *the guitarist goes spack while the flautist calmly noodles around him.*

7. 'Today (I Feel No Pain)' – Doug Parkinson In Focus **EP Track (December)** **Columbia: SEGO-70188**

Originally earmarked as the follow-up single to Doug Parkinson In Focus's highly successful cover version of 'Dear Prudence', 'Today (I Feel No Pain)' was given the catalogue number of DO-8858, and was even advertised in the music press, before everyone involved with the record suddenly got cold feet and realised they'd be better off putting out something more 'radio friendly' than this hunk of psychedelic jumble. As a result, the band went into Armstrong's studios and recorded 'Without You', which – with 'Hair' on the B-side – turned out to be a good commercial decision. 'Today (I Feel No Pain)' ended up on an EP that was issued around Christmas time.

members of the Australian Performance Group, opens in local theatres, making it the first all-Australian feature film to do so since 1958's *Jedda*.

3 A naked protestor wearing a Gorilla mask with the words 'The More I Make Love The More I Make Revolution' written on his chest disrupts the Sydney University Chancellor's Orientation Day speech.

5 Pop group Climax 5 are forced to split up after being stranded in Vietnam following a series of rip offs by Saigon agents.

5 The Brisbane home of sculptress Daphne Mayo is raided by two customs officials and nine policemen who, acting on an anonymous tip off, fail to find any obscene material.

9 A *Sydney Morning Herald* reporter complains of having a tooth filling knocked out by police while covering a rowdy anti-conscription march in the central city.

10 The annual Moomba pop concert draws 200 000 to the Myer Music Bowl to witness sets from The Zoot, Masters Apprentices, Dave Miller Set, Russell Morris, The Groop and others. The crowd on this occasion prove particularly wild as brawls and bottle throwing regularly interrupt the performances. Incidents during the day see Johnny Farnham booed by up to a third of the crowd and The Valentines' co-vocalist Vince Lovegrove arrested for pushing an over-zealous policeman offstage with his foot. Later fined $50,

Lovegrove is also put on a 12 month good behaviour bond.

14 US Evangelist Billy Graham begins a two week residency, spruiking for God at the Melbourne Music Bowl and the MCG. In an attempt to get with it, the preacher also presents a series of Youthquake concerts featuring a sermon on 'Youth, God and the Hippies'.

14 A number of people are arrested at the National Service Office in Sydney for trying to prevent police from throwing protestors down the stairs.

14 The *Trance Dance* is held at the Ironworkers Hall in Sydney with music from The Nutwood Rug Band.

16 American film maker Jonas Mekas' anti-war feature *The Brig* premieres in Australia at the Greek Cinema in Sydney, after being banned from television.

17 With the completion of a pipeline from Roma, Brisbane becomes the first capital city to receive natural gas on tap.

17 Having released their fourth single, 'Soothe Me', Battle of the Sounds winners The Groove head off for the UK. Working there until the end of the year they make little progress, returning home to reform as Eureka Stockade.

19 US hard rock band Steppenwolf cancel their Australian tour.

19 Seventies heartthrobs Sherbet make their debut at the New 2UW Spectacular at Sydney's Brookvale Oval.

20 Internal fighting within the Liberal Party sees Liberal backbencher Edward St John

Doug Parkinson In Focus (Newhill)

Laden with backward tapes, crashing harpsichords and a heavily treated vocal the disjointed 'Today (I Feel No Pain)' – written by guitarist Billy Green – was always going to be an ambitious choice for a single. And even though they chickened out on that account, I'm sure glad they made this record.

Killer Moment: 01.21, *Santa Claus's cynical 'Ho! Ho! Ho! Ho!'.*

8. 'Hypnotic Suggestion'/'Even Stevens' – Vegetable Garden **A/B-side (September)** **Clarion: MCK-3285**

'Hypnotic Suggestion' is one of those 'two songs in one' type of tracks, in which an energetic intro section segues directly into a druggy, dreamy echo/backward-tape/flanged second part. I'm not sure whether this song even works, but it's sure fun while it lasts – right down to the jaunty brass band ending. 'Even Stevens' on the flip-side is more throwaway and spontaneous, with flanging effects being used to the absolute MAXIMUM. I swear that even the studio's *wallpaper* ended up being flanged on this track!

The story goes that Clarion (a Perth label, distributed by Festival) boss Martin Clarke got local songwriter Bill Millar (aka Phil Green) to write and perform a couple of songs, which Clarke then interspersed with his own studio effects and audio cut ups in an attempt to match 'The Real Thing'. The result was no 'Real Thing' by any stretch of the imagination, but certainly was no dud either.

Killer Moment ('Even Stevens'): 02.33, *the tape edit from Hell.*

9. 'Lullaby (To Sleep I Go)' – The La De Das **LP Track (April)** **Columbia: SCXO-7899**

The La De Das' famously 'ambitious' concept album 'The Happy Prince' – based on the Ocsar Wilde fable – is fairly hard-going, to be honest. The musicianship is pretty much flawless, and poet Adrian Rawlins' narration is warm, tender and expressive, but the trouble with 'The Happy Prince' is that it just doesn't have any memorable *songs* on it. Even the album's single 'Come and Fly With Me' fails to stick in the memory.

However the third-last track, 'Lullaby (To Sleep I Go)' – a heartbreaker in context of the story (it's when the swallow dies) – is the most touching and best realised song of the album. It consists of nothing but a lone vocal over Kevin Borich's masterful sitar playing and a classical guitar. The perfectly simple 'Lullaby' contains more emotion in a mere 2 minutes and 44 seconds than the rest of the LP put together.

Killer Moment: 00.43, *'Death is the brother of sleep, calling me . . .'.*

10. 'Oceans of Fire' – Oakapple Day **B-side (September)** **Philips: BF-449**

The singer/guitarist of Oakapple Day was Rory O'Donoghue, a frizzy-haired fellow who would later find mega-fame as Grahame Bond's sidekick Thin Arthur on the legendary '70s TV series *The Aunty Jack Show*. 'Oceans of Fire' is a dramatic Hammond organ driven piece, which originally appeared as a B-side to a cover of Traffic's 'No Face, No Name, No Number'. Oakapple Day were all supreme musicians and 'Oceans of Fire' is a fine showcase of the band's restless intensity.

Killer Moment: 01.12, *a harpsichord starts twinkling away all Baroquely from out of nowhere.*

11. 'Long Live Sivananda' – Inside Looking Out **Single (August)** **Sunshine: QK-3115**

Inside Looking Out were an Adelaide band about whom very little is known. What I *can* tell you is that 'Long Live Sivananda' is a terrific amphetamine-driven psychedelic workout with some restless time changes, a treacle smooth fuzz guitar line and some righteous bass playing.

12. 'Peculiar Hole in the Sky' – The Easybeats **Single (September)** **Parlophone: A-8892**

The Easybeats' original demo version of 'Peculiar Hole in the Sky' was released by Parlophone as a single once the band had switched labels to Polydor. For a demo recording it is spectacular, and in this writer's opinion, better than The Valentines' 'properly recorded' version. It's certainly a little bit weirder, as Stevie Wright's vocals come across as more detached and strange than Bon Scott's professional soulful performance, and Tony Cahill's drumming is pure genius. The record was not a great hit, though, as #53 nationally was the best it could do.

13. 'The Wind' – The Groove **Single (June)** **Columbia: DO-8811**

After winning 1968 'Hoadley's Battle of the Sounds', The Groove got to lay down a couple of tracks in Britain and the best by far was the symphonic 'The Wind', written by vocalist Peter Williams and organist Tweed Harris.

A stately slow-paced number backed by harpsichord, piano, organ, bass, drums and an ethereal female choir – it is psychedelic in the way that 'A Whiter Shade of Pale' is psychedelic. Basically, though, 'The Wind' was a showcase for the outstanding singing voice of Peter Williams, who gives the vocal performance of a lifetime on this song – throaty, theatrical and truly emotional. Despite such genuine quality and an attractive half-page ad in *Go Set*, 'The Wind' only managed to make it to #48 on the Melbourne charts, before bowing out the following week.

Killer Moment: 02.50, *that scream.*

14. 'I'm On Fire'/'Watch Me Burn' – Mike Furber **A/B Side (December)** **Columbia: DO-9870**

With his long silky fringe, big brown puppy dog eyes and vulnerable 'take me home and mother me' poses, teenage pop star Mike Furber was the pin-up boy of choice for many a young Aussie female in the mid-'60s. Between 1966 and 1967 he (along with his former band The Bowery Boys) released no less than six singles, four EPs and an album and, for a while there, it looked as if Furber would usurp Normie Rowe's King of Australian Pop crown. However, it was not to be. Other equally pretty, but more talented boys, like Ronnie Burns, Jim Keays and Russell Morris would come along and steal Furber's screams. In fact, after his final single for Festival in late '67 he wasn't even heard of for over 18 months.

In 1969 Furber was signed by Columbia records and, desperately in need of a hit to put a spark back into his flagging career, he hooked up with Harry Vanda and George Young. Vanda and Young had written a fiery two song mini-suite, and it seemed that Mike Furber was the perfect artist to bring it to light. 'I'm on Fire' is a scintillating pop track underscored by a ripping lead fuzz guitar line and a solid rhythm section, but 'Watch Me Burn' is even wilder, with TWIN lead guitars (one fuzz and one wah-wah) wailing away beneath Furber's excellent vocal performance.

Unfortunately, the single didn't do a thing and Furber was soon dropped by Columbia. He later moved into musical theatre with mixed success, and in May 1973 was found hanged in a garage aged just 24.

accuse PM Gorton of personal impropriety over a trip he made to the US Embassy in the company of a 19-year-old girl.

23 With the Easter Show filling the AMP Pavilion, Ubu moves its latest Happening, entitled *The Second Intergalactic Festival Lightshow*, to the Greek Cinema in Sydney. Jazz musicians The John Sangster Band and acid rockers Nutwood Rug and Tamam Shud provide the aural accompaniment to Ubu's *Trip Without Glue* and *Crystal Trip* light shows.

26 New Zealand psych act The Hi-Revving Tongues tour Australia after winning the NZ Battle of the Bands.

27 Michael Powell's controversial film *Age of Consent* debuts at the Odeon Theatre in Brisbane. His second film, after the highly successful *They're A Weird Mob*, the feature updates Norman Lindsay's tale of a dissolute artist for the modern era. Starring American actor James Mason alongside Helen Mirren, the film narrowly avoids an X rating upon release in the US.

30 Australian amplifier manufacturers Strauss open a second store at Shop 12, Princess Gate Tower in Melbourne.

APRIL

- Popular documentary series *Chequerboard* makes its debut on ABC TV.
- Years in the making, The La De Das' *The Happy Prince*, Australia's first concept album, is finally released.
- Former Twilights singer/ songwriter Terry Britten leaves for the UK.

1 The first shipment of Australian iron ore leaves for Japan.

2 Party Machine singer Ross Wilson leaves Melbourne to join Procession in London.

9 The Melbourne City Council's By-Law 418 is repealed after months of protests in which over 100 people are arrested for circulating anti-Vietnam and anti-censorship leaflets.

11 The National Art Students' Union presents *Alexander Nevsky's Homecoming* at the Cellblock Theatre in Sydney. Orchestrated by David Humphries, the 'environmental theatre' piece involves Tully and the Arts Students Pop Orchestra providing the musical backing to an Ubu-lit Human Body ritual and performance.

11 100 are arrested at an anti conscription demonstration in Sydney as part of a 'get tough on protests' push by the conservative Askin government.

12 In Focus, The Zoot and The Valentines play to 15 000 at Melbourne's Princess Gate Tower.

13 The last tram runs in Brisbane.

16 ALP leader Gough Whitlam pledges that, if elected, a Labor government will abolish university fees.

15. 'Billie's Bikie Boys' – Wickedy Wak **Single (August)** **Sunshine: QK-3118**

Brought to us by the 'A' Team of Johnny Young (composer) and Ian 'Molly' Meldrum (producer), 'Billie's Bikie Boys' is a fun Shadow Morton-styled powerpop track laced with wah wah, motorbike sound effects and Rick Springfield's growling guitar. Producer Meldrum's signature piano/tambourine rhythm base provides the foundation, while guitarist/vocalist Springfield blasts off with some devastating lead.

Wickedy Wak were formed by ex-MPD Ltd bassist, the late Pete Watson. By the time of 'Billie's Bikie Boys' release, however, Rick Springfield had already joined The Zoot.

16. 'Mr Time' – Chain **B-side (October)** **Festival: FK-3331**

The B-side to their debut single, 'Mr Time' – written and sung by future Aztecs pianist Warren 'Pig' Morgan – is one of the least traditionally bluesy tracks that Chain ever recorded. A sumptuous, slow, almost hymn-like number, the Pat Aulton-produced 'Mr Time' is augmented by the astounding Hammond work of blind New Zealand organist Claude Papesch. 'Mr Time' is one of those tracks that seems to sound better the more often you hear it.

Killer Moment: 02.00, *That Hammond organ chord, which bubbles up like a cauldron full of molten gold.*

17. '2000 Weeks'/'Bargain Day' – Terry Britten **A/B Side (March)** **Columbia: DO-8711**

With the demise of The Twilights, guitarist/songwriter Terry Britten immediately set himself up as a songwriting 'gun for hire', penning tracks for The Zoot, Avengers, Cliffmores, Ronnie Burns and others. He also made this one vastly underrated solo single for The Twilights' old label Columbia, before heading off overseas to eventually write hits for the likes of Tina Turner, Cliff Richard and Michael Jackson.

'2000 Weeks' is an unused title song to a film by Tim Burstall, and it's a lovely piano ballad that could sit comfortably on the Zombies' classic *Odessey and Oracle* album. However, it's 'Bargain Day' on the flip that really earns its place on this psychedelic list. Like The Twilights' 'Comin' on Down', this one also delves into the subject of the Earth's destruction, with Britten going all Christian to espouse the *'Coming of the Lord.'* All the same, 'Bargain Day' is a way cookin' track with Britten's vocals in fine form and his biting guitar fed through a Leslie speaker (and some lead guitar ideas lifted from Clapton's work on 'While My Guitar Gently Weeps').

'2000 Weeks' charted in Melbourne, Adelaide and Brisbane, doing best in Melbourne, where it peaked at #19.

18. 'What a Scene' – Kevin McCann **Single (May)** **RCA: 101853**

An obscure artist from the RCA roster, Kevin McCann made two singles, but his first, the self-penned 'What a Scene', was the most musically interesting.

'What a Scene' is all about taking a hired balloon trip around the world, until the balloon in question unfortunately catches fire. (Oh, the *humanity*!) All manner of weird studio trickeries are got up to here, including flanging, echo rushes and mellotron-like violin bends. Apart from being a fascinating song in its own right, 'What A Scene' is worth hearing simply for the angelic Claire Pool Singers sounding as if they're singing at the bottom of a storm water drain.

19. 'Emily on a Sunday' – Clapham Junction **Single (October)** **Du Monde: SDM-309**

When Sydney band Clapham Junction (full of several expatriate Poms) came to record with DuMonde kingpin Martin Erdman, after winning a local radio station's 'Battle of the Bands', they only had one original song – a Who/Move-inspired pop art powerpop explosion entitled 'Emily on a Sunday'. Erdman later remarked that the band were constantly drunk and crazy throughout the entire recording session, and that the studio *'. . .was like a grog shop.'* Despite alcohol, and not LSD, inspiring the track, it's an absolute corker, with guitars slashing away right, left and centre and drums clambering all over the shop. Pure exhilaration.

Killer Moment: 00.23, *a mod powerchord that Pete Townshend would be proud of.*

20. 'Moonshot' – Oakapple Day plus The Deadly Pair | **Single (August)** | **RCA: 101864**

An unashamedly silly track by Rory O'Donoghue's band Oakapple Day, augmented by 'The Deadly Pair' (whoever *they* were – perhaps Bannerman and Stokes, who wrote both sides of the single). 'Moonshot' is interesting as an early stereo single put out on the RCA label, and as a song itself it's a cute li'l piece that compares the difficulty of getting your girlfriend to 'come across' to the complexity of launching a fully-fledged Moon mission. Lots of electronic sound effects, corny Earth-to-Moon dialogue (*'All systems A-OK! . . . Trajectory A-OK!'*) and some freaky guitar and organ sounds ensue – and all in magnificent stereo!
Killer Moment: 01.53, *The lunar climax.*

21. 'Tweedle-e-dee'/'Carolina Court' – The Avengers | **A/B Side (May)** | **Columbia: DO-8756**

Terry Britten wrote 'Tweedle-e-dee' for The Avengers (known as the 'Brisbane' Avengers during this period, due to a New Zealand band of the same name playing around). While it's basically a bubblegum number, 'Tweedle-e-dee' still has plenty of charm about it – particularly in the lyrical department: *'Plays the guitar like a Beatle, people come to feed their eagle eye/ Kids all think he looks much older, with his moustache and his shoulder hair . . .'*

'Carolina Court' on the B-side (co-written by vocalist Julian Jones) is more reflective and subdued, with a complex melody and some deft piano and organ lines. A quality double-sider all round, 'Tweedle-e-dee' made #27 on the Melbourne charts, and #13 in the band's home town.

22. 'Hey Bulldog' – Travis Wellington Hedge | **Single (September)** | **RCA: 101867**

The guitarist on this track is Graham Goble, a chap who later found fame with The Little River Band, whose 'Time Exposure' album was produced a certain George Martin. Well, back when he was still just a jobbing musician in an obscure Adelaide band called Travis Wellington Hedge Goble he had his first taste of chart success (#29 in Adelaide) with a cover version of 'Hey Bulldog' – a Beatles track originally produced by Martin. Travis Wellington Hedge's version of 'Hey Bulldog' is heavier and funkier than the original, with plenty of spacey echo to keep things tripping along nicely.

23. 'Lazy Life' – Heart 'n' Soul | **Single (June)** | **Festival: FK-2949**

'Little children playing in the park/ Catching butterflies before it gets too dark . . .'

This is a rosy-eyed take on the psychedelic experience, a stoned summery ode to dropping out and drifting away. Heart 'n' Soul were a seven piece (later 15-piece) jazz rock 'big band', who delighted festival audiences with rocked out versions of classical pieces such as *The 1812 Overture* and Bach's *Brandenburg Concerto*.

'Lazy Life' features the resonant velvety voice of Graeme Willington and a lush and drippy string arrangement. It made #18 in Sydney, but the languid sound of the song really connected in sunny Brisbane, where it peaked at #4 and spent 18 weeks in the charts.

24. 'Zoom Zoom Zoom'/ 'Getting Myself Together' – Cam-Pact | **A/B Side (August)** | **Festival: FK-3215**

The fifth and final single from Cam-Pact, recorded after founding members Keith Glass and Chris Stockley had left the group. 'Zoom Zoom Zoom' (originally done by an obscure US band, Our Patch of Blue) is a noisy bubblegum number with drummer Trevor Courtney on vocals, and is quite reminiscent of British pop art band The Creation. Better is the B-side, the Courtney-Cook penned 'Getting Myself Together'. With guitarist Greg Cook on lead vocals and new pianist Bill Blisset pounding away at the keys like Billy-o, 'Getting Myself Together' really hits its straps in the coda, where the band jam away loose 'n' loud for the final two and a half minutes of the song. Pat Aulton handled the production on this single, which explains the subtle yet expert touches of echo and reverb on both sides of the 45.
Killer Moment ('Getting Myself Together'): 04.08, *Cam-Pact collapse in a heap.*

18 25 people are arrested during an anti-war march from Sydney University to Chifley Square.

21 The Student Union at the University of NSW elects two Bailing Officers, whose sole job will be to arrange bail for students arrested at political demonstrations.

21 Channel 7 launches a new pop TV program entitled *Turning On*.

23 Draft resister Lou Christofides is arrested for delaying the arrival of a train load of conscripts heading from Newcastle to Sydney. He is later jailed for his sit-in on the rails and for refusing to register for conscription.

23 The arrests of peace protestors continue to mount in Sydney when six are locked up for demonstrating outside the Commonwealth Offices in Martin Place.

30 Sir Paul Hasluck takes over as Governor General.

MAY

- Conservationists begin a successful campaign to save the Little Desert in Victoria, by calling for it to be made a national park.
- Acting in solidarity with striking teachers, teenagers from the Victorian Socialist Secondary Students Union hang an effigy of Premier Bolte.
- John Romeril's agit-prop play *Mr Big The Big Big Pig* plays a short season at La Mama before being taken to the streets and protests of Melbourne. During the month La Mama also presents an Arts Festival Season, featuring 30 performances in 10 days.

1 Australia signs up to the Universal Copyright Convention.

1 Agit-prop band Semblance of Dignity become the first rock act to play a May Day march in Melbourne.

1 Brisbane's May Day march sees 300 young activists wave red and black flags and heckle Gough Whitlam with the chant 'Socialism Yes, Whitlam No!' Underlining the increasing gulf between the New Left and the old guard of the ALP and communist parties, Trades and Labour Council President Jack Egerton attacks the youngsters for 'subjecting Labor leaders to rude and unwarranted personal attacks.'

1 Radical students spend their May Day getting bashed by police after they attempt to disrupt a speech by the Governor of New South Wales for Sydney University's Army Regiment.

2 The Monkees film *Head* opens in Melbourne at the Forum Theatre.

7 During a visit to the US, PM Gorton embraces President Nixon wholeheartedly, stating 'Wherever there is a joint attempt to improve not only the material, but the spiritual standards of life of the peoples of the world, then we will go a Waltzing Matilda with you.' Anti-war protestors later expose the true meaning of the Australian-US alliance when they paraphrase Gorton by singing 'We'll go a bombing and burning with you.'

7 Having completed a frenetic tour of New Zealand and Australia,

25. 'Whole Lotta Shakin' Goin' On' – Doug Ashdown | **Single (March)** | **Philips: BF-430**

A bizarre rendering of the Jerry Lee Lewis Rock and Roll classic by the usually more 'serious' country/folk singer-songwriter Doug Ashdown. Ashdown plays it deadpan here, with his vocals heavily treated with distortion and EQ. The backing band are going through all the clichéd boogie-woogie licks, but meanwhile all these disembodied male and female voices continually name-check various artistic figures: *'Johann Sebastian Bach . . . Bob Dylan . . . Leonardo Da Vinci . . . Omar Khayyám . . .'* Odd.

26. 'Such A Lovely Way' – The Groop | **Single (January)** | **CBS: BA-221583**

A couple of months before providing the backing on 'The Real Thing', The Groop made a triumphant return to the charts in their own right with this, the sizzling 'Such a Lovely Way'. Led by the explosive vocal and organ work of Brian Cadd and the insane drumming of Richard Wright, 'Such A Lovely Way' is as catchy as the catchiest of bubblegum songs. It made the charts in both Melbourne and Sydney, but did best in Brisbane, where it peaked at #7.

27. 'A Tear Falls'/'Tabatha Crystilla' – The Society | **A/B-side (November)** | **Nationwide: Z4KM-0506**

A very classy one-off single by an Adelaide band called The Society, who were discovered by a Channel-9 TV big-wig named John Crossing, who set the group up with a recording date on the tiny Nationwide label. Crossing even provided some tasty keyboards for them on their recordings of two songs by the band's guitarist-vocalist Martin Goostrey.

'Tabatha Crystilla' has a loose goodtime jug band feel with banjo, harmonica and piano letting loose as clinking bottles, whoops and whistles fill out the atmosphere. It reached #34 on the Adelaide charts and stayed in the top 40 there for six weeks. 'A Tear Falls', on the other side, is a slower, moodier number with a mournful harmonica, melodic organ and some fine ensemble vocals.

28. 'Gentle Art'/'You've All Got To Go' – The Party Machine | **A/B-side (January)** | **Columbia: DO-8405**

Neither side of this single is as provocative as the legendary 'I Don't Believe All Your Kids Should Be Virgins', but The Party Machine's one and only single is a fine record in its own right. 'Gentle Art' is a smooth 'n' gentle soul number with some gorgeous airy chords and a seductive vocal performance by Ross Wilson. 'You've All Got To Go' is an existential theatre-piece about the inevitability of death, featuring some twisted Salvation Army-style brass. The distinctive vocals of Party Machine bassist (and future Spectrum main man) Mike Rudd are also well apparent in several sections of the song.

29. 'Walking and Talking' – R. Black and The Rockin' V's | **Single (January)** | **Sunshine: QK-2752**

A cute song that almost sounds as if its being made up as it goes along. 'Walking and Talking' was an unreleased Easybeats track by Vanda and Young, recorded by Wollongong's R. Black and The Rockin' V's. The best things about this song are Stuart Bedford's stinging main guitar motif and Dave Rossall's reedy vocals.

30. 'Hey! Watch Out'/'Girl in the Garden' – Hugo | **A/B-side (September)** | **Festival: FK-3159**

'Hey! Watch Out' is a slightly snarly and rather lascivious garage punker by obscure Adelaide power-trio Hugo, which is all done and dusted in just two minutes and ten seconds. The B-side 'Girl in the Garden' is more of the same, with a rather neat fade-in, some cool throbbing bass work, and a tight little drum break in the middle – and *it* only goes for 1 min 52 secs. Not until the punk era of almost a decade later would pop songs ever be this short again.

Honorable-ish Mention

'Incense' – Issy Dy | **Single (September)** | **Festival: FK-3254**

Issy Dy (real name Israel Dyzenhaus) had been a fixture on the Melbourne pop scene since the mid 1960s, performing with several bands as well as in the duo Issy and Adrienne (with Adrienne Russell). Dy's first solo single was a cover of Jimmy Miller's soul rave-up 'Incense', and it's a fairly telling indication that the flower pop movement – which had not all that long ago been a mysterious underground phenomenon – was now well and truly mainstream.

The Party Machine (Beard)

The B-side, the semi-bubblegum 'A Simple Song', was written by the brand-new Masters Apprentices songwriting duo of Jim Keays and Doug Ford, and features the latter on guitar. 'Incense' was a sizeable hit in Melbourne (highest pos. #14; 13 weeks in the charts).

Choice Australian Albums of 1969

	Artist	Title	Release date	Label: Cat. No
1.	Tamam Shud	*Evolution*	January	CBS: SBP-233761
2.	The La De Das	*The Happy Prince*	April	Columbia: SCXO-7899
3.	The Masters Apprentices	*Masterpiece*	December	Columbia: SCXO-7915
4.	Australian Cast (and Tully)	*Hair*	November	Spin:SEL-933544
5.	Pip Proud	*A Bird in the Engine*	December	Polydor: LPHM-109

Ian D. Marks

The La De Das relocate to London.

10 The last state not under conservative rule falls to the Coalition, as the ALP loses its first Tasmanian election in 35 years.

10 The President of the Western Australia Aboriginal Association, playwright Jack Davis, calls on the State and Federal Governments to give Indigenous people land rights, stating, 'Morally, Australia has committed robbery, violence and murder to confiscate this island continent . . . we want them to admit it was and still is the Aborigines' Australia.'

10 Following the release of their 'You Gotta Live Love' single, The Groop split up, with Brian Cadd talking up his next project, a super group that will eventually become Axiom.

14 A two day Happening featuring Russell Morris, The Valentines, The Avengers, The Iguana and The Zoot, sponsored by Radio 3XY, is held at the Melbourne Town Hall. Tickets for the shows are only made available through Clarks shoe stores.

15 Clarrie O'Shea, secretary of the Victorian Tram and Bus

Employees Union, is jailed by Judge, later Governor General, John Kerr after his union refuses to pay fines imposed under the penal provisions of the Commonwealth *Conciliation and Arbitration Act*. Strikes involving over a million workers erupt across Australia, effectively breaking the power of the Commonwealth Industrial Court to control union activities. O'Shea is eventually freed on 21 May after his fines are paid anonymously.

15 Lloyd O'Neil founds Lansdowne Press to fight the control of Australian publishing by overseas firms.

16 Richard A. Pennebaker's Bob Dylan documentary *Don't Look Back* opens in Australia.

17 The ultra-conservative Bjelke-Petersen government is re-elected in Queensland.

17 Ellis D. Fogg stages an Underground battle of the bands in Sydney.

23 Oakapple Day and Levi Smith's Clefs play the *Ubu Lightshow* at the Greek Theatre in Sydney.

24 Brisbane police carry out the first of three raids on the left wing Red and Black bookshop, seizing 'obscene' material including *The ABZ of Love*, *Circus* magazine and a book of Audrey Beardsley artwork. The Acting Mayor of Brisbane,

Diana modelling the Afghan look (Beard)

The year in Fashion

Crazy Legs

In January 1969, *Go Set* announced: 'Get set on the painted kick: whether you wear your canvas Levis as you buy them, paint them yourself or buy them already screened as Crazy Legs . . .' *Go Set* also mentioned that painted Op Art patterns on unisex jeans and bags were becoming popular, and in February 1969 described new vinyl clothes painted with psychedelic patterns, recommending readers paint motifs on their new vinyl jackets, dresses or suits. Pointing to the popularity of painted clothing, Waltons of Melbourne launched their new range of clothes with an in-store painting party, featuring music by The Zoot and artwork by Melbourne Pop Artist, Ian McCausland.

It is interesting to note that jeans are rarely mentioned during the late 1960s in the fashion press, and that they were not worn as they are today until the 1970s. An advertisement for Buscaderos jeans in a January 1969 edition of *Go Set* alerted the fashion conscious youth with, 'Hey Bambinos, Buscaderos are here. The high waist, skim hips, wide leg-look with extended band and a big bold buckle at the back. Jeans for guys and jeanies for girls cut in denim, dashing stretch denims in white, navy, sand, oatmeal, whiskey, sky, chilli or coffee . . . brought to you by Leisure Master from $5.25.' In April 1969 another advertisement appeared for Sterling brand jeans that were 'flares, hipsters or tubes' and 'plain, checked or houndstooth'.

The lead singer from Sons of Fred (Jonas)

By contrast, in the 9 June 1969 issue of *Woman's Day*, men's trousers were velvet and flared and worn with a pastel crepe loose shirt with full sleeves, a neck tie and a heavy gold medallion. This image was inspired by the film *Romeo and Juliet*, and the corresponding women's outfit was a braid trimmed jerkin with a velvet dress cap, velvet ribbons in braided hair and pearls. By May 1969, *Go Set* recommended taking 'a dash of Victoriana and the late twenties, a splash of Elizabethan colour, bring[ing] it up to date with loads of imagination . . .'

Mr Jim Jonas was working in Adelaide during 1969 and playing in bands such as Charcoal Lane, The Paper Sun and Sons of Fred. He remembers wearing a burgundy shirt, black flared trousers, a black leather vest and gold chains. He also remembers a 'puffy white shirt with a floppy collar'. He wore R.M. Williams black leather boots made in Adelaide and said some of his friends wore platform-soled shoes.

Sons of Fred drummer (Jonas)

Alderman Walsh, attacks the move, daring police to seize a copy of *The Best of Beardsley* from his office desk.

27 Paul Witzig's psychedelic surf movie *Evolution* opens at the Brighton Town Hall in Melbourne. Detailing the adventures of Australian surfing champions Nat Young and Wayne Lynch as they tour around Australia, Europe and the US, the film employs various experimental techniques. Dispensing with narration, it also features a soundtrack coordinated by *Go Set* magazine's David Elfick and played by Tamam Shud.

28 Descendants of the Kelly family and members of Actors Equity protest against the casting of Mick Jagger as Ned Kelly in the upcoming film of the bushranger's life.

31 Lynne Randell returns to Australia for a brief visit after 14 months spent in the US touring with bands such as The Monkees.

JUNE

- The 'Tribal Rock Musical' *Hair* makes its debut at the Metro Theatre in Kings Cross, with Tully providing the music, Ubu providing the lights and promoter Harry M. Miller providing the money.
- Three Sydney University academics are threatened by the Commonwealth Government with prosecution after they urge non-compliance with conscription. The charges are later withheld, when over 500 other Australian academics

put their name to a similar statement.

- The Liberation centre is opened in Manly to provide a base for local anti-war activities.
- Responding to newspaper editorials decrying Australia's outmoded censorship laws, the outgoing Minister for Customs Senator Malcolm Scott backs the status quo, arguing 'I would like to keep our young people as pure as possible for as long as possible.'
- Anti-racist protestors demonstrate in Sydney and Melbourne against a visit to Australia by the South African Economics Minister.
- The Dave Miller Set tour Indonesia alongside Mike Furber and Nikki Bradley, playing just three shows before dodgy dealings by promoters force them to flee the country.

2 PM Gorton is heckled and jeered by students whilst giving a speech at the Royal Melbourne Institute for Technology (RMIT).

3 The aircraft carrier *Melbourne* collides with the US Destroyer *Frank E. Evans* in the South China sea, killing 74.

4 Michael Robertson, Peter Weir and Chris McCullough withdraw their films from the Sydney Film Festival after the Commonwealth Censor prevents the Swedish film *I Love, You Love* from being shown.

12 Student activists occupy the Senate Room of the University of Queensland, condemning the institution as 'only existing to serve capitalism.'

Georgia-Lee Eames and friends in short mini dresses with ethnic embroidery (Newhill)

Jeff Crozier and friends model a collection of theatrical styled outfits (Newhill)

In May 1969, *Go Set* advertised girls' fashion outfits at Sportsgirl for 'every occasion' in velvet, wool, crepes and brocades. Typical outfits included a purple wool pantsuit with an emerald sequinned bolero jacket for contrast, a flowing mustard sleeved dress with flared skirt and a bodice laced in a 'peasant style', as well as ponchos in purple, green, red and yellow. Ponchos were part of the 'gaucho' look often referred to in the fashion press of the late 1960s and were probably attributed to late 1960s American western films, such as *Butch Cassidy and the Sun Dance Kid* that popularised native American, Mexican and frontier styles of clothes. As with many fashion conceptions of vintage or antique clothes, their historical accuracy could be dubious. Further, late 1960s fashion interest in ethnic inspired embroidery, jewellery and fabrics were considered highly fashionable details to typically western middle class dress. It seems too that ethnically inspired fashion details were the preserve of the young. It was uncommon for older women and especially older men to appear in clothes that had any ethnic detail.

In contrast by August 1969, *Go Set* reported Kinky message T-shirts, Indian embroidered shirts, hand printed kaftans and Afghan coats in goatskin or sheepskin as high fashion items. This perhaps marks the moment when clothes for the young moved away from being mini versions of clothes for their elders. The contrast could not have been more distinct from ideas of propriety and class association as seen in older peoples clothes to these younger clothes that embraced ethnic, political and class difference.

Indeed, Miss Gerry O'Reilly hand stitched a sheepskin jacket for her future husband, which was made so that the woolly side was worn on the inside and the skin on the outside. Peter Gerner, who was a student at Royal Melbourne Institute of Technology during 1969, also wore black hipster flannel bellbottomed trousers and a denim peaked hat that O'Reilly made. Some of his student friends wore corduroy, suede, paisley and big collared shirts.

Interestingly, while clothes seemed to be taking a rather theatrical direction during 1969, O'Reilly remembers wearing distinctly conservative clothes to work. She wore straight cut dresses and recalls a Sentex knitwear outfit that comprised a slacksuit with a tunic top and bell bottom pants. She also wore a sleeveless cream coloured dress with a drawstring waist and a slip underneath. Miss Kate Harman wore a cream wool crepe evening dress with a jewelled neckline. As cream was a suitably restrained colour for conservative events, middle aged women photographed in the *Woman's Day* and the *Australian Women's Weekly* wore coat dresses and jacket and dress sets in the colour with elbow length sleeves to the knee. For important events they still wore hats and sometimes gloves, though gloves were becoming far less visible than earlier in the decade.

Brigid Finlayson and Maria Sokratis

AMERICAN TRIBAL LOVE-ROCK

HAÏR

Hair: the 'Tribal Love Rock Musical'

1969

19 The Commonwealth Arbitration Court rules that women and men should be paid equally for doing work of the same value. However, the decision holds that pay increases are to be introduced over a three year period and fails to address under-representation of women in high income jobs.

17 Albie Thoms' experimental feature *Marinetti* makes its world premiere at the Wintergarden Theatre in Sydney. A quarter of the film's 2000-strong audience walk out during the screening, and the film is panned by mainstream critics for its incomprehensible plot and lack of structure. In response Thoms tells the *Sydney Morning Herald* 'I designed it so that those who didn't like it would actually walk out in the first 15 minutes. I am not offended. If more people walked out of shows you would not need to have the censor.'

19 ABC TV current affairs program *This Day Tonight* is attacked in a *Daily Telegraph* editorial for screening a 'sexy slice' from *Marinetti*.

19 An anti-conscription sit-in is held at Federal Treasurer Billy McMahon's offices in Sydney.

22 2000 attend the St Kilda Palais Theatre for the annual *Go Set* awards.

25 It is announced that around one third of Australian women aged between 15 and 49 are now taking the contraceptive pill.

JULY

- Ubu member Aggy Read is charged by the Commonwealth Customs Department for taking David Perry's banned *A Sketch on Abigayl's Belly* out of Australia for a screening in West Germany. Sydney's *Daily Telegraph* responds with an editorial calling on its readers to protest against the charges. Read is later found guilty and fined $10 plus costs.
- *Age* critic Colin Bennett publishes a list of 13 films recently banned by the Commonwealth Censor, including *Skidoo, Girl on a Motorcycle, Psych-Out, Three in the Attic, Born Losers, 100 Rifles* and *Pretty Poison.*
- Members of Students for a Democratic Society (SDS) hold three large anti-conscription rallies at Sydney University as part of their fifth 'Don't Register' campaign since 1967.
- Alexander Buzo's play *Norm and Ahmed* plays a short season at La Mama before touring the country. Actors in both Melbourne and Brisbane later incur the wrath of the law for the play's punch line, receiving convictions for obscene language. Also hitting the stage of La Mama this month is the debut of Jack Hibberd's *Dimboola* featuring Graeme Blundell, Bruce Spence and music from Semblance of Dignity.

Considered something of a period piece today, *Hair* was, upon its Broadway debut in 1968, hailed as 'a remarkable [example] of social protest' by cultural commentator Denis Altman. Depicting the conflict between 'the groovy generation' and its forebears, the play became a runaway success, spawning 29 separate productions in 17 countries by the early 1970s.

The musical premiered in Australia at Sydney's Metro Theatre during 1969. Produced by impresario Harry M. Miller and featuring the cream of Australia's pop crop it broke box office records and played for almost two years straight before touring the country. Drawing its share of controversy, the production was banned in Queensland, where leading Country Party politician Russ Hinze labelled it as being only of interest to 'lesbians, wife-swappers and spivs.' Former Cam-Pact front man and present day country musician Keith Glass recalls his time with the show.

I still don't know whatever possessed me to roll up and audition for *Hair*. Doing so was certainly flavour of the moment in 1969, it seems like someone from every band working around Melbourne and Sydney did. We were all caught up in the feeling there was some sort of revolution going on. So, laughable as it seems, we saw this event not as a corporate rip-off, but a genuine youth proclamation on the state of the world. Might seem deluded from this distance, but with the conflict over involvement in Vietnam, the hysteria over drugs, etc., just wearing your hair long was still an act of defiance almost guaranteed to get you clobbered in the wrong place or situation.

This was a generational thing as much as a factional, but the latter, youth sub-groups at each others' throats, was hardly new. Just in my time we'd had the rockers beating the shit out of the jazzers (a specifically Melbourne experience), then the skinheads/sharpie's running riot for a while without media detection, because these neatly dressed, short haired cretins didn't attract the attention the freaks they regularly beat up did. In the mid to late 1960s it was dangerous just to walk up Swanston Street as the sun went down for fear of sharpie attack – the media finally got the message and they were banned from a lot of venues and vilified in the newspapers – not unjustly.

In [Keith's psychedelic soul band] Cam-Pact we'd often put our lives in danger in country towns by just going to the local pub. I well remember the shouts of derision as the 'long haired pooftas' entered the bar. Amazingly, I never had a punch thrown at me, but came very, very close.

In any event, I must have been ready for a change so I showed up to the open call at (I think)

Keith Glass with Cam-Pact (Newhill)

the Melbourne Town Hall and sang a song or two. Guess I looked sort of the part, in the latter stages of Cam-Pact my hair was pretty long and bushy. So I was asked back the next day when I read a few lines from the script, jumped around a bit and was offered a place – simple as that. Nothing as drawn out as the *Australian Idol* auditions I can tell you. Director Jim Sharman told me he had the part of 'Berger' in mind for me and would I mind perming my hair into an afro?

Graham (Fluff) Matters and Keith Glass (Lofven)

That was small potatoes in relation to telling my parents I was 'deferring' the RMIT course I'd been trying to fit in around working four nights a week in the band, and of course, I had to tell the group members I was leaving too. I was signing on for an 18 month contract, and thought that would be enough to see out the show around Australia and maybe New Zealand too. How wrong I was!

As I was going to be paid far more than scale for this leading role, I weirdly enough had to fend for myself in (a) getting to Sydney, (b) finding accommodation and (c) negotiating the actual salary. If I had have had a theatrical agent things may have been easier, but coming from the rock/pop side of things, I knew virtually nothing about that, as various members of the regular cast, some of whom made a big deal of mentioning their years of study at NIDA, were quick to point out! Anyway I sorted out a suitable figure to ask for and it sounded like a fortune; after a bit of to and fro with Harry Miller's moneyman it was agreed. In the meantime I had to draw on my forthcoming salary, because as a lead I wasn't being paid for the four week rehearsal period!

The show was being put together in a small pavilion at the Sydney Showgrounds (now Fox Studios) right by Centennial Park. First day the media turned up and took shots of all the new cast members throwing their arms up in the air and generally doing an 'Age of Aquarius' type hippy celebratory dance on the spot – we hadn't even met each other yet. I had one friend who'd made the cut – Graham 'Fluffy' Matters, who had been in a band called Carnival; their demise meant Cam-Pact had a new recruit, bass player Chris Lofven, boy genius film maker who later directed the movie, the 'Aussie Rock' version of *Oz*.

I also met Wayne Matthews who was to play the other male lead 'Claude' – I was sort of Satan to his Jesus. There on that day also was John Waters, who would later share the role of Claude with Wayne. The four of us became pretty tight as the first few weeks rolled on, ultimately all moving into a house together when *Hair* settled in for the long haul at the Metro Theatre in Kings Cross.

Of particular interest to us (and the public) were the imports in the cast. The six African-Americans gathered mainly from New York, and what a strange set of personalities they were. The coolest was the beautiful Denni Piggot, whom Marcia Hines (not yet a cast member) named her daughter after. Denni, who dropped her last name for the show I think, is pretty cool to this day and pops up on a TV drama every so often.

Then there was Teddy Williams, almost Gary Coleman size, gay and proud. One time years later I remember turning on the television to be greeted with Teddy's beatific face beaming out in a scene from the Diana Ross movie vehicle, another *Oz* remake *The Wiz*. Sharon Redd was a pocket size singing sensation who went on to become a solo disco star back in the States in the '70s, and then a member of Bette Midler's 'Harlettes.'

Michael Angelo Springfield III – what an enigma! A Walter Mitty type character the expression 'jive ass' was tailor made for. He ended up as 'the man from Brash's' (in ads flogged to death on Victorian TV), and was so full of shit you had to admire him. According to him, he knew everyone and had done everything. Couldabeen an Olympic track and field star, but did a

KEITH GLASS
Virgo. Art — guitar — music. Write — sing — pulp. S. Z. Sakall — Buster Crabbe — Krazy Kat — Harvey Kurtzman — W. Elder — Van Dyke parks — Randy Newman — Tolkien — Gandalf — Stan Lee — Everyone.

- Liberal Minister Billy Snedden is temporarily trapped when anti-war protestors blockade his office.
- Doug Parkinson In Focus wins the Hoadley's Battle of the Sounds, but fail to join previous winners in heading to the UK, after their management runs off with the prize money. Runners-up The Masters Apprentices, however, do start packing their bags, after they are also awarded a prize of a return trip to England. In the same month the band also releases *5:10 Man*, their catchy tirade against the workaday life of 'straight' society.
- Original Sherbet singer Dennis Laughlin is replaced by Daryl Braithwaite.

2 Following the burning of conscription registration cards earlier in the day at the Monash and La Trobe universities, eight people are arrested for a sit-in at the Department for Labour and National Service offices in Melbourne.

4 Demonstrations against the Vietnam war occur in Sydney, Brisbane, Canberra and Adelaide. 11 people are arrested for occupying the

Canberra offices of the South Vietnamese Ambassador, whilst in Melbourne police prevent 3000 from storming the US consulate by erecting steel barricades. 30 are arrested en route to the Melbourne consulate, after mounted police charge the crowd prompting demonstrators to hurl firecrackers and marbles. During the protest one student sits across the road in the Chevron Hotel relaying police movements by walkie-talkie.

4 Rod Laver wins the Men's Singles title at Wimbeldon in a record length match, while John Newcombe and Tony Roche take out the Men's Doubles.

6 Just days after the death of former Rolling Stones guitarist Brian Jones and the holding of the massive *Stones in the Park* concert, Mick Jagger and Marianne Faithfull leave for Australia to star in *Ned Kelly*. Attacked from the outset, the pair ignite a media feeding frenzy when Faithfull drops out of the film after being hospitalised due to a drug overdose.

16 Students at the University of Queensland hold an Erotica Day, replete with Beardsley prints, nudity, graffiti and same-sex kissing.

17 The Sydney Filmmakers Co-operative Ltd is formed to take over underground film distribution from Ubu and give its artists legal standing.

21 The Parkes radio telescope in New South Wales relays the first pictures of the *Apollo XI* moon landing. On the same day

tendon at the trials, Daryl Zanuck was sending him scripts from Hollywood to check out, etc., etc. First day at rehearsals he collapsed claiming he had 'sickle cell' disease, which does affect blacks, but naturally we had no knowledge of. He didn't, it was just an attention grabber.

The final two black members of the cast didn't last too long and I can't remember much about the male, but the female was absolutely unforgettable for her schizophrenic behaviour. Charlene was her name, she stood about six feet tall and belted out a song with gospel intensity and fervour that matched most other elements of her life. She claimed to have recorded backup for The Stones, but unlike Venetta Fields, for example, I have never seen a credit or evidence of this. She was a glorious mess. Very hard to take for more than a few minutes, but riveting all the same. Possessing a complete lack of discipline, she was likely to do almost anything, be in tears or rapture.

Other imports came and went, including the lovely, very middle class and normal Karolynn Hill. She brought her mother out and she cooked us the greatest 'soul food' meal you could ever have. At one stage Karolynn went back to the US for a holiday and asked if there was anything I wanted. I said 'Can you get me a mojo?' She looked puzzled. When she returned she said she couldn't find one, but would a Hershey Bar (with almonds) do?

Marcia Hines turned up as a chubby 16-year-old who could really sing. We'd found out why she was chubby 6 months later. She was working the show right up to the birth of daughter Denni, then came straight on back – she's always been a very positive person, a hard worker and a great addition to the Australian population.

The final bro' who stays in my mind was Tomay (Jim) Fields, originally (well he said) from Memphis, Tennessee. He became Tomay once he'd settled in here and was the original, milk the audience, draw attention to yourself, ham. Long and lanky he'd roll his big eyes around and do a 'Steppin' Fetchit' routine, overstaying his part of the show by minutes, stretching it out, till we'd actually forgotten where we were in it (the drugs aiding and abetting that). Likeable enough though he was, there was only one love in Tomay's life – himself. He was one strange cat and when the show finally made it to New Zealand about three years later, Fields decided, in the best LSD induced tradition, he could fly and tried it off a cliff, jumping to his death. He was a unique individual and an audience favourite.

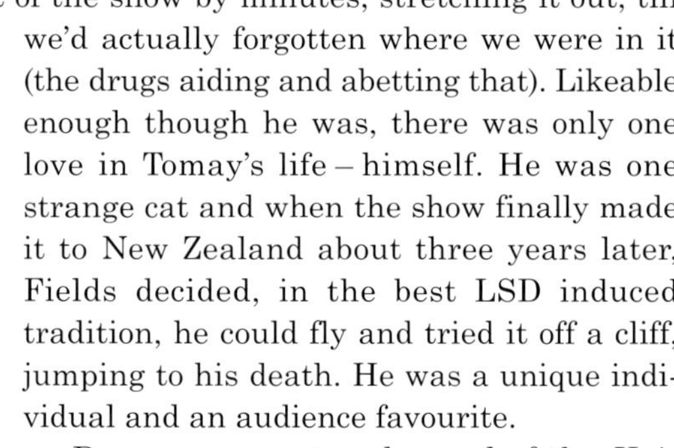

Drugs were part and parcel of the *Hair* experience, with management turning a blind eye to most activity, unless the law became involved. In the first months I must have been handed dope by someone most nights of the show at the stage door and there were no shortage of girls wanting to participate in the 'Tribal Love-Rock' experience either, although my girlfriend, later wife, moved up from Melbourne pretty quick-smart. So it mainly

The Metro Theatre (Lofven)

came down to drugs, and to be honest I rarely did the show straight in the early days. I did it tripping a few times and that was ridiculous, trying to clear away on-coming hallucinations to get back in sync with the script – I'm sorry if anyone had to endure that!

We mainly stuck to getting completely out of it at home in Gipps Street, Paddington and there was a party more nights than not. Strange people would turn up, Gerry Humphreys' ex-wife Claire was a constant. Broderick Smith used to spend weekend leave with us when he could (he'd been conscripted), so it was from one freak show to another for him. Richard Shara used to come and do weird make-up on people. Adrian Rawlins would try to clear out the fridge. He once turned into a giggling little forked tongue lizard on my shoulder. One night Graham Matters ran down the stairs yelling 'There's a sailor on the roof!' We went up to the attic and sure enough there was a guy out there, three floors up in a sailor suit. We dragged him in, all too out of it to actually find out who he was or how he got there, but I'm pretty sure it actually happened.

Another time John Waters and I were in Centennial Park tripping and a mounted policeman rode up to us and asked 'Seen anyone acting suspiciously?' Apart from us we hadn't, but he looked over our shoulder and said, 'Oh there he is,' and rode off to arrest a guy laying on his back in a flower bed, throwing flowers in the air.

Harry M. Miller—Michael Butler (U.S.A.)—Aztec Services
present

The American Tribal-Love Rock Musical

Produced by
HARRY M. MILLER

Entire production designed and directed by
JIM SHARMAN

Book & Lyrics by
GEROME RAGNI & JAMES RADO

Music by
GALT MacDERMOT

Executive Producer
STEFAN HAAG, O.B.E.

Stage Director
SANDRA McKENZIE

Musical Director
PATRICK FLYNN

Dance Director
JACK MANUEL

Sound Equipment by
SIMON GRAY PTY. LTD. and
AUSTRALIAN THEATRE MANAGEMENT

Lighting Equipment by
STRAND ELECTRIC

Costumes by
SUZIE MYLECHARANE

TRIBAL COUNCIL

NEIL BARTLEY JOHN BOWMAN IAN COOKESLEY CHRISTINE DOBINSON
MARGARET ENCHELMAIER JOHN FINLAY PATRICK FLYNN
FREDERICK J. GIBSON KEN GREGORY STEFAN HAAG DOUG HOWARD
SUE LAMBERT JERRY LUKE PETER MACKENNAL ANDREW MACKINTOSH
SANDRA McKENZIE JACK MANUEL HARRY M. MILLER JOAN MONAGHAN
COLLEEN MUCKERSIL SUZIE MYLECHARANE MARGARET NESTOR
RON PATON JUDITH RICH BILL SARGEANT JIM SHARMAN
BABETTE SMITH PETA SOUTHON

Sydney band The Jellallah hold a public exorcism in the Sydney Domain to 'aid the karma of the astronauts.' Accompanied by an audience of 50 the band play their own 'spatial brand of soul music' for two and a half hours.

22 SDS creates the John Sullivan Award for the highest number of false registration forms filled in and posted to the Department of Labour and National Service. Named after a particularly pernicious Commonwealth Police Chief, the award's prize includes a trip to the nearest penitentiary.

AUGUST

- Over 250 students invade the La Trobe University Council Chambers to prevent the expulsion of radical students by a disciplinary committee meeting.
- A Morgan Gallup poll finds, for the first time, that a 55% majority of those polled want Australian forces to withdraw from Vietnam, with only 40% remaining in favour of the war.
- Adelaide activists launch an anti-conscription campaign, setting up an advice line, leafleting Trade Schools and chaining themselves to the steps of State Parliament to protest the jailing of draft resister Bob Hall.
- The Federal government announces it will provide $300 000 in funding to the Australian film industry.
- The Masters Apprentices, Johnny Farnham, Ronnie Burns, Russell Morris, Johnny Young, The Zoot and The Valentines embark on the Operation Starlift

It was a bit of a charmed life taking this stuff, which thankfully was pretty pure Sandoz. Sometimes I was just totally discorporated, bodiless, floating around on another plane. Music came down to a big drone note and I managed to audio tape a group acid experience one night, but it was an unsettling experience, as what I'd sensed as communication while under the influence came out as a series of grunts and strange noises.

Meanwhile, back at the show, I was cutting notches on the bench of the dressing room and counting down the days till I could leave. The tedium was worse for me, because in bands I'd been used to moving around and also doing my own thing. The money was good, but it became a nightly ritual with little passion. Andy Anderson/James (ex Missing Links/Running Jumping Standing Still) had joined the cast and wanted my role. He didn't get it, but old Reggie Livermore did. At first he did it a few times a week and then we split it 4 shows each. In an effort to motivate the

Andy James/Anderson with The Andy James Asylum (Colbert)

tour. During the package's Brisbane show Masters' bass player Glenn Wheatley is forced by the police to leave the stage after his pants are torn off by a rampaging crowd.

- The ABC launches its Monday through Thursday youth program *GTK* (*Get To Know*), focusing on pop culture and featuring live-in-the-studio performances from numerous underground Australian acts.

7 The Commonwealth Censor rules that *Marinetti* is 'Not Suitable for Children – Not Suitable for Television', demanding director Albie Thoms delete various nude scenes before the film can be shown in Victoria.

8 The Australian Free Theatre troupe present a performance of their *Birth of Space* at the Cellblock Theatre in Sydney. Aiming to create 'revolutionary love theatre', the group are supported by the Foreday Blues Band, who feature former Id and Missing Links member Peter Anson.

12 Dr Norman Talbot writes to *The Australian* bemoaning the fact that Commonwealth

cast, roles were also being changed around, I did a few others and even played bass in the band for a few nights as a dep, just for something different. I was missing music and Graham and I had plans to form a part time band, but between the show, parties and drugs there wasn't enough time.

Tully, the *Hair* band, were even heavier on the drug intake than us, if that was possible. The band was augmented by a couple of jazz cats, Johnny Sangster on vibes and all sorts of miscellaneous instruments and Keith Stirling on trumpet. On guitar was Michael Barnes of The Nutwood Rug Band, a genuine ex-pat San Fran psychedelic outfit who had made their way out here a year or so before. He could play all that freakout stuff like a maniac, but apparently didn't know any chords.

Terry Wilson, the singer for Tully, was officially part of 'The Tribe' and sang 'Aquarius', which opened proceedings once we'd slithered our way to the stage through the audience. Then basically I came out and shook 'em all up jumping around and down into the seats, wearing nothin' but a lap lap and being obnoxious – it wasn't much of a stretch. One night I dislocated my toe on a seat. The toe was sticking out at a weird angle, and I was stoned, which made it worse. I also knocked my front tooth out with a microphone after someone stood on the lead as I was running forward with it on the giant peace symbol stage. It is not easy to sing with a tooth out, and I had to retire for the night.

A lot of celebs came to the show. Opening night was ridiculous – everybody who was anybody was there. At the end, when the audience jumped on stage, they all fell over each other to get in front for a picture. Graham Kennedy managed to hog the centre and me holding Gra Gra's hand made the front page of the paper next day. Graham Matters and I had the biggest afros, and so had our photo taken with a bunch of people. Dame Zara Bates (Prime Minister Holt's wife) was particularly venomous about us and the show as the media took snaps – wish I had one of those. Sir Robert Helpmann wore the most expensive flashy fringed jacket I've ever seen, must have cost a packet.

It was *Hair* mania – we were invited everywhere. Fame by association. Mobbed by thousands at Roselands Shopping Centre – a bizarre experience. We also went to Brisbane to do an 'arena' style performance of the music from *Hair* at Brisbane's Festival Hall, as talk was that the show would be banned in the deep north.

Various cast members would also do cameo TV spots as the instant celebrities we were – a breed still popular on the tube to this day. I did a late night show, which turned pretty ugly, with stand in host Maggie Britton deciding to tear strips off the musical and me. Even in my hippy, trippy state I shot a few back and managed to get Miller's clients 'banned' from appearing for six months.

Despite this, Sharon Redd and I got to do *Bandstand* (on another network) to promote the soundtrack album that came out a few months after the show started. We shared the single, one side each, which people still unearth a copy of from time to time. *Bandstand* was on it's last legs, and we simply did our spots and left, with Brian Henderson coming in later to intro us. I guess that footage is out there somewhere. As is the one and only gold record presented from the album. Last time I saw it was in the foyer of the old Festival Records building in Pyrmont and I kept threatening to rip it off!

After a while things settled down and the crowd turned more suburban, although the visiting celebs would still come backstage to say 'hello' and 'you were wonderful.' Eddie Albert and his son Eddie Jr, both Oscar winners, trotted that line out whilst more 'flash in the pan' identities such as Poncy Pounce (from *Hawaiian Eye*) and Lobo (*You And Me And A Dog Named Boo*) paid a

Customs officials continue to impound numerous imported books, including Henry Miller's *Sexus*, Frank Harris's *My Life* and Norman Douglas's *Some Limericks*.

14 30 anti-war protestors occupy the Newcastle Office of the Minister for Defence for 14 and a half hours.

18 Russell Morris receives a Gold Record for *The Real Thing*.

25 Ubu hosts Australia's first Underground festival at the Union Theatre and Argyle Bond in Sydney billing it as a *Seven Day Happening* featuring 'lovefreedompeacehappiness.' Cafe La Mama and Tribe travel up from Melbourne to present the controversial *Norm and Ahmed*, while local troupe the Human Body present their own brand of performance art. Numerous poets also perform on the bill, which is topped off by a light show and performances from Tamam Shud, The Nutwood Rug Band and Lindsay Bourke.

28 Having been championed by *Oz* artist Martin Sharp, Tiny Tim plays a 10 night stand in Sydney.

29 The Web discotheque runs for nine days as part of the

A SEVEN - DAY HAPPENING
lovefreedompeacehappiness

AN UNDERGROUND FESTIVAL

music films lightshows
poetry happenings plays
a continuous happening
be - in for one week
UNION THEATRE: AUG.25to28
ARGYLE BOND : AUG.29to31
attend participat perform
presented by ubu 699-1285
proceeds benefit UBU NEWS
australia 's underground
newspapernewspapernewspap

AN UNDERGROUND FESTIVAL

lovefreedompeacehappiness
A SEVEN - DAY HAPPENING

Melbourne Home Show at the Melbourne Exhibition Centre. Featuring local bands, Go-Go girls and a light show, the disco draws up to 5000 punters.

SEPTEMBER

- Bob Evans' surf movie *Splashdown* premieres at Sydney University's Union Theatre bearing the banner 'The world of living is ours, until we splashdown!'
- Bee Gees drummer Colin Petersen is sacked from the band, leaving Maurice and Barry Gibb to continue as a duo.
- Having been offered the chance to pick any track from the forthcoming Beatles 'White' album, The La De Das record and release a scorching version of 'Come Together' in the UK, only to see it knocked out of contention by the release of the Fab Four's original take.
- Anti development activists hang out their dirty underwear in North Melbourne's Abbotsford Street during a protest against the Victorian Housing Commission's decision to demolish the only laundromat in the area.

8 Bruce Paling, a feature writer for the *Age*, is fined $50 plus $31.50 court costs in Melbourne for refusing to register for conscription.

10 Daring the police to try and catch them, the SDS newspaper *Resist* publishes the names of over 70 draft resisters.

20 Balmain defeats South Sydney to win the Rugby League Grand Final.

FAMILY
formerly "Traffik"
OPENING SAT.,19th DEC., 8.30 TILL LATE
* KING HARVEST
* DADDY COOL
* PIG FACE
Exclusive appearance of ★ KEITH GLASS
star of "HAIR"
Also open Sunday afternoon with guest group
FLINDERS LANE, CITY

visit, but I was most excited when Darlene Love and The Crystals came by.

Billy Preston sort of embraced the *Hair* cast as his crowd during a season at Chequers night club, and he turned it on at his shows especially for us. Mick Jagger also turned up while making the movie *Ned Kelly*, as one of the cast members and a some-time resident of our house, Geoff Gilmour, had a part in the movie. The greatest celebrity *Hair* hanger-on was Frank Thring, who really loved being around the tribe and would often be there at the end asking in his unique way 'Where are we going tonight?'

Most of the time I wasn't going anywhere but home. The second year was a drag. We had a new band, Luke's Walnut, a much straighter outfit than Tully, but with a few rough edges, namely Reno Tehei ex-Compulsion (an uncannily accurate Jimi Hendrix tribute band) on 'borrowed' bass (from me actually), and the great Bobby Gebert on piano. There was a huge pile of Bex powder wrappers by Bobby's piano stool every night after the show, while Reno (who briefly joined The La De Das) disappeared a little later.

We'd also moved on from the communal Paddington address. We were in fact packing up to go when the police came calling one day, finding only myself and girlfriend Helena at home. It was a beautiful sunny day, we were painting in the backyard, and they were looking for drugs. It was a veritable task force and they moved through the premises with a fine tooth comb. One member from the *Hair* cast arrived as the hunt was on and cheerfully sat in the front room soaking it all in in the middle of a trip!

Wayne Matthews' suitcase was the subject of intense scrutinisation by an officer as he extracted a lock of hair from it tied with a blue bow. 'What's this?' he asked me. I answered (truthfully) 'That's a lock of Joan Sutherland's hair.' He looked at me quizzically – Wayne was an opera freak and there were photos, records and other mementoes to support my answer, but somehow it just didn't compute with our image!

On the way out, someone checked a leather jacket slung over a chair and 'found' a block of hash. I was immediately bundled out to the police car and taken downtown. It wasn't my jacket and it certainly wasn't my hash. Over the next two hours I was subjected to the good cop, bad cop routine. I'd seen enough movies to have found it laughable if it hadn't been my freedom in the balance. The bad cop came rushing in and said 'You'd better tell us all about it, you're high now and you need a fix don't you?' He threw open a drawer and grabbed an ancient rusty metal hypodermic with dried blood on the tip of the needle and made jabbing motions at my arm. Good cop came in and said 'Give him a break.' He then told me I'd better come clean as they had been reading my girlfriend's diary, which detailed the various times I'd taken acid. Helena had never even touched a cigarette herself, and I was unaware of the existence of this document. I denied, denied, denied and eventually they let me go. There were other occasions and other people not so lucky.

Catty in-fighting was replacing any peace-love feeling among the cast, so the night my contract was up I had all our possessions packed into a Transit van and headed out back to Melbourne. I had the vague notion that I wanted to play country music.

Keith indeed went on to play country music, and also opened a series of Melbourne import record shops during the 1970s, including the legendary Archie and Jughead's and Missing Link. The latter spawned a record label, which saw Keith release albums in the 1980s by such Australian alternative mainstays as the Go Betweens and The Birthday Party. During the 1990s Keith could be heard on ABC Radio, and he currently resides in the US where he continues to tour and play music.

RUSSELL MORRIS

1969

20 The Valentines are arrested at the Jan Juc Surf Lifesaving Club for the possession of marijuana. Having been watched for days by the Geelong police, the arrests earn the band much publicity. Speaking out in the pages of *Go Set*, the band lambast Australian society for its backwardness, with Bon Scott stating 'The Australian government deserves a few ripples. It'll be the last to legalise homosexuality, and pot will be the same.'

26 Pro-choice campaigner Dr Bertrum Wainer quits the Australian Medical Association (AMA), revealing that Victorian police have been receiving pay-offs to permit doctors to perform illegal abortions.

27 Richmond beats Carlton to win the VFL Grand Final.

27 Russell Morris becomes the latest Australian artist to seek fame and fortune in the UK.

29 Three actors from the play *The Boys in the Band* are convicted on nine charges of using obscene language in a public place, when Supreme Court Justice Little overturns an earlier decision to clear them of all charges.

29 Flinders University student Andrew Ellerman is arrested, and later spends 28 days in prison, for taking part in a raid on the Labour and National

• • • Russell Morris (Newhill)

Service Department in Adelaide, during which he and eight others poured pig's blood over desks and files.

29 Mining company Poseidon announce the discovery of a massive lode of nickel at Windarra, Western Australia, triggering a boom in resources shares. By February 1970 the value of the company will rise from $1 per share to $280, before once again crashing.

31 Federal Labor party front-bencher Jim Cairns and his wife are attacked when gatecrashers storm a party in Melbourne.

OCTOBER

- Tug boat workers bring Melbourne's shipping to a halt when they strike for 18 hours in response to Commonwealth Government threats to jail Laurie Carmichael Jr for his failure to attend a call-up for National Service.
- Cementing the band's reputation as Australia's premier blues rock outfit former Thursday's Children and latter day Wild Cherries members Barry 'Big Goose' Sullivan (Bass) and Barry 'Little Goose' Harvey (drums) take over rhythm section duties for Chain.

In 1969 Russell Morris produced the definitive Australian psychedelic hit 'The Real Thing'. The song was an immediate smash, topping the charts in many states and spawning the follow up single 'Part Three: Into Paper Walls'. Whilst Russell Morris's career was never to span these heights again, the song he is most famous for has been kept alive through consistent radio airplay, and covers by the likes of Third Eye and Midnight Oil. Paul Culnane traces how the song was discovered and transformed for Morris by maverick journalist-cum-producer Ian Meldrum.

Russell Morris with Somebody's Image (Beard)

'The Real Thing' was born with Johnny Young (born John De Jong), a fading mid-'60s pop idol who was fast becoming an important pop/rock songwriter. Ensconced in London at the peak of the psychedelic era, he worked closely with (and picked up valuable tips on songwriting from) his British-based mates The Bee Gees. Young began noodling around with a chord pattern on an acoustic guitar, and gradually evolved a melody not too far removed from that of Donovan's 'Hurdy Gurdy Man'. The song was, by Young's own account, an oblique swipe at the advertising industry inspired by the 1967 Coca-Cola advertising campaign, which declared the ubiquitous soft-drink to be 'the real thing'. Young's song started out as a skeletal, simple, plaintive ditty, which he intended to record as a Strawberry Fields-style chamber piece with acoustic guitar and a few strings. It developed into the full-blown widescreen extravaganza we know and love via the intervention of Russell Morris' manager and mentor, Ian 'Molly' Meldrum.

When he arrived back in Australia in early 1968, Young began concentrating on developing his songwriting career and finding singers for his material. 'The Real Thing' was originally earmarked for Ronnie Burns, former lead singer of The Flies, by then a major solo star. Young was playing it to Burns in the dressing room of the Channel 0 studios in Melbourne during the taping of pop show *Uptight*, when as luck would have it, Molly chanced by, heard the song and was smitten. Here was the vehicle he'd been searching for to launch the career of his young protégé – he had to have it for Russell Morris, he decided, and nothing was going to stop him. Young wasn't particularly keen, but according to legend, Molly turned up at Young's house in the early hours of the morning armed with a tape recorder and refused to leave until Young had taped a demo of the song for him.

In late 1968, Meldrum, as producer for this landmark recording, assembled a group of friends, all denizens of Melbourne's healthy and congenial rock fraternity, at Armstrong's studio, then the pre-eminent recording facility in the country. Enlisting the seasoned skills of engineer John Sayers and arranger John Farrar (former guitarist with The Strangers), Meldrum began to fashion some basic tracks. He built the musical 'bed' with The Groop's rhythm section: Brian Cadd (organ, piano), Richard Wright (drums) and Don Mudie (bass). The track was augmented with guitar embellishments from The Zoot's Roger Hicks, along with backing vocals from Russell's mate Ronnie Charles (also from The Groop), and falsettos courtesy of Maureen Elkner (who later became famous for her Bob Hudson-penned novelty hit 'Rack Off Normie'!).

Tracking began in late 1968 and continued over several months into early 1969. As the sessions progressed, Meldrum built a sound collage in his mind. The musicians could not have envisioned how their short recorded segments would eventually fit into the greater scheme of things since, as with Brian Wilson's 'Pet Sounds' and Lennon's 'Strawberry Fields Forever', 'The Real Thing' was built from composite parts. The headphone-wearing trainspotters among us might, in retrospect, be able to detect a number of edit points where the disparate song elements

The Groop (Beard)

were patched together, but it was a deftly-accomplished job of sonic juggling, much to the credit of patient engineer Sayers. Even tambourines and maracas were recorded with uncanny fastidiousness and given prominence in the lavish final mix.

And lavish is indeed the word – Molly reputedly spent far more on this one track than was usually budgeted for an entire LP at that time – over $10 000, which in 1969 was a serious amount of money! It was far and away the most expensive and complex single ever recorded to that time, setting new standards of production for Australian rock music. As a result of his profligacy, Meldrum was supposedly sacked from the project, but refused to let it go. When EMI decided to release the single only in Victoria, Meldrum personally took it to Sydney to get it played on local radio stations.

When interviewed by John Doyle on Sydney radio station 2BL several years ago, John Sayers recounted some fascinating details of this epic production. According to Sayers the basic track was laid down in only a few takes, and was intended to be much shorter than what was eventually released. The Groop and Hicks played the basic track through and then began to jam and improvise on it. The quick ears of Molly and Sayers picked up that this was sterling material, and they wisely kept the tapes rolling, exhorting the musos to 'keep going' until the take eventually broke down after about ten minutes. It was this spontaneous jam that provided the foundation for the extended 'freakout' sound collage that makes up the second half of the song.

The finished recording begins with a lovely acoustic guitar motif supplied by Roger Hicks (actually one of the last pieces added to the mix), before folding out into Russell's breathy delivery of the main refrain. As the song develops, so too do the startling sound treatments that Meldrum and Sayers had designed to bring the song into an other-worldly, epic realm.

Russell Morris (Beard)

1 Shifting his stance in response to recent polls, ALP leader Gough Whitlam promises that if elected, his government will withdraw all troops from Vietnam by June 1970.

3 Melbourne activist Phil Twomey is fined $40 for filling in two false National Service forms, before being sentenced to 14 days jail for also 'damaging a door knob' worth 50 cents.

11 Australia's last passenger steam train makes its final run between Sydney and Goulburn.

12 Even though it is never shown on air, *This Day Tonight* executive producer Bruce Buchanan is suspended by ABC management for producing a satirical segment on Chairman Mao.

13 Ross Ceaves, an Executive Officer of the Standing Committee on Technical Studies, reveals he has recently been approached by ASIO to spy on the Communist Party of Australia in return for an exemption from National Service.

18 Despite releasing a series of strong singles and gigging regularly in the UK, Procession split up after failing to crack the European market.

21 Sick of the unwillingness of Victorian unions to effectively take up women's rights as an issue, Melbourne activist Zelda D' Aprano chains herself to the doors of the Commonwealth Centre in La Trobe Street. Demanding wage parity with men, D'Aprano spends hours addressing the media before police step in with bolt cutters to remove her.

23 The Melbourne Royal Show features performances from The Zoot, Axiom, Ronnie Burns and Johnny Farnham. Adding to the pop element, *Go Set* produces a show bag featuring stickers bearing the likenesses of Doug Parkinson, Wendy Saddington, Russell Morris and The Valentines, as well as posters, records and 'Indian In-things' (beads, incense, sandalwood soaps).

25 A strong 7.5% swing to Labor in the Federal elections sees it pick up 18 seats, but the ALP is kept out of power by Democratic Labor Party preferences.

26 The *Great Happening* at the Liverpool Speedway, Sydney, features sets from the likes of Doug Parkinson In Focus, The Valentines, Mecca, The Flying Circus, The Dave Miller Set, Aesop's Fables, Mike Furber and Tamam Shud.

28 Pop artist Christo puts together his 'Wrapped Coast' installation, wrapping 2.4 km of Sydney's Little Bay in fabric for 10 weeks.

29 Brian Ross, a 22-year-old farmer from Orbost, is sentenced to two years jail for refusing to obey a call-up notice for National Service.

30 The Family Planning association of Victoria is founded to provide unbiased advice on contraception, abortion and associated health issues.

31 During a Victorian teachers' strike, Zelda D' Aprano and two

Band manager Bill Joseph helps hold the crowd back (Newhill)

The first verse has an almost pastoral feel – Morris' gentle vocal, backed only by Mudie's beautifully plunky bass, and some fluid acoustic guitar by Hicks. In the second verse, the groove unfolds, with drums added and Cadd supplying supremely mod Hammond organ; the overall sound tight and close. The spacey, raga-flavoured middle eight section opens out with an ethereal choral backing, and various Eastern embellishments such as sitar. In the third verse the sound gets much broader and heavier; Cadd switches to grand piano, with its signal heavily compressed and equalised to remove the 'bottom-end', and fed through an echo chamber, creating the tinny yet dramatic sound so popular at the time. A reprise of the middle-eight occurs and then it's off into the freakout zone.

Another unsettling effect utilised is the dual vocal in the later verses, with Morris' voice mixed to the fore and another strange, whispery vocal behind it. It's an effective trick, later used by The Doors on their classic 'Riders on the Storm'. Funnily enough, according to Sayers, the other voice was actually a guide vocal prepared by Molly to instruct Russell as to how he wanted the singing to go. Molly is by all accounts a fairly awful singer, and the tape was apparently received with some scorn. Morris sang pretty much as he pleased, but Sayers and/or Meldrum had the bright idea of keeping the guide track, and mixing it into the second verse.

Then there's the phasing. Although there had been examples of the use of 'phasing' on Aussie records before this (The Wild Cherries' 'That's Life', Cam-Pact's 'Drawing Room' and The Twilights' 'Comin' on Down'), 'The Real Thing' was the first major Australian recording to successfully employ this trick to such devastating effect.

Phasing is a recording technique in which the original sound signal is fed back upon itself with a miniscule delay, creating a swooshing, 'out-of-phase' distortion of the original signal, which sounds to the listener like his or her head is immersed in a large sea-shell. Phasing creates a lush, turbulent wash of sound, akin to the disorientating sensory effects some people have reported experiencing while under the influence of LSD or similar hallucinogens. Along with reverse tape effects, it became one of the hot studio tricks of the psychedelic era. It's also called sometimes called 'flanging' because the effect was (in those days) obtained by playing two synchronised tape recordings of the same sound source. Meldrum loved it and slapped the effect all over 'The Real Thing', which imparted an alien, tripped out feel to what, after all, had begun as a simple acoustic ballad.

Another production hallmark Meldrum employed was the massed choir effect. The vocal call-and-response arrangement that is introduced early in the piece ('I am the real – REAL!', etc.) reaches an apotheosis in the song's closing stages, which throws in everything including the

Ian Meldrum in the offices of *Go Set* magazine (Colbert)

kitchen sink. Underpinning this glorious melange is the solid and driving sound of The Groop rhythm section rocking out, embellished with insistent bleating guitar squalls and heavily processed vocal and percussive decorations (including what sounds suspiciously like a crazed Molly delivering a 'buyer beware' message to potential trippers). Another notable feature is the way the second section is punctuated by deliberate edits and 'dropouts' of various instruments, anticipating the studio explorations of dub music in the 1970s.

At the end of its heady six-plus minutes (unheard of for an Australian single then, as only the Fabs' 'Hey Jude' had previously managed to break the 3-minute constraint for airplay 45s), 'The Real Thing' ascends through a wild spiral of sound and fury. As the song concludes, the vocal chorus reaches its climactic note, which is provocatively undercut by a wartime recording of a choir of the Hitler Youth singing their anthem, the *Horst Wessel Lied*. And then – as the massed German voices shouting 'Seig Heil!' – the song simply explodes, ending with the apocalyptic sound of an atomic bomb blast!

The sequel to 'The Real Thing' maintained this production ethic, but took it to further extremes. 'Part Three: Into Paper Walls' sounded similar, but was sonically far superior, utilising as it did the rhythm section from The Groop, along with most of the other musicians featured on 'The Real Thing'. However, this track was recorded with even more punch and clarity than the first single. 'Part Three' picks up where 'The Real Thing' left off, opening with an explosion followed by a brief, heavily phased reprise of the guitar coda from 'The Real Thing'. It then moves into Russell's introspective examination of the power of bright colours, sung over a rich blend of softly phased strings and choral pleading, with freaky ghost-vocals replicating Russell's vocal parts, before unfurling into the brass-laden bravura finale. And, in a neat touch tying it all together, the song fades once more into a reprise of the gorgeous, phase-drenched acoustic guitar figure that introduced 'The Real Thing'.

As previously stated, the two Morris singles were recorded and mixed at Armstrong's Studios in South Melbourne. Both were mixed from the master multi-track tapes to mono, a common practice of the day, as AM radio play was the prime consideration (although, in this case, it might also have been necessary to achieve the full phasing effects). Therefore, sadly, no stereo mixes were ever made for the two songs. The American release of 'The Real Thing', on the Diamond label, was spread over two sides (Parts One and Two), and was emblazoned with the legend 'stereo', though it wasn't. It was issued with the appalling mono-reprocessed-for-stereo gambit peculiar to US pressings at the time. Even the so-called remix issued by EMI on 12 inch vinyl in 1990 was not, strictly-speaking, a true remix at all. Rather, it was the original tape of 'The Real

young teachers chain themselves to the doors of the Arbitration Court in a protest over women's rights. Recalling the events in her autobiography *Zelda*, D' Aprano points out that 'There was just sufficient chain to allow the door to open slightly and people had to bend down and crawl in sideways to enter the building.'

NOVEMBER

- Film director Philip Noyce is arrested for selling *Ubunews* on the streets of Sydney.
- Waterside workers refuse to unload the Vietnam supply ship *Jepparit*, after four union officials are threatened with jail for signing a 'declaration of defiance' to the National Service Act.
- Radical group Provo open the Adelaide Draft Resistance Centre at 238 Rundle Street to provide locals with an advice centre, workshop space and bookshop.
- An appeal by Aggy Read over the banning of his film *Boobs a Lot* (set to The Fugs' song of the same name) is upheld, allowing it to be shown in Victoria.
- Inspired equally by local experiments at La Mama as by

the international trends chronicled by New York's *Tulane Drama Review*, the Australian Performing Group (APG) comes together to craft their own brand of performance art. Under the auspices of the Australian Metal Workers Union (AMWU), one of the APG's first acts is to perform the radical play *The Developing Story of Mr Big* at various factories across Melbourne.

- Sydney singer Mike Furber releases 'I'm on Fire'/'Watch Me Burn', a pairing of two killer Vanda/Young compositions recently written for him in London.

1 Former Pogs member Peter Best independently releases his 'Who Said Love?' single as a protest against the banning of the Swedish film *I Love, You Love.*

4 Melbourne Cup favourite Big Philo is pulled out of the race at the last minute, delivering a huge windfall to bookies. Weeks later it is revealed that tests had shown the horse was doped.

7 PM Gorton holds onto the leadership of the Federal Liberal Party after receiving a challenge from Billy McMahon.

11 Bob Gould and Keith James of Sydney's left wing Third World bookshop are charged under obscenity laws for publishing three prints by nineteenth century artist Audrey Beardsley. Gould is eventually found guilty, but on appeal the fines are dropped and his posters returned under the provision that he keep them for 'personal use.'

Thing' with added drumbeats and studio-enhanced effects. Supported by a bizarre video clip that mixed wartime footage with original black and white inserts of a young, spot-lit Morris miming the song, this re-release had little impact and only really served as a pale reminder of the original.

The impact of 'The Real Thing' and 'Part Three: Into Paper Walls' was undoubtedly most strongly felt when the two seminal singles were first released. While their influence and stature can be measured in the terms of the remarkable new music that was surrounding them in late 1969, their effect continues to be felt even now. In 1990, Ollie Olsen's trance/electro outfit Third Eye released a lovingly recreated version of 'The Real Thing' as a single, dedicating it (fittingly) to acid guru Timothy Leary. That single was only a moderate chart success, but a recording triumph. Other, dodgier, adaptations of 'The Real Thing' later abounded. In July 1999 on variety TV show *Hey Hey It's Saturday*, Molly expressed his disdain for the quite tacky and inept use of the song in a canned fruit advert that excruciatingly mangled the main chorus. Original composer Johnny Young also did the song few favours when he unashamedly re-created it for use in a kitsch promo trailer for his pay-TV programme, *Cavalcade of Stars*.

Following the success of 'The Real Thing', Russell Morris headed to the UK, where he recorded the song 'Rachel' with former Bee Gee/Aztec Vince Melouney. Returning home to Australia, he re-entered the Top 10 with 'Mr America', before recording his seminal *Bloodstone* album. Since the early 1970s he has continued to record and tour with a variety of bands.

Molly Meldrum continued to write for *Go Set* before becoming an Australian cultural icon by hosting the TV pop show *Countdown* from 1974 to 1987.

Russell Morris and fans (Beard)

Jeff Crozier 1969

13 The New South Wales government moves to prevent doctors from prescribing amphetamines except in 'exceptional circumstances.'

21 Australian icon, bush poet and rebel author Norman Lindsay dies, aged 90.

24 The day before his official call up for National Service, draft resister Laurie Carmichael Jr disrupts the opening of Commonwealth Parliament in a bid to present an anti-war petition to the new Minister for Labour and National Service Billy Snedden.

25 A national anti-war conference held in Canberra brings together representatives from 36 groups across Australia to organise a mass protest along the lines of the recent US Moratorium.

26 *Pelican*, the paper of the Student Guild at the University of Western Australia, is charged with obscenity after it flaunts West Australian law by producing a special anti-censorship edition. Editor Alistair McKinley and printer Don Chosid are later fined $50 each, while Guild President and future Opposition Leader Kim Beazley launches an appeal fund.

27 Peter Clifton's pioneering surf movie *Fluid Journey* opens in Australia. Described by Clifton

• • • Jeff Crozier (Newhill)

as a 'surf, drugs and rock 'n' roll' film, it features 'a band of young Australians in the last summer of the 1960s who follow the waves and sounds of rock 'n' roll to Hawaii and California.' Starring various Australian surfers, the film utilises psychedelic effects such as solarisation, pixilation, coloured lights and oils.

29 The last of the standard-gauge railway line is completed between Port Pirie and Broken Hill, allowing freight trains and the Indian-Pacific passenger train to travel continuously between Sydney and Perth.

DECEMBER

- The Fire Brigade is called out to Melbourne's La Trobe University after locals mistake plumes billowing from visiting Sydney light show master Ellis D. Fogg's smoke machine for a full blown fire.
- Sydney's Greek Theatre is reopened as the Mandala Theatre by Tully and The Nutwood Rug Band.

10 Police halt the outdoor Amco pop show at the Myer Music Bowl for a half hour while they arrest and bash young drinkers amongst the 40 000 strong crowd. During the fracas a teenage girl is run over by a police vehicle.

Illusionist Jeff Crozier remains one of the most enigmatic and bizarre characters to ever grace the Australian stage. Fascinated by magic from a young age, he graduated from set painting to live performance after winning an episode of the *New Faces* talent show in 1969. Plugging into the experimental side of Melbourne's rock scene, Crozier put together The Magic Word and, combining tricks, poetry and lighting effects, created an arresting live show. With band in tow he was soon performing at Melbourne venues such as Traffik and the Thumpin' Tum as well as appearing on television and running his own season of shows at Fitzroy's Cathedral Hall. Magic Word guitarist Duncan Fry recalls how he met Crozier, and some of the adventures that followed.

Jeff Crozier and members of the Indian Medicine Magik Show (Newhill)

In 1969 or thereabouts I answered an ad in *Go Set* magazine along the lines of 'musicians wanted for sensational new act'. The previous band I was in had imploded and I was looking around for something to do. So I went along to the audition, not really expecting much.

The auditions were held in a rambling guesthouse in Hawthorn, run by Jeff's parents, on a huge block leading down to the river. Jeff lived in a large subterranean closet underneath the house that was jammed to the roof with magic tricks and props. There was barely enough room for three people to stand, let alone set up drums and guitar amps. Various musicians turned up all through the afternoon; some took one look and left immediately, some played a few notes and then left and some just stood and stared as Jeff whirled around doing magic tricks.

What Jeff wanted was free-form continuous music for the 30 minutes or so that he performed, while clouds of oily smoke, flashpots, and strobe lights would alternately choke and dazzle the audience. Most of the musicians who turned up for the audition couldn't handle such a laissez-faire attitude to the musical side of things.

'But what songs are we going to play?' they would whine. 'No songs, just play, play,' Jeff would reply, setting off another flashpot.

By a process of attrition the band was whittled down to me, a bass player called Cal, and a drummer called Tom. We just banged around on various chords for a while in a no holds barred continuous solo reminiscent of the final chaos of *My Generation*. Tuneful it wasn't, but I think it had just the right amount of anarchy for Jeff, and by having no fixed form, it could be stretched out or shortened as required.

So that was it. We called ourselves The Magic Word, although that was a bit risqué for some dance promoters and on some occasions we were billed as The Magic Pudding. Who would have thought promoters, an avaricious breed who would sell tickets to their grandmother's cremation if they thought they'd get away with it, could be so precious?

Every week we worked the Melbourne dance circuit, although just what audiences made of the whole thing I don't know. The shows always ended in absolute chaos – things would fall over, unintentional sparks would fly from electrical bits and pieces, while sometimes the smoke machine refused to smoke and just squirted hot oil over everything and everyone. Pity the act that came on after us!

Jeff Crozier (Porter)

Jeff's daytime job was as a set painter at Channel 9, so with his connections there we did quite a few TV performances. At first they were live, but the production people had a hard time coping with the lack of a fixed, rehearsable format, so later TV appearances were mimed to a couple of tracks we put down in their recording studio.

Many people, I'm sure, thought Jeff was as mad as a cut snake, and it's true, he did occasionally appear to have a tenuous grip on reality, but he was a hell of a nice guy to work for. I never once saw him crack the shits with anybody, apart from the occasional promoter who richly deserved it, and he never had a bad word to say about anybody.

He was also a shit hot magician and very well respected by his peers in the magic biz. One night after a gig we were having a bite to eat at Leo's Spaghetti Bar in St Kilda, when he bumped into a fellow magician. Well, fair dinkum, the two of them had the whole restaurant entranced as they did endless close-up magic tricks involving coins, spoons, knives and forks,

Jeff Crozier and bassist Phil Stone (Newhill)

12 Anti-conscription activists are attacked by locals in Sale when they travel there to protest the imprisonment of Brian Ross for draft resistance.

15 Delegates from 27 unions, supported by 200 Victorian shop stewards, issue a statement urging Australian soldiers in Vietnam to lay down their arms.

15 Having formed earlier in the year, Sydney's Women's Liberation collective makes its first public stand, marching as part of a 3000 strong anti-war mobilisation in the central city. Within months similar feminist organisations pop up in Melbourne, Adelaide, Canberra, Newcastle and Brisbane. Drawn largely from the anti-war movement, these groups confront male dominance within both the Left and wider society.

16 PM Gorton announces that Australia will begin to withdraw troops from Vietnam in the near future.

19 The management of the Paddington Town Hall allows Ubu to return to the venue for its *Living Lightshow* featuring The Nutwood Rug Band and Plastic Tears.

21 Vice-squad police raid the La Mama theatre during a performance of John Romeril's *Whatever Happened To Realism*, arresting nine people and charging them with using obscene language. In response to the arrests the 150 strong audience heckle the police chanting with the offending words 'Shitcuntfartbuggeroffwillya!'

23 The King of Television, Graham Kennedy, retires, but not for the last time, as it turns out.

27 The Valentines are greeted by 4000 fans at Perth Airport when they arrive home to play a 6KY New Years Concert.

Iain McIntyre

Jeff Crozier (Newhill)

plus the inevitable pack of cards. Just as guitarists always seem to have a plectrum in their pocket, so do magicians always have a pack of cards about their person.

Like all good things, it eventually came to an end. They say you can't stand too close to genius without getting burned, and I was certainly feeling its heat. Playing in the band seemed to be costing me much more money than I was earning from it (some things in the music biz never change), and the amount of stage equipment and sets we were carting around was getting out of hand. I'd also had my prized Rickenbacker 360 12 string guitar stolen during one of the TV appearances. It was a rare early export model with 'F' holes instead of the curved dagger ones – absolutely priceless today. Think early Who or George Harrison. I replaced it with the cheapest Fender Telecaster copy I could afford – nick-named the 'East Doncaster' – and was a bit pissed off over the whole deal.

So one day I told him I was leaving just to get my brain back in some kind of order. He shook my hand, we parted on amicable terms, and I never saw him again. I'd follow his career from time to time, and see his name on posters with The Indian Medicine Magik Show, and then the business of getting on with my life took over.

When I read of his death in 1981 I felt just as sad as I did when Jimi Hendrix died. A great talent had suddenly passed. But hey, although I don't think in his wildest dreams Jeff would have expected to be compared to Hendrix, at least people are still talking about him and his influence on the face of Australian live music. Can't really ask for more than that, can you?

In 1970 The Magic Word was replaced by The Indian Medicine Magik Show. Managed by 'hip' booking agency Let It Be, Crozier maintained a steady pace of live performances, regularly appearing at the TF Much Ballroom as well as outdoor rock festivals. Problems with local authorities and conservative promoters, over issues such as the potential fire hazard posed by his pyrotechnic effects, saw bookings dwindle, prompting a move to the US in 1973. Over the coming years, Crozier would build an international reputation for the innovative and bizarre, before his untimely death (while practicing a self-hanging illusion) in 1981.

Part Five
1970

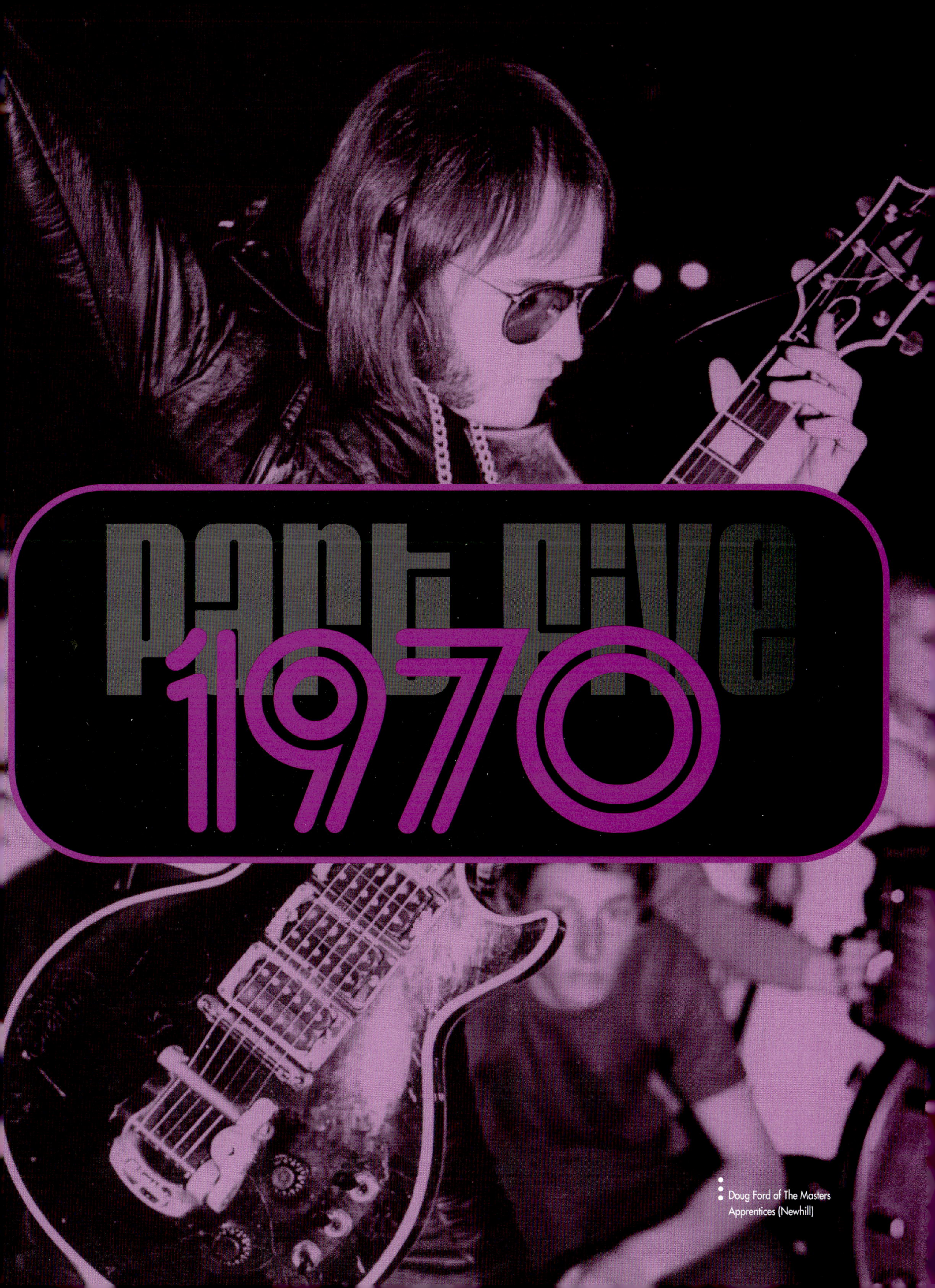

Doug Ford of The Masters Apprentices (Newhill)

1970 MUSIC

WORLD

- President Nixon admits that the US military has invaded Cambodia and carpet-bombed Laos.
- Four students are killed at Kent State University and two at Jackson State University during anti-war protests in the US.
- Jordan expels PLO guerillas after they hi-jack and destroy four airliners.
- British troops battle the Irish Republican Army (IRA) and other guerilla groups in Belfast.
- The Soviet Union lands an unmanned spacecraft on Venus.
- *Oz* magazine releases its infamous *Schoolkids* edition, leading to one of the longest obscenity trials in British history.
- Tonga (4 June) and Fiji (10 October) gain independence from Britain.
- Rhodesia severs its last ties with the British Crown to declare itself a racially segregated republic.
- Jimi Hendrix and Janis Joplin die in separate drug related incidents.
- The first International Earth Day is launched in New York, with more than 100 000 people attending an ecology fair in Central Park.

Billy Thorpe and The Aztecs (Porter)

A new decade dawns . . .

The beginning of the 1970s was an age of questioning. It was a time of spiritual quests, of God-Rock stage musicals, Krishna freaks and odes to Meher Baba. It was a time to lose your clothes and 'get it together in the country'; of anti-Vietnam War moratoriums that would see previously taciturn Australians taking it to the streets in massive numbers. Indeed, one of the finest Australian pop singles of the 1970 was an anti-Vietnam song written by Johnny Young and inspired by former pop star, now conscripted soldier, Normie Rowe. 'Smiley', by Ronnie Burns, was a personal rather than political statement. It didn't mention death or dismemberment, merely disillusionment and the loss of innocence. It said a lot about what was happening in Australia.

The TF Much Ballroom crowd (Porter)

1970 was also the year that radio stations decided that big record companies should pay them a royalty for the privilege of having their records played on air. When record companies (such as EMI and RCA) retorted with the resounding 'up yours', the radio stations stopped playing their records on air, particularly by British bands. This infamous stand off became known as the 'radio ban'. Radio stations stopped compiling their charts and the commercial pop world was temporarily plunged into chaos. But within every problem there lies an opportunity, and no one was more able to capitalise on this strange stalemate than Melbourne record label boss Ron Tudor and his fledgling Fable label and Martin Erdman in Sydney with Du Monde. Thanks to the radio ban (which lasted for six months), local artists on Fable and Du Monde got to issue their own cover versions of British hits that were often as good as the originals – and they *sold*. It was a good time for original artists on these labels too.

But for the real rock fan in 1970, a new form of vinyl currency had taken effect – the *album*. With bands such as Tamam Shud, Tully, Kahvas Jute and Spectrum now performing elongated musical pieces in smoke-hazed venues such as the TF Much Ballroom in Melbourne or Paddington Town Hall in Sydney, the humble 45 rpm single was simply not going to cut it any more. Some radio stations even began to air programs late at night that focused exclusively on LP tracks. And for the first time in Australian pop history, comprehensive album charts were being compiled.

New publications emerged to cater for this new generation of serious music fan. *Revolution*, *Daily Planet* and *Sound Blast* tended not to include glossy pin up shots of pop acts like New Dream, The Town Criers and Johnny Farnham, but instead featured 'heavy' bands, who seemed to sport enough facial hair to provide an eco-system for entire species of small mammals. Even TV personalities such as Bert Newton and Graham Kennedy were now wearing paisley ties, blow-waving their hair and growing fuzzy mutton-chop sideburns. Fortunately they kept their clothes on.

International Album Releases

Syd Barrett – *The Madcap Laughs*
The Doors – *Morrison Hotel*
Simon and Garfunkel – *Bridge Over Troubled Water*
Jimi Hendrix – *Band of Gypsys*

AUSTRALIAN EVENTS

- An explosion of strikes, demonstrations and occupations hit Australian cities as unions, anti-war and anti-racist protestors embrace militant tactics unseen since the 1930s.
- Western Australia and New South Wales lower the voting age to 18.
- Australian academic Germaine Greer's groundbreaking treatise *The Female Eunuch* is published. A controversial figure, Greer is lambasted in the mainstream media as a 'man hater', and derided by radical feminists for supporting individual defiance over collective action.
- Exhibitions held at the National Gallery of Victoria include *Lloyd Rees Retrospective, Paradise Garden* (*Sidney Nolan*) and *Recent British Painting.*
- Former Surfing World writers John Witzig and Alby Fanzon begin publishing *Tracks* magazine. Appealing to the growing demographic of 'soul surfers', *Tracks* features articles on environmentalism, drugs, spirituality and macrobiotics.
- Tim Burstall's *Getting Back to Nothing* becomes the first surf film to be shown at the Sydney Film Festival.
- Following the success of his *A Salute to the Great McCarthy*, Melbourne writer Barry Oakley's *Let's Hear it for Prendergrast* is published by William Heinemann

Australia. Satirising the Carlton radical arts scene, the novel details a young hippy's campaign against the bourgeois values of the suburban 'Glen Waverly Man.'

- Anti-war protestors confront Defence Minister Andrew Peacock with banners reading 'Thou Shalt Not Kill Vietnamese' as he leaves the Sunday service at St Silas's Church in North Balwyn.
- The Sydney Women's Liberation Centre is opened at 67 Glebe Point Road.
- Vice Chancellor Sir Zelman Cowen steps in to prevent the University of Queensland from publishing Frank Moorhouse's *It's the Americans Baby* on the grounds of supposed obscenity.
- New Australian television productions include *The Long Arm* (ATV-0), *Phoenix Five* (ABC), *Dynasty* (ABC), *Mrs Finnegan* (ATN-7) and *The Link Men* (TCN-9).

JANUARY

- Students at the University of NSW (UNSW) defoliate trees in the Commerce Quadrangle to illustrate the effect of herbicides in Vietnam.
- La Mama hosts a Season of Experimental music featuring works from Barry McKimm, Robert Rooney and Jean-Charles François.
- Having added young hotshot guitarist Rick Springfield to their line up, The Zoot ditch their pink suits and pop songs in favour of a harder, more contemporary rock sound, churning out

Van Morrison – *Moondance*
Eric Burdon & War – *Eric Burdon Declares War*
Crosby, Stills, Nash & Young – *Deja Vu*
Joni Mitchell – *Ladies of the Canyon*
Randy Newman – *12 Songs*
The Beatles – *Let It Be*
Deep Purple – *In Rock*
Free – *Fire & Water*
Traffic – *John Barleycorn Must Die*
Humble Pie – *Humble Pie*
Yes – *Time and a Word*
Neil Young – *After the Gold Rush*
Can – *Monster Movie*
The Grateful Dead – *Workingman's Dead*
Black Sabbath – *Paranoid*
The Byrds – *(Untitled)*
James Brown – *Sex Machine*
Joe Cocker – *Mad Dogs & Englishmen*
Led Zeppelin – *Led Zeppelin III*
John Lennon – *Imagine*
Santana – *Abraxas*
Derek and the Dominoes – *Layla and Other Assorted Love Songs*
George Harrison – *All Things Must Pass*
The Kinks – *Lola Versus Powerman and the Moneygoround Vol. 1*

The Charts

Melbourne

The first #1 hit in Melbourne for the 1970s was the Johnny Young penned 'I Thank You', performed by boxer Lionel Rose. 'I Thank You' held top spot for the first eight weeks of the year, before eventually being knocked off by Led Zeppelin's 'Whole Lotta Love'. The only other Australian composition to top the Melbourne charts in 1970 was 'New Faces' winner John Williamson's novelty song 'Old Man Emu' in August.

The Beatles' 'Let It Be' was the biggest hit of the year, with 3 weeks at #1 and an amazing 29 weeks in the charts. Second was the similarly hymn-like 'Bridge Over Troubled Water' by Simon and Garfunkel (highest pos. #4; 29 weeks in). Other biggies included 'Close to You' by The Carpenters (#1 for nine weeks; 28 weeks in) and 'The Wonder of You' by Elvis Presley (highest pos. #3; 23 weeks in – this was Elvis' 66th Melbourne chart hit in only 15 years).

The radio ban was well in evidence among the top ten biggest hits of the year, as no less than three of the top seven singles for 1970 were Australian covers of British songs on Ron Tudor's Fable label. 'In the Summertime' by The Mixtures (original by Mungo Jerry), #1 for four weeks, 30 weeks in; 'Yellow River' by Jigsaw (original by Christie), highest pos. #2, 27 weeks in; and the Eurovision runner-up tune 'Knock Knock Who's There' by Liv Maessen (original by Mary Hopkin), highest pos. #3, 27 weeks in.

Some cool overseas tracks to top the Melbourne charts included 'Venus' by Shocking Blue (highest pos. #1, 19 weeks in) and 'Spirit in the Sky' by Norman Greenbaum (#1 for four weeks, 19 weeks in). Creedence Clearwater Revival had a fine run of three big hits: 'Travelling Band'/ 'Who'll Stop the Rain' (highest pos. #4); 'Up Around the Bend' (#1 for four weeks) and 'Lookin' Out My Back Door' (#2). The Beach Boys had their first Melbourne #1 in July, with their cover of Leadbelly's 'Cottonfields'. The final #1 hit for 1970 was 'I Think I Love You' by The Partridge Family, which remained at the top spot for five weeks, and would eventually stay in the charts for 32 weeks.

Some big Australian-made singles included 'A Little Ray of Sunshine' by Axiom (#2), 'Boom Sha La La Lo' by Hans Poulsen (#8), 'Turn Up Your Radio' by The Masters Apprentices (#2) and 'Smiley' by Ronnie Burns (#3).

Sydney

Roy Orbison's 'Penny Arcade' was the first #1 for the 1970s in Sydney. It was eventually usurped by Johnny Farnham's (shared with B.J. Thomas) 'Raindrops Keep Falling on my Head' (#1 for four weeks, 23 weeks in). The only Australian composition to reach #1 was 'Smiley' by Ronnie Burns, which stayed in the charts for a very respectable 20 weeks.

As in Melbourne, 'Bridge Over Troubled Water' and 'Let it Be' were the two biggest hits for the year. Some Sydney chart-toppers that didn't achieve the same feat in Melbourne included 'Sascha' by Hank B. Marvin (#1 for three weeks during March);' 'He Ain't Heavy He's My Brother' by The Hollies (February); 'Spill the Wine' by Eric Burdon's War (November); and 'Love Grows (Where My Rosemary Goes)' (April) by Edison Lightshow. 'Yellow River' hit the top spot for four weeks over October–November, but interestingly, the original by English band Christie was never even listed on the charts – the Sydney radio surveys instead listed Melbourne band Jigsaw alongside Sydney's own Autumn.

Local band Flake had a sizeable hit with Bob Dylan's 'This Wheel's on Fire' (highest pos. #4, 22 weeks in), but apart from that, no major Australian-made hits were particularly unique to the Sydney charts. Adelaide and Brisbane, too, were remarkably in line with Melbourne and Sydney during 1970.

The 1970 *Go Set* Pop Poll Winners (as voted by the readers of *Go Set*)

Male Vocal:	1969	1968
Johnny Farnham: Gold	1st	2nd
Russell Morris: Silver	2nd	1st
Ronnie Burns: Bronze	3rd	3rd

Female Vocal:	1969	1968
Allison Durbin: Gold	1st	–
Wendy Saddington: Silver	4th	–
Colleen Hewett: Bronze	–	–

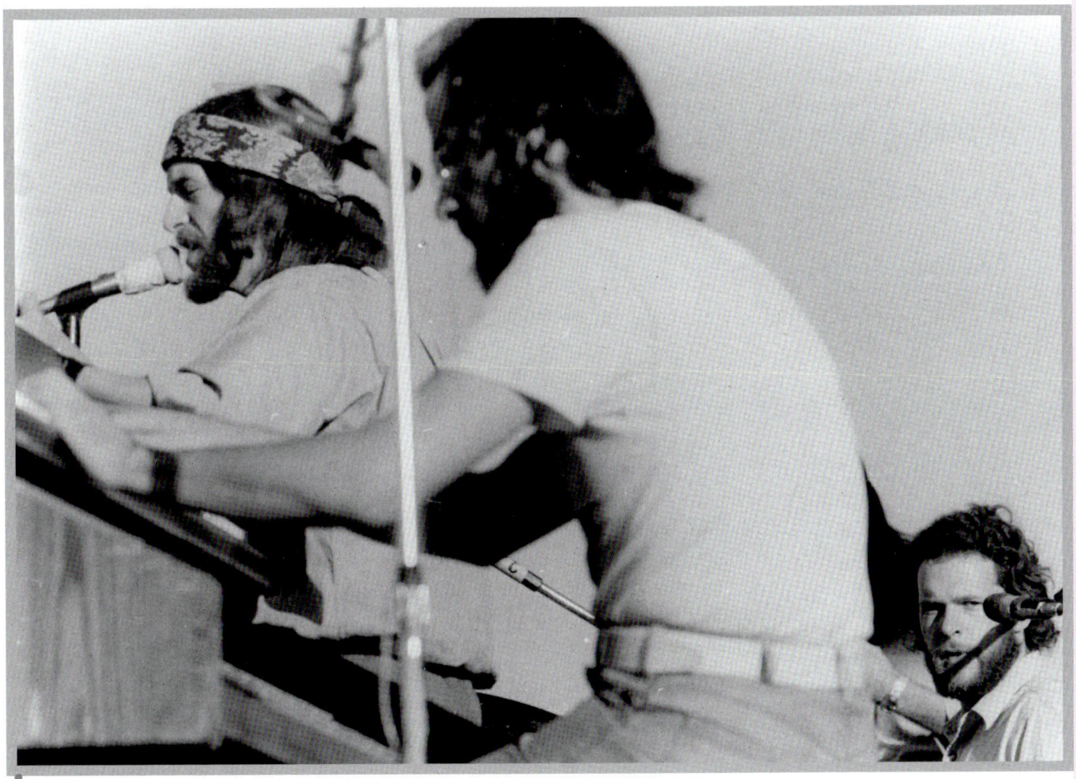

Spectrum in the great outdoors (Porter)

'heavy' versions of such classics as 'Eleanor Rigby'.

- Tired of mismanagement at the hands of Daryl Sambell, The Masters Apprentices set up their own DRUM booking agency in an old terrace house in Drummond Street, Carlton.

5 The Aboriginal and Islanders Council in Queensland demands the state government stop removing activists from Palm Island and hand over control of the area to Indigenous residents.

5 Hippy squatters are given five days to vacate camping spots on Fitzroy Island.

5 A Victorian inquiry into the state's abortion rackets begins. In the coming weeks witnesses reveal that doctors have been paying $1000s to police, including the former chief of the Homicide Squad, Superintendent Jack Matthews.

9 Auditions for the controversial play *Oh! Calcutta* are halted when the owners of Melbourne's Phillip Theatre, a Roman Catholic sect known as the Knights of the Southern Cross, discover that the play contains nudity and swear words.

9 Julie Ingleby is separated from her children and jailed for contempt, after protesting in the City Court against the sentencing of her husband for holding a placard reading 'Fuck the Draft – Not the Vietnamese.' Sentenced to three days of 'mending socks' at Fairlea Prison, Ms Ingleby learns that in addition to her prison stay, she has also been sacked by the Education Department.

In a separate case also heard at the City Court, three ministers of religion claim that a mock crucifixion held on Christmas Eve was not offensive, and indeed may have prompted parishioners 'to ponder the true meaning of Christmas.' Regardless of this interpretation, the Court fines two men $50 for offensive behaviour in displaying placards reading 'Born at Christmas, Killed in Vietnam.'

10 During a protest against the Queensland Government, Pastor Douglas Brady sets alight and throws into the gutter a copy of the repressive *Aboriginal and Torres Islander Act*.

12 Police reveal they are baffled as to how a recent intruder got past a police guard and a seven foot 'man-proof' fence to throw a bluish-brown substance into the Prime Minister's swimming pool in Canberra.

14 Five are arrested during a Canberra demonstration against visiting US Vice President Spiro Agnew.

17 Cyclone Ada rips through the Great Barrier Reef, killing 13 and causing millions of dollars damage to holiday homes.

17 The *Age* reports that police have been regularly stopping and searching trucks for amphetamines hidden in magnetic containers and stashed in hollow bolts.

19 Magician Jeff Crozier opens his own show at Fitzroy's Cathedral Hall, featuring an Ellis D. Fogg light show, the pop band Cast, members of the Australian Society of Magicians and

Australian Groups:	1969	1968
The Masters Apprentices: Gold	2nd	2nd
Axiom: Silver	–	–
New Dream: Bronze	4th	–

1970 Hoadley's Battle of the Sounds Winners

Flying Circus: Gold
The Zoot: Silver
Autumn: Bronze

The Sonic Landscape

The biggest Australian advances in sound technology during 1970 were being made, not so much for the recording studios, but for the massive outdoor music festivals that were beginning to happen in Australia. Starting with the *Pilgrimage for Pop* festival in Ourimbah New South Wales, and eventually culminating in the legendary *Sunbury Pop Festivals* of 1972–75, concert production companies, such as Jands in Sydney, were forced to keep up with the ever-expanding wattage required to put such monster shows on the road. This explosion in skyscraper-like PA stacks, multi-channelled mixing desks, sub-mixing facilities and hitherto unheard of foldback monitors (i.e. onstage speakers that allowed musicians and vocalists to hear themselves and each other while performing) would change forever the sound quality a punter could expect to hear in a live setting. It also helped improve the quality of live recordings – a medium that would become all the more important as the decade progressed.

Instrumentally, the most radical new sound to emerge for Australian bands was the Moog synthesiser. Named after its creator Robert Moog, the monophonic (i.e. only one note could be played at a time) keyboard instrument was first used in Australia by Tully. So integral was the Moog synth to Tully's sound and image that the band would even be billed as Tully and The Moog on gig posters.

1970 Top 10 Psychedelic Pselections

Title – Artist	Status (release date)	Label: Cat. No
1. 'You Realise You Realise' – Tully	**LP Track (July)**	**Columbia: SCXO-7926**

Robert Taylor and Richard Lockwood of Tully (*Go Set*)

Tully have been described as the Australian equivalent to Pink Floyd, and one listen to the superbly spacey 'You Realise You Realise' from their self-titled debut album reveals that they certainly resided within a similar head-space. Genuinely trippy and more than a little bit spooky – particularly in its weird rushy bits that sound like ghosts coming back from beyond to claim back their souls. Or maybe that's just me.

Tully boasted a degree of musical prowess that other bands could only sit back and envy, and 'You Realise You Realise' represents a perfect bridge between the psychedelic sounds of the '60s and the headier, more sophisticated progressive sound of the early 1970s. This was a new frontier of Australian music, and as far away from the 'suck more piss' attitude as you could possibly get.

Killer Moment: 01.15 and 04.38, *those ghosts want their souls back.*

2. **'The Garden Party' – Sons of the Vegetal Mother**
EP (November) **Custom Pressing: MP-465**

This well-recorded stereo EP was given away by Sons of the Vegetal Mother at a multimedia event/art exhibition/happening organised by artist Warren Knight, and was never commercially released. Sons of the Vegetal Mother consisted of the four chaps who would soon become Daddy Cool – Ross Wilson, Ross Hannaford, Gary Young and Wayne Duncan – plus Spectrum king-pin Mike Rudd, keyboardist Trevor Griffin and a brass section containing saxophonist Jerry Noone (who would also later become a member of Daddy Cool).

On one side of the record there's the delicate instrumental 'The Garden Party' and the fractured Frank Zappa-esque 'Make it Begin'. But it's the eight minutes plus 'Love is the Law' on the other side that makes the trip truly worthwhile. A medium-paced hypnotic piece, 'Love is the Law' (based on the Aleister Crowley dictum: 'Do what thou wilt shall be the whole of the law') consists of a joyous chant interspersed with some spiky guitar/saxophone interjections that then branches off into a free-flowing instrumental jam that manages to take you somewhere else without you even noticing it. Daddy Cool would later revisit this style on their 1972 masterpiece 'Make Your Stash'.

Gary Young of The Sons of the Vegetal Mother and Daddy Cool (Porter)

Killer Moment: 05.40, *Ross Hannaford's guitar in one speaker, Mike Rudd's guitar the other, with both trading snaky finger-picking licks. Transcendental bliss.*

3. **'Naturally' – Alison Gros** **Single (June)** **Gamba: GA-1**

If you were to listen to this track and suspect that the harmonies and musicianship sounded just a little too good to belong to some Adelaide band that no one's ever heard of, then you'd be right. The personnel of Alison Gros – namely Messrs John Mower, Graham Goble and Russ Johnson – went on to become Mississippi (and also Drummond, who had a big hit with the Chipmunky 'Daddy Cool' – but that's another story). Mississippi had great success with their harmony-laden 1972 hit 'Kings of the World', and Graham Goble eventually became a major creative force behind The Little River Band.

'Naturally' is a sunny melodic number featuring some outstanding sitar playing and sparkling harmonies. Its breezy wide-eyed optimism certainly keeps one foot firmly back in the '60s. The single peaked at #2 on the Adelaide charts, made #4 in Brisbane, but did zip everywhere else.

Killer Moment: 01.21, *Best sitar solo EVER.*

4. **'Goolutionites Theme Parts 1 and 2' – Tamam Shud** **LP Tracks (October)** **Warner Bros: WS-20001**

The centrepiece to Tamam Shud's concept suite *Goolutionites and The Real People*, 'Goolutionites Theme' features only clean electric guitars, bass and vocals – and it is this simplicity in arrangement that makes the track so powerful. With an intense haunting melody and passionate lyrics about the preservation of nature and the evil of greed, 'Goolutionites Theme' uses atmospheric vocal reverbs to devastating effect. Singer-songwriter Lindsay Bjerre told Ian McFarlane in *Freedom Train* magazine that the track was all about LSD: 'That's why the music's all pretty and then turns ugly. That's an acid trip turning bad'.

cameos from the likes of Wendy Saddington.

24 Ronnie Burns leaves Melbourne to record in the UK with The Bee Gees' Barry Gibb.

25 Australia's first major outdoor rock festival, The Ourimbah Pop Pilgrimage, is held in New South Wales. Organised by US expatriates The Nutwood Rug Band and MCed by Adrian Rawlins, the event draws 11 000 to hear music from Chain, Doug Parkinson In Focus, Billy Thorpe and The Aztecs, Max Merritt and The Meteors, Tully, Wendy Saddington, Stevie Wright, Copperwine and Leo De Castro and Friends. Over the long weekend an impromptu group called If perform The Who's 'Tommy', Heart 'n' Soul perform 'Thus Spake Zarathutsra' and a hybrid Meteors/Aztecs big band pump out the blues.

27 Melbourne's Lord Mayor presents Aboriginal boxing champion Lionel Rose with a Gold Record for his Johnny Young composed country pop smash 'I Thank You'.

FEBRUARY

- Having confronted the public with guerilla theatre in the streets, schools and parks of Melbourne, the APG hits the Perth festival, performing works by Melbourne playwrights Jack Hibberd, John Romeril and Alex Buzo.
- The La De Das become the latest in a long line of Australian bands to return from the UK empty handed. Lacking a manager, the

band had struggled to find gigs, and after a proposed American tour fell through are left with little option but to borrow money and return home.

- Mid 1960s pop hopeful Marty Rhone is conscripted into the Army, where he spends the next two years playing flute in the military band at Duntroon Academy.
- The Victorian country town of Deniliquin hosts a *Love-In* concert, drawing 400 to see local act The Young Generation.
- The Masters Apprentices release their second album, *Masterpiece.*

14 Former Melbourne psych-pop act Cam-Pact reform as a blues band.

14 The premiere of Peter Sculthorpe's *Love 200*, by Tully and the Sydney Symphony Orchestra, at the Sydney Proms ends in chaos when Ellis D. Fogg's light show and smoke machine scatter concert goers.

15 Adopting long hair and a psychedelic makeover, harmony pop group The Executives change their name to Inner Sense. Signing to Buddah Records in the US, the band prepare to leave Sydney for Los Angeles.

16 Protesting against state support for private schools, members of the Defence Of Government Schools (DOGS) group disrupt the opening of the Waverly Christian Brothers College in New South Wales.

20 Premier Sydney acid rock band Tully play their first Melbourne show at the Dallas Brooks Hall.

5. 'H.M.S. Buffalo'/'Morning Sun' – Inside Looking Out — **A/B Side (January)** — **Festival: FK-3468**

Obscure Adelaide band Inside Looking Out managed to score a minor hit (#33) in their home town in 1970 with the odd 'H.M.S. Buffalo'. Alternating between atmospheric lilting passages (imagine you're drifting along in the ocean, the waves lapping at your side) and an upbeat section, it features some weird sounding organ and a vocalist who is clearly singing out of his natural register. The band's cover of The Spencer Davis Group album track 'Morning Sun' on the other side is a lot more pleasing to the ear, with the lead guitar particularly raw and shredded.
Killer Moment ('H.M.S. Buffalo'): 01.24, *everything suddenly* stops.

6. 'Start of A New Day' – Ray Brown and Moonstone — **LP Track (October)** — **Festival: SFL-933958**

It's almost impossible to believe that the guy responsible for this tripped out hunk of plastic is the same Ray Brown who made records like 'Fool Fool Fool', 'Pride' and '20 Miles' only five years earlier. 'Start of a New Day' is Brown and his, post American sojourn, band Moonstone, and it's a bizarre blend of country music with sitars and tablas jamming away in the background. It's one of those 'yearning for meaning' type of songs typical of the era (sample lyric: *'Give us a helping hand/ Don't put us down/ Give us a reason for life . . .'*). Despite the seemingly odd mish-mash of conflicting styles, this track actually works. Sort of.

Several tracks from Moonstone's *Madhouse* LP could have been included here, such as 'Story of Ali', 'Mr Blue' – or the completely wigged out 'Flight of the Gulls', which contains all sorts whacko psychedelic effects, including seagull sounds done with backwards feedback.
Killer Moment: 02.37, *the tandoori noodling starts to get ridiculously out of hand.*

7. 'Satan'/'Satan's Woman' – Freshwater — **A/B Side (May)** — **Caesar's Palace: CP-001**

Highly controversial double-sided 'mini-suite' by the Sydney band Freshwater, who were managed by John Jennings, owner of the Caesar's Palace discotheque and founder of the record label of the same name. 'Satan' is a lyrically explicit track written by organist Peter Sheehan about the Manson murders: *'Satan said, you must die Sharon Tate!/ Come with me little girl, lay down your sexy body on my big brass bed . . .'* Intense stuff indeed.

With Peter Sheehan's piping-hot Hammond organ simmering over a funky backing and vocalist Ian Johnson providing plenty of wavering Arthur Brown style wails, 'Satan' is a unique slice of bizarro psychedelic funk. In 1990, oddball goth band Box The Jesuit included a cover version of 'Satan' on the Black Eye label's various artists album *Waste Sausage*. The B-side, 'Satan's Woman', penned by guitarist Murray Partridge, is more of the same plus a few more dramatic musical interludes than the A-side. Despite (or because of) calls from outraged Christians to ban the single, 'Satan' made #24 on the Sydney charts.
Killer Moment ('Satan'): 03.04, *that final emphatic,* 'DIE!!!' *Time to take a chill pill I reckon.*

8. 'Crimson Ships' – Sherbet — **Single (March)** — **Festival: FK-3286**

These days the name Sherbet conjures up images of satin bomber jackets, flares and a bare-chested Daryl Braithwaite wielding half a mike-stand over the *Countdown* studio audience. However back in the late-'60s/early-'70s, Sherbet were a different band altogether – both musically and personnel-wise. There was no Daryl Braithwaite yet – the lead singer was a guy called Dennis Laughlin – and journeyman Sam See was behind the keyboards, before his place was taken by Garth Porter. The only two members familiar to most Sherbet fans would be guitarist Clive Shakespeare and drummer Alan Sandow.

Sherbet's debut single was a Badfinger cover entitled 'Crimson Ships', and it is a very British-sounding psychedelic record with fluttery drum fills, Bach-like organ lines, gimmicky handclaps and some bitey guitar playing.

9. 'In a Year or So'/'Two Faced Woman' – Glassweb — **A/B Side (December)** — **Nationwide: NSP-010**

'In a Year or So' and 'Two Faced Woman' are two raw garagey '60s punk tracks, which – if it wasn't for the wah-wah guitar – you'd swear had been made in about 1966 at the very *latest*. Glassweb were either five years behind the times or else really early in anticipating the '60s revival of the mid-1980s. Either way, this is a very cool record.

10. 'Somebody to Love' – The Velvet Underground | **Single (January)** | **Festival: FK-3466**

Cover of the Darby Slick/Jefferson Airplane classic by a Newcastle band, who were apparently unaware of the New York group also called The Velvet Underground. 'Somebody To Love' begins promisingly enough with some howling feedback and squelchy wah-wah guitar, but it soon becomes a fairly stock-standard affair – until right near the very end when the band starts chanting *'Love! Love! Love!'* under lots of reverb and echo. Oh, and speaking of Love, the B-side of this single is cover of Arthur Lee's 'She Comes in Colours', but the less said about that the better.

Two members of this band – drummer Herman Kovacs and guitarist Les Hall – later joined The Ted Mulry Gang. Interestingly enough, Malcolm Young was briefly a member of The Velvet Underground as well, before he left to form a subtle li'l combo called AC/DC. And AC/DC's first national tour in 1974 was as support act to Lou Reed – founding member of the original Velvet Underground.

Choice Australian Albums of 1970

Artist	Title	Label: Cat. No
1. Tamam Shud	*Goolutionites and The Real People*	Warner Bros: WS-20001
2. Axiom	*Fool's Gold*	Parlophone: PSCO-7561
3. Tully	*Tully*	Columbia: SCXO-7926
4. Chain	*Live Chain*	Festival: SFL-933926
5. The Zoot	*Just Zoot*	Columbia: SCXO-7916
6. Doug Ashdown	*The Age of Mouse*	Sweet Peach: SP-12001
7. Jeff St John's Copperwine	*Joint Effort*	Spin: SEL-933742
8. Ray Brown and Moonstone	*Madhouse*	Festival: SFL-933958
9. Dave Miller/Leith Corbett and Friends	*Reflections of a Pioneer*	Spin: SEL-934008
10. Flying Circus	*Prepared in Peace*	Columbia: SCXO-7925
11. Hans Poulsen	*Natural High*	Fable: FBS-A-004
12. Levi Smith's Clefs	*Empty Monkey*	Sweet Peach: SPB-504

Ian D. Marks

25 The Valentines face court over their recent dope bust. Pleading guilty the band members each receive a $150 fine and a good behaviour bond. Speaking with *Go Set*, the band talk up the legalisation of drugs, with singer Vince Lovegrove recommending 'Supervised centres like Hotels where people with a license could smoke.'

28 Nine Australian soldiers are killed and 28 wounded in fighting around the Long Hai mountains in Vietnam.

28 Anti-apartheid activists protest against the presence of South African athletes at the Australian Swimming Championships in New South Wales by throwing black dye into the pool.

28 Journalist Wilfred Burchett arrives back in Australia for the first time in 15 years. Addressing the National Press Club, he lambasts the Federal Government for forcing him into exile on the basis of spurious claims he had 'brainwashed' POWs for China during the Korean War.

28 Thieves steal recording equipment and demo tapes belonging to Melbourne bubblegum band The Mixtures.

28 Protestors hold a torchlight vigil outside Federal Parliament in memory of all the Indigenous Australians killed since colonisation.

29 Power black-outs hit Melbourne after State Electricity Commission (SEC) workers go on strike.

1970 Fashion

MARCH

- Following the failure of their final single 'Does Anyone Really Know What Time it is?'/'No Need to Cry', The Dave Miller Set split up.
- Pioneering Adelaide independent label Sweet Peach, run by American expatriate Pam Coleman and English producer Jimmy Stewart, release the Levi Smith's Clefs' debut album, *Empty Monkey*. Despite *Go Set* hailing the release as 'The best rock album ever produced in Australia', the record sells poorly, leading most of the band members (like Tully before them) to break away from singer Barry McAskill and form Fraternity.
- Progressive pop vocalists The Cleves play a small outdoor festival in Cowra with Nutwood Rug.
- After a series of media and legal battles between the program's producers and Channel 10, pop show *Uptight* is cancelled and replaced with *Happening 70*.
- Company Caine is formed in Melbourne, bringing together former teen sensation (Little) Gulliver Smith with members of Cam-Pact.
- The first Australian Women's Liberation conference is held in Melbourne.

Bon Scott in velvet jacket with beads • • •
(Newhill)

The year in fashion

The Hair Generation

In January 1970 *Go Set* set the tone for the next part of the 1970s when they announced the 'hair generation'. Throughout the rest of the year, photographs of boys show that hair was getting longer and longer, with sideburns becoming ever more pronounced. Girls' hair was still worn long, as in previous years, but the fashion press started showing distinctly centre parted dead straight hair, un-set and free flowing.

In April 1970 *Go Set* touted the colours of the season as 'Raspberry fool, Gran green, Zane grey', and the materials as 'velvet, fur, cord [and] ponyskin'. A *Go Set* advertisement for Peter Jackson, known as 'the traditional men's outfitters', in February saw them selling 'psychedelic pants' in the colours of 'wild cherry, vanilla or lime'.

While men still wore suits to work and conservative dress conventions applied to women in the workplace, such as not wearing trousers, clothes for both men and women became less structured

A hairy Jim Keays (Newhill)

- *Go Set* magazine claims its circulation has now reached 57 000 copies per week.

2 The Women's Action Committee is formed in Melbourne to oppose sexist advertising, campaign against discriminatory hiring policies and fight for the right to clean, safe and affordable abortion. One of the group's first actions is to protest at the Miss Teenage Quest, where they drop leaflets into the crowd and hoist a banner denouncing the 'exploitation of women's bodies for charitable purposes.'

4 Wendy Saddington defends her *Go Set* Taking Care of Business advice column on Radio 3DB, telling angry talk-back callers that they are unable to 'face reality.'

6 Psych-folk band Extradition, featuring members of Tully, play a free concert in the Coffee Lounge at UNSW.

7 The Masters Apprentices headline the *Stateside 70 Pop Spectacular*, taking in country towns such as Colac, Warrnambool, Portland, Swan Hill, Wagga and Wangararatta. Issy Dy and The Sect fill the support slots, with the latter recently releasing their own version of The Masters' track 'St John's Wood'.

7 New Zealander Clive Coulsen stops road managing for The Pretty Things and Led Zeppelin in order to join Sydney's Mecca on vocals.

8 Victoria's first outdoor rock festival, *The Miracle*, ends in igmony after the state's notoriously fickle weather floods the festival site at Launching Place. Lacking any shelter, festival-goers huddle over camp fires for two days, catching occasional sets from Company Caine, Wendy Saddington, Chain and The Adderly Smith Blues Band, before the police and organisers finally pull the pin.

14 African American session player Billy Preston begins a residency at Sydney's Chequers nightclub. Originally starting out with Little Richard, the piano man has more recently worked on recordings by Ray Charles and The Beatles.

18 UNSW student paper *Tharunka* decides to challenge New South Wales' censorship laws by publishing the bawdy poem 'Eskimo Nell'. Drawing a storm of condemnation from the mainstream media, politicians and other student papers, *Tharunka*'s editors are charged with obscenity over the sexual content of the paper, whilst their decision to also print instructions for the creation of thermite bombs, napalm and chlorine gas goes strangely unnoticed. Upon her appearance at Sydney Central Court, *Tharunka* editor Wendy Bacon racks up yet more charges for wearing a nun's habit emblazoned with the words (from her banned poem 'Cunt is a Christian Word') 'I've been fucked by God's steel prick.'

19 ABC TV's pioneering rock program *GTK* clocks up its 100th show.

than those worn in previous years. By 1970, work wear had absorbed some of the fashion themes of the late 1960s – lapels on jackets became generally wider, trousers more flared and higher waisted. This applied to clothes worn by both the young and older generations. During 1970, it became uncommon to see the young and the old in work suits, for example, that featured narrow legged trousers, narrow ties, or narrow lapelled fitted jackets that had been the height of fashion in 1966.

Doug Parkinson wearing ethnic patterns and necklace (Newhill)

In Sydney, the House of Merivale reflected this shift. The fashion house was established in 1960 by Merivale and John Hemmes with the youth market in mind. Initially, their stores carried designs by overseas designers and local Australian designers such as Prue Acton, Norma Tullo, Kenneth Pirrie. Later the designs of John Hemmes and Merivale were made locally in their own factory and sold exclusively in their shops. The House of Merivale sold women's clothes, but from 1967, menswear was carried by their subsidiary, Mr. John. Mr. John catered for young men and by the end of 1970, many of their clothes were considered quite daring by the older generation but quite suave and sophisticated by the young. These sorts of clothes were theatrical and highly coloured.

The under thirty-year-old fashion buying public seemed to have viewed these theatrical clothes as perfectly acceptable, and wore them as a reflection of individuality rather than of earlier 1960s ideas of social conformity. As we have seen in 1969, clothes in 1970 for young men and women continued an interest in ethnic patterns, textures and materials. While the hippy look was clearly a popular fashion look, especially amongst students, it could also be said that it represented a continuing politicisation of the young in the context of the anti-Vietnam protest movement, indigenous land rights, and the rise of the Women's Movement and Gay Liberation.

For example, the January and February 1970 issues of *Go Set* described the seminal 'hippy look' as crushed velvet jackets, Swedish clogs and Indian bangles, Mexican dresses and blouses,

Johnny Dick from The Aztecs in a unisex T-shirt (Newhill)

fringed moccasins, flowing scarves, oversized sunglasses, crocheted bolero vests, and floppy felt hats. Popular fabrics included velvet, corduroy, cottons such as cheesecloth and seersucker satin, lace and chiffon.

Boy's trousers were worn tight on the top and loose on the bottom with grandfather shirts or close fitted body shirts in 'electric new colours'. Big leather belts were advocated for a 'masculine image'. But, ideas of gender were being renegotiated through fashion with uni-sex wear – uni-sex T-shirts were particularly popular. Androgyny and ideas of gender identity were explored through clothes, popularised through mass media images of contemporary pop culture. These fashion explorations were, however, in the minority of the fashion for the young. These ideas did not displace entrenched ideas about appropriate attire for appropriate events amongst the middle classes.

In 1970 Miss Elisabeth White married, and her wedding dress was cream coloured Swiss cotton with a simple cross over fitted top and a long skirt. It was a home made dress, and the material was purchased at Buckley and Nunn in Melbourne. Her husband, Mr Robin Grove, wore a mismatched suit with only slightly flared trousers. During this year, the new Mrs Grove began working at Monash University, and remembers wearing a tweedy suit with the skirt above the knee on the first day of her new job.

At the same time, Miss Gerry O'Reilly remembers going to a conservative evening function wearing a glamorous homemade black lace evening dress with high frilled neck, cuffs and hem to the floor. She wore this dress with flat black pointy shoes.

Thus, fashion for women in the workplace and at formal events reinforced traditional gender constructions of femininity, modesty and social status. For men suits were important reflections of middle class propriety and status in the work place and at formal events. By contrast, fashion at discos and nightclubs was, for the young, a place to freely express new, non-conformist ideas. These were places where individuality and theatricality could rework notions of conventional dress codes.

1970 marks, therefore, the beginning of a more relaxed Australian view of fashion that continued throughout the decade and beyond. Now we see equal numbers of men and women wearing jeans. Few men now own dinner suits, indeed, many men today do not even own a suit. Far fewer men wear a tie to work today than before 1970 and ideas of female modesty have been radically rethought since then. Co-ordinated shoes and handbags, hosiery, hats and gloves are not worn today because of a sense of correctness, but rather, they are worn for solely practical reasons. Perhaps the clothes that one would have seen walking around Australian streets during the late 1960s were the last time our society responded en masse to class defined overseas imported conservatism. Now, one might make the case that Australian fashion better reflects our more relaxed egalitarian lifestyle.

Brigid Finlayson and Maria Sokratis.

20 A rally to commemorate the massacre of anti-apartheid protestors at Sharpeville meets at Wynyard Park in Sydney. Scuffles with police break out when a South African flag, stolen from the Apartheid regime's Canberra Embassy, is burnt.

24 Following cuts from the censor, Italian director Michelangelo Antonioni's stylish tale of the American counter-culture, *Zabriske Point*, opens in Sydney.

28 After being banned for six months, US counterculture smash *Easy Rider* opens at Sydney's Gala Cinema.

APRIL

- The Melbourne Vietnam Moratorium Committee, *Sunday Observer* and *Go Set* run a Victorian Peace Poster competition judged by Phillip Adams of the *Australian* and Alan McCullough of the *Herald Sun*. The competition soon spawns a national version judged by cartoonist Bruce Petty.
- The ABC censors the broadcast of radical author Frank Hardy's speech at the Adelaide Festival, after he issues a blistering condemnation of censorship, liberally peppered with swear words, to the assembled dignitaries.
- Pioneering progressive rock act Blackfeather form in Sydney.
- Michael Dransfield's second book of drug influenced poetry is issued by the University of Queensland, but a line in the poem 'Fugue in G Minor' sees the collection banned.

1970 Spectrum

- The Masters Apprentices release their classic 'Turn Up Your Radio' single.
- The Committee for Action Against Censorship holds a Festival of Banned Works at Sydney University's Wallace Theatre, drawing over 2000 people and turning another 2000 away. During the festival performers read banned pieces by Norman Mailer, the Marquis de Sade, Henry Miller and others.
- Social commentator and gay rights activist Denis Altman launches the first successful legal challenge against a decision by the Commonwealth Censor to ban the importation of a book, in this case Sandford Friedman's *Totem Pole*.
- Nothing less than versatile, harmony group The Cleves record a batch of songs for both a children's puppet show and the soundtrack of *Revolution*, a short feature made by the Commonwealth Film Unit.
- Ronnie Burns receives a Gold Record after his anti-Vietnam ballad 'Smiley', a Johnny Young composition, sells more than 50 000 copies.

11 *Go Set* collects thousands of Vote For Peace coupons to send on to John Lennon and Yoko Ono as part of their War is Over campaign.

Spectrum live at the TF Much Ballroom (Porter)

Fresh and inventive where many of their progressive peers were ponderous and overblown, Spectrum emerged from Melbourne's inner city rock scene in 1969. Combining slabs of Hammond organ with ironic lyrics and a crack rhythm section, the band went on to release a series of albums before breaking up in 1973. Iain McIntyre spoke with founding members Mike Rudd and Bill Putt about the band's early days and groundbreaking hit 'I'll be Gone'.

Tell us how Spectrum first came together in 1969?

Mike Rudd: The impetus for me was that The Party Machine, which I played bass in, was splitting up because Ross Wilson had received the call to go and play in the UK with Procession. By that time the band had been together for a few years and had moved from doing a small percentage of originals to nearly 100% of Ross's songs. This was unusual in itself, and more so because Ross's influences were from the US, whereas as most local bands were more British oriented.

Once the band split up I thought 'I'm going to have to get a band together otherwise I'll have to get a job, again.' I met up with this keyboard player first, David Skewes, who had a Hammond, and the idea I had was to form a band based around the Hammond, because I was knocked out by Traffic and Vanilla Fudge.

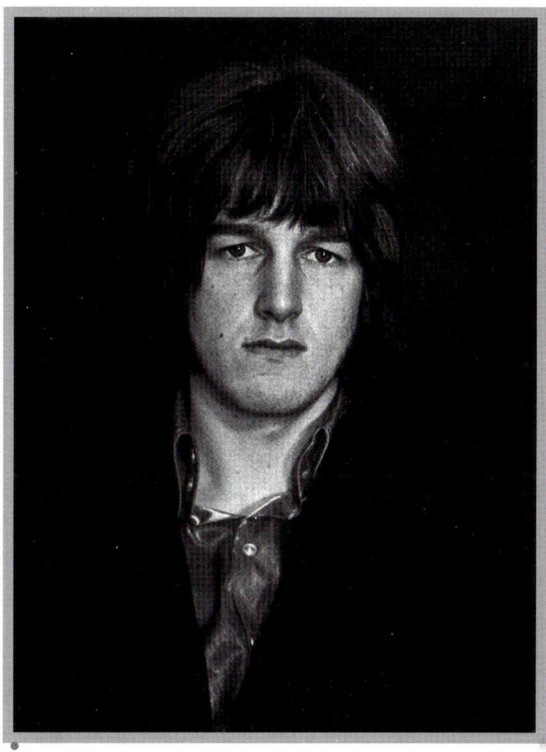

Mike Rudd during his time with The Party Machine (Beard)

Bill Putt: I was originally in The Lost Souls and after that joined a band called The Gallery, which was Mark Kennedey on drums, me on guitar and Ray Finlay on bass backing three girls in short dresses. I think we were playing Ormond Hall when Mike saw us. Mike approached Mark to join his new project, which was fine with us because our little trio wasn't anything serious and was there to be poached.

Mike: After a while of working on things I decided to expand the band by inviting Bill in.

Bill: I had a bass and he had a guitar so we swapped those and our amps. We had a play in Lee Neale's lounge room in Doncaster and that was it.

Mike: Lee [who had by this time replaced Skewes on keys] was in a band called 1987, which in those days was considered pretty modern (laughter). We started with a few Traffic covers to ground things, but we didn't have a huge repertoire because I was still feeling my way so far as writing was concerned. Luckily Mark, who was only 17, was a prodigy, and when we did eventually begin playing in August 1969, he just filled out the set with solos.

Where did you first play?

Mike: We started at The Thumpin' Tum and played a few shows there until Michael Gudinski, who was a still a schoolboy hanging around the AMBO agency being fed scraps, booked us a residency at a place called, quite ominously, The Punchbowl. It was a sharpie hang out in Degreaves Street, but fortunately at the first gig we got adopted by the biggest sharpie there who put his arms around a terrified me and said 'I like you guys.' (laughter)

The good thing about playing there was that a bunch of bands came through who saw us, thought 'Gee they're quite weird,' and passed on the word. After that we were adopted by some of the guys at *Go Set* and so received fame way beyond our actual status because we were barely playing anywhere.

Bill: The thing was that because we were playing wholly original stuff once we got regular bookings it read Sebastian's, Berties, Berties, Sebastian's.

14 Customs and Excise Minister Don Chipp attends a Canberra screening of scenes deleted from recent films by the Chief Censor.

15 The publishers of Sydney's *Arena* magazine are summoned to the Court of Petty sessions over the publication of a 'Smokers' Guide' to marijuana. Two of those charged with 'Inciting, urging, aiding or encouraging the commission of crimes, to wit the smoking of Indian Hemp' turn up to court dressed in cowboy outfits.

17 In a protest against unequal wages, a number of women ride trams in Melbourne, refusing to pay more than 80% of the fare.

18 Peter Andrews, formerly of the Michael Browning Booking Company, sets up Let It Be productions to promote bands, anti-war demonstrations, art exhibitions and other 'underground' events. In Melbourne the agency handles business for such progressive rock acts as Spectrum, Chain, Gerry Humphreys (ex Loved Ones) and magician Jeff Crozier.

22 The Federal government announces it will soon remove the Chief Censor's power to vet films for overseas export.

23 Battles between school authorities and radical teens accelerate, following an inaccurate report in the *Australian* asserting that permission has been given for New South Wales high school

Principals to allow the 'passive wearing of Moratorium badges.' Despite a retraction from the newspaper, students refuse to remove said badges and are expelled or suspended from several schools. Some schools, such as Seven Hills, threaten to also suspend teachers wearing anti-war badges, while a few progressive minded institutions, such as Hunters Hill and Pittwater, allow their students to wear whatever they like.

25 With their management going belly up, Doug Parkinson In Focus lose all of their savings, scotching any chance of them touring the UK. At the launch of their own booking agency, entitled Malcolm X, Parkinson talks up the need for bands to get organised, telling *Go Set* 'Pop musicians are putting out the most productive music in Australia right now, but the Muso's Union just aren't interested in us. I'd like to see a separate association for pop musicians that would fight for our rights.'

27 Future Labor Environment Minister Dr Moss Cass calls for the abolition of penalties arising from the possession and sale of illicit drugs.

28 Aboriginal protestors throw wreaths into Botany Bay as tens of thousands, including the Royal Family, attend a re-enactment of Captain Cook's landing.

30 The Federal Government announces it will spend $500 000 on drug education in the coming year.

What were those places like?

Bill: There was no alcohol, the stages were usually small and the venue not much bigger.

Mike: The size of Sebastian's was tiny, and with all the people crammed in there it was pretty hard to get three bands and all their gear on and off the stage. It was absurd really. There was a particular Victoriana thing in Melbourne when I arrived [1966], which continued for a couple of years and which the Knight brothers exploited in a big way. Both Berties and Sebastian's had that Victorian atmosphere.

Bill: For us to play there all the time was fantastic. It wasn't until we went overseas many years later that we realised how lucky we were once we got rolling to play 5 or 6 nights a week.

Mike: There was a Jewish crowd as well that hung around Sebastian's who were the basis of a lot of the TV shows that were on. They liked us and so once again even though the crowds weren't very big we tapped into a group of people who were very influential.

The Thumpin' Tum was also quite a venue. When I arrived in Melbourne it was the mod venue and then it became the Stylist place, which was even more up itself, but the venue was cool. They followed the hippy thing and used to show movies during the bands.

How did the crowd react to your music?

Bill: They tended to just plonk themselves down and sit there while we did our thing, because some of our songs were pretty long.

Mike: And quite often had a drum solo, as we exploited Mark's talents as much as we could.

Spectrum's first line-up. L–R: Bill Putt, Mike Rudd, Mark Kennedey, Lee Neale (Rudd)

So there was a fair bit of improvisation involved?

Bill: There was lots as Mike would bring an idea to us and we'd expand on it. One particular track, 'Fiddling Fool', was originally three and a half minutes and wound up being over fifteen. A real ingredient in that was the keyboard playing of Lee Neale, who was one of the most unique players I've ever come across.

Mike: Lee was also different from most of the Hammond organ players of the time in that he didn't use a Leslie speaker, so he used to make a feature of playing around with the bars on it. The audience would end up pushed against the back wall at Sebastian's, because he'd be playing away on one super high frequency. It was quite wild. He was truly central to the band's live performance – it was very much *the* Hammond and then the band.

Given you could have gotten a lot more work just doing covers what was the impetus to do your own songs?

Mike: Essentially I'm a musical snob, and after playing in The Party Machine I was genuinely enthusiastic about the possibilities of doing my own stuff. In many ways those were the days in which the possibilities were there. Because there were no track records as such, the horizons were limitless.

Tell us about your involvement with managers Let It Be.

Mike: Let It Be evolved from an association we had with Michael Browning and Peter Andrews and they worked with a bunch of people including John Pinder, Phil Jacobsen, Warren Knight and a woman called Roxy. The idea of it was to unify the arts and it was a very wacko idea (laughter), but it had its moments, which really came to fruition with the TF Much project. The TF Much Ballroom exploited the suburban hippy thing, as by this point the mods had evolved into hippies.

Spectrum's second line-up, with Ray Arnold on drums, at the TF Much Ballroom (Porter)

Bill: We played pretty much all of the shows. They were not just musical, but had things like the Leaping McSpedden Brothers, which featured 11 guys dressed in funny red skin tight suits who would do acrobat tricks and fall about and crash and do a human alphabet and all that. They were incredibly funny and would perform in between acts or there would be a magician or something. It was very much like a circus in a way.
Mike: Very vaudevillian.
Bill: And they didn't want cover bands. There was Lipp Arthur, who were so out there, and The Captain Matchbox Whoopee Band who could vary from a band of eight to 40 depending on what they were doing at the time. It was a bizarre period of time and again there was no alcohol.
Mike: But they did have vegie burgers. They brought in food . . .
Bill: It was a little bit like a festival brought indoors. One time to get into the place they had all this plastic stuff and it was like walking in through a womb and being reborn.
Mike: That was the idea, but it very quickly changed, because the first one was trying to be really arty, but once they realised where their audience was at it all devolved rather quickly.

It must have been exciting playing those events after tiny discotheques.

Bill: We looked at it as an opportunity to expand and try out silly ideas and get extra people involved. We had Jeremy Noone playing saxophone at one and at another show in the same hall we based our whole set around playing a card game called Misere.
Mike: We also did some work with [theatrical group] Tribe.
Bill: On the [1971] *Milesago* album there's a whole sequence of songs called the *Crab Saga*. We gave Tribe the record and they came along and did this bizarre thing while we played the segments. I was seeing it for the first time on the day. It was fabulous, all these weirdoes crawling around on their hands and knees half naked looking like crabs and things.
Mike: We also had the Edison Lightshow, which was Hugh McSpedden's thing, which was projected over the stage and made it a very heady, acidy thing. It's hard to put a name to the music we were playing and the description psychedelic is wrong, but with all those other visual things that were going on you could say the live events were psychedelic.

Tell us about Sons of the Vegetal Mother.

Mike: Well one of the only vestiges of that period that survives is the *Garden Party* EP. Ross Wilson came back from London with this macrobiotic idea of a band that was meant to be anyone who turned up playing the material that Ross had written. So on any given night there could be two bass players and three drummers or whatever. It very rarely worked out to be that chaotic, but nevertheless the band recorded an EP that was combined with an art installation. Out of that came the nucleus of Daddy Cool.

What are your memories of the Launching Place Festival in 1970?

MAY

- The Bee Gees officially break up, with Barry Gibb releasing his first solo single 'I'll Kiss Your Memory'. With Maurice foundering and Barry and Robin failing to achieve chart success, the band reforms shortly after, going on to release two more albums, *Marley Purt Drive* and *Two Years On*, before the end of the year.
- Fourteen teachers and a number of students at Frankston High School stage a protest against plans by Federal Minister Philip Lynch to present the school with an Australian flag.
- The conservative Bolte government is re-elected in Victoria.
- German composer Karl Stockhausen visits Melbourne to present a three day lecture series on avant-garde electronic music. Misunderstood and lambasted by local arts critics, he derides them as a 'quaint race peculiar only to Melbourne, South Africa and Russia.'

1 The APG perform John Romeril's *Dr Karl's Kure* as part of the traditional May Day march before going on to appear at the Footscray Institute of Technology and a series of factories (with support from the Amalgamated Engineers Union).

2 Promoting Copperwine's new *Joint Effort* album, Jeff St John dismisses the Melbourne rock scene, telling *Go Set* 'I can't get over the huge gap between Melbourne and Sydney . . . the musical side of the scene in Melbourne is played down to the point where it is non-existent.'

5 In the run up to the anti-Vietnam Moratorium march, jumpy Melbourne police race to the US consulate in response to (false) reports that it has been invaded by students. In the meantime, US computer company Honeywell begins moving sensitive equipment out of their offices for fear that marchers may target them over their ties to the US military.

5 The ABC is threatened with cuts, clearly aimed at penalising the public broadcaster for the production of such contentious programs such as *Four Corners* and *This Day Tonight*. Following public protests and industrial action by staff, the government backs down, increasing the station's funding by $5 million.

8 Following an eight month organising effort, involving branches throughout the suburbs, 100 000 demonstrate against the Vietnam War in Melbourne as part of nation wide Moratorium marches. At the height of the march, a mass sit-down outside Parliament in Bourke Street brings the city to a halt. Despite a quarter of Victoria's police force showing up, many armed with shotguns and pistols, the only violence occurs when RSL members throw a rock at protest organiser and future Deputy PM Jim Cairns. Regardless of Billy Snedden, the Minister responsible for conscription, deriding the organisers as

Mike: I don't think we actually played. I remember waiting for hours and hours in the mini Moke while it rained.
Bill: Chain played and they were nearly electrocuted and came off swearing and carrying on and we all decided it was very dangerous and went home.
Mike: The idea had been to have a festival in a rain shadow, which was really stupid.
Bill: They wanted to have a lovely, groovy festival . . .
Mike: And Launching Place was a great name . . .
Bill: And it was a beautiful place, but with an extremely high rainfall.
Mike: It was a Let It Be thing and it was their idea to move the whole trip out of the city, but they were foiled. It was the second time in a row so they gave that away.
Bill: The good thing for us was that Mike wrote two tunes, 'Launching Place Part One' and 'Part Two' to help promote the event.
Mike: That got us into the studio for the first time. We happened to meet up with Howard Gable who'd arrived from Auckland and been put on a roving commission by EMI. We recorded 'Parts One' and 'Two' with him. I don't know if he was impressed or not, but he asked us if we had anything else. Since 'I'll Be Gone' was the one that went down with the crowds the best we put that down.

Because the recording coincided with the Radio Ban on all the major international record companies and we were on EMI, unsigned I might add, there was a gap of six months before it was released. We were up in Sydney [in 1971] playing at Caesar's Palace and had just finished a sound check when suddenly we heard our song on the radio.
Bill: We had no idea it was coming out and had no idea that they had edited it down.
Mike: Well I knew, but I hadn't heard the end result. It was two verses, a middle eight, two verses and they thought two verses, middle eight, one verse was the way to go (laughter).

When you chose to record 'I'll Be Gone' did you have any conception that it would be such a huge Australian hit?

Mike: No, we had no expectations at all. What had happened in the six months since we had recorded it was that the band had evolved from the short snappy songs that the single represented to doing the really stretched out songs. The band had moved on and when it came to recording and releasing the album I felt that the song didn't really fit and asked that it be left off and the record company foolishly agreed.
Bill: The record still did okay, but would have gone mega had it had 'I'll Be Gone' on it (laughter).
Mike: A silly move commercially, but we had our moment in the sun and it happened to coincide with a number of Australian bands opening the floodgates. The Whitlam era had kind of started and things opened up for a while creatively before they closed once again. Daddy Cool and us were both at the top of the charts together, so we did a very unlikely tour called the Aquarius Tour around the whole of Australia. We swapped headlines and although the two bands didn't really fit together in any musical way the audience accepted it either way around, although it was nicer if it finished with the madcap antics of Daddy Cool.

Did you find on that tour that the hippy ideals had gone national?

Mike: There was a lot of hope in the idea of the counterculture. In fact, at one point in the early 1970s I went up to Canberra to some sort of government-inspired conference to put the perspective from a band point of view as to whether there was any credibility in the counterculture. It showed that they were concerned as to whether it existed, and I don't think it did in any organised sense, but there was a feeling, and I think the Whitlam era tapped into that, that things were changing and that there was hope for different points of view and macrobiotics and all that kind of stuff (laughter). A different way of approaching things anyway. It lasted a few years, but when reality set in and the Whitlam government was tipped up it really tipped up all those counterculture ideas. All of the guys who had come through uni with those ideas suddenly became rabid capitalists and exploited everybody (laughter).

Did you guys identify closely with the countercultural, hippy movement?

Mike: I think it was different here to many places, in that all the bands were sort of isolated and we were more isolationist than most. We had a few social contacts with other bands, but musically didn't mix with anybody. We just did our own thing, but somehow I guess we were pushing in the same direction as other people.

There was a period in the early 1970s when Billy Thorpe, Daddy Cool, Chain, us and other local bands were at the top of the charts, and it seemed as if there was a genuine Australian voice emerging minus the cultural cringe. We were lucky in those days because the record company would say 'We don't know what you're doing, we do not have a clue, but we'll put it out anyway.' These days they say 'We know everything, you don't have a clue and this is what you are going to put out.' And then they wonder why nothing's happening.

Spectrum relaxing at home (Porter)

Had you guys been living fairly hand to mouth before 'I'll Be Gone' hit?

Mike: It didn't change that much to be honest.

Bill: We just worked a lot and lived from gig to gig.

Mike: And that was why recording was such a trial, because we had to stop playing for a week or two and that put a lot of pressure on us to complete our recordings in a short period of time.

Bill: It was usually one week of recording, one week of mixing and then back on the road. That was the case with every Spectrum and Ariel recording we did.

Mike: We were lucky with our recordings in that in those days we weren't getting advances, loans in effect, but EMI were just paying for it and we were counting on the deal to eventually pay it all off. That worked for us at the time, but it didn't stop that compression, time equals money feeling, which wasn't very helpful on the creative side. On the other hand, our open ended jamming had moved on into arrangements so we could go in and if the first take didn't work then we'd just do it again. Our recordings were virtually live so we didn't waste any time in the studio.

Tell us about recording *Spectrum Part One*.

Mike: That was at Bill Armstrong's studio at Albert Road, Albert Park.

Bill: He was like a little garden gnome with glasses who used to turn the lights off all the time. I remember recording all day and then Doug Parkinson's band would come in after hours.

Mike: I wrote one song, 'Drifting', for the album, but the rest of it was all in the repertoire at the time.

Bill: It was all pretty straight forward. There were no arguments and no drugs and no boozing or anything.

Did drugs play much of a role in the song writing at this point?

Mike: No. By the first album I hadn't even taken any drugs. By the time we got to the next album, *Milesago*, I might have dabbled a little bit, maybe. It kept the rhythm section going, though (laughter).

Bill: I'd watched it happening around me for many years and saw the negative side of it. Mainly

'political bikies who pack-rape democracy', the event defies the usual clichés in bringing churchgoing pensioners together with headband wearing hippies.

During the march Tribe perform street theatre, whilst acts such as Spectrum, Wendy Saddington, Ronnie Burns and Company Caine play an outdoor festival in the Treasury Gardens.

Meanwhile, protests in the other capitals see 30 000 march in Sydney, 8000 in Brisbane, 3000 in Hobart, 3000 in Perth and 2000 in Newcastle, whilst hundreds protest in smaller towns across the country. An unofficial march in Adelaide, organised by the Worker-Student Alliance and Students for Democratic Action, draws 2000 onto the streets.

9 The official Adelaide Moratorium march, held on the weekend so as to avoid disrupting city traffic, sees 12 000 march against the Vietnam war.

9 *Go Set* reports that The Valentines are experiencing various hassles, with Paddy Beach threatened with deportation and Vince Lovegrove facing court over the breaking of his good behaviour bond. In an attempt to ditch their former bubblegum image, the now hard rocking act amp up their genuinely rebellious side, with Lovegrove saying 'We're still very image conscious, but it's no longer a fabricated one . . . We're always in trouble so why shouldn't we let people know it. That's what we're like . . . We're honest. A lot of people smoke [dope], but don't admit it.'

21 Martin Sharp launches the Yellow House multi-media space in Potts Point Sydney with an exhibition of his recent work for *Oz* and others.

22 The Beach Boys tour Australia for the first time.

23 Indian sitar master Ravi Shankar performs at Melbourne's Dallas Brook Hall.

24 The Masters Apprentices play a huge farewell gig at the Camberwell Civic Centre in Melbourne, before heading off on the first of two UK jaunts.

31 Former RSL President, Sir William Yeo, delivers a speech in New South Wales in which he fondly recalls watching police beat students during a recent visit to France. Revealing much about his tastes, he declares it to have been 'the loveliest thing I've seen in all my life.'

JUNE

- Following the success of the Moratorium march, Melbourne activists open the Super Dove store in Little Lonsdale Street, selling anti-war posters, flags and badges, as well as left wing books and hippy clothing.
- A new microwave trunk dialling system allows Western Australia to be linked to the eastern states for regular interstate telephone calls.
- Blues act Chain record their *Live Chain* album at Caesar's Palace disco in Sydney.
- Motown superstar Stevie Wonder tours Australia.

lethargy, people sitting around being too stoned to do anything and being paranoid all the time. I made sure none of that happened to me, but had fun with it. Overall we kept it pretty clean and have always played straight and kept it straight in public. What you do at home is your own business.

A lot of bands were playing high schools at this time. Were you guys involved in that?

Mike: Yes and the kids were terrific. Occasionally the teachers were reactionary, but by and large music teachers loved us. Sometimes they were concerned that we were going to cause a riot . . .
Bill: Or corrupt the kids or mention drugs. I remember being in Hobart and we did a show at one of their private colleges, all boys, and were told to finish right on one o'clock. We were playing away and it was a couple of minutes to one and we thought 'Well we'll finish and be right on cue.' Then storming down the centre of the hall came the principal. Sweeping past these rows of little grey uniformed boys he came on to the stage and pulled the plug. I wanted to punch his head in

Spectrum live (Porter)

of course, but instead of that we danced around him in a circle, which made it all seem even sillier. The kids all laughed and he looked like a fool.

TV exposure had been really important for bands in the mid 1960s. Was this still the case heading into the 1970s?

Bill: Yes and it has never changed. It gets bigger every second. We did all the shows at least once or twice and got kicked off a few.

Mike: *GTK* in combination with *Go Set* was what made us famous really. We were so lucky in that they were looking for things of value, and for some reason we became their darlings in terms of saying something and being serious. We got on the front cover of *Go Set* and played a lot on *GTK*.

So which shows did you get kicked off?

Mike: Well the Ernie Sigley incident in 1970/71 made the papers around the country.

Bill: We got more publicity by not doing a show than if we had done it.

Mike: He wanted us to play in suits.

Bill: Tuxedos.

Mike: And we said 'We'd rather not thank you. We'd rather perform like this.'

Bill: A little guy went off and came back and said 'We're going to have to call it off' and we said 'Cool.' We had no problem with that, and I remember thinking 'Great, we've got the afternoon and the night off. We can have a rest.' So we went off and played pool and relaxed. Then when we got to the hotel that night there was all sorts of newspaper people there asking bizarre questions about us storming off the show.

Mike: It was another pivotal incident in the history of the band (laughter).

Bill: And Ernie has never forgotten it.

Tell us about the film clip you had made for 'I'll be Gone'.

Mike: I think Chris Lofven approached us. We did it over a few weekends. It came across as being very hippy, especially with the bit at the end where we were walking down a country road and stopped to say hello to some horses. The mini-Moke got in there as well (laughter). The clip got shown on every TV station, because they were hungry for it. There weren't many clips around, so any little fillers they needed, bang on went the clip. The song slowly grew as a hit in lots of different places around the country, and I think the clip really helped with that.

Following the success of 'I'll be Gone' and *Spectrum Part One* the band went on to release the *Milesago, Warts Up Your Nose* (as The Indelible Murtceps), *Testimonial* and *Terminal Buzz* albums before evolving into Ariel in 1973. Bill and Mike continued to play together in bands such as Instant Replay, The Heaters, W.H.Y. and Number 9 during the 1980s and 1990s before reforming Spectrum in 1998.

Spectrum at the TF Much Ballroom. (Porter)

- Unhappy with the band's lack of success, Danny Robinson breaks up the Virgil Brothers by returning to Australia from the UK.

2 The ALP retakes power in South Australia. Riding a left-wards shift in the general community, flamboyant Premier Don Dunstan institutes a series of reforms affecting Aboriginal land rights, consumer protection, education, housing, licensing laws and welfare.

4 Police attack an anti-apartheid demonstration outside the Women's Recreation Centre in Melbourne's Royal Park. Two weeks later, nine are arrested in Canberra when they attempt to stop another basketball game involving the South African women's team.

6 Anarchists are arrested in Melbourne for selling copies of a magazine called *Solidarity*, which includes an article on 'Fucking the System', outlining simple tips for 'living without money, engaging in sabotage and shocking the citizenry.'

11 Women from the Wollongong Save Our Sons (SOS) group bring Parliamentary proceedings to a halt during a demonstration in Canberra.

12 In a speech to the House of Representatives, Don Chipp outlines proposals for a new system of censorship, which will introduce a classification system allowing adults to view many previously banned films under a 'Restricted' or 'R' rating.

12 A former conscript is fined $1200 in Sydney for smuggling

Wendy Saddington

marijuana from Vietnam in a stereo speaker cabinet.

16 Doug Parkinson and Teddy Toi break up In Focus with 'No fanfares, no goodbye stories – just a quick split for England' as they prepare to join former Bee Gees guitarist Vince Melouney's new band Fanny Adams.

20 The Four Tops tour Australia.

30 The *Go Set* Pop Poll awards are shown on TV for the first time, with Ian 'Molly' Meldrum and the Bee Gees' Barry Gibb hosting proceedings at the Dallas Brooks Hall.

JULY

- The Federal government allows Aborigines to lease land in the Northern Territory from the Commonwealth on a 99 year basis, putting them, for the first time, on equal terms with pastoralists. The first two land lease schemes in the Northern Territory give Indigenous locals control of 243 201 square kilometers of land, but are criticised for falling short of true compensation for dispossession and genocide.
- Having suffered for years under archaic laws that condemn gays and lesbians to undergo psychiatric treatment or face up to 14 years prison for engaging in 'homosexual activity', Sydney activists form the Campaign

Wendy Saddington (Newhill) • • •

Sporting heavy mascara, faded jeans, a blue tank top and the biggest Afro this side of Jimi Hendrix, Wendy Saddington could not help but stand out amongst the bloke ridden world of late 1960s Australian rock. Possessed of a superlative blues voice and inspired by soul heavyweights such as Nina Simone and Aretha Franklin, Saddington constantly drew comparisons to Janis Joplin, but in truth held little in common with either the white blues belter's voice or lifestyle. Crowned Australia's 'Queen of the Blues', Wendy performed solo and with a variety of Australia's leading psychedelic, soul and blues bands, including The James Taylor Move, Chain and Copperwine. However, despite her arresting appearance, outspoken attitude and the enthusiastic support of *Go Set*, for whom she also wrote, her music failed to appear on vinyl until 1971. Iain McIntyre traces the somewhat haphazard trail of her early years on the Australian scene.

By Wendy Saddington's own admission, she could be at times a somewhat confrontational, stubborn and terrifying prospect for audiences, friends and enemies – a fact that was to both help and hinder her musical career. Despite having what she described as loving, supportive parents, she was a troubled teenager, bored and annoyed at the constrictions of school, and yet fearful of escaping them. Nevertheless, leave she did at the age of 15, drifting through a series of dead-end jobs until one night in 1967, when she saw Levi Smith's Clefs singer Inez Amaya live on TV. Entranced by the singer's performance and demeanour she realised she had finally found her calling.

I thought 'Yeah, I want to be a singer.' I've always, as long as I remember gotten what I wanted.
Wendy Saddington, *Revolution*, May 1970.

Inez Amaya and Doug Stirling (Colbert)

Having practiced at home for a month, she plucked up the courage to make her debut at the Love-In Coffee Shop in Carlton. Accompanied by a friend on guitar, her powerful voice caught the attention of the café's regulars, and her performances rapidly became one of the venue's draw cards. Before long her obvious talent saw her picked up by local soul act Revolution.

We were really good friends. We only played once a week and I used to dance about on stage and everything. I was happy in those days. People would die if I moved on stage at all now, or even smiled. I act like I'm crapped off, and I usually am.
Wendy Saddington, *Go Set*, November 1969.

Playing with Revolution until the middle of 1968, Wendy began hankering for more live work, and soon found it in the form of the somewhat more professional James Taylor Move. Originally hailing from Adelaide, the band had moved to Melbourne in 1967 and released two premier Australian psychedelic singles in the harmonious 'Magic Eyes' and Eastern influenced 'Still I Can Go On'. With singer and namesake Robert Taylor quitting the band to sell shirts in the city and pioneering guitarist Kevin Peek (later of Sky) heading off to the jazz world, the band was in pursuit of a new direction. Poaching Saddington they soon found it, switching from incendiary psychedelia to rippling soul and gaining a new crowd in the process. Despite the input of new members John Pugh (ex Cam-Pact) and Lance Dixon, Wendy quickly became the star of the show, garnering the lion's share of critical attention. In the eyes of influential *Go Set* music writer Ian 'Molly' Meldrum, she had most certainly arrived.

Wendy Saddington is a sight to be seen before believed. Her frail, electric haired figure stands poised on stage waiting for Trevor, Allan, Lance and John to tune their instruments. The

Against Moral Persecution (CAMP) Inc. The organisation initially focuses on law reform and media monitoring, before some members break away to form the more militantly 'Out and Proud' Gay Liberation organisation in the early 1970s.

- The Meter Movement hits Sydney with the defacing and destruction of parking meters.
- Doug Ashdown releases Australia's first double album *The Age of Mouse* on Sweet Peach. Backed by Fraternity on a number of tracks, the album is picked up by US label MCA, prompting Ashdown and producer Jimmy Stewart to move to Nashville.

1 The Federal government introduces a new health insurance scheme, increasing benefits to ensure that most services do not incur a fee of more than $5.

3 On the same day that tutors and professors help barricade occupied offices at Monash university, The Bakery, an organising centre run by the Monash University Labor Club in Prahran, is raided by police with warrants to search for explosives, drugs and pamphlets. Despite this and another raid four days later, all the police come away with is a pillow case full of cotton wool, the inside of a toilet roll and the label off an ink bottle.

3 Demonstrators invade the Sydney Stock Exchange, burning US and Australian flags and wiping clean the tally boards to spray paint

'Fuck Capitalism' and 'Merchants of Death' in place of the usual company names.

4 The Metric Conversion board is set up to begin a nation wide switch over to metric measurements.

4 John Newcombe wins the Men's Single's Title at Wimbeldon and Margaret Court wins the Women's Singles.

4 The annual July Fourth protests see anti-war protestors rally outside the Melbourne offices of American Airline Pan Am.

6 A group calling itself the People's Liberation Army throws a brick through the Prime Minister's electoral offices in Malvern, before setting alight McPhersons Ltd's motor parts factory over its ties to the military.

9 During a visit to Papua New Guinea, Australian PM Gorton is booed by 10 000 Tolai tribespeople, demanding an end to Australian colonial rule.

9 A newly formed Melbourne Public Servants anti-war group stages an all night vigil in support of conscientious objector Bob Bissett.

11 Having issued a challenge to police to arrest him at Monash University, draft resister Adrian Bissett and 200 supporters draw attention to his case by blocking Dandenong Road.

16 Bales of marijuana wash up on Melbourne beaches after being dumped by smugglers escaping police.

19 The Zoot's Beeb Birtles is taken to hospital after being bashed by three youths at a Werribee dance.

pulsating beat begins and Wendy's voice hits the air. It was at this stage that I started to get shivers down my back. Her voice is unbelievable . . . to compare it with any other would be a criminal act. It is Wendy's and that is that.
Ian Meldrum, *Go Set*, July 1968.

Wendy's time with The James Taylor Quartet, however, was only to last four months. Dissatisfied with playing with what she later termed 'creepy thin suits', she opted to go solo, and not for the first time, as it turned out. Jamming on a regular basis with R&B heavyweights Max Merritt and The Meteors, she turned her back on the psychedelic finery of Melbourne's stylist set, embracing an earthy style that anticipated the hippy countercultural wave of the coming years.

Rapidly tiring of solo work, Wendy next turned her attention to a West Australian blues group named Beaten Tracks. The band had visited Melbourne as the winners of their state's Hoadley Battle of the Bands in mid 1968, and realising that they could only take things so

Wendy Saddington with Chain (Newhill)

far in Perth they returned later in the year. Undergoing the first of what would be innumerable line-up changes over the next three decades, the band at this point comprised of original members Warren 'Pig' Morgan (piano/keyboards), Murray Wilkins (bass) and Ace Follington (drums), plus guitar journeyman Phil Manning (ex Bay City Union, Laurie Allen Revue). Joining the band in December 1968, Wendy renamed them Chain after Aretha Franklin's 'Chain Of Fools', thereby christening what would go on to become a mainstay of Australian electric blues.

During her time with Chain, Saddington not only sealed her reputation as Australia's foremost female blues/soul singer, but also became known as one of nation's most prickly and aggressive. Some of this was no doubt the result of being an outspoken woman in a male dominated scene, but Saddington rarely pulled her punches on stage or in print, castigating fellow musicians for their unoriginality and taking on any audience she felt was unresponsive or disrespectful.

Sometimes when I'm singing a slow number all those people who rave about my voice start talking through my singing. I've been known to swear at them and tell them to shut up . . . People call me tough, but they've only seen the fighting side of me, not the loving side. The ones who condemn me for being tough and rough are the people who've made me tough and rough.
Wendy Saddington, *Go Set*, June 1969.

In June 1969 Wendy once again found herself chafing under the constraints of group work and quit Chain. Citing financial and creative differences, she wished her former band mates luck with the new material they had been unable to explore with her. Repudiating the heavy workload she had undertaken with Chain and rejecting the need for a manager, she laid low, only occasionally turning out to jam with friends, as well as making an appearance on the ABC TV program *Fusion* alongside Sydney acid rockers Tully.

I only want to be in it up to my waist, not up to my neck. You can only take so much of working your guts out five lousy nights a week for some pathetic amount of money which when split five ways becomes even worse . . . My attitude was all wrong in the end. I didn't care if I turned up late or drunk for a job. At first the boys gave me dirty looks, but after a while they pretended not to notice. They knew I was unhappy, but they were powerless in the circumstances for it was the promoters who handed out the money and they're all a pack of misers.

Wendy Saddington, *Go Set*, June 1969.

Just as Wendy was taking a break from her musical career, new opportunities arose. Having already interviewed Max Merritt for *Go Set* in 1968, she was now offered the chance to come on board as a full time staff member. Announcing the arrival of their 'wild new *Go Set* girl' with a full page cover shot in September 1969, the publication nurtured her writing abilities, whilst she in turn assisted in pushing the paper in an increasingly countercultural direction. Over the next twelve months, Wendy would interview bands, write opinion pieces calling for such things as free festivals, and also pen a brief news column for *Go Set*'s progressive Core section. Most famously, though, she took over the paper's advice column from Leslie Pixie renaming it *Taking Care of Business*.

WENDY SADDINGTON
takes care of business

Wendy was so distinctive in her presentation of her personal life and her music that she had developed a cult following that included some of our gay female staff members. They came to me and said 'Wendy's having trouble paying the rent' and I thought the idea of Wendy, a working class girl from the suburbs, giving advice to the kids was great. She and Jean Gollan, who was a pretty sophisticated feminist, worked together and it was very successful.

Philip Frazer, 3CR interview, June 2005.

Acting as agony aunt for *Go Set*, Wendy fielded questions and dispensed advice on matters as varied as allowances, sibling rivalries, intergenerational bickering and, of course, the trials and tribulations of teenage love affairs. While some of the queries were somewhat laughable, such as the case of one girl who claimed to develop hiccups every time a boy tried to kiss her, others were more serious. Advising young teenagers on how to deal with drug addiction, rape and pregnancy was not a task to be approached lightly, but Saddington and Gollan handled all of it, as well as attacks from parent and mainstream media commentators, with poise and aplomb.

I remember one of the last things I wrote was that if they could talk more to their mothers then they wouldn't have to write to me.

Wendy Saddington, ABC Radio, 2002.

Having only performed intermittently during her early days at *Go Set*, Wendy began to plug back into the music scene during the middle of 1970. Hailing what she saw as the rise of 'dedicated musicians who really live and are completely involved in their music', she attended and performed at Australia's first outdoor festival, the New South Wales *Ourimbah Pop Pilgrimage*. Blown away by the festival's heady atmosphere and peeved at the mainstream media's dismissal of it, she used her semi-regular spot in Core to compose a call to arms.

20 Customs and Excise Minister Don Chipp announces that the amount of illicit drugs already seized in 1970 is 18 times higher than the total amount for the previous year.

25 New South Wales Builders Labourers Federation (BLF) members begin occupying work sites employing non-union labour. In the coming years the BLF will campaign for the right of women to work on sites, and launch a series of green bans to protect important heritage sites across Sydney.

25 Sydney's Flying Circus release *Prepared In Peace*, their second album, on Columbia records. Featuring all original compositions, the album sees the band steer away from earlier bubblegum efforts, returning to their original country rock sound. Shifting their sound yet again towards commerciality, the band moves to Canada in 1971.

25 A youth is charged with assault after hitting Russell Morris in the head with a well aimed ashtray during a gig in Adelaide.

25 Hans Poulsen, The Carson County Band and Flying Circus present a night of country rock at Melbourne's Thumpin' Tum.

25 Actors from popular TV police dramas *Homicide* and *Division Four* protest at the Melbourne Civic Square, calling for an increase in the number of Australian productions on TV.

27 Touching on an increasing interest in environmental issues, a senior research officer at ANU, the Reverend Elzo Vandermark, warns that Australia may only have a few decades in which to turn around the 'ticking time bomb of ecological destruction.'

29 Three home-made bombs explode in Glenrowan as local youths protest over their exclusion from the premiere of the film *Ned Kelly*.

30 Eight mothers from the Save Our Sons organisation hold an anti-conscription protest at the Doncaster Shopping Town in Melbourne.

30 Five students resign and another is expelled after the New South Wales Drug Squad raids the Wagga Teachers' College.

31 Students jostle the Federal Attorney General Tom Hughes and let down the tires of his car during a visit to Sydney University.

AUGUST

- Power blackouts hit Melbourne as the conservative Bolte government goes head to head with SEC workers over the right to unionise.

1 Despite attempts to rebrand themselves as a hard rock outfit, The Valentines find their bubblegum image impossible to shake. Finishing an extensive East Coast tour in Newcastle, the band go their separate ways, with Bon Scott joining Fraternity and Vince Lovegrove heading into print and television journalism, before managing The Divinyls during the 1980s.

1 70 protestors, including noted author Frank Hardy, are arrested during a wild land rights demonstration in Sydney.

Ourimbah was simply a flash, a quick look at how life should be and a brilliant weekend proving that one can be so much happier without the ridiculous constrictions and conventions which society insists upon. A time, place where policemen could be people and people could be humans, not just indoctrinated representatives of ammunition and targets . . . No we are not freaks. We are human beings grasping at freedom and for one weekend it wasn't simply a dream.

Wendy Saddington, *Go Set*, February1970.

With her interest in live performance now fully revived, Wendy linked up with Sydney soul act Copperwine in March 1970. Led by the arresting Jeff St John, who had previously fronted The Id and Yama, the band had emerged from Sydney's underground ranks in early 1969. Melding energetic soul with extended rock work-outs, the band had already released a successful album in Sydney with their debut *Joint Effort*. Adding Saddington to the mix, they now began what was later described by St John as an 'insane' amount of touring, playing up and down the East Coast of Australia.

When they start their session, nobody dances. For once the reason is understandable – Jeff St John, Wendy Saddington and Copperwine are playing and the reaction is incredible . . . From the moment [Wendy] walks on stage with that strange teetering trot you're aware of a strong presence. With a handful of rings clutching the microphone she began to sing and the back of my neck began to tingle – and that's the best way to judge any singer's capability of exciting an audience. Wendy has a thousand different facets to her personality and they all go into her singing. Among other things Wendy is tough, sensitive, vulgar and shy – she's a million things and it all shows when she starts singing, so she is fascinating to watch and listen to.

Caught in the Act, *Go Set*, January 1970.

Having always contended that her music was more readily accepted in the cosmopolitan Sydney scene, and with her collaboration with Copperwine proving so successful, Wendy moved out of her parents home and headed north. Continuing to occasionally write for *Go Set*, the demands of intensive live work saw her take a complete break in 1971, handing over the advisory role to Pat Wilson, aka Mummy Cool.

With their new single 'I'll Teach You How To Fly' hitting #3 on Sydney's charts, Copperwine headed into the studio in late 1970 to begin work on their second, never to be released, album. Heading off to play the Wallacia festival in January 1971, the band also took the opportunity to record their live set with Wendy. Although she was unhappy with the results, the band's new label, Festival's progressive imprint Infinity, began gearing up to release it as an album in the new year.

Whilst the band's feet were firmly planted in the soil of the underground, their new-found success found them playing all manner of venues. Sydney may have been in the forefront of Australia's progressive rock movement, but the city still possessed a lot of old-style cabaret clubs, and Copperwine could occasionally be found playing them, not always with the best of results. One particularly fateful show saw them teamed up with fading British pop stars The Hollies. Before the night was through, Copperwine had been kicked off stage for 'killing the audience', and were accused the following day in Sydney's dailies of being 'half whacked on stage.'

Just because we've got a hit record doesn't mean we have to play it all night. They accuse us of not playing to the crowd, but we've proved we can make a commercial record and we've even played it on stage. If that's not playing to the audience I don't know what is . . . [When] they yelled out 'last song' we made sure our last song ended up being 20 minutes long.

Copperwine drummer Peter Figures, *Go Set*, February 1971.

Having moved beyond the confines of the inner city circuit, Wendy found herself increasingly disillusioned with both the music industry and the teenagers whose tastes it so often moulded. Annoyed at the resurgence of bubblegum pop, her love/hate relationship with audiences continued with her railing that '[Kids] have had so much bull put on them that they wouldn't know good music if it fell on them.'

Seeking a way out of what she saw as an increasingly commercial dead-end Wendy quit Copperwine in February 1971. Despite her fractious relationship with Infinity, she now teamed up with former Chain member turned Aztec Warren Morgan to finally commit her voice to record with the soaring 'Looking Through a Window'/'We Need a Song'. Released in July with a writing credit to Billy Thorpe (who played on the recording and apparently had a 'what's mine is yours' relationship with Morgan), the single hit #22 on the national charts.

Slagged off in the pop pages of the Melbourne *Sun* as a 'pretentious put on' sounding like 'Mrs Miller', the single was predictably enough hailed by *Go Set*'s Stephen MacLean as 'the best Australian song I've heard.' Giving more qualified praise, the magazine's chief rock writer Ed Nimmervoll pointed out that whilst he felt the song was a 'little out of [Wendy's] range', it captured 'the feeling in her voice.' Furthermore he gave the thumbs up for her overall performance, saying the single was 'Emotional to the point where you think you can hear a tear as she sings the sadness.'

Not long after the single hit the charts,

4 Melbourne police announce they have already arrested 207 people on drugs charges this year, as opposed to only nine during the whole of 1969.

5 Australia becomes the first country to censor the film *Woodstock* when up to an hour of the original film is excised to remove swear words, drug references and nudity.

8 Despite Melbourne being the centre of Australian pop for most of the 1960s, the Sydney rock scene's growing ascendancy is crowned when the Hoadley's Battle of the Sounds grand final moves northwards.

8 Ushering in a new era of 'Head' oriented events, the Let It Be agency presents the first *TF Much Ballroom* concert at the Cathedral Hall in Fitzroy. Hundreds pack in to see the cream of Melbourne's progressive rock scene, including Spectrum (featuring new drummer Ray Arnott), Sons of the Vegetal Mother, Captain Matchbox Whoopee Band, Gerry Humphreys and the New Joy Boys, Lipp Arthur, Adderley Smith and Margaret Roadknight. Tribe, Jeff Crozier's Indian Medicine Magik Show and the Flash Light Show provide the visuals, and local dealers bring the dope.

12 Five men are arrested in Melbourne for shooting out the windows of US multinational computer company Honeywell during a night time raid.

17 Nine are arrested during an anti-conscription demonstration held outside the home of Federal

Attorney General Tom Hughes. At one point Hughes comes after the protestors with a cricket bat, prompting 50 others to stage a match outside his home the following weekend.

18 Robert Muntz is sacked from the Commonwealth Public Service after an update of his security file reveals he has been active in the anti-war movement.

19 Customs agents raid the Melbourne docks, seizing marijuana bales from the *Aranda*. One week later a raid on the *Ronaat* at the Yarraville docks yields another massive drug haul.

27 Peter Nixon, Minister for the Interior, announces the government will fight Aboriginal land rights claims at Wave Hill, Northern Territory.

27 30-year-old Arts teacher Craig Forster buys 10 acres of land in Eltham to set up an alternative school opposed to the 'present system oriented towards exam results and the school routine.'

SEPTEMBER

- After spending months in London haggling with various record companies, The Masters Apprentices finally enter the Abbey Road studios to begin recording. Working with Jeff Jarratt and Pink Floyd engineer Pete Brown, the band completes their *Choice Cuts* album within a month, before shooting a film clip for 'Because I Love You' at Hampstead Heath.
- Having fully reinvented himself as a blues rocker, Billy Thorpe and the latest incarnation of his

Infinity finally released the live album with Copperwine. Wendy had always opposed its release, and true to her word flatly refused to promote it. She certainly had plenty of reason to be unhappy with its shoddy packaging which featured somewhat unflattering photos of her singing at Wallacia, incorrectly attributed songs, and even failed to mention the members of Copperwine.

Adding to the overall cheapness of the package was the fact that it featured only six songs. Infinity's later attempt to bulk out the album with the single 'Looking Through a Window' was undermined by the fact they also included a reprise that was simply the track repeated minus it's extended ending. In a similar vein, the overall feel of the album was further let down by the dubbing of fake sounding mass cheering. Faded in and out rapidly at the beginning and ending of each song, it recalled a cheap laugh track, dwarfing Wendy's introductions and sounding completely out of place with the songs.

Wendy was glad to have been able to say on GTK that anyone who bought [the album] was an idiot and wasting their money. She said she had heard the edited tapes and that they'd cut one particular song so that you only heard the trailing climax. She's even offered to rerecord all the songs, but they're not willing to invest the money.
Ed Nimmervoll, *Go Set*, August 1971.

Despite the mishandling of the album by Infinity and Wendy's scathing attitude towards it, *Live With Copperwine* remains a classic of the period. Saddington's voice is in top form and backed by a crack band, comprised of Ross East on guitar, Barry Kelly on keyboard, Harry Brus on bass and Peter Figures on drums, she had undoubtedly been captured at the peak of her career. Australia's studio technicians may have still had some way to go before they perfected the craft of live recording, but where previous efforts from Procession and The Masters Apprentices had sounded thin and unbalanced, the overall sound here is weighty and full, adding presence to an inspired performance.

Opening with a superbly funky take on Nina Simone's 'Backlash Blues' before flowing into an intense version of Bob Dylan's 'Just Like Tom Thumb's Blues', the first side of the album closes with a muscular, acid tinged reinvention of The Beatles' 'Tomorrow Never Knows'. On the flip, some of Wendy's own compositions finally make it on to record with the slightly pedestrian 'Blues In "A"' dwarfed by the mighty 'Five People Said I Was Crazy'. Clearly autobiographical, the song sees Copperwine rocking with the best of them while Wendy takes on her critics. Unsurprisingly, *Go Set* once more sang her praises.

Wendy Saddington performing in the early 1970s (Porter)

The first time I played this album I thought it was one of the worst I'd ever heard. Then came a realisation. If it was that bad, how come I kept playing it over and over . . . Despite its faults this is an album so real that it's unlike any other record I've ever heard. Wendy Saddington's singing lifts every barrier and there's such a reality to the feeling placed into the words she sings that not for a second do you doubt her sincerity.
Stephen MacLean, *Go Set*, September 1971.

Having moved back to Melbourne, Wendy could soon be found jamming with local bands such as Company Caine. For the most part, though, she was well and truly tired of Australia, and with Infinity scoring her a deal with United Artists in the US, she was ready to fly the coop. By December 1971 she was in San Francisco, and with her *Go Set* press credentials still intact, could soon be found interviewing the likes of Jefferson Airplane.

Wendy Saddington returned to Australia in late 1972, working with backing band Teardrop before appearing in Peter Weir's *Three Directions In Pop* and the film of the Sunbury rock festival. Playing the 'Nurse' in the 1973 Australian production of Tommy she branched into theatre and continued to perform with bands such as Blues Assembly, Shango and The Jeff Crozier Band throughout the rest of the decade. Embracing the teachings of the Hare Krishna sect she formed The Wendy Saddington Band in the 1980s, recording an album, which sadly was never released. More recently she has made appearances performing alongside Chain, The Kevin Borich Blues Express and Mick Conway's National Junk Band.

Aztecs enter the studio to record *The Hoax is Over* album. Failing to capture their live prowess, the album is marred both by poor production and the presence of interminable LSD fueled blues jams.

- The first issue of Sydney's *Sound Blast* magazine is published, profiling the heavier end of Australia's musical landscape.

1 Queensland Mines Ltd reports it has discovered a large amount of uranium at Narbalek in Northern Territory. Two weeks later the Gorton government announces it will pass emergency legislation to prevent any overseas takeover of the reserves.

1 The Federal government bans African-American comedian Dick Gregory from visiting Australia to take part in anti-war protests.

9 Leaked documents reveal that the Federal government is aware of at least 3000 people who have knowingly breached the *National Service Act* in order to avoid conscription.

11 Roman Catholic Priest Father Carrigan is dismissed from the post of Parish Curate for his role in helping organise the upcoming Tasmanian Vietnam Moratorium march. After protests from supporters in and out of the church, he is reinstated a month later.

11 500 students from La Trobe University are savagely beaten by police during a march down Waterdale Road Resevoir. The policeman in charge of

1970

operations, Inspector Platpuss, who is later demoted, tells reporters 'They got some baton today and they'll get plenty more in the future.'

12 The opening of the Pink Pig at 115 Little Bourke Street in Melbourne echoes a slow shift towards open alcohol consumption at gigs by allowing BYOG seven days a week.

15 Members of the Australian Ballet Company hold stop work meetings in Canberra over a pay dispute.

18 A second Vietnam Moratorium march is held, with over 100 000 marching nationally. Violence breaks out in Adelaide and Sydney, where police arrest over 300 people during an attempt to push marchers off the streets and onto the footpath. During the Melbourne march, a Jam For Peace is held outside Princes Gate Tower featuring sets from Lotus, Company Caine, Spectrum and Gerry Humphreys.

18 The Melbourne Royal Show features an 'In Stall' selling head bands, grandpa shirts, peace buttons, incense and 'burn it yourself' Premier Bolte candles.

19 South Sydney defeat Manly-Warringah in the Rugby League Grand Final.

22 Former Australian swimming champion John Pick is sentenced

ROSS WILSON

Ross Wilson (Porter)

Even from a young age, Melbourne performer Ross Wilson seemed destined for a life in music. Forming his first band, The Pink Finks, at 16, he went on to head up a number of acts, including The Party Machine, Mighty Kong and Mondo Rock, before enjoying success as a solo performer. Nick Black, Melthoid and Iain McIntyre talked with Ross about the evolution of his most famous band, Daddy Cool.

The Party Machine (Beard)

What was the history behind Daddy Cool?

Ross Wilson: After The Pink Finks I had a band called The Party Machine with Ross Hannaford on lead guitar. We'd evolved from The Pink Finks, where we were teenagers playing old R&B songs, to a point where we wrote our own material. Mike Rudd, who later went onto Spectrum, was on bass. I was the main writer, and also wrote a bit with Hannaford, and we created all this weird and wonderful music. We played a lot of gigs and most people didn't like us because were a bit out there (laughter).

It was quite unusual for Australian bands to play their own material in the 1960s. What motivated you to do so with The Party Machine, and how did the crowds and promoters react?

Ross: There were a lot of bands writing their own songs (e.g. Twilights, Masters Apprentices, etc.), but The Party Machine weren't afraid to go out on a limb by trying out weird stuff that wasn't exactly commercial. To keep the punters and promoters happy, our live repertoire also included whatever current Top 40 or soul songs we liked. In general we went over okay in Melbourne, even though we played a lot of original songs, but, at one gig, on our only trip to Sydney, Hannaford and I were attacked by some disgruntled sharpies after the show, and I scored a black eye and some free publicity!

The Party Machine. L–R: Mike Rudd, Ross Hannaford, Peter Curtain and Ross Wilson (Beard)

to 18 months jail for importing LSD into New South Wales.

26 The Commonwealth Censor cuts five minutes from John Murray's landmark study of Australian sexuality, *The Naked Bunyip*. Featuring Russell Morris (singing to a striptease), Barry Humphries, Malcolm Muggeridge, Jacki Weaver and others, the film exposes and satirises Australian attitudes towards prostitution, abortion and homosexuality.

26 Carlton come from 44 points behind at half time to defeat traditional rivals Collingwood in the VFL Grand Final.

26 3XY DJ Graham Berry follows a US trend in radio programming by hosting a Saturday night show, playing album and extended tracks instead of the usual three minute singles.

28 A New Zealand schoolteacher is arrested at Essendon Airport for importing marijuana and LSD.

OCTOBER

- David Williamson's *The Coming of Stork* premieres at La Mama. Detailing the sexual proclivities of a young troublemaker, the play stars Bruce Spence, who goes on to play the lead role in Tim Burstall's highly successful 1971 film adaptation.

7 Axiom return from the UK.

11 400 students chanting 'Cops off Campus!' remove police officers after they enter the La Trobe University grounds.

11 Max Merritt and The Meteors prepare to leave for the UK to mix down their new recordings.

11 Following a spate of sit-in protests at Commonwealth offices across the country, the Federal government introduces a Law and Order Bill imposing maximum penalties of three months' jail or a $250 fine for the occupation of buildings.

15 The construction of the West Gate bridge, linking Footscray to central Melbourne, is halted when scaffolding collapses, killing 35 workers.

15 Instituting Australia's first Green Ban, Victorian unions block redevelopment in the historic Melbourne suburb of Carlton.

15 The first Boeing 747 Jumbo Jet lands in Australia.

16 Oil workers become some of the first in Australia to win four weeks paid annual leave.

21 Albert Park's Riveria Theatre hosts the *Acid Test* event, featuring sets from Chain, Spectrum, Blackfeather, Ken White and Margaret Roadknight.

22 In the wake of the revelation that Queensland university student John Geil was paid by Commonwealth police to spy on his fellow alumni, the Minister for the Interior admits that photos taken by police at demonstrations are not just used for evidence, but also to build files on activists.

28 The Sons of the Vegetal Mother give away copies of a recently recorded EP at the four week long *Garden Party* 'environment' held at the Age Gallery in Melbourne.

29 After a long struggle, Aborigines at Lake Tyers and

Some of The Party Machine songs later turned up as other things. 'Please America' off the second Daddy Cool album was originally part of something I wrote with Hanna called 'The Camel Suite'. Don't ask why, but it was about Camels and Camel farms and all this stuff (laughter). When we rewrote it, it went from being 'We all live on a camel farm, We just got off the apple farm', or something stupid like that, to having lyrics you could understand.

Tell us about The Party Machine's songbook and the raid on *Go Set* that occurred because of it.

Ross: We printed the songbook to give the punters more insight into what we were doing. Our manager, Gavin Anderson [ex-Loved Ones drummer], had connections at *Go Set*, so he got them to print them. Because the books were lying around their office, somebody at *Go Set* decided to put a copy in with every competition's give away prize. Then some prize winning kid's mother took exception to the book's contents and called the vice squad, who raided *Go Set* and seized the remaining books. That got us in the papers and the *Truth Weekly*, and enabled me to go on to Channel 7 news to defend the band, free speech, etc.

Then I went to UK and when I returned, over six months later, the case was only just going to court. The magistrate ruled that, although he didn't think the book was particularly outrageous, they would destroy them anyway, probably to please the cops. I didn't get charged with anything as the case was against *Go Set* for distributing an unsolicited obscene publication, or something like that, and read about the verdict in the paper. 35 years later people are still talking about it!

How did the band come to an end?

Ross: The Party Machine broke up in 1969 because I received an invitation to go overseas and play with Procession in London. They'd gone there in search of fame and fortune and decided they needed an injection of fresh blood. They'd seen The Party Machine live in Melbourne and liked the original songs and the sound of my voice. I mucked around there for around six months over the summer and had a great time. I then trekked back to Australia and arrived home totally broke with my new bride (laughter).

I had a whole load of songs I'd written overseas, and the genesis of Daddy Cool had occurred while I was away, as I'd been looking at early R&B and Doo Wop, sounds that had never really had much of a run in Australia.

Go Set writer Ed Nimmervoll in 1970 compared your work to Frank Zappa . . .

Ross: There was a big Frank Zappa influence. I would never claim to be as accomplished a musician as him, but his whole approach was that some musical styles have an innate humour built into them. He was one of the few Americans at the time to use irony and satire in his music, and I love to do that, so he appealed to me greatly. Also through him I helped to ignite my interest in Doo Wop music.

Daddy Cool live (Porter)

Framlingham are finally granted full ownership of the reserves they have been forced to live on for years.

31 Daddy Cool make their debut at a Jimi Hendrix Memorial held at the TF Much Ballroom, playing alongside Spectrum, Chain and King Harvest.

NOVEMBER

- Tim Daly is jailed after attempting to set Sydney's Imperial War Museum on fire.
- The wearing of seat belts becomes compulsory in Victoria.
- The Australian Record Ban ends. One Melbourne radio station celebrates by playing 24 hours of The Beatles, while others opt to reintegrate major label material more slowly.
- Pope Paul VI embarks on the first papal visit to Australia, using several speeches to attack Australia's racist immigration policies and 'isolationism'.
- A half Senate election sees the ultra-conservative DLP continue to hold the balance of power federally.
- The 'Killer' Jerry Lee Lewis undertakes a tour of Australia, with 100s walking out on a drunken and chaotic performance in Melbourne.
- Lilydale High School students threaten to riot when their principal pulls the plug on a lunch time concert by progressive rock act Lotus.

1 300 students at the Mordialloc-Chelsea High School in

Daddy Cool's extended line-up. F–B: Gary Young, Ross Wilson, Jeremy Noone, Wayne Duncan, Ross Hannaford (Porter)

Melbourne strike over the issue of hair length for boys.

3 Baghdad Note wins the Melbourne Cup.

12 Australian troop numbers in Vietnam are reduced for the first time when a returning battalion is not replaced. Following the lead of the US, the Federal Coalition government will withdraw the last of Australia's soldiers from Vietnam by 1972, although support for the war is only formally ended with the election of the Whitlam government in the same year.

12 *The Naked Bunyip* premieres at the St Kilda Palais Theatre, with director John Murray blacking out dialogue and images with an image of a cavorting Bunyip to illustrate the effect of the Censor's cuts. Following the path laid down by surf movie makers, Murray chooses to side step traditional forms of distribution by hiring out halls and independent theatres to screen the film himself.

21 Johnny O'Keefe is released on $100 bail after facing a Sydney court on charges arising from the possession of Indian Hemp.

DECEMBER

- After months of renovations the APG opens the Pram Factory performance space in Melbourne. Located at 323/325 Drummond Street, Carlton, it plays host to a series of plays, exhibitions and events, before becoming the home of Circus Oz in 1978.

Tell us a bit about Doo Wop.

Ross: It evolved [in the US] from 1948 and kind of led to rock 'n' roll. It was very much a vocal thing. In the post war years there was a lot of small combo work going on with big beat drums and saxophones where electric guitars also started to appear. Barber Shop Quartets and hip jazz sounds began to turn into Doo Wop, which was very much born out of the ghetto thing, where guys were following a tradition of harmonising together on street corners. It typically featured a bass voice, a couple of tenors and an alto or falsetto voice on top. The chords of so much Doo Wop stuff would go from the tonic to the relative minor to the four chord to the five chord. That was a progression they would apply to any kind of melody (laughter). A lot of people would now say it all sounds the same, but that wasn't the point, it was a simple kind of music that had up tempo feel along with the ballads.

During that period there was a rash of what they all called 'bird groups' – The Ravens and The Robins and others named after birds. One of the first big hits that crossed over in the US was by The Crows with a song called 'Gee', which Daddy Cool later did. As so often happens, the black people were doing it for some time before the white people absorbed it, and you started to get Elvis and Buddy Holly and all the rest of them, which was what we then heard in Australia. I got really excited about all of this and started to ferret out this whole era of early 1950s Doo Wop, which I'd missed out on.

What band did you first put together when you returned from the UK?

Ross: When I got back I found that all my pals were involved in the emerging progressive/hippy rock scene around the TF Much Ballroom. I hooked up with Mike Rudd's manager Peter Andrews [of Let It Be] and started to put together this super-group, experimental rock thing called The Sons of the Vegetal Mother. We were doing some of my new songs, which included 'Eagle Rock', but most of them were more out there, Zappaish, hard rock.

At the same time, though, I was also researching all this Doo Wop stuff and thinking 'It'd be great to do this live.' Knowing that Sons of the Vegetal Mother members Gary Young and Wayne Duncan had come up through '50s instrumental bands and into playing with Bobby and Laurie, they'd been famous a few times already, I knew they had a great knowledge of rock 'n' roll. Hanna and I had also evolved from R&B, so I decided to get the four of us together to do a Doo Wop thing. During our first rehearsal, Peter Andrews came around and heard us blasting away and said 'Wow! You've got to play at the TF Much Ballroom.'

So at the next event The Sons of the Vegetal Mother did their thing. It was very much a hippy scene with people sitting there listening to all these long solos. Then Daddy Cool came out and all started dancing. We turned the scene on its head because we were a lot of fun and not just concerned with absorbing, long, boring solos, which was the trend in prog-rock at the time. That was our template from day one.

Daddy Cool formed during the Australian Record Ban of 1970. Would it be a fair call to say that Daddy Cool were the biggest band in Australia during the most difficult period for the Australian music industry?

Ross: I guess so, although at the time I wasn't thinking much about that. In hindsight there were a lot of things going in our favour. The Record Ban was on and we signed with an independent so that didn't affect us. The TF Much Ballroom scene was also going, which was a hot bed of new talent with weirder bands like Spectrum and The Captain Matchbox Whoopee Band. The whole flavour of the new bands influenced us, we were a product of the same swimming pool they were all swimming in at the time (laughter).

Also we were lucky in that our management was forward thinking. Back then most bands didn't do national tours, they just went out and did whatever was available. However, our management managed to get us in with this Aquarius group who were coordinating all the student bodies around Australia. Somehow through them there was money available to take us and Spectrum, who had just had a number One hit while we were still climbing the charts, on this tour, which started off in Western Australia. While we were there we'd play one or two Uni gigs as part of the contract and then we were able to play public gigs. So we'd book a bunch of those and blow everyone away and then move on to South Australia and then Victoria and so on, so that within the space of six weeks or something we'd done this national tour just at the time we had a single and album out. That was *unheard of* back then and broke us overnight practically everywhere.

And so *Daddy Who* became one of the first really big selling Australian albums.

Ross: Yeah. The other fortunate thing was that our friends Spectrum had had a film clip done for 'I'll Be Gone', and we said 'Well we want a film clip too.' So we got Chris Lofven to make one, and he followed us all around getting live footage, which we stitched together with a few more scenes. For $300 we got a real cool clip. Our single went to Number One, but it wasn't until years later that we realised that the clip had anything to do with it. We just wanted one because our mates had one (laughter). Later on when we came to do our second album, Bob Weiss did a TV documentary on the band as well. Bob's got great footage of us playing live in funny locations like a farm and at the drive-in movies and in a tiny room.

Daddy Cool in the studio (Porter)

Did you feel in the early 1970s that Australia was still a conservative place?

Ross: Well Australia had been very conservative in the late 1960s. When The Party Machine was playing it was the Henry Bolte era with his sidekick Arthur Rylah running the Vice Squad so it wasn't a very fun time at all.

By the early 1970s everyone was in ferment about the Vietnam war. Pot was very popular and acid was everywhere, so things began to loosen up a bit. Nevertheless, when Daddy Cool's second album *Sex, Dope and Rock 'n' Roll: Teenage Heaven* came out (in 1972), it was removed from Myers because the Catholic Mother's Association, housewives groups and others took exception to the title.

Tell us about the band signing to Sparmac, as *Daddy Who* was the first album on the label.

Ross: It was Robbie Porter's label, but the connection came through John McDonald who ran the Disc shop in Bourke Street, Melbourne where I'd buy imported records. Spectrum, and this is another link to them, had signed to EMI, and in typical alternative muso fashion were a bit annoyed at being told what to do, so we thought we'd try an indie company instead. John had made an overture and we met up with him and his partner at the time, the DJ Ken Sparks. The name came from Sparks and MacDonald, hence Sparmac.

By this time, though, Sparks was pulling out and had sold his share to Robbie Porter, who was living half the time in the US. Of course I knew who he was because he'd been Robbie G., the teenage prodigy of the steel guitar and had many Number One hits of his own. He'd turned into a producer with all these American connections. He came to see us at Melbourne Town Hall and was just blown away.

Sparmac said Robbie would produce it, then take it to America to get it mixed. They didn't want to muck around with a single, but wanted to do an album. All of that appealed to us so we went ahead and did it. Next thing we knew we were in the studio and two and a half days later we had the first album. Robbie whipped it off to America and brought it back and out came the first single and that was that.

In 1971 the band went to America. This was long before Australian bands hit it big in the US. Did you have a plan to try and break you over there?

Ross: Robbie Porter had a business partner over there called Steve Binder, who is a well known TV director. At that time he was doing the *TAMI Show* with James Brown, The Rolling Stones, whoever was hot at the time, but his biggest success had been the *Elvis '68 Comeback Special*. We went over there and signed our lives away to him, and then didn't end up getting along because he wanted us to do things we wouldn't do.

- The Environment Protection Agency (EPA) is set up in Victoria.
- The Sydney City Council appoints four wardens to guard shoppers in Martin Place from 'Extremes of behaviour that are deemed offensive.' As part of their remit, the Wardens move on hippies, break up kissing couples and evict chanting Hare Krishnas.
- Tully vocalist Terry Wilson and drummer Robert Taylor leave the band after the rest of its members become heavily involved in the Meher Baba Sect. Carrying on without a drummer, the remaining members sign to EMI's Harvest label, releasing an explicitly spiritual single 'Krishna Came' and two albums, before splitting up in 1972.
- The Melbourne Arts Cooperative starts a regular Sunday night show, featuring lights from Ellis D. Fogg and music from Spectrum, Pig Face (featuring Laurie Pryor from The Twilights) and The King Hippo Poetry Band. During the week the Cooperative's space at 336 Nicholson Street, Carlton plays host to poetry workshops, mixed media concerts and dance events.

9 Having engaged in strikes throughout the year, Victorian Secondary School unions prepare for a busy year ahead by asking teachers to contribute one day's pay per month towards a strike fund for 1971.

11 Ellis D. Fogg presents *Tully by Fogglight* at the University of Queensland.

12 The third TF Much Ballroom night is held at Cathedral Hall, with sets from Spectrum, Lipp Arthur, Gerry Humphreys and The Joy Boys, Daddy Cool, Pig Face and King Harvest.

15 Sirius, the first Eastern Bloc rock band to visit Australia, begin a national tour of Hungarian clubs and pop venues.

19 The Masters Apprentices return home from the UK to begin a national tour in support of their 'Because I Love You' single. Returning to London the following year, the band record the *A Toast to Panama Red* album, before breaking up in 1972.

26 Having been signed up by wealthy promoter Hamish Henry (of the Grape Organisation), Fraternity announce they are leaving Sydney to live communally in the Adelaide Hills. Band leader Bruce Howe tells *Go Set* that the city is 'Too dirty, it chokes you. There are too many hassles, it's not worth it.'

31 Having lost access to the Cathedral Hall due a combination of pressure from health authorities and the police, Let It Be's plans to holds an outdoor concert at Launching Place are scuppered by high rainfall. Attempting to shift the line up, including Spectrum, Daddy Cool, Billy Thorpe and The Aztecs and The Captain Matchbox Whoopee Band, to Ashton's circus tent in St Kilda, the organisers meet resistance from the local council and the event is eventually cancelled.

Iain McIntyre

They did, however, get us a deal with Reprise records, so our first two albums came out in the US with slight track changes. Reprise gave 'Eagle Rock' and the band a lot of promotional support and we did break out quite heavily in a few areas. We toured on a bill with Fleetwood Mac and were later able to go back and headline some college towns. On the West Coast we had a good reputation and did very well on some local charts, but not enough to make it all over.

The big difference between us and the Australian bands that had come before was that, having been to England with Procession, I knew I didn't want to go there again. Every Australian band was going there because The Beatles were from there and so on, but every single English band was trying to get to America.

Later on it was proved that in order to make it in the US you just had to keep going back and tour non stop and I was prepared to do that, but not with Daddy Cool. After the second album came out (in 1972) I felt my interest in Doo Wop had been satisfied and the well was running dry. Also, having done contemporary music with The Party Machine and Sons of the Vegetal Mother I felt that taking a retro act to the US was a bit like selling coal to Newcastle (laughter). They had all the retro acts they needed.

In many ways I saw Daddy Cool as like going to Rock 'n' Roll High School (laughter). I learnt how to do four part harmonies and play the roots of rock and how to apply that to country pickin' blues, Stonesy things and wild out on the edge stuff. By the end of the band, though, I'd felt that I'd fully explored the innocent side of rock 'n' roll and wanted to get back to the nasty side again (laughter).

Wayne Duncan (Porter)

In 1972 Wilson formed The Mighty Kong with long time collaborator Ross Hannaford, before the pair accepted the lure of money to reform Daddy Cool in 1974. After playing for two years and releasing the live album *The Last Drive-In Movie Show*, Daddy Cool once more called it a day. Heading in a polished, modern pop direction Wilson scored a number of Australian Top Ten hits during the 1980s with Mondo Rock. Since the 1990s he has continued to play with a variety of backing bands, and recently rejoined the former members of Daddy Cool for a one off benefit for victims of the 2004 Asian Tsunami and a number of shows to promote *The Complete Daddy Cool* DVD.

Sources and Further Reading

Advertiser
Age
Drift
Everybody's/EB's
Foffle (Ed.: Ian Marks)
Freedom Train (Ed.: Ian McFarlane)
Go Set
Herald
Livin' End (Ed.: Dean Mittlehauser)
Lucifer
Resist
Sound Blast
Sun
Sydney Morning Herald
Tom Thum' (Ed.: Jackie Vidot)
Truth
Ubunews
West Australian
Barker, A. *When Was That?*, John Ferguson, Sydney, 1988.
Beilby, P. (ed.) *Australian TV: The First 25 Years*. Thomas Nelson Australia, Melbourne, 1981.
Bassett, J. and Gerster, R. *Seizures Of Youth: 'The Sixties' and Australia*. Hyland House, Melbourne, 1991.
Dutton, G. and Harris, M. (eds) *Australia's Censorship Crisis*. Sun Books, Sydney, 1970.
Fraser, B. *The McQuarie Book of Events*. MacQuarie Library, Sydney, 1983.
Gilbert, A. and Inglis, K. (eds), *Australians: Events and Places*, Fairfax, Sync and Weldon Assoc, 1987.
Harrison, T. *The Australian Film and Television Companion*. Simon and Schuster, Sydney, 1995.
Horne, D. (ed.) *Time Of Hope: Australia in the 1960s*. Angus & Robertson, Sydney, 1980
Jarratt, S. *Permissive Australia*. Jack De Lissa Pty Ltd, Sydney, 1970.
Jay Jay and Friends, *Marijuana Australiana*. The Marijuana Australiana Project, Kent Town, 2001.
Jones, L. *La Mama: Story Of A Theatre*. McPhee Gribble, Fitzroy, 1988.
Kent, David. *Australian Chart Book 1940–1969*, Australian Chart Book Pty Ltd, Bendigo, 2005.
Langley, G. *Decade of Dissent*. Allen and Unwin, North Sydney, 1992.
McFarlane, I. *The Encyclopedia of Australian Rock and Pop*. Allen and Unwin, North Sydney, 1999.
McGrath, N. *Australian Encyclopedia of Rock*. Outback Press, Melbourne, 1978.
McIntyre, I. *Australian Troublemaker's Calendar 2005*. 3CR, Melbourne, 2004.
Manderson, D. *From Mr Sin to Mr Big*. Oxford University Press, Oxford, 1993.
Marks, I. and McIntyre, *Wild About You: Tales From The Australian Rock Underground, 1963–68*, Community Radio Federation, Melbourne, 2004.
Mudie, P. *Ubu Films: 1965–70*. UNSW Press, Sydney, 1997.
Percy, J. *Resistance: A History of the DSP and Resistance, Volume 1*. Resistance Books, Sydney, 2005.
Ross, John (ed.), *Chronicle of Australia*, Chronicle Australiasia, 1993.
Ryan, G. *Adelaide Chart Book – 1959–2002*, Moonlight Publications, Bendigo, 2003.
Ryan, G. *Brisbane Chart Book – 1956–2002*, Moonlight Publications, Bendigo, 2003.
Ryan, G. *Melbourne Chart Book – 1956–2002*, Moonlight Publications, Bendigo. 2003.
Ryan, G. *Sydney Pop Music Charts – 1953–2003,* Moonlight Publications, Bendigo, 2004.
Smith, Y. *Taking Time: A Women's Historical Data Kit*. Union of Australian Women, Melbourne, 1988.
Spencer, C. *Australian Rock Discography 1956–1969*, Moonlight Publishing, Bendigo, 1998.
Spencer, C. *Australian Rock Discography 1970–1979*. Moonlight Publishing, Bendigo, 1998.
Spencer, C, Nowara, Z. and McHenry, P. *Who's Who of Australian Rock (5th Edition)*. The Five Mile Press, Melbourne, 2002.
Sparrow, J. and Sparrow, J. *Radical Melbourne 2: The Enemy Within*, Vulgar Press, Fitzroy, 2004.
www.milesago.com
www.howlspace.com.au
www.morningoftheearth.net

Key Contributors

Iain McIntyre is a Melbourne writer and community radio presenter. He has contributed to the publications *Wild About You: Tales from the Australian Rock Underground, 1963–68*, *Disturbing The Peace: Australian Rebel History* and 3CR's *2006 Seeds of Dissent* calendar.

Ian D. Marks co-wrote *Wild About You: Tales from the Australian Rock Underground 1963–68* (www.3cr.org.au/way) and is the editor of the tragic pop culture zine *Foffle*. He can be contacted at fofflemag@yahoo.com.au.

Maria Sokratis is the former coordinator of the Melbourne '60's Appreciation Society. She currently plays in Melbourne bands Thee Mystaken and Pinchu Macha.

Brigid Finlayson is a Melbourne based architectural historian who has been published in *Heritage Australia*, *Trust News* and is a member of the National Trust of Australia's (Victoria) Building Committee. She has had a long interest in the fashion of the 1960s.

Keith Glass is a music writer/researcher/songwriter/musician/vinyl record buyer and seller now based in Mobile, Alabama. He has worked as a producer/label owner/retailer/tour promoter/shop owner/distributor and tree loper.

Paul Culnane is a Canberra-based freelance music journalist, who regularly contributes to a variety of music-related websites, magazines and biographical books. He is also a songwriter, musician, record producer, collector and archivist. During 2005, Paul has been heavily involved with promotional activities on behalf of bands based, respectively, in London, Dublin and Newcastle, New South Wales. He can be contacted via paulculnane@yahoo.co.uk.

Nick Black is a script editor in the Film and TV industry. He also co-hosts Melbourne's 88.3 Southern FM's psychedelic music programme 'Purple Haze'.

Duncan Fry finds it hard to believe that a small piece of his late teenage years is now part of history. After playing in a few more bands after Geoff Crozier, he discovered that many more people were willing to pay him to mix than to play! The subsequent book *Live Sound Mixing* is now in its 4th Edition and is the preferred text for audio courses around the world. He can be contacted via www.dunkworld.com.

Tagdh Taylor is the Melbourne based author of *Top Fellas*, the definitive guide to Australian Sharpie culture. He is also a filmmaker who is currently completing production on his first feature film *One For The Money*.

Jim Colbert has been taking pics round the music trade off and on (with a lot more off) since the '60s as well as messing about with graphics, the international bond market and other nefarious but hopefully legal activities? He can be contacted via jcolbert@bigpond.net.au.

Colin Beard has been a successful fashion and advertising photographer winning many international awards. He has also worked as a lecturer in photography at The Sydney College of the Arts and at The University of Technology, Sydney and produced a number of large format books on aspects of Australian life. He has held major solo exhibitions throughout Australia and overseas. He is currently living in semi-retirement in South-eastern Queensland.

David Porter a.k.a Jacques L'affrique worked in Melbourne during the surge in rock & roll in the 1970s, and in particular during the rise of Daddy Cool and Spectrum, providing photographs for their record albums. As a freelance journalist for *Go Set*, *Planet* and *Rolling Stone*, he compiled a great deal of photographs. He now works in New South Wales teaching art in the Blue Mountains. An exhibition of his work entitled 'Unreal Rock' opened at Penrith Regional Gallery and has toured various galleries in New South Wales, Victoria and Canberra. David can be contacted at davidivan@westnet.com.au.

John Newhill is a Melbourne based freelance photographer who has been documenting Melbourne's live blues and rock scene since the late 1960s. He can be contacted on 0424 018 447.

Thanks to all the contributors, everyone at 3CR, staff at the City of Yarra, Bree McKilligan, Brona Keenan, Philip Frazer, the Marks family, the McIntyres, Laura and Astrid MacFarlane, Meg Butler, Rockin' Ronnie, Mrs Gerry Gerner, Ms Kate Harman, Mrs Robin Mellors, Mr Jim Jonas, Mrs Joy Cassidy, Dr Robin Grove and Mrs Elisabeth Grove.

Index

This index is arranged alphabetically, word for word. Songs are within single quotation marks and albums and other titles in italic. *Italic* page numbers indicate photographs.

C

E

F

Q

R

W

X

Y

Z